The Rising Tide of Cultural Pluralism

The Rising Tide of Cultural Pluralism

The Nation-State at Bay?

■ ■ ■

Edited by

Crawford Young

THE UNIVERSITY OF WISCONSIN PRESS

The University of Wisconsin Press
114 North Murray Street
Madison, Wisconsin 53715

3 Henrietta Street
London WC2E 8LU, England

2 4 5 3 1

Printed in the United States of America

Library of Congress Cataloging-in-Publication Data
The Rising tide of cultural pluralism : the nation-state at bay? /
edited by Crawford Young.
318 p. cm.
Includes bibliographical references and index.
ISBN 0-299-13880-1 ISBN 0-299-13884-4 (pbk.)
1. Nationalism—Congresses. 2. Pluralism (Social sciences)—Congresses.
3. Ethnic groups—Political activity—Congresses.
4. Ethnic relations—Political aspects—Congresses.
5. Ethnicity—Political aspects—Congresses.
I. Young, Crawford, 1931–
JC311.R474 1993
306.2—dc20 93-7103

Contents

CONTRIBUTORS vii

PREFACE xi

1. The Dialectics of Cultural Pluralism: Concept and Reality 3
Crawford Young

2. Engendering Cultural Differences 36
Virginia Sapiro

3. To Polarize a Nation: Racism, Labor Markets, and the State in the U.S. Political Economy, 1965–1986 55
Noel Jacob Kent

4. Language Policy Conflict in the United States 73
Ronald J. Schmidt

5. Demise of an Empire-State: Identity, Legitimacy, and the Deconstruction of Soviet Politics 93
Mark R. Beissinger

6. Azeri Nationalism in the Former Soviet Union and Iran 116
Nader Entessar

7. Nationalism and Ethnic Conflict in Ethiopia 138
Solomon Gashaw

8. Ethnicity in Ethiopia: The View from Below (and from the South, East, and West) 158
Herbert S. Lewis

9. The Cultural Construction of Eritrean Nationalist Movements 179
Tekle M. Woldemikael

10. Ethnicity, Caste, Class, and State in Ethiopian History: The Case of the Beta Israel (Falasha) 200
James Quirin

11. Ethnic Identity and the De-Nationalization and Democratization of Leninist States 222
Edward Friedman

12. Cultural Pluralism, Revivalism, and Modernity in South Asia: The Rashtriya Swayamsevak Sangh 242
Douglas Spitz

13. The Creation of the Modern Maya 265
Alan LeBaron

INDEX 287

Contributors

MARK R. BEISSINGER is Associate Professor of Political Science and Chair of the Russian and East European Studies Program at the University of Wisconsin–Madison. He is the author of *Scientific Management, Socialist Discipline, and Soviet Power* (1988), and a contributing co-editor of *The Nationalities Factor in Soviet Politics and Society* (1990). He is currently working on a study of protest mobilization in the former Soviet Union.

NADER ENTESSAR is Professor of Political Science and Chair of the Social Science Division at Spring Hill College in Mobile, Alabama. His most recent publications include *Kurdish Ethnonationalism* (1992), *Reconstruction and Regional Diplomacy in the Persian Gulf* (1992), and *Iran and the Arab World* (1993).

EDWARD FRIEDMAN, Professor of Political Science at the University of Wisconsin–Madison, specializes in the comparative politics of Leninist and post-Leninist states, with an expertise in East Asian affairs. His next book is *The Politics of Democratization: Vicissitudes and Universals in the East Asian Experience* (1993). His most recent works are *Chinese Village, Socialist State* (1991) and *New Nationalist Identities in Post-Leninist Transformations* (1992).

SOLOMON GASHAW is Assistant Professor of Sociology at the University of Minnesota–Morris and received his Ph.D. and an SJD degree from the University of Wisconsin–Madison. During the Ethiopian revolution, he worked as Land Reform Administrative Director of Showa. For a brief period he participated in the initial deliberations of experts appointed by an inter-ministerial subcommittee on nationalities issues. Currently he is writing a book on "The Ethnicization of the Ethiopian State."

NOEL JACOB KENT is Associate Professor of Ethnic Studies at the University of Hawaii–Manoa. He is the author of *Hawaii, Islands under the Influence* (1983) and is currently interested in the impact of the U.S. economic crisis on politics and race relations.

ALAN LEBARON received his Ph.D. in Latin American History from the University of Florida in 1988. He has taught for the University of Maryland's Overseas division, and currently is Assistant Professor of History at Kennesaw State College. He visited Guatemala for the first time in 1972 and has returned many times since.

HERBERT S. LEWIS is Professor of Anthropology at the University of Wisconsin–Madison. He has carried out field research in Ethiopia, Israel, the West Indies, and Somalia. Among his publications are *After the Eagles Landed: The Yemenites of Israel* (1989) and *A Galla Monarchy: Jimma Abba Jifar, Ethiopia, 1830–1932* (1965).

JAMES QUIRIN is Associate Professor at Fisk University. His primary teaching has been in African and world history, with research on Ethiopia and the Horn of Africa. He has recently published *The Evolution of the Ethiopian Jews: A History of the Beta Israel (Falasha) to 1920* (1992).

VIRGINIA SAPIRO, Professor of Political Science and Women's Studies at the University of Wisconsin–Madison, is interested in political psychology, gender politics, and feminist theory. Her books include *The Political Integration of Women* (1983) and *A Vindication of Political Virtue: The Political Theory of Mary Wollstonecraft* (1992).

RONALD J. SCHMIDT is Professor of Political Science at California State University–Long Beach. He specializes in U.S. minority politics and public policy and has published articles on Latino politics and on language policy issues in the U.S. and Canada. He is currently completing a book on "Cultural Pluralism and the Politics of Language in the United States."

DOUGLAS SPITZ is Professor of History at Monmouth College, Illinois. After completing his Ph.D. at the University of Nebraska in 1964, he did postdoctoral work at the University of Chicago, University of Wisconsin, University of Pennsylvania, and at the Central Institute of Hindi in Delhi. His special area of interest is South Asian religious-political movements.

TEKLE M. WOLDEMIKAEL is currently a visiting Associate Professor of Sociology at the University of California–Irvine. His research interests are ethnicity and nationalism in the Horn of Africa, and race and ethnic relations in the United States.

CRAWFORD YOUNG is Rupert Emerson Professor of Political Science at the University of Wisconsin–Madison, and, during 1992–93, Acting Dean of the College of Letters & Science. Among other works, he is author of *The Politics of Cultural Pluralism* (1976), *Ideology and Development in Africa* (1982), *Politics in the Congo* (1965), and co-author of *The Rise and Decline of the Zairian State* (1985). *The Politics of Cultural Pluralism* won the Herskovits Award of the African Studies Association in 1977 and was co-winner of the Ralph Bunche Award of the American Political Science Association in 1979.

Preface

SOME YEARS AGO, Allen Fitchen, director of the University of Wisconsin Press, queried whether I might be interested in undertaking a companion volume to my 1976 book, *The Politics of Cultural Pluralism*. Many important changes had occurred in the years intervening since the drafting of this work, both in the world at large and in our theoretical understandings of this array of phenomena. The idea was attractive, but other large projects stood ahead of such an undertaking. Thus the welcome suggestion was filed away in the directory of distant intentions.

In summer 1990, I had the opportunity to direct a Summer Seminar for College Teachers, under the sponsorship of the National Endowment for the Humanities (NEH). A dozen excellent scholars from several disciplines and diverse regional specializations joined in an intense eight-week dialogue on the politics of cultural pluralism in comparative perspective. Most of the participants brought years of research endeavor to the seminar and drew upon a rich fund of knowledge, grounded in field inquiry in the countries concerned. Our seminar benefited from presentations by a number of my faculty colleagues at the University of Wisconsin–Madison.

The exceptional quality of a number of the seminar papers summoned from mental storage the Fitchen invitation. A practical response to his suggestion now appeared; the best of the seminar papers could be developed into a collective volume, completed by contributions from several of the University of Wisconsin–Madison specialists. The challenge of integrating these essays offered me an opportunity to organize my own reflections into an overview chapter. Our summer of sustained intellectual exchange had created a shared analytical discourse, one which might assure the common problematic necessary to lend cohesion to the volume as a whole. We owe a large debt of gratitude to Allen Fitchen for his initial suggestion and his subsequent encouragement when the project was broached to him shortly after the conclusion of the seminar.

Nine of the seminar participants were then invited to develop their contributions into articles for publication, building upon the framework employed during our discussions. One of these articles, a sociolinguistic analysis of the former Soviet Union by David Marshall, was so overtaken by the stunning collapse of that state that it could not be included; we nonetheless greatly benefited by his collaboration. Four scholars from our faculty were asked to develop their presentations into chapters for this volume, a task which they somehow fit into their crowded agendas with exemplary punctuality. I set to work on the introductory overview chapter; this was available to most authors only after their first drafts were completed. However, two rounds of revision were undertaken to strengthen the overall integration of the volume. In the second, we benefited from the incisive critiques of the two external readers for the University of Wisconsin Press, to whom we are most grateful.

Two of our contributors have in the last year published major books drawing upon their years of research in their regions of specialization (Nader Entessar and James Quirin). Five had the opportunity to return to their countries of focus to update their materials subsequent to the invitation to contribute (Alan LeBaron, Douglas Spitz, Edward Friedman, Herbert Lewis, and Mark Beissinger). Three are indigenous to the countries they analyze (Entessar, Solomon Gashaw, and Tekle Woldemikael—plus, of course, Noel Kent and Ronald Schmidt). All speak with the authority of prolonged immersion in their subjects of inquiry.

The diversity of contributors, and the many sources of support which we collectively have enjoyed over the years for our research, make impossible a comprehensive listing of all of our benefactors. However, we do wish to give particular acknowledgement to the NEH for its financial support for the 1990 Seminar, birthplace of this volume. We hope that the volume may serve as a tribute to the invaluable program of Summer Seminars for College Teachers, which has provided for many years crucial opportunities for many scholars located at non-doctoral institutions which often lack the internal resources to adequately support the research endeavors of their faculties.

Madison, Wisconsin
July, 1992

CRAWFORD YOUNG

The Rising Tide of Cultural Pluralism

1

The Dialectics of Cultural Pluralism: Concept and Reality

■ ■ ■

CRAWFORD YOUNG

NEARLY TWO DECADES have passed since I initially drafted the manuscript eventually published as *The Politics of Cultural Pluralism* (Young 1976). The rise of ethnicity as a central political variable, which first became apparent in the 1960s, was at that time just starting to attract comparative attention (for example, Enloe 1973; Olorunsola 1972; Connor 1972; Rabushka and Shepsle 1972). In retrospect, one might locate that analytical moment as lying halfway between the serene self-confidence of the 1950s concerning the nation-state system and the apprehensions of the early 1990s. In the early postwar years, even though two deeply hostile ideological visions—welfare state liberalism and state socialism—engaged in a titanic struggle to control the body of the nation-state, the sturdiness of its soul was not in question. Both camps shared the secular faith in the idea of progress, whose philosophic antecedents were brilliantly delineated by Bury (1955), however sharp their differences in rendering its message (Almond, Chodorow, and Pearce 1982).

By the 1990s, the mood was utterly transformed. Gone with the cold war were the comfortable certainties concerning the nation-state. Both "nation" and "state" were now subject to relentless interrogation: the former by deepening cultural cleavages in many lands, the latter by currents of economic and political liberalization now girdling the globe. The potent force of politicized and mobilized cultural pluralism is now universally conceded. Laments the *Economist*, ". . . the force of tribalism, whose potency has been one of the surprises—and, in its extreme nationalist form, one of the scourges—of the 20th century" (29 June 1991, 9). A new, more apocalyptic strain enters the analysis; one of the most prolific and influential contributors to this field of inquiry, Ralph Premdas (1991, 35), captures this mood:

> I think protracted ethnic conflicts can engender a level of solidarity that over-saturates the need for belongingness. It brings into play, after a certain threshold of solidarity intensity is attained, a new set of adverse effects which negate the initial value of group cohesion . . . *"the collective insanity threshold."* When group consciousness attains a certain critical mass, it thereafter destroys the carriers themselves.[1]

In my 1976 effort to extrapolate from the comparative experience in the contemporary politics of cultural pluralism to identify future trends, I reconfirmed the distinction between political science and prophecy. Part of the prognostication did conform to subsequent events; in the unfolding encounter between nation-state and cultural pluralism, the forecast that the latter would play an increasing role has proved reasonably accurate:

> . . . there is a continuous process of broadening and consolidation of identities at the periphery. The state impinges increasingly upon the field of social vision of the individual. . . . Through the prism of the broadened unit of self-awareness, conflict bounded by the territorial arena is likely to occur with other similarly extended communities, over scarce values within the broader system. Various aspects of change are reinforcing this trend. (Young 1976, 521)

My expectations with respect to the state system, however, can only be reread with embarrassment. The nation-state, I argued, enjoys a steady growth in its capacities, "a powerful tide of central power." Further, potent currents of autocracy flowed; in the third world, "Although the routes might vary, most political roads carried the polity to an authoritarian destination" (ibid., 518–520). In such observations, we are very far from the "probabilistic theory of the polity" which Gabriel Almond once proclaimed as our vocation (Almond 1960, 58). The sunny hues of optimism pervading my manuscript concerning the collective capacity of nation-states and civil societies to harmoniously manage cultural pluralism now seem several shades too bright.

In short, a transforming relationship between cultural pluralism and the nation-state is a central drama of our times. In returning to this theme in the present volume, I benefit from the collaboration of scholars with a number of regional, disciplinary, and conceptual perspectives. Together, we seek to capture the essence of these alterations both substantively and theoretically.

In selecting contributors, and in definition of our task, I wish to remedy what I now regard as a defect of the earlier work: the restriction of the field of observation to the third world. Comparative reflection on this topic, I now believe, is better served by moving beyond the largely artificial compartmentalization of the world into "developed" and "developing" areas. The global generality of the trend toward higher saliency of communal politics summons us to draw upon all human experience in our search for patterns and understandings. Thus included are several studies focusing upon the United States and former Soviet Union, along with chapters on China, India, Ethiopia, and Guatemala.

Although we aspire to a world perspective, no effort is made to select cases on the basis of comprehensive regional coverage. Indeed, more than half the chapters are devoted to aspects of cultural pluralism in only three countries. Although this partly is an accidental reflection of the specializations of the collaborators, it also reflects a belief that these three cases in the different dimensions examined cumulatively represent many of the most crucial issues. The breakup of the Soviet Union in 1991, above all because of the "national question," is one of the epochal events of our century, whose lessons will be studied for many years. Mark Beissinger deftly performs the autopsy, showing how the ultimately irreconcilable contradictions between the state personality of this gigantic polity—empire-state, nation-state, or socialist state—proved fatal. The politics of identity on the non-Russian periphery are illuminated by Nader Entessar's comparison between Azeri consciousness in Iran and Soviet Azerbaijan—diffuse and intertwined with Shi'a-Iranian affiliation in the former, recently politicized and mobilized but sharply differentiated from the Russian core in the latter.

The very nature of national identity in the United States, explored by Noel Kent and Ronald Schmidt, appears on the threshold of major transformations of uncertain implication; their topics, race and language, address crucial dimensions. New patterns of immigration, and far more assertive articulation of group claims by long marginalized and submerged groups, are rapidly altering cultural geography. Highly charged debates arise over "multi-culturalism," and the adoption of "Afrocentric" school curricula in a number of cities whose public schools have predominately African-American enrollments. Such metamorphoses are not entirely new; the initially Anglo "shining city on a hill" was profoundly marked by the "great immigration." Oscar Handlin, in his powerfully moving ode to the immigrant essence of America, could write that, "to describe the course and effects of immigration involved no less a task than to set down the whole history of the United States" (1951, 3). The European immigrant, in short, was America, a plausible interpretation at that apogee of an assimilationist, integrationist dominant vision. Today, when "minorities" are now a quarter of the American population, and seem likely to number at least 30 percent by the turn of the century, constituting a majority of school children shortly thereafter, the obsolescence of such an imaged America seems clear.[2]

Ethiopia, which claims a three-thousand-year lineage, witnessed like the Soviet Union convulsive changes in 1991. Guerrilla forces of the former province of Eritrea, after a three-decade struggle, drove the Ethiopian army out. The collapse of the Marxist-Leninist imperial regime of Mengistu Haile Mariam in May 1991 opens the door to a self-determination referendum in that territory, virtually certain to result in independence. Meanwhile, the conquest of the center by insurgent armies of the periphery destroys the existing cultural basis of the Ethiopian state. Here as well, the pace and scope of change are extraordinary. The rise of ethnic consciousness as an active political force really begins in the 1960s, as our contributors show in different ways. Solomon Gashaw examines this process from an Ethiopian nationalist perspective, whose contrast with the Herbert Lewis chapter captures the dilemmas now facing that country. The large and important Oromo group, long the object of Lewis's research, is perhaps 40 percent of the population and crucial to the survival of a reconstructed Ethiopia resting upon the active consent of its peripheral communities.[3] Tekle Woldemikael, in his painstaking examination of the ethnic and religious dimensions of cultural pluralism in Eritrea, shows what large challenges lie ahead for that prospective new state, now that the unifying struggle against what most came to see as a foreign occupant is supplanted by everyday competition over relative shares and leadership by the constituent elements of a nascent Eritrean civil society. James Quirin explores an ethnoreligious community whose recent flight to Israel attracted world attention, the Beta Israel (Ethiopian Jews, or Falasha). His arresting and solidly documented interpretation of the construction of identity amongst the Beta Israel—controversial in Israel as it calls into question application of the "law of return" and the justification for the spectacular airlifts which transplanted the great majority to the Jewish homeland—skillfully demonstrates the complexity and contingency of group formation over the *longue durée*.

The chapters on India and Guatemala bring important correctives to some passages in my 1976 book. Douglas Spitz argues the declining force of the secular vision of India associated with Nehru and many of the independence generation of Indian nationalists. Alan LeBaron, in his monograph on the crystallization of a Mayan consciousness in Guatemala, shows convincingly that cultural politics amongst Indian groups in at least parts of Latin America has moved beyond the "fugitive ethnicity" which was my earlier thesis. Edward Friedman, in his first published contribution on what is known in China as the "minority" question, enters a powerful brief for the thesis that, far from "solving" the nationality question, the Leninist state greatly exacerbates, if not creates, burning tensions between core culture and periphery.

Finally, my earlier study was entirely silent on the issue of gender. Virginia Sapiro enlarges upon her earlier work on this theme, tracing a pathway toward systematic consideration of the interaction of gender and cultural pluralism. Each interrogates the other, in ways whose complex patterns we are only beginning to explore.

In the balance of this chapter, I propose a comparative overview of the politics of cultural pluralism, with a focus upon change in the global historical context and theoretical perspective. There is a crucial dialectic between empirical event and conceptual interpretation. On the one hand, the political world daily enacts history, in its perpetual journey from past to future. On the other, our knowledge of reality is partial and transformative, conditioned by the selectivity of our perception, the cognitive maps which chart our understandings, the conceptual frameworks which guide our interpretation—and, ultimately, the cultures which enclose us. In this overview essay, I wish to explore both poles of the dialectic: major changes in the global arena, and evolutions in theoretical discourse concerning cultural pluralism.

The Emergence of the Nation-State

As we look backward on the early postwar years, it becomes clear that we witnessed the apotheosis of the nation-state. A confluence of circumstances, whose particularity emerges only in retrospect, yielded a historic moment when this form of polity appeared astonishingly ascendant. With the idea of progress still robust, those polities which were perceived as leading humanity's march to a better future had singular power as authoritative models. Analytical vocabulary was saturated with such imagery: "modernity" versus "traditionality"; "developed" versus "underdeveloped" (or "developing"); "advanced" versus "backwards." In 1960 Gabriel Almond spoke for a generation: "The political scientist who wishes to study political modernization in the non-Western areas will have to master the model of the modern, which in turn can only be derived from the most careful empirical and formal analysis of the functions of the modern Western polities" (Almond 1960, 64). Many would have added the Soviet Union as an alternative model of modernity in construction, inspirational to large numbers at that time.

The pacesetter polity, the beacon of progress was self-consciously a nation-state. Nationalism, to be sure, could take pathological forms, in the aggressive, militaristic, fascist states of prewar Germany, Italy, or Japan. But the national ideal as summons to citizen loyalty, as indispensable ideological cement binding the polity, as imperative component in legitimating doctrine of the state were cherished notions, in most cases highly developed and well anchored, in all the Western industrial democracies. The Soviet Union fully shared the self-concept of the advanced polity as axiomatically a nation-state. Leading Soviet students of the nationality question, of the pre-*perestroika* age, expressed the dominant view of the socialist commonwealth as midwife to the "new Soviet people":

> The socio-economic integration of the peoples of the USSR is closely linked to their political integration in the framework of a federated state, which is not a conglomerate of national administrative units, but an organic whole. . . . All these radical transformations equally signify that the national question . . . is irrevocably resolved. . . . The socio-economic and political transformations in the country have brought about the birth of a new historical community, the Soviet people. (Bromlei et al. 1982, 299)

Elsewhere, Bromlei unwittingly pointed to the fragility of this concept, arguing that the "essential factor" in the edification of this new trans-ethnic community "is the integration of the spiritual life of the peoples of our country [based on] Marxist-Leninist ideology" (Bromlei 1983, 141).

Yet, rather than a natural culmination of human progress and fulfillment of historic destiny, the nation-state was a recent and novel development in European history, which appeared on the scene at the time of the French Revolution, strongly influenced by the intellectual currents of that time. With the demise of the absolute state, the spread of the doctrine of popular sovereignty, and the crystallization of organized civil societies activated by a steadily enlarging franchise, the idea of the "nation" doubtless played a crucial role in providing emotional content to the purely juridical concept of citizenship (Seton-Watson 1977; Smith 1971; Hobsbawm 1990; Anderson 1983; Gellner 1983). Over time, the doctrine became so fully incorporated into statehood as to make the words interchangeable and frequently married by hyphenation. So powerful did this assimilation become, writes Ernest Gellner (1983, 6), that the very notion of a "man without a nation" strains

> the modern imagination . . . defies the recognized categories and provokes revulsion. . . . A man must have a nationality as he must have a nose and two ears; a deficiency in any of these particulars is not inconceivable and does from time to time occur, but only as a result of some disaster, and it is itself a disaster of a kind. . . . nations, like states, are a contingency, and not a universal necessity. . . . [yet they] hold that they were destined for each other; that either without the other is incomplete, and constitutes a tragedy.

The compulsive urge to nationhood applied equally to states, whose numbers multiplied rapidly with the swift crumbling of colonial empires following World War II. Rupert Emerson (1960, 96), in his classic study of the "rise to self-assertion of Asian and African peoples," well captured this unanimous mood that statehood won by anticolonial struggle required completion by the construction of nationality:

> Since the state is in modern times the most significant form of organization of men and embodies the greatest concentration of power, it is inevitable that there should have been, and should still be, a great and revolutionary struggle to secure a coincidence between state and nation. The nation seeks to take over the state as the political instrument through which it can protect and assert itself. . . . the nation has in fact become the body which legitimizes the state. . . . Where the state is based on any principle other than the national one, as is by definition the case in any imperial system, its foundations are immediately suspect in a nationalist age.

"Nation-building" and "national integration" became sacred vocations of new states; realization of this quest opened the door to "development" and "modernity." Nationhood achieved (or in process) was as much a mark of sovereignty as a flag, a United Nations seat, or an army.

The nation-building norm of statecraft drew sustenance from a universe of historical experience broader than simply the advanced industrial countries of Europe. The first wave of anticolonial revolt, in the eighteenth- and nineteenth-century Western hemisphere, had brought in its wake a state system, initially fragile, stabilized through internalization of the national idea. These independence movements, led except in Haiti by settlers who had previously conceived of themselves only as overseas fragments of a "mother" imperium (Hartz 1964), over time realized the metamorphosis into nationhood. The thirteen colonies, at the moment of the Declaration of Independence in 1776, were still accustomed to conceiving of their "rights" as inhering in their status as "Englishmen" and as separately rooted through the individual colonies. By the time of de Tocqueville, the idea of an American nation, embedded in popular sovereignty, was clearly established. " 'The will of the nation,' " he wrote, "is one of those phrases that have been most largely abused by the wily and the despotic of every age . . . In America the principle of the sovereignty of the people is . . . recognized by the customs and proclaimed by the laws; it spreads freely, and arrives without impediment at its most remote consequences" (1835, 1: 57).[4] In Latin America, the diverse administrative units of empire, led by the creole (American-born of Iberian antecedents) elites who spearheaded the independence movements, became by the close of the nineteenth century indisputable repositories of national sentiment. "The original shaping of the American administrative units," notes Benedict Anderson, "was to some extent arbitrary and fortuitous, marking the spatial limits of particular military conquests. But over time they developed a firmer reality. . . . To see how administrative units could, over time, come to be conceived as fatherlands . . . one has to look at the ways in which administrative organizations create meaning" (1983, 54–55). The central hold was especially precarious at the frontier periphery; "Mexico" was in the nineteenth century too weak an idea to retain Central America within its boundaries. Only over time did a powerful national ideology emerge, weaving together a mestizo myth consolidated by the Mexican Revolution (Portes and Rumbaut 1990, 106).

The successful assimilation of nation doctrine by states outside the pacesetter core demonstrated its utility as anti-imperial weapon as well. Those Asian and African states which eluded the triumphant march of imperial expansion—Japan, China, Thailand, Ethiopia—all reinvented themselves as nations. Japan, after the Meiji Restoration, transformed the millennial but feeble institution of emperorship into a resonating symbol of newly imagined nationhood and translated an ancient but societally rooted religious heritage into the potent text of state Shinto. The generation of Sun Yat-Sen imbued the Middle Kingdom with the radical new identity of Chinese nationalism, redefining the Han Chinese self and the barbarian "other" in ways that failed in the short run to build a stable polity but did help avert the fate then contemplated by covetous colonial statesmen, who in the late nineteenth century saw a decadent China as ripe for "carving like a melon." The much weaker but long-standing kingdoms of Siam and Abyssinia were reborn as the national states of Thailand and Ethiopia. In both places, diplomatic skill and simple good fortune were combined in a defensive appropriation of an alien doctrine of statehood to permit escape from the colonial yoke.

Also exemplary was the fate of the old multi-national empires after World War I; the classic empire-state was no longer a viable form of polity in the age of nationalism. Austria-Hungary was reduced to its residual Germanic core, bitterly torn by ideological strife, fatally tempted by the pan-German idea of *anschluss*. The once mighty Ottoman state, which for centuries domesticated both religious and ethnic diversity, was reduced to its Turkish inner ramparts and then rebuilt on an assertive version of the national idea. Only the giant Czarist empire was largely salvaged by Lenin, with an adroit mixture of cunning, coercion, and socialism. The idea of nation, resonating powerfully within the "prison of peoples," was co-opted and long tamed by the lapidary formula of "national in form, socialist in content," although, as Beissinger elegantly demonstrates, a submerged reality of empire remained embedded within the Soviet polity. The primal force of radical nationalism around the periphery of the empire was initially captured by the promise of self-determination, but domesticated by the assertion of a higher claim of proletarian internationalism, through which a superior form of nation-state as socialist commonwealth could take form: what Walker Connor in his seminal study of the "national question" in state socialist polities identifies as "the lengthy process of assimilation via the dialectical route of territorial autonomy for all compact national groups" (Connor 1984, 38). Stalin (1936, 168) stated this doctrine with characteristic candor in 1923:

> It should be borne in mind that besides the right of nations to self-determination there is also the right of the working class to consolidate its power, and to this latter right the right of self-determination is subordinate. There are occasions when the right of self-determination conflicts with the other, the higher right—the right of a working class that has assumed power to consolidate its power. In such cases—this must be said bluntly—the right of self-determination cannot and must not serve as an obstacle to the exercise by the working class of its right to dictatorship.

It was this same explosive doctrine of self-determination seized by anticolonial forces on the march first in Asia, then in Africa, which proved a supremely effective detonator of the imperial order and a defining element in Afro-Asian nationalism. The imperial partition itself gave territorial shape to the claims of self-determination. The "nation" which gave voice to this right by tactical necessity had to be the administrative units defined by the colonizers. In Asia, there was frequently a cultural or historical logic to the units of imperial rule: Burma, Malaysia, Vietnam, Cambodia, Laos, even India (but not Indonesia or the Philippines). Also in Asia, the number of units was limited. In Africa, colonial territories only rarely had the slightest historical pedigree or cultural coherence (Morocco, Tunisia, Egypt, Rwanda, Burundi, Swaziland, Lesotho are the exceptions).[5] They were also far more fragmented.

But in both cases the preservation of the frame of partition bears witness to the commanding force of practical circumstance. The concept of self-determination entered the pantheon of international norms through the United Nations Charter. Yet it could only be invoked territorially. Political struggle was driven into the compartments imposed by the steel grid of colonial partition. With rare exceptions, such as Pakistan and the Palestine mandate, political struggle could not be pursued in the name of a communal group smaller than the colonial territory. Nor could a pan-territorial ethnocultural solidarity serve as grounding for self-determination; here the seminal case is the failure of pan-Arabism, despite the potency of the historical myth upon which it rests. In this vast expanse from the Senegal River to the shores of Oman, eighteen states share an Arab core to their national identity; among them, but a single boundary (Saudi-Arabia and Yemen) was actually drawn by Arabs, yet all have "an astounding sanctity" (Akins 1991, 40).

The victorious combat with a dying colonial order was thus carried out under banners emblazoned as nationalism. Although in the language of everyday discourse, nationalism was "African" or "Asian," on the battlefield it was territorialized. With victory won, territories which had perhaps been units of convenience in struggle now required that collective act of historical imagination to meet the requirements of nationhood; success at that moment seemed to open the door to the "modernity" of the "advanced" polities, while failure left the new polity mired in "backwardness." This drama is illustrated in the intellectual pilgrimage of Nigerian nationalist Obafemi Awolowo; in 1947, he wrote: "Nigeria is not a nation. It is a mere geographical expression" (Young 1976, 274). But in later life he was a tireless partisan of Nigerian unity and a powerful voice for a radical nationalist vision of Nigeria's future. This nationalist vision is eloquently illustrated in the richly evocative title of the magistral nationalist text of India's first prime minister, Jawaharlal Nehru, *The Discovery of India* (1946). An Indian nation, politically constructed in battle with the British Raj, was given doctrinal foundations by historical exegesis, a new *lecture* of the past by a contemporary imagination.

Nationalism: Attempts at Assimilation

As we weave together these various strands of history, we can understand why the ideology of the nation-state had such a powerful grasp upon the human imagination in the 1950s and 1960s. To complete the portrait, we need to sketch in some background features which place in relief the singularity of that epoch as a historical moment. In western Europe—heartland of the exemplary modern state—ethnonationalism was at a low ebb. The "time of troubles" in Ulster began only in 1969. Although Flemish ethnic claims were voiced, Belgium was still a unitary state. Catalan and Basque ethnonationalism were still underground, and the illusion that "guest workers" were merely sojourners remained intact. Ethnonationalism was an archaism, the province of the small-town antiquarian or the clerical reactionary.

The United States, in the 1950s, stood at an exceptional point in its cultural history. "Melting pot" as master metaphor was at an apex of credibility; only in the 1960s did it come under attack (Glazer and Moynihan 1963; Parenti 1967; Novak 1971). Cultural pluralism had roiled the political waters in earlier periods, when the large influx of Catholic Irish and German immigrants in the 1840s and 1850s threatened the Protestant ascendancy in national identity, then again when the "great immigration" from the 1880s to World War I vastly diversified the European stock. It was in the wake of the latter phenomenon that the very term "cultural pluralism" first entered the sociological lexicon.[6]

The 1924 immigration act, however, all but choked off the flow of eastern and southern Europeans. The country then experienced two traumatizing events, which in different ways occulted cultural plurality. The great depression interrogated society in terms of social class; there was little public reflection upon the differential impact of distress in ethnic terms, and almost none concerning uneven racial effects. The Second World War was a profoundly unifying event, far more than World War I. Thus, by the 1950s the highly assimilative pedagogy of the school systems, the integrative impact of exceptional historical episodes, and the momentary end of a dynamic of differentiation produced a highly incorporative conjuncture, the unchallenged predominance of an integrative mood. The supreme confidence in the assimilative capacities of American society found reflection in the short-lived policy of "termination" of reservation status for native American tribal communities and in the profound commitment to integration of the civil rights movement in its early days. "Multi-culturalism" as public policy would have been unimaginable; polarizing racial conflict assumed importance only in the 1960s. The very vocabulary of cultural pluralism has completely changed since the 1950s; terminology such as "minorities," "persons of color," "Chicano," "Latino," "African-American" were yet to achieve currency.

A similar historical moment of apparent unification prevailed in the Soviet Union, indeed endured into the 1980s. In 1979, at a panel on ethnic conflict in the Moscow meetings of the International Political Science Association, a leading French scholar, Mattei Dogan, opened the session with the statement that the Soviet Union had "solved" the nationality question; none in the audience (myself included) publicly challenged this assertion. Such was the settled view of the Soviet leadership. Mikhail Gorbachev, the first Soviet leader who had never served outside the Russian republic, clearly had little notion of the nationalist ferment which would explode once *glasnost* opened the door. The long years of terror under Stalin, and more subtle despotism in the Brezhnev years of stagnation, seemed to have solidified the Soviet state. Nationality consciousness was clearly present, and its longer term evolution was a matter of speculation. Even if the optimism of Bromlei and Kozlov concerning the potency of an attachment to a "new Soviet people" evoked skepticism, few anticipated that the survival of the Soviet Union would be at issue, and none could have remotely imagined the cataclysmic events of August 1991; the prophetic study by Hélène Carrère d'Encausse, *L'empire éclate* (1978), was a dissident voice when it appeared.[7] Consult any text on Soviet politics of the early postwar years, and the chapter on "nationalities" invariably appears at the end with other residual topics. As Beissinger argues, the "overwhelming opinion" amongst Western experts as late as 1986 held that dissolution of the Soviet state was virtually impossible.

Finally, the moment of independence in Asia and Africa was an hour of confidence in the integrative power of the national idea. There was, particularly in Africa, some sense of the possible fragility of the new sovereignties, which made muscular nation-building imperative and frequently justified autocratic formulas of governance (single party systems, military rule). Sekou Toure of Guinea was perhaps incautious in his 1959 statement that, "In three or four years, no one will remember the tribal, ethnic or religious rivalries which, in the recent past, caused so much damage to our country and its population" (1959, 28). But most agreed that ethnicity, stigmatized as "tribalism," was synonymous with backwardness, an unwanted intrusion of traditionality into the drive for modernity.

Not only was the quintessentially progressive nature of nationalism axiomatic, but so also was its secular character. Secularism had become a component of state doctrine in the western European states as a means of ending the religious civil wars which raged in England, France, and Germany in the sixteenth and seventeenth centuries. The most influential political creeds of the nineteenth and twentieth centuries—liberalism and socialism—were resolutely secular in content. Although religious cleavage continued to influence partisan alignments in continental Europe (Lipset and Rokkan 1967), the idea of the nation, in its form for global export, was largely secular. Thus, in the great debate over the decolonization of British India, although "Muslim" and "Hindu" were represented as separate nations, neither of the major parties, Congress or the Muslim League, built upon religion as theological obligation. The Congress party, which articulated a vision of a united Indian state which could only be secular, after independence developed the national doctrine that language might be a permissible basis for solidarity claims, provided these claims stopped short of secession, but that regional demands based upon religious community were *ultra vires* (Brass 1974, 17–18).

The Muslim League spoke for an essentially secular Muslim "nation"; Pakistan in the original vision was to have a political Islam as its unifying element, but was not to be an integral Islamic state. In the vast zone of Asia and Africa where Islam was predominant, it was invoked as a component of national identity, but intended to be subordinated to a secular vision; those like the Muslim Brotherhood in Egypt and Sudan, the maraboutic movements in Algeria or Senegal, and Islamic extremists in Tunisia or Indonesia were viewed by dominant elements in nationalist movements as menacing voices of a resurrected past, obstacles to modernity, akin to "tribalists" in the ethnic domain. The influential synthesis by Donald Smith, *Religion and Political Development,* argued a three-pronged thrust of modernization imperatively linked to secularization: the separation of the polity from religious ideology and ecclesiastical structure, the expansion of the state to perform socioeconomic functions once carried out by religious structures, and transvaluation of political culture to emphasize secular goals and means. "These three aspects of secularization," he wrote, "are universal in the development of modern polities over the past century and a half" (1964, 85).

Disuniting the Nation

These, then, were the parameters of what appears in retrospect as the zenith of the nation-state as exemplary model. "National integration" and "nation-building" have all but vanished from the repertory of progressive statecraft. The United States gropes toward a multi-cultural future. The Soviet Union simply dissolved in 1991, with astonishing speed and with its only pallbearers being residual elements from its *nomenklatura* beneficiaries. "No one needs it," was the Russian press requiem cited by Beissinger; the all-powerful empire vanishes into an unmarked grave. A belated effort, beginning in 1989, was made to define a new treaty of union bringing together the fifteen nationality-based republics enjoying the full (though previously fictitious) right of self-determination. The pathetic farce of the August 1991 coup carried out by the custodians of an irretrievable past, triggered by the imminent signature of such a pact, proved to be its death warrant. Valery Tishkov, director of the Soviet Institute of Ethnography and Anthropology, writing in early 1991, glimpsed the end of empire, concluding that the Soviet state "cannot be salvaged . . . within the framework of the existing constitutional system and the dominant political and conceptual postulates on which it is based." The fruitless efforts of the Soviet leadership to save the Soviet state, from 1989 when the depth of its crisis was recognized, were bedeviled by "the profound polarization and obsessive intransigence that characterize our thinking, our manner of speaking, and our argumentation in the field of nationalities issues, and by the absence of the requisite sense among the citizenry that they belong to a unitary civil society" (Tishkov 1991, 1–2). In such settings, when a vacuum is created by abandonment of coercive central management of the national question, ethnonationalist forces are likely to fill the void. The 1991 fragmentation of Yugoslavia followed a similar logic. Ethiopia, perceived in its periphery, as Lewis shows, as empire-state rather than as the nation-state imagined by its largely Amharic central elite, faced the certain loss of Eritrea and a difficult challenge in redefining its identity with the collapse of its centralizing, autocratic rule in 1991.

In western Europe, new latitude has been granted ethnonational movements in recent years. Impressive statecraft in Spain provided a still uneasy accommodation in a democratized framework for Catalans and Basques; even Jacobin France tolerates a less *une et indivisible* concept of itself, allowing some cultural space for Bretons and Corsicans. The long-standing unitary state in Belgium has been supplanted by a bicultural, consociational federation. But a whole new set of issues now arises concerning immigrant communities far more differentiated from the ethnocultural basis for "nationhood" than groups absorbed or accommodated in the past. In Belgium, for example, immigrants now total 9 percent of the population and are projected to reach 37 percent in the Brussels region by the beginning of the next decade. A new reality casts its shadow over the laborious and painful compromises reached in federalizing Belgium: the immigrants are a permanent part of the population; they must eventually win citizenship; their numbers are likely to grow (Bockstael and Feinstein 1991). Commissions on "integration" (although, significantly, not assimilation) are at work in several European countries.

In Latin America, a crucial new trend observable in several countries is an emergent Indian consciousness. In my 1976 book, I presented Latin American Indians as the intriguing case where racial and cultural difference appeared not to give rise to politically expressed identity. Although this interpretation reflected conventional wisdom at that time, there are clearly portentous new currents emergent, as Alan LeBaron shows. The Maya are not an isolated case, although not all native American communities have such rich historical materials to draw upon for their contemporary "imagined community." Similar processes have been observed in Mexico, Nicaragua, Brazil, Ecuador, and Peru.

In Asia and Africa, the initial illusions concerning the transformative force of nationalism were swiftly dispelled; this indeed was the central argument of *The Politics of Cultural Pluralism*. Particularly in south Asia (Pakistan, India, Sri Lanka, Malaysia) and the Horn of Africa (Ethiopia, Sudan, Somalia), the intervening period witnesses an intensification of ethnic and regional pressures and the emergence of endemic civil war in Sri Lanka and the Horn. Religion joins ethnicity and regionalism, as the earlier vision of the secular state tends to fade. Islamists constitute a far more assertive political force in many (though not all) parts of the Muslim world and promote a more comprehensive vision of the Islamic state. The triumph of the Islamic revolution in Iran over an *ancien régime* which sought to root a secular doctrine of state in Persian historical origins rather than in its Islamic personality was a watershed event. Spitz, in tracing the rise of the Hindu revivalist *Rashtriya Swayamsevak Sangh* (RSS), shows how the gradual decay of Congress as a secular integrative force has opened space for an alternative conceptualization of the Indian polity. Stephen Graubard, in introducing a special 1991 issue of *Daedalus* devoted to religion and politics, cogently observes that, contrary to expectations three decades ago, there is now "little evidence to suggest that religion as a universal force is declining." Rather, he argues, "the experiences of this hard century" suggest "the remarkable capacity of the world religions to survive in very different social settings, and with quite new dimensions and forms . . . modernity, while influencing all established institutions, cannot destroy those that continue to respond to man's deepest needs, to understand suffering, age, and death, to respond to new societal cravings, but to do so in quite distinctive and different ways" (1991, vii–viii).

These patterns of change may be related to some overarching trends which merit recapitulation. The sheer scale of population movement—driven by both political and economic factors—and demographic change deserve stress. More than 200 million persons now live in countries in which they were not born—a staggering figure.[8] The opening of the Soviet borders to emigration has already produced a migration to Israel which alters the parameters of the Palestine conflict; the long period of economic decline in prospect for the former Soviet Union and much of eastern Europe before the adjustment to market economies can take hold—if indeed it does—suggests the clear potential for much larger movements toward western Europe and North America. The rapidly swelling populations along the northern rim of Africa will continue to find the European Community a magnet, however vigorous the efforts to exclude them. Central America, the Caribbean, and Mexico have potentially mobile populations unlikely to find satisfying opportunities in their present locations.

Differential reproductive rates join with population movements to bring dramatic changes in cultural geography. When South Africa became independent in 1910, the white population was 25 percent and growing, utterly confident of its manifest destiny of dominating all of southern Africa. By 1990, no more than 11 percent of the citizens of South Africa were white, and the figure was rapidly shrinking—a factor of fundamental importance in explaining the 1990 decision of the white regime to seek accommodation with the black majority. In the former Soviet Union, at the point of its dissolution, ethnic Russians were becoming, for the first time historically, a minority of the total population. Between 1979 and 1989, the three major Slavic groups increased by figures ranging from 4.2 percent to 6 percent while Muslim nationalities increased at rates ranging from 24 percent (Azeris) to 45 percent (Tadzhiks) (Tishkov 1991, 9). A consciousness of changing demographics was one of the elements raising questions about the future of the Soviet polity, even before the upsurge of secessionist ethnonationalism.

A comparable dynamic of astonishing demographic alteration is revealed in the United States by relative rates of increase among the major racial groupings. Between the 1980 and 1990 censuses, the number of Euroamericans rose by just under 8 percent, while African-Americans increased by almost 13 percent, native Americans by 38 percent, Hispanic-Americans by 53 percent, and Asian-Americans by 103 percent. Three different processes were at work: some difference in reproductive rates; immigration patterns, for Latinos and Asians; and self-reclassification, for native Americans. Each of these racial categories is internally differentiated and has distinctive interests as a totality; there is little warrant for the expectation that a monolithic "minority" political block will coalesce. Yet with "minorities" now a quarter of the total and rapidly increasing, important shifts in cultural politics in the United States in the decades ahead seem certain.

The stunning collapse of state socialism as a form of rule seems certain to have major consequences, not all yet perceptible. The most immediate has been the loss of a legitimating doctrine for the state as previously constituted in the most multi-national: the fragmentation of the USSR and Yugoslavia followed at once, and is likely in Czechoslvakia. Less obvious but perhaps equally important are the implications for the world state system of the end of the cold war. In the global competition, the two camps sought third world clientele and were driven by their rivalry to nurture their affiliates. The removal of this logic was at once apparent in the collapse of regimes in Ethiopia, Somalia, Liberia, Afghanistan, and Cambodia, partly explicable by the removal of security support from external patrons.

In the place of a security-driven bipolar world state system, there appears to emerge an international regime defined by mercantile blocks, with the "trading state" enjoying an ascendancy unknown since the decline of Venice (Rosecrance 1986). A parallel trend toward the globalization of private economic organizations similarly devalues the currency of the nation-state. Yet another dimension of this transformation is the broad-front assault upon "statism" in the 1980s, of which Ronald Reagan and Margaret Thatcher were only the most spectacular leaders of the attack party. Economic as well as political liberalization became global processes: privatization, deregulation, "structural adjustment" in endebted third world countries. So many watershed events symbolize the force of these trends: the loss of innocence by advanced social democratic states such as Sweden; the spectacular abandonment of core elements of its classical social and economic program by the French Socialist Party in 1982, only a year after the left won its first clear majority; the retreat from populism in Mexico and Argentina led by populist parties which were the very architects of such strategies.

Less clear are the implications for the politics of cultural pluralism. If earlier arguments that the politization of communal cleavages was partly driven by the steady rise in the stakes of the national political arena are accurate, one might speculate that a depolitization of the political economy through a reduced state role might over time lower the temperature of cultural politics. However, this impact would only come gradually and might well be overwhelmed by those trends which have tended to exacerbate communal tensions.

The powerful currents of liberalization were not just economic, but increasingly political. A complex and imperfectly understood relationship grew apparent between the democratic polity and the market economy. Charles Lindblom noted in his influential work, *Politics and Markets,* that no democratic polity existed without a significant role for the market in the economic sphere (1977, 162–166). Robert Dahl, a lifelong student of democratic theory, notes at the end of a long career in a new chapter for the 1990 reissue of *After the Revolution: Authority in a Good Society* that, "It is an historical fact that modern democratic institutions . . . have existed only in countries with predominantly privately owned, market-oriented economies, or capitalism if you prefer that name" (cited in Almond 1991, 468). Such a proposition may have a plausible ring in the 1990s; it clearly did not appear as axiomatic "historical fact" in the 1970s, when scholars such as Guillermo O'Donnell developed powerful briefs for the claim that the "deepening" of capitalism required a "bureaucratic-authoritarian state" (1973). In the impasse in the world of state socialism becoming evident by the end of the 1970s, the inseparability of political and economic reform over time grew apparent, even (one suspects) to the Leninist gerontocracy in China that summoned the army to Tienanmien Square in 1989 to defer the day of reckoning. The passing of the "bureaucratic-authoritarian" state in Latin America, the stunning sweep of democratization in Africa in 1990, the demise of the last dictatorships in western Europe: these momentous transformations left islands of autocracy in the Middle East and southeast Asia, but seemed to announce a global pattern for the 1990s. Scholars such as Juan Linz, who had barely completed major comparative inquests into the rise of authoritarianism, now redirected their energies to the explication of liberalization (Linz 1978; Diamond, Linz, and Lipset 1988).

The momentum toward political liberalization, and the relative institutional vacuum within newly empowered civil societies which it often encountered, created a context in which cultural solidarities might most readily serve as nodal points of structuration; this was clearly the case in Yugoslavia and the Soviet Union. At a minimum, communal claims upon the polity would find new avenues for expression. A prolonged period of uncertainty seemed in prospect, while class, interest, and shared values might (or might not) give rise to complementary or cross-cutting bases for political expression and organization. Were cultural pluralism to monopolize the political arena, to serve as the sole basis for organizing societal consciousness, democratization would face painful obstacles to consolidation. Such apprehensions, however, cannot arrest the contemporary currents of political liberalization. For much of the globe, a great experiment in reconciling democratic governance and cultural pluralism is already in course—doubtless with a variety of outcomes.

The Dynamism of Self-Determination

Intersecting the issue of political liberalization is the changing meaning of self-determination. This potent elixir, discovered in the nineteenth century as a by-product of the idea of nationalism, has always been viewed with unease by the managers of the world system of states, who are instinctively drawn toward the stability of world system's component units as an organizing value. At the time of World War I, two suddenly influential outsiders to global statecraft, Vladimir Lenin and Woodrow Wilson, gave to this potential dissolvant of international order new normative standing. Lenin had purely tactical objectives and believed he had enclosed the concept's volatility within the sturdy container of proletarian internationalism and Bolshevik dictatorship. *Perestroika* and *glasnost* shattered the bottle seven decades later, and self-determination escaped to haunt Lenin's successors. Wilson believed he had discovered an ethical principle for democratic disposition of the European domains of the multi-national empires of Austria-Hungary, Ottoman Turkey, and Czarist Russia. Never imagining that such a principle could find application outside Europe, he was shocked at the parade of would-be nationalities he beckoned from obscurity by his words, many hitherto unbeknownst to him. In subsequent testimony to the Senate Committee on Foreign Relations, he confessed: "When I gave utterance to those words [that all nations had a right to self-determination], I said them without the knowledge that nationalities existed, which are coming to us day after day. . . . You do not know and cannot appreciate the anxieties that I have experienced as a result of many millions of people having their hopes raised by what I have said" (Cobban 1970, 64–65).

The idea of self-determination returned to the international agenda with a vengeance following World War II, finding its way into Articles 1 and 73 of the United Nations Charter. Yet the Charter gave simultaneous sanctuary to the contradictory norms of territorial integrity and the inherent right of a state to self-defense. For a time, self-determination doctrines were above all a weapon in the struggle of African, Asian, and Caribbean lands for liberation from colonial rule. A broad consensus emerged in the international system by the 1960s, accepting anticolonial self-determination, but seeking to confine the application of the doctrine to such situations. Fundamental contradictions subsisted in all efforts to codify such a containment of self-determination, well illustrated in the contrast between Articles 1 and 6 of the 1960 UN General Assembly solemn Declaration on the

Granting of Independence to Colonial Countries and Peoples (UN Resolution 1514 [XV]):

> Article 1: All peoples have the right to self-determination; by virtue of that right they freely determine their political status and freely pursue their economic, social and cultural development.
>
> Article 6: Any attempt aimed at the partial or whole disruption of the national unity and the territorial integrity of a country is incompatible with the purposes and principles of the Charter of the United Nations.

The shared interest of new states and old polities in caging the incubus of unrestricted self-determination served for more than four decades to circumscribe its reach. Until 1991, only Bangladesh managed to escape the custody of an independent state resisting "disruption" of its "national unity and territorial integrity."[9] "Captive nations" such as the Baltic republics of the Soviet Union, no matter how dubious their mode of incorporation, received no succor from the international system.[10] Particularly revealing is the case of Eritrea (carefully examined in the Woldemikael chapter), which carried out a lonely war of liberation for three decades in the face of virtually universal hostility to its claims by the international state system. The terms of its original attachment to Ethiopia in 1952 by the United Nations (a decision largely determined by the play of great power interests unrelated to the principle of self-determination for formerly colonized territories) were swiftly and grossly violated by Ethiopia, with nary a whimper from the United Nations or its membership. So strong was the aversion of the international system to what Ethiopians argued was a dismemberment of their territory that Eritreans could find no audience for any argument other than the force of arms, which in 1991 ultimately prevailed (Lewis 1983; Sherman 1980; Markakis 1987; Selassie 1988).

In 1991, self-determination slipped its chains in the Soviet Union, Yugoslavia, and the Horn, profiting from a sudden collapse of the political order. In Ethiopia, the disintegration of the Leninist regime of Mengistu Haile Mariam brought to power an insurgent formation pledged to accept the results of a referendum on self-determination in Eritrea by 1993; the outcome of such an exercise of popular sovereignty is not in doubt. In Somalia, after a particularly brutal civil war shaped by shifting clan alignments, the northern regions—roughly former British Somaliland—dissolved the voluntarily created union of 1960 and proclaimed an independent Somaliland in June 1991. Although this forlorn entity lacked international recognition, residual Somalia equally lacked the capacity to end the separation by force. Add to these developments the disintegration of the Soviet Union and Yugoslavia, and we find international law interrogated by a new set of political facts. As one student of international jurisprudence recently put the matter, *faits accomplis* are "creative of values regardless of previous conceptions of rights" (Vincent 1978, 27). The bonds tying self-determination solely to "colonial peoples and territories" are thus dissolved.

Yet another aspect of the changing meanings of the self-determination doctrine was an emergent international jurisprudence related to "native peoples" in states whose dominant population stock originated in settlement—essentially the Western hemisphere and parts of Australasia. In a slowly enlarging codification of rights of indigenous minorities, begun by the International Labor Organization in 1957 and the UN Commission on Human Rights from 1971 on, the idea of "self-determination" as a normative entitlement of such groups won growing recognition. Although those speaking for native peoples generally denied that "self-determination" meant a demand for secession, the scope of potential meanings embedded in this doctrine implied an array of status issues confronting such states in the years ahead. The summons to a reconstruction, if not dissolution, of Canada initiated by Quebec has been picked up by Inuit and Algonquian communities in northern Canada. The contested content of "domestic sovereignty" for American Indian communities in the United States, and self-determination claims for indigenous Hawaiians not covered by treaty relations, will figure on future political agendas, as will Maori rights in New Zealand and those of Aboriginal communities in Australia. Where the immigrant stock is of smaller proportions, "indigenous rights" becomes a claim to preferential political treatment for *bumiputera* (sons of the soil) in Malaysia, Fiji, and New Caledonia.

Summing the altered scope of self-determination and the new surge of political liberalization, we face the likelihood of resurrected or novel assertions of sovereignty claims by cultural groups in many parts of the world. All of the excruciating ambiguities in the doctrine of self-determination will return to the political arena. What is a "people" entitled to make this claim? How can such a demand be validated? Is there some critical date at which self-determination is definitively exercised, or may it be repeatedly invoked? Simple coercion can no longer silence such demands, nor can an international normative order preclude their consideration.[11]

Three Conceptions of Cultural Pluralism

The postwar flow of political history has thus radically transformed the politics of cultural pluralism. An equally crucial metamorphosis has come in the conceptualization of this phenomenon since the 1950s. Three formative modes of theoretical discourse have emerged since that time, which for expository purposes I have labeled "instrumentalist," "primordialist," and "constructivist." In a very loose sense, these may be seen as chronologically ordered. Cumulatively, and conjointly, these schools of analysis have transformed our perspectives.

The "instrumentalist" orientation loomed large in many of the early wave studies rediscovering ethnicity (Rothschild 1981; Enloe 1973; Young 1976; Kasfir 1975; Melson and Wolpe 1971; Glazer and Moynihan 1975; Olzak and Nagel 1986). "Instrumentalists" hinged their analysis upon the uses of ethnicity in political and social competition. Cultural pluralism offered a repertory of social roles available for use in pursuit of material advantage. In the well-turned phrase of Daniel Bell, the greater saliency of ethnicity occurs "because it can combine an interest with an affective tie" (1975, 169). From this vantagepoint, cultural pluralism becomes contingent, situational, and circumstantial. The task of analysis was to identify the political factors which might activate it, to discover the cultural entrepreneurs who supplied its doctrine, and the activists who exploited such solidarities.

The "instrumentalist" perspective played an important part in restoring cultural pluralism to the social science agenda, from which it had been all but removed by the paradigmatic preoccupation with nationalism in third world studies and by a dominant focus on "national integration." From these standpoints, cultural pluralism was an artifact of traditionality and backwardness, an inanimate "obstacle" to integration. "Instrumentalism" suggested a way by which analytical recognition could be accorded to cultural pluralism which was compatible with an array of influential paradigms. Structural-functionalists could add communal groups as one additional entry to the roster of "input" groupings on their organic charts of "political system." For the neo-Marxist, the stress upon material factors in instrumental activation of cultural solidarity offered an analytical bridge to class theory. The suzerainty of class could be upheld while recognition was granted to ethnicity as a subsidiary factor—a form of consciousness which, if not false, was at least not fundamental. Cultural pluralism was a serviceable weapon in the hands of petit bourgeois politicians pursuing class interests (Saul 1979; Nnoli 1978). For the rational choice theorist, "instrumentalism" nurtured the notion that ethnic groups were calculating, self-interested collective actors, maximizing material values through the vehicle of communal identity, rational because the ethnic group was at once large enough to seek an effective voice but provided an exclusionary principle permitting limitation of benefits to group members (Bates 1983; Rabushka and Shepsle 1972; Hechter 1986).

However compelling in illuminating the contemporary dynamics of cultural competition and conflict, something important was missing in the material focus of the instrumentalist. A "primordialist" school—in reality an older perspective but now renovated by its dialogue with instrumentalism—emerged to explore the psychological and cultural dimensions necessary to grasp the intensities which might surround ethnic conflict. A. L. Epstein, in summoning analysis to go beyond instrumentalism, points to its inability to explain "the powerful emotional charge that appears to surround or to underlie so much of ethnic behavior; and it is this affective dimension of the problem that seems to me lacking in so many recent attempts to tackle it" (1978, xi). Harold Isaacs, in an influential comparative exploration, insisted upon the "ineffable significance" and "peculiarly coercive powers" of ethnic identity whose social force lay in its psychic properties: ". . . a desperate effort to regain the condition of life in which certain needs were met, to get behind walls that enclose them once more, if only in their minds, in a place where they can feel they belong, and where, grouped with their kind, they can regain some measure of what feels like physical and emotional safety" (1975, 28).

The primordial interpretation of cultural pluralism draws as well from the cultural anthropologist. Human beings, argues Clifford Geertz, are born as incomplete animals, who fulfill themselves through the culture they create, which assumes the role of a primordial "given" of social existence (1973). Frederik Barth (1969) perceives the essence of identity in the array of cues, symbols, and basic values orientations through which groups understand their distinctiveness from "the other"; boundary is the core of consciousness. For Charles Keyes, the primordial root of ethnicity "derives from a cultural interpretation of descent" (1981, 5).

In its extreme form, "primordialism" wanders into the zoological gardens of sociobiology. Pierre Van den Berghe (1978) suggests that ethnicity should be understood as "an extended form of kin selection," best grasped as an elemental instinctual impulse. Paul Shaw and Yuwa Wong (1989) make the provocative claim that a consciousness of group affinity is imprinted in the genetic code, as a product of the many millennia of prehistorical existence when the capacity to recognize members of the kindred was crucial to survival.

Primordialism usefully completes instrumentalism by explaining the force of the "affective tie" through which interest is instrumentally pursued. It helps make comprehensible the emotionality latent in ethnic conflict, its disposition to arouse deep-seated anxieties, fears, and insecurities, or to trigger a degree of aggressiveness not explicable in purely material interest terms. Episodes such as the conflict over Ayodhya temple which inflamed India for weeks in 1990, evoking what Ashis Nandy (1991) calls "the discreet charms of Indian terrorism," can only find explanation in a "primordialist" framework.

The most recent of the three analytical streams, which I label "constructivist," bears the mark of post-structuralist theoretical discourse (Onuf 1989; Berger and Luckmann 1967). The ethnic group, analogous to the Anderson (1983) theory of "nation," is above all an "imagined community." Both instrumentalists and primordialists need to be stood on their heads; what is problematic is not what drives ethnic group action, but the existence of the group itself. Otherwise put, argues Jean-Loup Amselle, ethnicity requires "deconstruction": "Rather than beginning with given ethnonyms, as empty notions requiring filling with economic, political and religious structures, it would be preferable to demonstrate how a term located in time and space acquires progressively a multiplicity of meanings, in sum to establish the genesis of symbols in the realm of ideas" (1985, 44).

Leroy Vail (1989, 11), in his introduction to a remarkable collection of essays, gives exemplary statement to the "constructivist" approach:

> The creation of ethnicity as an ideological statement of popular appeal in the context of profound social, economic and political change in southern Africa was the result of the differential conjunction of various historical forces and phenomena. It is the very unevenness of their co-appearance and dynamic interaction that accounts for the unevenness of ethnic consciousness in the region. One may discern three such variables in the creation and implanting of the ethnic message. First, as was the case in the creation of such ideologies elsewhere, for example in nineteenth century European nationalism, it was essential to have a group of intellectuals involved in formulating it—a group of culture brokers. Second, there was the widespread use of African intermediaries to administer the subordinate peoples, a system usually summed up in the phrase "indirect rule," and this served to define the boundaries and texture of the new ideologies. Third, ordinary people had a real need for so-called "traditional values" at a time of rapid social change, thus opening the way for the wide acceptance of the new ideologies.

The heart of the matter, then, was to perceive ethnicity as manufactured, rather than as given, an innovative act of creative imagination. In complex ways, through multiple mechanisms, consciousness once germinated evolved through progressive redefinitions at all levels of state and society. Over time, it tended to project itself upon larger social spaces (Roosens 1989). The process of social construction proceeds at an individual as well as group level; in the innumerable transactions of daily life, individuals are engaged in a constant process of defining and redefining themselves; identity thus understood is not a "fixed essence" but a "strategic assertion" (Kondo 1990, 9–10). This view is essentially shared by the Sapiro chapter.

A noteworthy merit of the constructivist perspective is the linkages it suggests with other categories of identity creation. The volume by Dorinne Kondo, *Crafting Selves,* is a valuable case in point. Its primary interrogation lies in transacting gender, but it is equally arresting in its insights into the construction of ethnic consciousness, through its partly autobiographical cultural anthropology of a Japanese-American female scholar engaged in a research role within a Japanese milieu. Another virtue is its innate historicism; in problematizing the ethnic category, inquiry is drawn to close inspection of its origins and temporal fluctuations.

Cumulatively, these three modes of conceptualization define much of the universe of theory relating to cultural pluralism. All three, to varying degrees, have shaped the essays which compose this volume. Some, such as the Kent and Schmidt chapters on the United States, are predominately shaped by instrumentalist concerns. Others, such as the Spitz chapter on Hindu revivalism in India, deal more in the primordial dimension. Yet others, such as Entessar's comparison of Azeris in the USSR and Iran, Quirin's exploration of ethnogenesis among the Beta Israel ("Falashas") in Ethiopia, and LeBaron's examination of emergent ethnoracial self-assertion among Guatemalan Maya, exhibit a clear constructivist imprint.

Class and Gender: Are They in Opposition to Cultural Pluralism?

Particularly important to further conceptual development is the terrain of encounter with theoretical perspectives rooted in class and gender. The former confrontation—cultural pluralism versus class—has many decades of unresolved interaction (Young 1986). The latter—represented in this volume by the Sapiro exploratory essay—is only beginning.

Class—most extensively conjoined with cultural pluralism by Kent in this volume—proposes a mode of interrogation of whole societies (normally those defined by a state unit) which perceives as fundamental the principles of inequality rooted in differential material circumstance, resource control, and status. Buttressed by the rich analytical tradition informed by the innumerable strains of Marxist discourse, class theory in a broad sense clearly defines critical dimensions of conflict in any society.[12] Axiomatically, class describes the vertical, hierarchical cleavages in a political society, whereas cultural pluralism is frequently largely a horizontal division; indeed, a recent magistral monograph of comparative synthesis explicitly excludes hierarchical relationships from its study of ethnicity (Horowitz 1985). The conceptual grasp of analysis privileging class, however, is contingent upon the presence of consciousness: the classical class-in-itself versus class-for-itself distinction in Marxist theory. Where social classes rest upon widely diffused and generationally self-reproducing ideologies of identity, as has often been the case in western Europe, and where they become incorporated in the panoply of formal political and social organizations structuring societal conflict, then the analytical force of class analysis is clear. However, in many parts of the globe, ideologies of class identity are diffuse at best; as Benjamin DeMott (1990) has recently lamented in the American case, the citizenry is unable to "think straight" about class. Where, as in Africa, social flux stands out most sharply, and relative wealth or elite status for most is no more than a generation deep, class consciousness is neither deeply rooted nor well centered upon the established categories of classical class theory, as best articulated in Marxist theory. When all is flux, then class—like ethnicity—can be captured as situational, circumstantial, and contingent (Schatzberg 1980).

In my view, the core of the contrast between class and cultural pluralism as political variables lies in the primordial dimension. A linkage between class divisions and patterns of social consciousness is problematic; ethnicity is defined by consciousness. Cultural pluralism more readily supplies an ideological framework evoking powerful psychic responses. Large-scale violence in recent decades within polities has in the great majority of instances followed cultural and not class lines; in the limiting case, genocide is the ultimate pathology of cultural pluralism, not class struggle.

In conceptual exchange between class and cultural pluralism, it is no accident that the most important contributions revolve around race and class. Race, as a form of cultural pluralism, shares with class some critical characteristics. It is rooted in domination and hierarchy and originates in organized systems of labor exploitation (African slavery, indentured Asian labor, coerced Amerindian servitude). Thus, in societies such as South Africa and the United States, the overlap between race and class is strong. Analysis of conflict inevitably leads to reflection upon the race and class components; the claim that political dynamics can find exclusive interpretation in terms of only one of these dimensions is difficult to sustain.[13]

Assimilation of recent feminist scholarship into the understanding of cultural pluralism is only beginning. Sapiro's essay is a stimulating contribution. Like race and class, gender relationships in virtually all cultures have been hierarchical. If one relates the vector of patriarchy which has characterized diverse societies to the distinction between male-dominated public realms and a private sphere into which the female is relegated, one might suggest that politization of cultural pluralism is gendered, like the conduct of warfare. Leadership in organized religion—from Buddhist monks to Catholic priests—is universally male; the cultural entrepreneurs and political activists who have been the builders of ethnic consciousness are overwhelmingly so. Leroy Vail cites the arresting Tswana proverb: "a woman has no tribe" (1989, 15). To the extent that instrumental uses of ethnicity were located predominantly in male realms, this aphorism reveals a broader pattern.

However, male and female are joined through the family structure. Intensely held competing cultural identities within the household unit introduce serious discords, generally managed by deferring to the ethnic or religious affiliation of the dominant partner, or following widely held societal norms (as in patrilineal or matrilineal descent prescriptions in sub-Saharan Africa). Identity definition issues are particularly important in the transmission of consciousness to the next generation, above all in the religious sphere; whereas dual ethnic consciousness is possible, as Mary Waters (1990) elegantly demonstrates in her study of "ethnic options" in America, active membership in two religious systems is an oxymoron. Generally speaking, within the family, the dominant pattern globally is for either a community of cultural identity within the household, or an acknowledged ascendant one.

There are, however, noteworthy instances where dominant employment or household patterns sharply separate male and female, creating at least the possibility of divergent identity systems. In southern Africa, the widespread use of migrant male labor in mines and urban employment, with women remaining in the rural areas, places male and female in radically different circumstances for the construction and transaction of identity. In American cities, the growing phenomenon of the single mother household gives conceptual force to an emergent literature on "women of color." Insights from this and other feminist scholarship will undoubtedly chart new pathways and compel reconsideration of some old ones in the years ahead.

Empirical Insights into the Dynamics of Cultural Pluralism

My discussion thus far in this introduction has been general; the remaining chapters (except for Sapiro) are all specific in their country or regional setting. The particularity of historic circumstance powerfully shapes the form taken by cultural pluralism. However serviceable general and comparative concepts may be in grasping its dynamics, cultural pluralism in operation is contingent upon its immediate environment. The historical trajectory of a given polity provides one set of defining parameters. The imprint of the past persists through the embedded collective memory of traumatic or inspirational moments or events, patterns over time by which broadening elements in civil society have been incorporated into an active political realm, and evolving structures of political organization, conflict, and cooperation.

Dominant modes of discourse concerning cultural pluralism likewise condition the forms which communal solidarities may take. The Soviet Union in its terminal 1989–91 crisis was hostage to a state discourse created by its founders in their dialectical design to capture, subdue, and domesticate ethnonationalism. "National in form, socialist in content" became an explosive doctrine when the credibility of socialism crumbled, leaving only the "national" form in the guise of the fifteen nationality-based republics whose "right" to self-determination could no longer be trivialized by the centralized autocracy of state socialism. Beissinger demonstrates, in different ways, the impact of a state discourse of legitimation which contained a hidden detonator. The importance of this factor clearly emerges from the Entessar chapter comparing Azeri ethnicity under two sovereignties. As a peripheral nationality in an empire-state, Azeri self-consciousness deepened over time and became increasingly assertive. In so doing, it increasingly diverged from that of Iranian Azeris, bound to the Iranian state by sharing in its religious discourse, in its historic mythology, and in its dynastic succession; ruling families from the Safavids (who introduced state Shi'ism) to the Qajars were of Azeri origin.

In China, a state in its third millennia has created a powerful cultural ideology:

in a unique way, the construction of a Chinese people from a diverse set of origins bears the cachet of the "Middle Kingdom." The richly significant ethnonym of "Han Chinese" is emblematic of ethnogenesis; the first enduring unifying and state-building dynasty lives on in this widely employed identifier. The republican heirs to the empire rejuvenated and redefined "Han Chinese" as a doctrine of nationality in a threatening world of nation-states, rather than as a statement of civilized status juxtaposed to a barbarian "other" beyond the Great Wall. In the era of state socialism, examined by Friedman, dominant discourse again changed, absorbing elements of Soviet nationality theory to the management of relations with a geographically large (60 percent of the territory) but demographically small (9 percent) portion of the citizenry.

In Southeast Asia the dominant discourse represented the cultural domain as composed of a core community, historically associated with and currently dominating the central institutions of the state, and "minorities," "hill tribes," or a Chinese immigrant mercantile group. In the Caribbean states, originating in slave plantations, race gradations and classifications defined the cultural universe. In the eighteen states where Arabic is the dominant medium and Arabhood is a defining component of national identity, the discourse of identity is profoundly shaped by the religious and historical experiences which have marked this vast reach of territory, and the frequently painful effort to relate them to modernity and the multiplicity of state units within the Arab cultural zone (Hourani 1991).

In Latin America, the discourse of state has long supplied a powerfully assimilative idiom. Cultural and racial differences constitute a spectrum of status, and not sharp compartments of identity. Ladinoization was ultimately possible. The dual origins of the Mexican soul are transcended in the fusion of the Quetzalcoatl and Guadalupe myths (Lafaye 1976); the Spanish conquerers appropriated an indigenous legend foretelling the imminent return of Quetzalcoatl, mysterious god of the sea, while in 1531 an Indian maiden convert at Guadalupe internalized the alien Christian doctrine through her miraculous visions of the Virgin Mary. Only in very recent times does the commanding power of this discourse over an indigenous periphery begin to weaken in those Andean and Central American polities where the Indian population component remains large; the LeBaron chapter provides fascinating documentation of this process in Guatemala.

In the American case, historically the pedagogy of state at once integrated and differentiated. A powerful, and largely successful, discourse of assimilation applied to immigrants of European ancestry. Native Americans, by contrast, were long constituted as a hostile other; citizenship was accorded to Indians only in 1924, and the Declaration of Independence cites provocation of "savage Indian tribes" in its bill of particulars against George III as justifying the revolt against the crown. African Americans as well were largely excluded from the "shining city on the hill" evoked by the discourse of American national identity: the "blessings of liberty" promised by the framers of the Constitution were somehow compatible with the abomination of slavery which they discovered ways of accommodating. In reaction, in recent times, a discourse of dissent emerges which deconstructs the assimilative ideology into an alternative project of multi-culturalism. Kent and Schmidt effectively capture different aspects of this dynamic.

Africa stands out in the degree to which, in both state doctrine and most intellectual discourse, ethnicity is thoroughly stigmatized. The use of ethnicity as a basis for political organization is formally banned in many states. Usually characterized as "tribalism," ethnic self-assertion is pejoratively viewed as subversive, juvenile, and backward. Clearly the pervasive sense of the possible fragility of the African state system undergirds this concerted assault on formally organized ethnicity. Not without reason: by my count, in the first years of African independence, secessionist movements appeared in eighteen of the fifty-two states. At least until now, the stigmatization of ethnicity has succeeded in limiting open challenges to the current state system itself; the major self-determination movements after the immediate period of transition have invariably grounded their claims in the right of a colonial territory, or one of its administrative subdivisions, to acquire sovereignty as a unit (Biafra, southern Sudan, Eritrea, Western Sahara).

The Ethiopian case deviates from the African pattern in several illuminating respects. State mythology builds upon a three-thousand-year history to create an unusually powerful discourse of nationhood, at least to the intelligentsia, as Gashaw well argues. In this century, ideas of state were transformed by the appropriation of the European nation-state model, especially by Emperor Haile Selassie. The Shoan Amharic core to this rewoven state was partly concealed by the nature of its discourse but became more visible after the 1974 ouster of the emperor and the subsequent imposition of Marxism-Leninism as the doctrine of state—including, *inter alia,* elements of Soviet nationality theory and Leninist lexicon concerning cultural pluralism. At this juncture, in Ethiopia—alone in Africa—the term "nationality" has begun to be used for ethnolinguistic units; elsewhere, "tribe" (in everyday conversation) or "ethnic group" (in more formal contexts) are the terms employed. The growing intensification of the civil war with Eritrean insurgents, whose struggle was rooted in the "colonial territory" theory of self-determination, and policy flaws which (as Friedman insists) seem endemic to Leninist regimes brought a progressive militarization and degeneration of the central polity, culminating in its collapse in May 1991. In its wake, a far-reaching redefinition of political arrangements is in course, in which cultural identities will play a major role—not only in Ethiopia, but, as Woldemikael effectively shows, in an independent Eritrea.

In sum, the world enters a period of exceptional fluidity—of the sort which historically has usually come about through the dislocation of a major war. Nation and state, as we have known them, are interrogated by history and alternative visions of the future. In this process, the politics of cultural pluralism will influence the outcomes in many important ways. In turn, the prospective impact of cultural pluralism beckons us to continue our quest for a more complete understanding of its inner workings.

NOTES

1. The 1989 initiative of the United Nations Research Institute for Social Development (UNRISD) (for which the cited Premdas article was drafted) to undertake a large-scale collective study of ethnic conflict is in itself a significant barometer registering a difference in atmosphere. Earlier studies by this small international agency had been exclusively centered upon conventional "development" issues. Probing into communal strife engages the organization with highly sensitive issues, given the nation-state membership base of its parent body.

2. As one illustration among many of how the changing cultural demographics of the United States may alter the political landscape, one may cite the warning by Arthur Hertzberg (1992, 22) to the Israeli leadership:

> Especially since 1967, Israel's leaders thought that the political power of American Jews would remain more than sufficient to protect Israel's interests in the US. . . . The Israelis believed that American society was permanently dominated by white Christians of European origin, by the descendents of people who had long historical connection with Jews and who harbor some guilt for Jewish suffering through the ages—and support for Israel was "safe" in America.
>
> This confidence is becoming less and less justified. . . . The African Americans, Hispanics, and Asians who are increasingly numerous have no long history of connection to Jews, and they have no special sense of guilt or obligation toward them. On the contrary, in the jostling competition of American life, Jews, both in America and in Israel, are perceived by these newcomers to the political process as an elite to be challenged, not as an endangered species to be protected . . . in not so many years, Israel might even be negotiating with a president who reflects a multi-ethnic coalition of non-white voters.

3. Consolidation of Oromo consciousness is a critical dimension of this change, well documented by Lewis. One measure of the pace of change is that Lewis in his 1966 monograph still used the Amharic ethnonym for the Oromo, "Galla," in his title. Today, as he indicates, this label is angrily rejected by Oromo as a prejudicial Amharic imposition.

4. Alexis de Tocqueville, in a less well known chapter, provides one of the most prescient analyses of the situation of the two racial groups then excluded from the emergent concept of the American nation, "Indian tribes" and "black population" (2: 343–97).

5. Somalia is a more ambiguous case. In the colonial era, there were two Somali-speaking territories, British and Italian Somaliland. In addition, Somali-speaking populations were present in Djibouti, Kenya—and, of course, in Ethiopia. The former British and Italian territories fused with independence in 1960, only to break apart again in 1991.

6. To my knowledge, the first usage of this term was by Horace Kallen in his 1915 work, *Culture and Democracy in the United States,* which appeared in the *Nation*. See Milton Gordon, *Assimilation in American Life* (1964).

7. There were some other long-standing skeptics, such as Robert Conquest, Richard Pipes, and John Armstrong. But those who three decades ago anticipated a break-up of the Soviet Union were few indeed.

8. I am endebted to Kumar Rupesinghe of the International Peace Research Institute in Oslo, Norway, for this figure.

9. Some other examples exist of states breaking apart (Mali and Senegal, Singapore and Malaysia, Syria and Egypt), but these scissions always occurred by mutual consent. Beissinger points out that, if we look beyond the postwar years, a number of examples of negotiated divorce may be found: Ireland from the United Kingdom (1937); Norway from Sweden (1905); Iceland from Denmark (1941).

10. Although the United States officially did not recognize the legality of the 1940 annexation, until 1991 no real encouragement was given to Baltic nationalists. For all practical purposes their incorporation into the Soviet Union was treated as an accomplished and irreversible fact.

11. One may note, as Beissinger and Lewis stress, that in the Soviet and Ethiopian cases, the self-determination claims were partly grounded in the argument that the groups asserting a right to choose their future were unwillingly locked in a colonial relationship by an empire-state. However, the implications of the breakup of these states, and Yugoslavia, go beyond the vindication of the right of colonized peoples to independence.

12. I find particularly useful the succinct discussion of class and ethnicity put forward by Brass (1985, 1–56).

13. For a review of the abundant race versus class literature with relation to South Africa, see Young (1986) and Rex and Mason (1986).

REFERENCES

Akins, James E. 1991. The New Arabia. *Foreign Affairs* 70, 3: 36–49.

Almond, Gabriel A. 1991. Capitalism and Democracy. *PS* 24, 3: 467–74.

Almond, Gabriel A. 1960. Introduction. In *The Politics of Developing Areas,* edited by Almond and James S. Coleman, 3–64. Princeton: Princeton University Press.

Almond, Gabriel A., Marvin Chodorow, and Roy Harvey Pearce, eds. 1982. *Progress and Its Discontents*. Berkeley: University of California Press.

Amselle, Jean-Loup. 1985. Ethnies et espaces: pour une anthropologie topologique. In *Au coeur de l'ethnie: ethnies, tribalisme et état en Afrique,* edited by Amselle and Elikia M'bokolo, 11–48. Paris: Editions de la Découverte.

Anderson, Benedict. 1983. *Imagined Communities: Reflections on the Origin and Spread of Nationalism*. London: Verso Editions.

Barth, Frederik, ed. 1969. *Ethnic Groups and Boundaries*. Boston: Little, Brown and Company.

Bates, Robert H. 1983. Modernization, Ethnic Competition and the Rationality of Politics in Contemporary Africa. In *State Versus Ethnic Claims: African Policy Dilemmas,* edited by Donald Rothchild and Victor Olorunsola, 152–71. Boulder: Westview Press.

Bell, Daniel. 1975. Ethnicity and Social Change. In *Ethnicity: Theory and Experience*, edited by Nathan Glazer and Daniel P. Moynihan, 141–74. Cambridge: Harvard University Press.

Berger, Peter, and Thomas Luckmann. 1967. *The Social Construction of Reality*. Harmondsworth: Penguin Press.

Bockstael, E., and O. Feinstein. 1991. Ethnic Conflict and Development: A Belgian Case Study. Conference on Ethnic Conflict, United Nations Research Institute for Social Development, Dubrovnik, Yugoslavia, 3–6 June.

Brass, Paul R., ed. 1985. *Ethnic Groups and the State*. London: Croon Helm.

Brass, Paul R. 1974. *Language, Religion and Politics in North India*. Cambridge: Cambridge University Press.

Bromlei, Y. V. 1983. *Processus ethniques*. Moscow: Academy of Sciences of the USSR.

Bromlei, Y. V., et al. 1982. *Processus ethniques en U.R.S.S.* Moscow: Progress Publishers.

Bury, J. B. 1955. *The Idea of Progress*. New York: Dover.

Carrère d'Encausse, Hélène. 1978. *L'empire éclate: la révolte des nations en l'U.R.S.S.* Paris: Flammarion.

Cobban, Alfred. 1970. *The Nation State and National Self-Determination*. New York: Thomas Y. Crowell Company.

Connor, Walker. 1984. *The National Question in Marxist-Leninist Theory and Practice*. Princeton: Princeton University Press.

Connor, Walker. 1972. Nation-Building or Nation-Destroying. *World Politics* 24, 3: 319–55.

de Tocqueville, Alexis. 1835. *Democracy in America*. 1954 ed. New York: Vintage Books.

DeMott, Benjamin. 1990. *The Imperial Middle: Why Can't Americans Think Straight about Class*. New York: Morrow.

Diamond, Larry, Juan Linz, and Seymour Martin Lipset, eds. 1988. *Democracy in Developing Countries*. Boulder: Lynne Rienner.

Emerson, Rupert. 1960. *From Empire to Nation: The Rise of Self-Assertion of Asian and African Peoples*. Cambridge: Harvard University Press.

Enloe, Cynthia H. 1973. *Ethnic Conflict and Political Development*. Boston: Little, Brown and Company.

Epstein, A. L. 1978. *Ethos and Identity*. London: Tavistock Publications.

Geertz, Clifford. 1973. *The Interpretation of Cultures*. New York: Basic Books.

Gellner, Ernest. 1983. *Nations and Nationalism*. Ithaca: Cornell University Press.

Glazer, Nathaniel, and Daniel P. Moynihan, eds. 1975. *Ethnicity: Theory and Experience*. Cambridge: Harvard University Press.

Glazer, Nathan, and Daniel P. Moynihan. 1963. *Beyond the Melting Pot*. Cambridge: MIT and Harvard University Press.

Gordon, Milton M. 1964. *Assimilation in American Life*. New York: Oxford University Press.

Graubard, Stephen. 1991. Preface. *Daedalus* 120, 3: v–viii.

Handlin, Oscar. 1951. *The Uprooted*. Boston: Little, Brown and Company.

Hartz, Louis, ed. 1964. *The Founding of New Societies*. New York: Harcourt, Brace & World.

Hechter, Michael. 1986. Rational Choice Theory and the Study of Race and Ethnic Relations. In *Theories of Ethnic and Race Relations,* edited by John Rex and David Mason, 264–79. Cambridge: Cambridge University Press.

Hertzberg, Arthur. 1992. A Lost Chance for Peace. *New York Review of Books* 39, 5: 20–23.

Hobsbawm, E. J. 1990. *Nations and Nationalism since 1780.* Cambridge: Cambridge University Press.

Horowitz, Donald. 1985. *Ethnic Groups in Conflict.* Berkeley: University of California Press.

Hourani, Albert. 1991. *A History of the Arab Peoples.* Cambridge: Harvard University Press.

Isaacs, Harold R. 1975. *Idols of the Tribe: Group Identity and Political Change.* New York: Harper & Row.

Kasfir, Nelson. 1975. *The Shrinking Political Arena: Participation and Ethnicity in African Politics, with a Case Study of Uganda.* Berkeley: University of California Press.

Keyes, Charles F., ed. 1981. *Ethnic Change.* Seattle: University of Washington Press.

Kondo, Dorinne K. 1990. *Crafting Selves: Power, Gender, and Discourses of Identity in a Japanese Workplace.* Chicago: University of Chicago Press.

Lafaye, Jacques. 1976. *Quezalcoatl and Guadalupe: The Formation of Mexican National Consciousness 1531–1813.* Chicago: University of Chicago Press.

Lewis, Herbert S. 1966. *A Galla Monarchy: Jimma Abbe Jifar, Ethiopia 1830–1932.* Madison: University of Wisconsin Press.

Lewis, I. M., ed. 1983. *Nationalism and Self-Determination in the Horn of Africa.* London: Ithaca Press.

Lindblom, Charles E. 1977. *Politics and Markets: The World's Political-Economic Systems.* New York: Basic Books.

Linz, Juan, ed. 1978. *The Breakdown of Democratic Regimes: Crisis, Breakdown and Reequilibration.* Baltimore: Johns Hopkins University Press.

Lipset, Seymour M., and Stein Rokkan. 1967. Cleavage Structures, Party Systems, and Voter Alignments: An Introduction. In *Party Systems and Voter Alignments,* edited by Lipset and Rokkan, 1–64. New York: Free Press.

Markakis, John. 1987. The Nationalist Revolution in Eritrea. *Journal of Modern African Studies* 25, 4: 643–68.

Melson, Robert, and Howard Wolpe, eds. 1971. *Nigeria: Modernization and the Politics of Communalism.* East Lansing: Michigan State University Press.

Nandy, Ashis. 1991. Ethnic Conflict: A Report from India. Conference on Ethnic Conflict, United Nations Research Institute for Social Development, Dubrovnik, Yugoslavia, 3–6 June.

Nehru, Jawaharlal. 1946. *The Discovery of India.* London: Meridian Books.

Nnoli, O. 1978. *Ethnic Politics in Nigeria.* Enugu: Fourth Dimension Publishing Company.

Novak, Michael. 1971. *The Rise of the Unmeltable Ethnics.* New York: Macmillan.

O'Donnell, Guillermo. 1973. *Modernization and Bureaucratic Authoritarian States in South America.* Berkeley: Institute of International Studies, University of California.

Olorunsola, Victor, ed. 1972. *The Politics of Cultural Sub-nationalism in Africa.* Garden City, New York: Doubleday.

Olzak, Susan, and Joane Nagel, eds. 1986. *Competitive Ethnic Relations*. Orlando: Academic Press.

Onuf, Nicholas. 1989. *World of Our Making: Rules and Rule in Social Theory and International Relations*. Columbia: University of South Carolina Press.

Parenti, Michael. 1967. Ethnic Politics and the Persistence of Ethnic Identifications. *American Political Science Review* 61, 3: 717–26.

Portes, Alejandro, and Ruben G. Rumbaut. 1990. *Immigrant America: A Portrait*. Berkeley: University of California Press.

Premdas, Ralph. 1991. Ethnic Conflict and Development: The Guyana Case. Conference on Ethnic Conflict, United Nations Research Institute for Social Development, Dubrovnik, Yugoslavia, 3–6 June.

Rabushka, Alvin, and Kenneth A. Shepsle. 1972. *Politics in Plural Societies: A Theory of Political Instability*. Columbus, Ohio: Charles E. Merrill Publishing Company.

Rex, John, and David Mason, eds. 1986. *Theories of Ethnic and Race Relations*. Cambridge: Cambridge University Press.

Roosens, Eugene E. 1989. *Creating Ethnicity: The Process of Ethnogenesis*. Newbury Park, California: Sage Publications.

Rosecrance, Richard. 1986. *The Rise of the Trading State: Commerce and Conquest in the Modern World*. New York: Basic Books.

Rothschild, Joseph. 1981. *Ethnopolitics: A Conceptual Framework*. New York: Columbia University Press.

Saul, John. 1979. *State and Revolution in Eastern Africa*. New York: Monthly Review Press.

Schatzberg, Michael G. 1980. *Politics and Class in Zaire: Bureaucracy, Business, and Beer in Lisala*. New York: Holmes & Meier.

Selassie, Bereket H. 1988. *Eritrea and the United Nations*. Trenton: Red Sea Press.

Seton-Watson, Hugh. 1977. *Nations and States*. Boulder: Westview Press.

Shaw, R. Paul, and Yuwa Wong. 1989. *Genetic Seeds of Warfare: Evolution, Nationalism, and Patriotism*. Boston: Unwin Hyman.

Sherman, Richard. 1980. *Eritrea: The Unfinished Revolution*. New York: Praeger.

Smith, Anthony D. 1971. *Theories of Nationalism*. New York: Harper Torchbooks.

Smith, Donald. 1964. *Religion and Political Development*. Boston: Little, Brown and Company.

Stalin, Joseph. 1936. *Marxism and the National and Colonial Question*. London: Lawrence & Wisher.

Tishkov, Valery. 1991. The Soviet Empire Before and After Perestroika. Conference on Ethnic Conflict, United Nations Research Institute for Social Development, Dubrovnik, Yugoslavia, 3–6 June.

Toure, Sekou. 1959. *Toward Full Reafricanisation*. Paris: Présence Africaine.

Vail, Leroy, ed. 1989. *The Creation of Tribalism in Southern Africa*. Berkeley: University of California Press.

Van den Berghe, Pierre. 1978. Race and Ethnicity: A Sociobiological Perspective. *Ethnic and Racial Studies* 1: 401–11.

Vincent, R. J. 1978. Western Conceptions of a Universal Moral Order. *British Journal of International Studies* 4, 1: 20–46.

Waters, Mary C. 1990. *Ethnic Options: Choosing Identities in America*. Berkeley: University of California Press.

Young, Crawford. 1986. Nationalism, Ethnicity, and Class in Africa: A Retrospective. *Cahiers d'Etudes Africaines* 26, 3: 421–95.

Young, Crawford. 1976. *The Politics of Cultural Pluralism*. Madison: University of Wisconsin Press.

2

Engendering Cultural Differences

■ ■ ■

VIRGINIA SAPIRO

Women haven't had an easy relationship with nationalism.

Cynthia Enloe, *Bananas, Beaches, and Bases*

IN ONE of the most powerful essays posing a constructivist view of gender, race, and rights, among other things, Patricia Williams writes about the "secret of my blood" (1988, 6). When Williams went off to law school as a young black woman, her mother comforted her by telling her she had nothing to fear in law school; law was "in her blood." The "blood" in question was that created by the rape of Williams's great-great-grandmother by the white judge who owned her. Family ties are real, they are natural and primordial. An obvious trick a parent might use to comfort a child about to enter a highly competitive law school would be to remind that child of the family precedent and succession. The great-great-grandfather, the judge, should ease the way for the great-great-grandchild, the law student.

The stunning part of this story, of course, is that it is not "natural" for the great-great-grandchild to claim such a right of succession when the ancestor was a white male slave owner and the grandchild is a black woman in a white- and male-dominated society and profession. As Williams understood, although her mother pushed her to reclaim her heritage as a source of strength, that heritage was located in the European and masculine part of her history. It is "a heritage the weft of whose genesis is my own disinheritance" (Williams 1988, 7). Somewhere, Williams may have a white-skinned female cousin who used her great-great-grandfather's status as a judge to give her the confidence to face law school. But if there is a white-skinned male cousin who faced the same prospect, it was surely the most "natural" move for him; after all, his great-great-grandfather was a judge.

At one time it would have been typical for the story of Patricia Williams's inheritance to be understood through the lens of race and, at least explicitly, race alone. But that would be a fragmented and most partial understanding. This particular story was conceived in a rape, pregnancy, childbirth, and a customary and legal construction of kinship rights that all depended on both race and gender.

Expansions of the study of gender, on the one hand, and of race and ethnicity, on the other, have occurred simultaneously, but these areas have existed primarily as parallel subfields, and only recently has there been serious attempt at theoretical integration and synthesis. Of course there have long been efforts that might be characterized as "add women and stir" or "sprinkle in some blacks," but understanding the role of gender in cultural pluralism, or the significance of cultural divisions for the lives of women and men *as* women and men, requires more. At the core of creating a more nuanced and complex understanding of the relationship between gender and cultural pluralism is the necessity of understanding the relationship between gender and cultural identity. The two are considerably more entangled than is often appreciated in the scholarly literature.

Elsa Barkley Brown, for example, poses a crucial question in analyzing the political history of black women in the United States: what constitutes a "race" issue and what constitutes a "gender" issue (Brown 1989)? Political movements conventionally place a priority on one or another form of identity, suppressing the significance of others. Thus, as Brown points out, at the beginning of the twentieth century, when neither women nor blacks had the right to vote, black women's status appeared incomprehensible to many of the political organizations with which they were allied. Black women who worked to gain the vote for black men and women were not regarded as "woman suffragists" by white-dominated "women's suffrage" organizations because the black women did not separate struggles on the basis of race and gender. Likewise, as Deborah King has written in an influential article on multiple consciousness, "In a curious twist of fate, we find ourselves marginal to both the movements for women's liberation and black liberation irrespective of our victimization under the dual discriminations of racism and sexism" (King 1988, 52).

This fragmented perspective has been widely held among scholars and activists, even though it places black women in an untenable situation, treating them as though "while we are both black and female, we occupy those roles sequentially, as if one cannot have the two simultaneously in one's consciousness of being" (Brown 1989, 612). Black women are cloaked in "theoretical invisibility" (King 1988, 42). As much as its negative impact should be clear in the American context for black women, it should not be overlooked that this fragmenting approach does not only affect people who share subaltern gender and cultural status. In any society incorporating gender divisions of labor and assignment of status—which includes almost all known societies—the specific significance of race or ethnicity for lived experience must be conditioned in part by the specificity of gender. Even in apartheid society, being the white wife of a white business or political leader is not the same as being a white business or political leader.

The linkage between gender and cultural identity is more profound than the multiple jeopardies encountered in the distribution of economic and political goods. Gender and cultural terms often inform the construction of each other. In an effort to explain the seriousness of women's oppression in society, feminists have often relied on racial metaphors, especially by drawing comparisons between race-based slavery and the historic power of men over women regardless of race. The reverse has also been true. The treatment of American blacks by whites has often been described as "emasculation," while the struggle for liberation has been termed a struggle for "manhood." The gendered construction of race oppression and the racial construction of gender oppression are not precisely parallel, and both reflect crucial assumptions that come into play in these usually unselfconscious uses of language. For feminists the racial metaphor places all the negative connotation on the oppressor. The import of the sexual metaphor in the case of race is different because emasculation or the loss of manhood is culturally understood to mean one is being turned into a naturally weaker and less significant being: a woman.

The literature on the politics of cultural pluralism suffers from the linked problems of the relative absence of women as contributors and of gender as a theoretical category.[1] In the remainder of this chapter, I suggest elements of feminist theory that might be especially useful in the endeavor to bring gender into focus in the politics of cultural pluralism. In doing so, I have used illustrations from recent literature on different national and cultural settings. These elements of feminist theory are simply bases for theoretical and empirical work that might be integrated in different ways. My purpose is not to offer "a theory" of gender and the politics of cultural pluralism, nor to explain the relationships fully in any specific national setting, but rather to suggest ways in which gender might be incorporated into analysis.

In taking a "constructivist" approach to both conventionally understood cultural categories and gender, my argument is that although comparative and historical research suggests that there are discernible patterns in the way gender and, for example, ethnicity are linked together in the construction of political claims and responses, the specific shape of these links is determined by the differing matrix of historical memory, material conditions, and contemporary problems in which they are found. The notion of the "eternal feminine" may be widely held and, most often, associated with closeness to nature as compared with culture and civilization, which is male (Ortner 1974), but in the history of cultural construction it is also possible to witness the varying construction of what constitutes the "eternal" and "natural" (Lerner 1986). As natural and primordial as many have viewed ethnic boundaries and differences to be, gender boundaries and differences are generally understood to be immutable. Thus the significance of constructions of gender for other cultural categories has usually been overlooked, much to the detriment of understanding either.

A Macrological Framework: Sex/Gender Systems

Incorporating a gendered perspective is not just a matter of including women in research where they have been excluded before. Rather, it means understanding the ways in which gender norms and divisions of labor help to structure the full range of social activity and organization. A useful concept that has been widely adopted within the social sciences and history as a framework for organizing and understanding of the significance of gender is the *sex/gender system,* first introduced by Gayle Rubin (1974). This term, similar in its construction to the related terms *political system* or *economic system,* refers to the institutionalization of norms that are constructed from and provide the evidence of biological sex with an elaborated cultural and social significance.

The notion of a sex/gender system requires distinguishing between *sex,* the biological distinctions between female and male, and *gender,* or the culturally constructed norms and activities that are associated with sex. In the most common illustration of this distinction, it is one's sex that determines whether one is a childbearer or semen contributor in the process of reproduction. It is one's gender that is used to determine what child-rearing roles one should play as well as what other activities are appropriate for an individual who is the parent of a small child. *Masculinity* and *femininity* are the terms commonly used to refer to those cultural norms, although in most cultures most of what is identified as masculine or feminine is assumed to be natural; that is, directly determined by biology.

Just as political and economic systems may be understood as variable and historically contingent allocation systems, so sex/gender systems also allocate value and structure divisions of labor. One of the main tasks of research on sex/gender systems is the investigation of the relationship between political and economic conditions and structures and the institutionalization of gender.

One important question, then, in the study of cultural pluralism is a very basic one: how is gender implicated in the allocation of group membership including, for example, ethnicity, religion, or nationality? Even where "blood" determines membership, not all "blood" is equal, either on grounds of cultural categorization or gender. With some exceptions (such as in Confucian societies) where there is a clearly dominant race or ethnic group, the subordinate group is usually seen, in a sense, as the stronger in passing on ethnicity, at least through a process of pollution. Thus in white-dominant societies, the child of a black and white parent is designated black. In Nazi Germany a self-defined Christian with one Jewish parent, grandparent, or great-grandparent was defined as Jewish.

It is also true, of course, that ethnic and religious groups and nations often hold women and men not equally capable of passing on group membership, or even of maintaining their own group membership if they marry outside the group or nation. The principles of lineality and ownership of membership rights not only can change, but also can be the subject of explicit policy debate and law, as in the United States in the last half of the nineteenth and beginning of the twentieth centuries (Sapiro 1984). Earlier in U.S. history, law and convention treated sex between a black slave and white freeperson differently depending on the race *and* gender of each participant. If the white was female she lost her freedom by having sexual relations with a black slave; if the white was male there was no such punishment.

The definition and preservation of access to membership in the group is an important function of any cultural group; that importance only increases in plural societies or in other situations in which one group comes in close contact with another. One of the key means of controlling group membership is through regulation of sexuality, reproduction, and the group identification and socialization of the young. Thus the activity of defending and fulfilling prescribed norms of masculinity and femininity becomes intertwined with fulfilling the prescribed norms of membership within a particular cultural community.

Although gender thus plays a role in the cultural status of both men and women, in a male-dominated or patriarchal sex/gender system, the regulation of women will be far more strict than the regulation of men. Where valuables such as group membership and property are defined as passing primarily by birth inheritance from father to son, it is especially important to control women's sexuality in order to be sure the inheritors are indeed legitimate. The recognition of this principle played an important role in European political theory on the distinct citizenship rights of men and women. Jean-Jacques Rousseau, for example, noted that while adultery among married men was not acceptable, among women it was tantamount to treason insofar as it resulted in "stealing" a man's inheritance from him if a child conceived in adultery could be passed off as the husband's (Rousseau 1780).[2]

The control over women's sexuality has often been played out in inter-group conflict through the dynamics of rape (Brownmiller 1975). Indeed, all too commonly it is possible to see what we might call the "politics of honor" played out between groups through the medium of women's sexuality. The assault on the enemy involves a wide range of physical and psychological tactics, but one of the most notable means of assaulting the honor or pride of a nation or community is to assault the "honor" of its women through rape.[3]

A searing illustration is offered by the twin examples of Pakistan and Bangladesh. As Ayesha Jalal writes, the frenzy of bloodletting at the time of partition had additional effects on women and "underlined the vulnerability of women deprived of the protection of male family members" (1991, 85). But the special form of violence committed against women was not just a "private" issue of the difficulty of maintaining a patriarchal family structure in the midst of such massive violence. Rather, it had more lasting social and political ramifications within Pakistani society, both in terms of communal memory and certainly, for the women involved, of survival. "The mere presence on Pakistani soil of tens of thousands of women who had been abducted and raped was an ignominious blot on the conscience of a social order that made a fetish of safeguarding female honor" (ibid.). The "rehabilitation" of the "fallen" women was slow to get underway and remains incomplete not just because of the difficulty of the task, but presumably, also because as long as the women had been stripped of their "honor," even if against their will, they would remain an internal sign of the opponent's success in taking that honor.

The tragedy was played out again in Bangladesh when perhaps thirty thousand women were raped by Pakistani soldiers, a campaign of terror that seemed so comprehensive that there was a widespread belief that part of the purpose was to "improve" the gene pool of the Bengalis. In order to avoid the likelihood that the victims would be rejected by their own families and communities, the women were declared war heroines, and some government jobs were reserved for them. Few took advantage of this program because it would mean identifying themselves as rape victims. This was one of the few cases of massive war-related rape in which the international community became involved, but in the end it seems that the women involved were seen less as victims who needed to be nurtured by their communities, and more as signs of a communal loss of honor (Brownmiller 1975; Kabeer 1991). A similar reluctance to identify women as the victims of war-related rape can be seen in Korea, where only in the early 1990s did the plight and long-lasting anger of the Korean girls and young women who were forced to "work for" Japanese soldiers in World War II become acknowledged, even in their own country. In a discussion of abuses of women in the context of nationalist struggles, Cynthia Enloe notes that the abuse of women often seems recast as more a problem for men than women. "Many nationalists have assumed, too, that the significance of the community's women being raped or vulgarly photographed by foreign men is that the honor of the community's men has been assaulted" (Enloe 1989, 62).

Allegations of rape are sometimes used as justifications for the men of one community to commit violent attacks on the men of another. The history of lynching of black men by whites in the United States shows the degree to which sexuality and gender help to frame the specific history of racism. The pivotal role played by the charge of rape in Paul Scott's novel, *Jewel in the Crown* (1966), suggests that the symbolic framing of racism by sexual and gender stories can be a powerful mechanism for excusing violence. This is not to say, of course, that the construction of sexuality or gender in any way *causes* inter-community violence, but rather, that that violence cannot be fully explained without understanding this frame. We can begin with simple questions that lead, inevitably, to more complicated answers. If a community must make up and believe a story to justify and excuse its violence, why do they "choose" a story of gender and sexuality?

There are many examples of (male) community and national identity being exercised and developed through the sexual symbolism of the protection of "its" women from the corruption and abuse by men from outside the community. In addition to the many examples of physical sexual violence against women, we can also see the politics of honor played out in terms of other kinds of violations. Kumari Jayawardena, for example, mentions the backlash following the end of the French occupation of Egypt against women who had been influenced by French style on the grounds that they had been "corrupted." As Jayawardena remarks, "It is significant that one does not hear of such violence being used against Egyptian men who had adopted European ways" (1986, 45).

Certainly the centrality of the "woman question" in the recent history of Iran reveals women and the regulation of their sexuality as the symbolic site of the contest for communal loyalty. Here as elsewhere, the emancipation of women and, as elsewhere in the Muslim world, the unveiling of women had become a symbol of a new modern community. When in 1936 the compulsory unveiling of women in public places was decreed, it was largely because " 'the traditional woman' became the most visible symbol of backwardness. Correspondingly the journey into modernity was defined as one of educating and unveiling this backward subject" (Najmabadi 1991, 51). After the fall of the Shah in 1979, Iranian women's sexuality and the means of regulating it took on even greater importance, as the day of enforced unveiling came to be recast as "a day of shame, symbolizing the assault of corrupt Western culture upon Islamic values, whose effect has been the undermining of public morality" (ibid., 49).

Why does the regulation of women and their sexuality take on such importance as symbolic turf in community-defining struggles? Enloe suggests five linked reasons for the importance of women's sexuality as both symbolic and instrumental grounds for regulation by men involved in community-defining and preservation. Women are regarded as valuable community possessions; they are principal vehicles for transmitting values from one generation to the next; they are bearers of the community's future generations; they are regarded as particularly vulnerable to defilement and exploitation by oppressive others; and they are seen as most susceptible to assimilation and co-optation by insidious outsiders (Enloe 1989, 53–54). These views revolve around women's roles as mothers and carriers of culture and morality, but in the last analysis, rest upon the notion that they are weaker by nature than men, not just physically, but culturally and morally as well.[4]

The argument is well exemplified by an editorial in an Iranian women's journal attacking the secular notion of enlightenment: "Colonialism was fully aware of the sensitive and vital role of women in the formation of the individual and of human society. They considered her the best tool for subjugation of the nations. Therefore, under such pretexts as social activity, the arts, freedom, etc., they pushed her to degeneracy and degradation and made of her a doll. . . ." (cited in Najmabadi 1991, 67). The article continues, ". . . woman is the best means of destroying the indigenous culture to the benefit of imperialists" and claims that indeed, women had been "unconscious accomplices" in the attempted destruction of their own culture (ibid.).

Enloe makes a telling point about the politics of cultural conflict and gender in her analysis of Malek Alloula's *The Colonial Harem* (1986), in which he uses colonialists' postcard images of Arab women to explore his identity as a male nationalist. She quotes him as saying, "Becoming a nationalist requires a man to resist the foreigner's use and abuse of his women" (Enloe 1989, 42). She notes that Alloula does not attempt to understand the dynamics of the situation from the women's point of view. He considers neither material questions: Who are the women in these pictures? How did they get there? Did they ever see the postcards later? Nor does he explore the psychological dimensions of their experience. "Malek Alloula and other male nationalists seem remarkably *un*curious about the abused women's own thoughts—about the meaning they might have assigned to foreign conquest" (ibid., 42). To consider these questions, we must turn to a more individual approach to the problem of the politics of gender and culture.

A Micrological Framework: "Doing Gender"

During the recent decades of women's studies research, scholars have searched for means of understanding the connection of the larger sex/gender system to individual behavior and experience. Most commonly, theoretical work has been based on the concepts of socialization and gender roles. The focus on socialization emphasizes the learning of cultural gender norms including the definitions of masculinity, femininity, and appropriate sexuality. Gender roles, on the other hand, draw attention to complexes of behavior linked to particular status and institutional positions. Most important of these in industrialized societies has been the distinction between (female) homemakers and (male) workers, or nurturers and producers, that shapes the way people think about what women and men do in society.

The conventional use of socialization and gender roles has sometimes been criticized for providing an overdetermined, oversocialized picture of how gender works in everyday life. In particular, as West and Zimmerman (1987) point out, much of the literature obscures the amount of work it takes in many circumstances to perform as a man or woman appropriately. In contrast, they draw on social interaction theory to pose the concept of "doing gender," which emphasizes gender as "a routine, methodical, and recurring accomplishment. We contend that the 'doing' of gender is undertaken by women and men whose competence as members of society is hostage to its production. Doing gender involves a complex of socially guided perceptual, interactional, and micropolitical activities that cast particular pursuits as expressions of masculine and feminine 'natures' " (West and Zimmerman 1987, 126). "Doing gender" does not refer just to acting within large role complexes, such as working in appropriately gender-segregated jobs. It includes even the minute details of dress, demeanor, and social ritual that not only may be done in appropriately feminine or masculine ways, but may be done precisely in order to signal that one is appropriately masculine or feminine.

West and Zimmerman argue that focusing on how people "do" gender focuses attention on what *individuals* do, but in contrast to the common, almost trait-like appearance of gender conceived purely as internalized norms, "we conceive of gender as an emergent feature of social arrangements and as a means of legitimating one of the most fundamental divisions of society" (West and Zimmerman 1987, 126). Two further points flow from this notion of "doing gender." Where being male or female is fundamental to social identity, "then a person engaged in virtually any activity may be held accountable for performance of that activity as a woman or a man, and their incumbency in one or the other sex category can be used to legitimate or discredit their other activities. Accordingly, virtually any activity can be assessed as to its womanly or manly nature" (ibid., 136). The symbolic interactionist basis of this view means that doing gender appropriately can become merged and reconstructed as, for example, doing ethnicity appropriately. Under certain circumstances, to violate one norm is to violate the other.

Perhaps one of the most obvious illustrations of a merging of the significance of gender and cultural or national membership is the history of political control over women's dress and demeanor. I have already referred to the historical controversy over veiling in Iran and other Islamic countries. There are other examples of situations in which there is a merging of the communal and gender significance of dress or demeanor for women and also for men, although usually not with the consequences found in contemporary Islamic politics.

The fact that ethnic or religious communities often identify themselves with physical markers—sometimes in clothing, sometimes hair styles, and sometimes in bodily alteration—is clear, but these markers are rarely similar for men and women. Individuals can thus be assessed with regard to doing *both* gender and ethnicity or religion in the way they dress, cut their hair or cover their head, pierce their ear or nose, or accept "circumcision" for their sons or daughters.[5] Entire political movements have been named after articles of clothing or hairstyles, but usually the clothing was intended for men rather than women. Consider the *sans-culottes,* brown shirts and black shirts, the roundheads, or even, in the United States in the 1960s, the hardhats. In the politics of dress and demeanor women and men are rarely treated similarly. Despite the support of Westernization of male dress in Korea in the 1890s, women who adopted Western hairstyles and dress were attacked as being savage.

If one does any of these daily rituals incorrectly, one is acting inappropriately as a member of the community, but also for one's gender. To do cultural categorization inappropriately is usually seen as having sexual implications. For men, it makes one unattractive as a sexual or marital partner as generally defined within the culture. For women, it may make one unattractive in these same ways, but very often the violator is accused of promiscuity or prostitution because of the symbolism of the regulation of women's sexuality by men. A woman out of line is also out of control which, ironically, makes her public goods.[6]

The daily rituals of dress and demeanor can be identified as the site at which community membership becomes integrated most directly into individuals' everyday consciousness and behavior, where the political and communal becomes personalized and moralized. The Iranian example offers an especially clear field for study. Afsaneh Najmabadi points out that, although the Islamic militant and secular radical might differ on a number of important issues, including how to define the range of women who might be classified as *gharbzadeh* (westoxicated) *women,* both would agree not just on criticizing "the painted dolls of the Pahlavi regime," but also on making these women a central symbol in the reconstruction of Iran. The charge of *gharbzadegi* (westoxication) has to do with a basic shared concern about the transgression of the norms of the community, most apparent among those who display their transgression and who are most charged with not displaying themselves: women. Najmabadi identifies the commonality between the contenders for a new Iranian order:

> First and possibly most important, was the common acceptance of the legitimacy of the community's prerogative to set the limits of individual moral behavior. Second, although the actual limits were vastly different between the two extremes of political opposition, there was a connecting thread that made sense of the common denunciations of the *gharbzadeh* woman: the preservation of "modesty" as a desirable characteristic of a woman (1991, 65).

It should be understood that although the Iranian example may appear especially stark to non-Islamic eyes, it is quite common for those engaged in cultural conflict to moralize politics through representations about the sexuality of the opponent's women. This commonly occurs, for example, between the dominant groups in society and new immigrant groups.[7] It is also used to rationalize away rape of women of subordinate groups in society by men of the dominant groups, by accusing the women of promiscuity or prostitution (see, e.g., hooks 1981, 33).

As West and Zimmerman alert us, we can be assessed in our performance of gender and community membership in any activity. Thus, the politics of control over personal behavior is the politics of gender and community. The Hindu practice of *sati* is a persistent example. For those who continue to support *sati,* the practice is certainly regarded as the appropriate way for a widow to behave; that is, it is the sign of female self-sacrifice and wifely devotion. But attacks on *sati* are taken as attacks on the Hindu community as a whole; as Amrita Chhachhi points out, in Hindu communities that feel threatened, "the ability of a Hindu woman to commit *sati* became a symbol for independence" (Chhachhi 1991, 155). This apparent independence takes some unraveling to appreciate fully. For the men who witness and defend *sati* and gain this sense of independence (as opposed to the woman who is cremated), the independence is in one sense vicarious: they see a (female) member of the community be courageous enough to give up her life as prescribed by the community, but in a way that cannot threaten the men themselves. To the contrary, indeed, for the men who feel their community threatened the source of the strength they draw must be double: the sacrificial devotion of their fellow Hindus to the community, and the sacrificial devotion of their wives to them.

Deniz Kandiyoti's conclusions about the importance of women in what we might call gender performance as focal points for larger social debates are drawn from her review of work on women, the state, and Islam, but they are much more broadly applicable. She argues that the anti-imperialistic pronouncements about the West in the Islamic world are often "thinly disguised metaphors" for painful internal social divisions made on the basis of class and cultural or other interests. She argues that "Discourses on women's authenticity are therefore at the heart of a utopian populism which attempts to obliterate such division by demarcating the boundaries of the 'true' community and excluding the 'Other within' " (Kandiyoti 1991, 8). Although women and sexuality will not necessarily be such a major center of attention in a transforming state, "women continue to represent the 'privacy' of the group and the focal point of kinship-based primary solidarities as against a more abstract and problematic allegiance to the state" (ibid., 9).

Gender-Based Divisions of Labor and Women's Activity

Although I have emphasized the symbolic role of women in the politics of cultural relations, it would be a mistake to see this as the only way to analyze the role of women and gender. Indeed, some observers have pointed out that as in most other realms of life women have too often been interpreted as passive or overdetermined subjects of their cultures, or as mere victims. Historians and social scientists in a variety of areas increasingly emphasize the need to uncover the women's active communal roles which have usually been ignored or passed over by scholars.

Women are often recognized as culture carriers—as we have seen, one of the reasons the regulation of women seems so important is because of this role—but the specifics of women's cultural labor has not received due attention. No known society is free of gender-based divisions of labor in at least some of the major social arenas such as the family, labor market, political system, or other social activities. The work of creating and maintaining culture is also marked by gender divisions of labor.

Some recent research on familial divisions of labor point to a concept that should be useful in examining the integration of family and personal life with the politics of cultural pluralism. In the course of her work on the life histories of Italian-American families in northern California, Micaela di Leonardo (1987, 442–43) has introduced the idea of the "work of kinship" or "kin work," defined as

> the conception, maintenance, and ritual celebration of cross-household kin ties, including visits, letters, telephone calls, presents, and cards to kin, the organization of holiday gatherings, the creation and maintenance of quasi-kin relations; decision to neglect or to intensify particular ties, the mental work of reflection about all these activities; and the creation and communication of altering images of family and kin vis à vis the images of others, both folk and mass media.

Di Leonardo finds in her own work and in her reading of ethnographies from widely divergent cultures that "kin work . . . is like housework and child care: men in the aggregate do not do it" (ibid., 443). She even found that over time women developed greater knowledge of their husband's kin than their husbands had. On the basis of her review of other research she concludes that kin-work is not nearly as much an ethnic, racial, or class phenomenon as it is a gender phenomenon; that is, she sees this gender-based division of labor across ethnic, racial, and class groups.

The idea of kin-work can expand and enhance our understanding of women's role in cultural production and maintenance beyond the usual recognition of women as socializers of the young. Even if men hold the authority in most public cultural institutions such as religion and education,[8] and even where they are regarded as the head of the family, women carry out what may be the most important day-to-day culture work. To the degree that the daily behavioral expression of community membership is embedded in such things as how one eats, dresses, and uses household space and is threaded through the cycles of daily, yearly, and lifespan rituals including especially family-based celebrations, women's kin-work translates also as culture work.

Women's work naturalizes culture. It helps make historically shaped cultural expressions feel primordial. Ritual foods offer good illustrations. Among Jews around the world, for example, it is traditional to eat something cooked in oil during the festival of Hanukkah. Although this is a matter of convention and tradition rather than law or formal prescription, Jews know they "should" eat this special dish at the appropriate time, and mothers teach their daughters how to prepare it, often taking pride in their special recipe for it. The interesting feature of this expression of heritage for our purposes is that the dish that is prepared is very different in different parts of the world. Most European Jews know that one "must" eat *latkes,* a potato pancake. But North African Jews eat an entirely different dish. Nevertheless, because the knowledge and *creation* of this dish passes from generation to generation within the family, one dish is not a suitable substitute for the other as a mechanism for making one "feel" Jewish when consuming it. Only the dish one's mother made (or, in some "modern" areas, purchases and serves) is the real one.

Sarah Deutsch's (1987) study of change within a Hispanic community of the southwest United States offers an example of the role of women not just in the history and maintenance of one culture, but in inter-cultural relations. Using the last part of the nineteenth century and the first half of the twentieth as her frame, Deutsch studied the community lives of the Hispanic community in northern New Mexico and then, following migration, in Colorado. In the earlier period, the divisions of labor helped to structure the daily life of the Hispanic community and its pattern of interaction with the Anglos. Women were important in maintaining communal ties through their interaction in food production, sharing and borrowing, and through the activities surrounding birth, in which the midwife served an important communal role. Looking further afield, their work helped maintain kin relationships with those in other villages.

Economic factors combined to lead to migration and to a different structure of family and community life. The communal links among the women unraveled and, in addition, Anglo missionaries and social workers engaged in efforts to "Americanize" the Chicanas. As a result, the women's former powers were lost as were some of the bonds of culture within the community.

Deutsch's story points to another important element in the history of women's relationship to cultural politics. Just as women have played important roles in the family and community through their activities as wives, mothers, and homemakers, so they have often played an active role in inter-cultural relations through other gender-based roles as teachers, missionaries, and social workers. Deutsch follows the work of the women who served as missionaries and social workers and who were intent on Americanizing the Chicano women, a project which entailed, among other things, enacting domestic roles that the Anglos thought proper, thus creating American homes that would also Americanize husbands and children. Women in the United States from the northeast variously went south and west as missionaries to teach, "civilize," Americanize, and otherwise culturally transform Hispanic, black, native, and European settler communities during the course of the nineteenth century. Women have also been active in international missionary work. Researchers who have gone beyond the conventional view that dismisses these efforts as being either a type of deviant angel work or merely derivative of the work of men (usually husbands), have made important contributions by revealing the gendered dimensions of inter-cultural activities.[9]

Feminism and Cultural Politics

Thus far I have suggested some leads to considering the relationship between gender and the politics of culture. Here I will turn more directly to the relationship between what is explicitly gender-based and what is culture-based, drawing especially on some of the current literature on feminism, nationalism, and state building.

As discussed above, women have often been transformed symbolically during the course of community and nation-building to represent the modernized nation or the timeless heritage of traditional values—or both. As Kumari Jayawardena points out, even nations which are creating a new modern image cannot totally abandon the old or they lose the psychological and cultural bond of nationhood itself. Therefore, even while reshaping women's dress and demeanor or education or work to become "modern" and "enlightened," many nations also construct or invoke a lost egalitarian past (Jayawardena 1986, 14). Thus, in a story common to revolutionary movements, the struggle for change is transformed into a struggle to regain lost authenticity.[10]

Just as some European political theorists and activists from the later eighteenth to the mid-nineteenth century argued that the status of women was a good clue to the general condition of a civilization or state,[11] so from the late nineteenth to well into the twentieth century in many third world nations a minimalist form of feminism became an instrumental part of the efforts of a sometimes odd coalition of missionaries, colonial administrators, male reformers, nationalists, and women themselves.

Not surprisingly, in nations intent on creating a new citizenship, women's citizenship has become an important focus of attention, although often for the instrumental purpose of being able to nurture citizenship through their domestic work. This phenomenon has often been documented by those who have studied European and U.S. political history of the late eighteenth and early nineteenth century and has been labeled "republican motherhood" in that context (see, e.g., Kerber 1986; Landes 1988). Similarly, Jayawardena reports on a 1927 textbook written by a Vietnamese nationalist who used "Mme. Roland" as a revolutionary model to urge young women to become "mothers to the nation." [12] If asked, "Do you have a husband," they were encouraged to reply, "Yes, his surname is Viet and his given name is Nam" (1991, 204).

Women's own feminist movements have grown up within and in the context of nationalist and other cultural movements. Just as women's individual identity cannot be fragmented into the part that is female and the part that belongs to a particular religious, ethnic, or other cultural group, so their political movements are not so easily fragmented. Even when women organize "as women," they do so in the context of the cultural and political conditions in which they live. Their social movements are often part of or instigated by more widespread social upheaval and demands for change; often the women who are most active in the early development of feminist movements began their political activism in other social movements. This was certainly the case in the nineteenth-century American suffrage movement, whose history is incomprehensible without understanding its relationship to the abolition movement, the Civil War, and the post-war politics of race (see, e.g., DuBois 1978), but studies of feminism elsewhere in the world reveal similar patterns (see, e.g., Jayawardena 1986; Kandiyoti 1991; Morgan 1975). And, as we have seen, the feminism of one political movement can become the focal point of rejection for the next.

Feminism has a much wider and longer history than most scholars outside of women's studies realize, and the history and politics of feminism are more directly linked to other important political problems and issues than is recognized. Despite the widely held view, for example, that feminism is a distinctly bourgeois and European phenomenon that has appeared in other parts of the world only through import or imitation, women's studies scholars show that there are varieties of feminisms, each marked clearly by their distinct national and historical origins. At the same time feminism has often also been internationalist in character. In its name women of different nations have met together in international organizations and meetings or have traveled to each others' countries to share their experiences. There are cases in which larger international organizations and other groups have sometimes facilitated and even initiated this feminist exchange, as was the case of the United Nations during the International Women's Decade, and also of labor organizations of the nineteenth and early twentieth centuries.[13]

One common claim shared by many political organizations and movements based on cultural categories, such as nation, ethnicity, race, or religion, is that women's status and thus feminism is a problem for *other* groups—not their own. Cynthia Enloe points out that although nationalist movements and struggles can open up new avenues for women's activism and lead women to organize on their own behalf as women as well as community members, political crisis can also lead to efforts to silence women. A shortage of resources, not to mention basic ideological resistance, often leads other political movements to tell women to wait for their turn, perhaps "after the revolution."

Conclusion: Up from Silence

In writing on the paucity of scholarly research on the history of Southern women in the United States, Jacqueline Dowd Hall noted that, "What gets written depends a great deal on who is doing the writing, and the South has not been notable for training and supporting female scholars" (1989, 902). She, like many others, notes that until the rise of the specialist field of women's studies, scholars were able to ignore the social significance of gender and, certainly, the historical significance of women, and thus never saw the whole picture. In many of the stories of the politics of culture and cultural pluralism, women seem hardly to exist at all, and when they do they are seen merely as passive carriers of culture rather than as active participants. At least some scholars have seen a parallel between the Euro-American treatment of third world cultural activity and male treatment of women's involvement in the development of culture: "Male historiographers of imperialism and popular writers have helped to create the stereotype of imperial gender and race relations as delimited by white men, creating a world in which the voices of white women and indigenous populations of both sexes rarely are heard" (Hansen 1989, 931).

Because women's lives have rarely until recently been taken up directly as subjects for serious scholarly research, their role in politics has often been understood through what people claim they believe about women and through ideal depictions. Deniz Kandiyoti shows the impact on the understanding of women, the state, and Islam which has been "dominated by ahistorical accounts of the main tenets of Muslim religion," sometimes through exegetical readings by "fundamentalist apologists," sometimes through progressive readings by Muslim feminists, and sometimes through radical readings arguing that Islam is "intrinsically patriarchal and inimical to women's rights." She argues that this has "produced a rather paradoxical convergence between Western orientalists . . . and Muslim feminists and scholars" (1991, 1). In any case, none of these approaches do much to increase an understanding of women, Islam, or the state.

The argument that scholars in this field make is that the condition of women and their political action on their own behalf as women cannot be understood except within the context of the broader political and economic history of which they are a part, including cultural politics and state-building. But at the same time, these scholars are claiming that the story of cultural politics and state-building is intrinsically gendered and can neither be ignored or assumed away. And in order to understand this more clearly, it is necessary not just to incorporate both women and men into research, but also to redevise theory to take account of gender.

Let us return to Patricia Williams and her musings about the creation and recreation of her own history. She uses the controversy about "surrogate motherhood" in the United States to probe ideas about senses of the natural and natural relationships. In the case she examines, the judge awards the child in question to the "natural" father and his wife and takes her away from her "natural" mother, saying that it is "natural" for people to want children "like" themselves, and that legal rights and connections should take account of these natural likenesses. But because of the realities of political and other institutions, the final designation of natural connections is one which is constructed by the court. In this case, as in the Williams's connection to "her" past and "her" history, the apparently natural and primordial connections of both race and gender are subject to human creativity, to a dynamic of social construction.

NOTES

1. But see, e.g., Giddings 1984; Jayawardena 1986; Kandiyoti 1991; Knapman 1986; Lissak 1989.

2. "No doubt every breach of faith is wrong, and every faithless husband . . . is cruel and unjust; but the faithless wife is worse; she destroys the family and breaks the bonds of nature; when she gives her husband children who are not his own, she is false both to him and them, her crime is not infidelity but treason" (Rousseau 1780:324–25).

3. A number of feminist scholars over the ages have noted the gender politics of the term *honor* and the different meanings of that term for women and men. See my *A Vindication of Political Virtue* (1992, ch. 4) and Rich (1979).

4. Regarding women as the carriers of both culture and morality but, at the same time, as having an essentially weaker grasp than men on culture and morality may appear a logical contradiction at first blush, but it is no cultural contradiction. It is a cornerstone of the views of women found in diverse pillars of cultural explanation, in Islamic, Christian, and Jewish theology, in Aristotle, and in Freud.

5. I use quotation marks around *circumcision* because, although the term is widely used for clitoridectomy, it is incorrect and suggests an unwarranted degree of similarity between the initiation rite performed on women and men.

6. See Gerda Lerner's (1986) discussion of the origins of veiling and its relation to sexuality.

7. For more discussion see Sapiro (1984).

8. The fact that women constitute a large proportion of teachers does not defeat my point about educational institutions. In the aggregate men hold more authority among those who create and administer education policy. The higher up one goes in the education system of any country, the larger is the proportion of men among those who do the teaching.

9. See, for example, Jeffrey 1979; Hill 1985; Hunter 1984.

10. Along these same lines it is interesting to recall in the early days of the new women's movement in the United States a considerable number of writers and scholars engaged in the search for the lost years of equality or even, female dominance. One popular early work was Elizabeth Gould Davis's *The First Sex* (1973).

11. Among them are Harriet Martineau, Charles Fourier, and John Stuart Mill. See, for example, Mill's *Subjection of Women* (1869).

12. The French revolutionary Mme. Roland has been adopted as a symbol for women in many countries around the globe, as has Ibsen's Nora.

13. An interesting example of the internationalist character of the women's rights movement is an article Ho Chi Minh wrote in 1922, when he was living in Paris, on the rape of Vietnamese women by the French. In it he appealed to Frenchwomen to come to the aid of their Vietnamese sisters (reported in Jayawardena 1986, 207).

REFERENCES

Brown, Elsa Barkley. 1989. Womanist Consciousness: Maggie Lena Walker and the Independent Order of St. Luke. *Signs* 14 (Spring): 610–33.

Brownmiller, Susan. 1975. *Against Our Will: Men, Women, and Rape*. New York: Bantam Books.

Chhachhi, Amrita. 1991. Forced Identities: The State, Communalism, Fundamentalism and Women in India. In *Women, Islam, and the State,* edited by Deniz Kandiyoti, 144–75. Philadelphia: Temple University Press.

Davis, Elizabeth Gould. 1973. *The First Sex*. Harmondsworth: Penguin Press.

Deutsch, Sarah. 1987. Women and Intercultural Relations: The Case of Hispanic New Mexico and Colorado. *Signs* 12 (Summer): 719–39.

di Leonardo, Micaela. 1987. The Female World of Cards and Holidays: Women, Families, and the Work of Kinship. *Signs* 12 (Spring): 440–53.

DuBois, Ellen Carol. 1978. *Feminism and Suffrage: The Emergence of an Independent Women's Movement in America, 1848–69*. Ithaca: Cornell University Press.

Enloe, Cynthia. 1989. *Bananas, Beaches, and Bases: Making Feminist Sense of International Politics*. London: Pandora.

Giddings, Paula. 1984. *When and Where I Enter: The Impact of Black Women on Race and Sex in America*. New York: Bantam Books.

Hall, Jacqueline Dowd. 1989. Partial truths. *Signs* 14 (Summer): 901–11.

Hansen, Karen Tranberg. 1989. Book Review. *Signs* 14 (Summer): 930–34.

Hill, Patricia R. 1985. *The World Their Household: The American Women's Foreign Mission Movement and Cultural Transformation, 1870–1920*. Ann Arbor: University of Michigan Press.

hooks, bell. 1983. *Ain't I a Woman: Black Women and Feminism*. Boston: South End Press.

Hunter, Jane. 1984. *The Gospel of Gentility: American Women Missionaries in Turn-of-the Century China*. New Haven: Yale University Press.

Jalal, Ayesha. 1991. The Convenience of Subservience: Women and the State of Pakistan. In *Women, Islam, and the State,* edited by Deniz Kandiyoti, 77–114. Philadelphia: Temple University Press.

Jayawardena, Kumari. 1986. *Feminism and Nationalism in the Third World*. London: Zed Books.

Jeffrey, Julie Roy. 1979. *Frontier Women: The Trans-Mississippi West, 1840–1880*. New York: Hill and Wang.

Kabeer, Naila. 1991. The Quest for National Identity: Women, Islam, and the State in Bangladesh. In *Women, Islam, and the State,* edited by Deniz Kandiyoti, 115–43. Philadelphia: Temple University Press.

Kandiyoti, Deniz, ed. 1991. *Women, Islam, and the State*. Philadelphia: Temple University Press.

Kerber, Linda K. 1986. *Women of the Republic: Intellect and Ideology in Revolutionary America*. New York: W. W. Norton.

King, Deborah H. 1988. Multiple Jeopardy, Multiple Consciousness: The Context of a Black Feminist Ideology. *Signs* 14 (Autumn): 42–72.

Knapman, Claudia. 1986. *White Women in Fiji, 1835–1930: The Ruin of Empire?* Boston: Allen and Unwin.

Landes, Joan B. 1988. *Women and the Public Sphere in the Age of the French Revolution.* Ithaca: Cornell University Press.

Lerner, Gerda. 1986. *The Creation of Patriarchy.* New York: Oxford University Press.

Lissak, Rivka Shpak. 1989. *Pluralism and Progressives: Hull House and the New Immigrants, 1890–1910.* Chicago: University of Chicago Press.

Morgan, David. 1975. *Suffragists and Liberals: The Politics of Women Suffrage in Britain.* Oxford: Basil Blackwell.

Najmabadi, Afsaneh. 1991. Hazards of Modernity and Morality: Women, State and Ideology in Contemporary Iran. In *Women, Islam, and the State,* edited by Deniz Kandiyoti, 48–76. Philadelphia: Temple University Press.

Ortner, Sherry. 1974. Is Female to Male as Nature is to Culture? In *Women, Culture, and Society,* edited by Michelle Z. Rosaldo and Louise Lamphere, 67–88. Stanford: Stanford University Press.

Rich, Adrienne. 1979. Women and Honor: Some Notes on Lying. In Adrienne Rich, ed., In *On Lies, Secrets, and Silence: Selected Prose, 1966–78,* edited by Adrienne Rich, 185–94. New York: Norton.

Rousseau, Jean-Jacques. 1780. New edition, 1974. *Émile.* London: Dent.

Rubin, Gayle. 1974. The Traffic in Women: Notes on the "Political Economy" of Sex. In *Toward an Anthropology of Women,* edited by Rayna Reiter, 157–210. New York: Monthly Review Press.

Sapiro, Virginia. 1992. *A Vindication of Political Virtue: The Political Theory of Mary Wollstonecraft.* Chicago: University of Chicago Press.

Sapiro, Virginia. 1984. Women, Citizenship, and Nationality: Immigration and Nationalization Policies in the United States. *Politics and Society* 13: 1–26.

West, Candace, and Don H. Zimmerman. 1987. Doing Gender. *Gender and Society* 1 (June): 125–51.

Williams, Patricia. 1988. On Being the Object of Property. *Signs* 14 (Autumn): 5–24.

3

To Polarize a Nation: Racism, Labor Markets, and the State in the U.S. Political Economy, 1965–1986

■ ■ ■

NOEL JACOB KENT

An Enduring American Dilemma

IN A NATION where nothing is said to endure or take root, the dilemmas and structures of race and racism surely have. In every historic period, racial dynamics have been central to the manner in which the U.S. political economy has functioned. Since the Indian "clearances" and antebellum slavery, racial discrimination and hierarchy have been intimately tied to the processes of capital accumulation and economic modernization. Race, in its complexity of forms, has evolved in concert with social structures, class formations, and state policies. African-American life chances have been deeply impacted by dominant racial ideologies and the policies they have legitimated; dark skin pigmentation has long carried a special onus and been a "rank sign" in the labor market. Ultimately, racial dynamics are quite revealing as to the fears and insecurities of a culture focused upon achievement through radical individualism.

If "race," as Michael Omni and Howard Winant suggest, is really "an unstable and decentered complex of social meanings constantly being transformed by political struggle," then the state becomes the political arena where those social meanings are shaped and defined (1986, 2–15). This was never more apparent than in the middle 1960s, when the culmination of a long train of changes in demography, social structure, and consciousness among both blacks and whites led to the interracial civil rights coalition that successfully overthrew officially sanctioned segregation. During the pre-1964 period, the ideological power of white supremacy ultimately lay in popular acceptance of black inferiority as expressed in biological stereotypes. What the civil rights movement did was to delegitimize such ideology and its categorization of African-Americans as natural racial inferiors appropriately relegated to lesser societal roles.

Significant as this accomplishment was, it amounted to but one facet of a more ambitious thrust on various fronts to redefine racial meanings and categories. If the nation were, and would remain, inherently pluralistic, American pluralism was envisioned as *nonantagonistic and noncoercive,* with an accent on the full inclusion of African-Americans as equal participants in U.S. society. Central here was the transformation of racially segmented labor markets which had acted to restrict access to opportunity and resources.

Has such a momentous change occurred? The "declining discrimination" school arose in the 1970s to enthusiastically avow that indeed it had. In sum, a complex of mutually reinforcing laws, social processes, and market mechanisms had made equality of opportunity an irreversible process. It was projected that as the structure of black-white relationships "normalized," racial perspectives would follow. What was being celebrated here was the integrative capacity of an open society.

There was, indeed, empirical evidence to make such a case. A considerable number of blacks had certainly experienced real upward mobility. One stream was comprised of unskilled workers moving into more stable working-class jobs–black employment in core goods-producing industries jumped sharply from 502,000 to 682,000 during the 1960s; a second found young blacks of working-class background gaining entry into lower white-collar jobs, as well as the professional-managerial-technical strata (Landry 1987, 21–63). The black middle class doubled during the sixties and continued to expand more rapidly than its white counterpart through the mid-1970s (ibid., 140–55; Farley 1981, 42, 80).

All of this was grist for scholars arguing the irrelevance of historic patterns of racism to contemporary African-American mobility potential. In several works forcefully setting out this argument, William Julius Wilson noted that "talented and educated blacks are experiencing unprecedented job opportunities" (1978, 120). Contending that the racial norms of exclusion no longer applied, he wrote: "The traditional patterns of interaction between blacks and whites, particularly in the labor market, have been altered" (ibid., xi). Class, not race, now constituted the key determinant of African-American opportunity. Another "convergence" advocate argued for "a virtual collapse in traditional discrimination patterns" (Darity and Shulman 1979, 50). In denying the salience of racial discrimination, some scholars ultimately chose to embrace a cultural determinism that placed the onus for continuing black poverty on black culture itself.

It is a grave flaw in any theory of ethnic/race relations in the United States to underestimate the extent to which racism is embedded in all levels of national culture. As befits the prototype of twentieth-century modernism, the United States is a strikingly diverse and highly individualistic, competitive, and transient nation. Bonds and "natural solidarities" are few and frail. In such a pervasively insecure society, racial identities and orderings become one of the main building blocks of the social stability and self-identity Americans possess. Antiblack sentiment can thus provide a basis of solidarity among the white population (Kovel 1970, 21–95). In a "classless" society marked by class hierarchies, race also functions as a vehicle onto which class conflicts are displaced so that the dominant social structure is preserved and legitimized.

Racial stereotyping and discriminatory structures have been an integral part of U.S. national mythology and folklore, institutional structures, everyday living arrangements, habits and humor, self-identity, and language. "Discrimination flows from reinforcing structural, personality and cultural sources . . . ," says John Milton Yinger, "and gets built into institutional patterns that intensify the vested interests of the dominant groups . . ." (1983, 399). A product of cultural conditioning, white racism has been constantly reinforced by the roles it has always performed for Euro-Americans: as a resource for their special privileges and a vehicle for the displacement of their internal conflicts.

So any movement to deracialize labor markets confronts an American racism which is multi-layered and of considerable density. It is quite compatible with larger societal dynamics: racism as a system provides material privileges for certain members of the majority. Moreover, as Gordon W. Allport showed in his classic work, *The Nature of Prejudice* (1979), many citizens, rather than confront "impersonal forces," easily turn their frustration, rage, and shame into the scapegoating of outgroups (1979, 21). Saying this is not to reduce racism to a material/psychological artifact of self-interest or psychological gratification; a venerable history in North America gives racism a strong measure of autonomy, its own special legitimizing mechanisms, rituals, and reference points.

Gunnar Myrdal argued in a seminal work, *The American Dilemma* (1944), that racism's vulnerability was the "universalistic" and "egalitarian" ethos lying at the core of "the American Creed." Two decades later, mobilized blacks were to utilize this ethos as a moral instrument in securing favorable white response to ending official segregation. But the Myrdal analysis minimizes the endurance and malleability of racism as a belief system, its neat fit with the Creed's individualistic emphasis, and its capacity as a "free-floating" phenomenon to bond with the myriad of hurts and dissatisfactions U.S. culture generates. If postwar white Americans did readjust their racial norms to accommodate new kinds of black participation, racial antipathy remained alive and well within an often contradictory and multiple-level consciousness.

Historically, labor market discrimination has been institutionalized in occupational segmentation by race. Dual labor markets have received the support of generations of employers and majority workers, alike, who drew tangible economic and psychological benefits from racial exclusion/segmentation (Bowser and Hunt 1981). Both the racially based trade union definition of who might constitute a skilled worker and capital's need to utilize a pool of cheap, pliable nonwhite labor raised a monolith against black workers. Attempts to challenge white labor market monopolies not infrequently met with violence and riots—witness East St. Louis, 1919; Chicago, 1919; Mobile, 1943.

What has accentuated racial animosities in the labor market is the modest opportunity available for social mobility for all workers. Contrary to the American Dream ideology, mobility has generally been sporadic, usually of short, horizontal distance, and most often a multi-generational project. Blue-collar and white-collar sons and daughters tend to inherit the class of their parents; the most accurate predictors of social class mobility remain parental occupational roles, support, and resources (Blau and Duncan 1967). Both majority workers and racial minorities seek betterment in a system whose normal tendency is to reproduce its class structure from generation to generation.

The logic of economic structure, compounded by American success ideology, exerts pressures on the dominant group to seek mechanisms for protecting labor market niches. African-Americans are doubly handicapped; a lack of resources due to historic discrimination is magnified by contemporary workplace biases (Darity and Shulman 1979, 190). Historically, black workers have had different entry level jobs than whites have had, different pay scales than whites, and have found promotion more difficult to obtain than whites have. They have been disproportionately located in low-paid, low-status, limited trajectory jobs within the secondary labor market (Althauser and Spivack 1975, 118).

From Civil Rights to the "Permanent Republican Majority"

It was no coincidence that the thrust for civil rights took hold at a unique historical juncture: the middle 1960s. The momentum supplied by new African-American assertiveness and political clout found itself powerfully buttressed by two forces. The first was an unprecedentedly buoyant economic prosperity, the heyday of the triumph of the "New Economics." Expansive economic growth meant enhanced real incomes, lessened job anxiety, and often better jobs for a wide cross-section of Americans. Since the civil rights movement occurred in a period when the economy was not merely a "zero-sum game," white antagonism to black labor market gains was blunted. Moreover, much of the black progress was concentrated in the areas of discrimination concerning law and custom which did not directly threaten white prerogatives. The mid-sixties, therefore, constituted one of those few moments when the burdens of racial equality were not to be borne by the sacrifices of the white working and lower middle classes.

The second favorable condition for continued minority mobility was the active support of the federal government. "The political system in recent years," wrote William Julius Wilson, "has tended to promote racial equality" (Wilson 1978, 12). The second Reconstruction, like the first, found the federal state the indispensable instrument for defending and enlarging minority rights. Transformation of policy-making Washington from "benign indifference" to legal white supremacy into the prime actor for minority inclusion and entitlement was essential to the process. Given the scarcity of minority resources, the continuance of such support was critical for ongoing progress in reducing labor market inequality.

Labor market breakthroughs were a major achievement of the civil rights movement. By 1970, blacks had access to a much wider spectrum of public and private positions. The presence of an educated professional-managerial elite gave the African-American occupational structure an increasing resemblance to the white occupational structure. A stable black working class seemed rooted in primary sector heavy industry.

What had *not* been achieved was the transformation of a racially segmented labor market into a nonracial one. As the momentum of civil rights waned during the late sixties and early seventies, the constraints of economic structures, racial hierarchies, and a thriving workplace racism became more visible. Social policy discourse of the period following the civil rights movement, profoundly influenced by the ethos of radical individualism, acted within narrow acceptable parameters; minimalist notions of "equality of opportunity" became dominant. Direct state interventionism to secure "outcomes" remained illegitimate (Marr and Ward 1976, 54).

In consequence, the new African-American labor market was at once hospitable *and* exclusionary—with membership determined, if not by race, then by level of skills. In 1970, the presence of over 60 percent of black workers in the secondary labor market pointed to the continuing strength of historic racial labor categories.

Racial issues were at the center of the political maelstrom that destroyed the civil rights coalition. Time magnified inherent instabilities. The legacy of racism bequeathed a shared inability to sustain meaningful dialogue and trust between white and black leaders and rank and file. Heightened expectations easily bred frustration; different perspectives on racism existed; varying levels of economic and political development had created differing political agendas and competition. If both black and white workers advocated meritocracy in principle, then blacks resented white attachment to a privileged status quo, while whites saw preferential hiring and promotions as undermining seniority protections and such. In the late 1960s, the broad, tentlike umbrella that was the Democratic Party proved unable to withstand divisiveness over the party's civil rights role (and Vietnam), and it split asunder (Hodgson 1976).

The earliest revelation of massive white countermobilization on a national basis came in the 1964 and 1968 presidential campaigns of Alabama Governor George Wallace. In addition to his segregationist southern base, Wallace's racial populism found many adherents among border state and northern white working and lower middle classes. This was the politics of *ressentiment,* American style. Wallace, the lightning rod for huge discontents in the country, used his bully pulpit to scapegoat black welfare recipients and white "New Class" professionals. The Wallace campaign's adroit manipulation of deep-rooted socioeconomic insecurities, including popular fears of white elite–ghetto black collusion, garnered 13.6 percent of the 1968 presidential vote (Burnham 1970, 27, 182).

What remained unindicted were the social structure and priorities of U.S. capitalism. Wallace's resonance with the lower middle and working classes reflected how conflicted they had become about their own tenuous roles in a transforming culture. Jim Sleeper has commented upon the "moral ambivalence of whites who find themselves fighting it out with blacks under pressures that are more powerful than any group" (1990, 171). The lack of an authentic, broad-based, democratic class politics meant race would continue to exercise its customary surrogate role.

One revelation of the Wallace phenomenon was the depth of alienation felt by northern (heavily Roman Catholic) blue-collar workers from liberal Democratic politics. On both interest and affective levels, they experienced black demands in their workplaces and neighborhoods as severely threatening. In response, New Ethnicity ideologists emerged, advocating themes of primordial ethnic solidarity, insisting upon the continued inferior status of their "peoples," and disclaiming responsibility for racial hierarchy and black poverty. To counter black claims to a unique "racial" experience, they cited traumatic "ethnic" histories. Black redefinition of history and identity called forth newly discovered "imagined communities" among other groups (Stein and Hill 1978; Anderson 1982; Warren 1978).

"Defensive ethnicity" was mobilized to defend their few areas of genuine influence. Among the earthworks thrown up to defend the "ethnic lock" on prized blue-collar jobs were work stoppages to protest black hiring on construction sites and trade union lawsuits filed to block affirmative action promotions (Darity and Shulman 1979, 215; Rubin 1972, 41).

While the "New Ethnicity" had modest ultimate impact, it did reveal the majority population's emergent mindset. The fortified communal ethic it espoused jibed with a stronger compartmentalism abroad in the land. The exhaustion it expressed with the ongoing demands and grievances of blacks was widespread also. Whites believed (or pretended to) that the end of U.S. apartheid had rendered blacks fully equal participants in the Great American Mobility Race. The clear desire was for closure to the civil rights era.

Kevin Phillips, the youthful 1968 Nixon campaign advisor whose celebrated "Southern Strategy" had helped defeat that embodiment of the civil rights coalition, Hubert Humphrey, recognized the power of the new racism early on. His "emerging Republican majority" was to be constructed from demographic changes, economic embourgeoisement, and resurgent social conservatism: an amalgam of southern whites, northern workers, the traditional Republican gentry, and new suburbanites everywhere. Racial fears and antagonisms provided the common reference point to keep the coalition intact. Indeed, the primacy of "ethnic and cultural animosities and divisions" was seen as crucial in determining party affiliations. Phillips counted on the fact of "the Negro problem having become a national . . . one" and the Democrats suicidal identification with black aspirations to guarantee long-term Republican dominance (Phillips 1969, 39–40).

In retrospect, Phillips has been the true political prophet of presidential realignment; he understood the political implications of the "social maladjustments" Walter Dean Burnham (1970) has called necessary for "critical realignments" to occur in American politics. But he foresaw neither the very partial nature of late-century "realignment," nor its failure to revitalize national politics. Likewise, he ignored how deeply the "Southern Strategy" would work toward racial polarization. The act of making the South, the region with the harshest racism, poverty, and labor market conditions in the country, presidential kingmaker, in effect handed over the future of black entitlement to rightest southerners fixed on a social control agenda.

While the Nixon and Ford administrations did not attempt to roll back the achievements of the civil rights era, they were content to view it as completed history. In the aftermath of the 1968 ghetto riots, "benign neglect" was substituted for the Kerner Commission Report's clarion call for "national action, compassionate, massive and sustained, backed by the resources of the most powerful and the richest nation on earth."

African-American votes arguably had made Jimmy Carter president in 1976, but his administration chose not to renew what commitments the Great Society had made to integrating the excluded. The tenuous nature of Carter's political base, amplified by the large and active white resistance to school busing and the generally cautious Carter approach to government, all served to inhibit radical innovations. In short, much of Carter's white constituency (unlike Lyndon Johnson's) was no longer even mildly sympathetic to African-American demands. By evolving from issues of voting rights and university admissions in Alabama to forced busing in Boston and Los Angeles and preferential hiring and promotions in plants, offices, and public employment, civil rights issues had estranged many whites.

It is not surprising, then, that throughout the 1970s, a curious silence pervaded the public discourse on minority rights in the labor market, a silence punctuated only by fierce debates about the ethics and efficacy of affirmative action policy.

The Role of Symbolic Racism

The Republican Party's Southern Strategy was viable because it recognized and exploited the newly dominant form of racism which appeared in the wake of the civil rights movement. The dismantling of official white supremacy in the *herrenvolk* southern states had a degree of general support from whites; yet, a large proportion were somewhat reluctant to accept the principle of complete equality and *very* reluctant to accept implementation of measures to bring it to fruition. The full humaneness of African-Americans was still only grudgingly accepted, if at all (Kovel 1970, 21–95). Since such views, however, ran counter to the new ethos in which overt (public) racism and biological inferiority had been discredited, "symbolic racism" emerged as the mediating instrument.

Indeed, more subtle racial explanations were inevitable in a society which had chosen to abandon the rhetoric and formal structures of white supremacy, while leaving most racial inequities intact. The transition from restrictive to competitive race relations produced new stereotypes; in place of the childlike, carefree, irresponsible, impulsive Negro appeared the "aggressive, uppity, insolent, . . . dangerous" black (Van den Berghe 1967, 20–35). Disadvantages once attributed to genes were now ascribed to culture.

In the post–civil rights era, argues Christopher Lasch, "de facto racism continues to flourish without an ideology of white supremacy" (Lasch 1978, 117). In the absence of credible white supremacy doctrines, the role of reprocessed stereotypes in influencing perceptions and performing the ritual (so necessary to racism) of depersonalization is all-important. Such stereotypes become absorbed as prejudicial markers into institutionalized settings, thus sustaining the racial division of labor.

An ascendant symbolic racism is really *another expression of resistance to both racial equality and equalization of opportunity.* At its core is a strong element of antiblack "affect" and negative black stereotypes (Katz and Taylor 1988, 70–80). It rigidly categorizes black demands for affirmative action processes in the hiring and promotion spheres as "reverse discrimination," while labor market failure is blamed on the lack of modern, salable African-American skills and sufficient motivation for "success" (Rothenberg 1988, 258–63).

What gives force and logic to "symbolic racism" is its appropriation of the rhetoric of a dominant American ideology which Michael Lewis refers to as "the culture of individualism . . . wherein advantage and disadvantage are explained and frequently justified" (Lewis 1978, 14). The national ethos does, indeed, place enormous responsibility upon the individual for personal economic "salvation" and tends to assign failure to personal, rather than market, inadequacies. Every individual is viewed as having the capacity to make her or his own way by utilizing specialized training, skills, cleverness, and the appetite for sustained hard work. What ties in symbolic racism here is its insistence on the existence of a post-1965 level playing field, a "color-blind marketplace," where the virtues of the work ethic are rewarded and inefficiencies and sloth penalized.

Thus, a mutually reinforcing dialectic exists between popular stereotypes of African-American culture/group characteristics—personified by the street hustler, welfare "chiseler," and "unqualified" professional—and the American meritocratic ideology. The logic is to attribute racial inequalities to the shortcomings of individual blacks, while affirming the elasticity and openess of the American opportunity structure to all who strive. Since 1964, such discourse has been used time and again to justify disproportionate black location in the secondary sector, black unemployment consistently double that of whites, and the large number of prime-age black males who leave the labor market. In its coded version, as "social control," symbolic racism contributed immeasureably to the Republican "lockhold" on the presidency. This, in turn, has tilted the "racial state" against African-American interests.

Race and the Crisis of American Abundance

The 1970s witnessed the traumatic end of the postwar economic miracle and with it the decline of a general rise in living standards and occupational mobility that had characterized the quarter-century since World War II. By decade's end, price escalation and three economic recessions had culminated in stagflation. At the core were profound and apparently irresolvable structural problems reflecting an altered American global position: the inability of major corporations to raise productivity and profit levels and their loss of global and domestic competitiveness; the wholesale disappearance of industrial jobs to export and automation strategies; instabilities in financial markets.

Around 1973, the real income of American working and lower-middle-class families began gradually declining; only the addition of huge numbers of new female workers to the labor force kept it from sliding further (Blumberg 1980; Bradbury 1986, 41–45). Large U.S. corporations responded to a crisis in profits and job site control by cutting labor costs; they jettisoned the postwar social contract and shipped production facilities overseas, forced domestic wages down, and outsourced for products at nonunion suppliers. The historical leaders of the heavy manufacturing sector diversified wildly and scrapped a considerable portion of their industrial capacity (Kolko 1988, 145–55; Bluestone and Harrison 1988, 1–10).

By 1980, workers confronted a labor market whose entry portals were clogged by an unduly large, better educated, and highly expectant baby boom generation, one for which "middle-class" jobs were increasingly at a premium and demanded special skills and training. General wage levels—especially for clerical, sales, and nonunion blue-collar workers—had not kept pace with a doubling of prices between 1967 and 1978 (Blumberg 1980).

Meanwhile, contrary to popular belief, the tide of black progress in the labor market had peaked and receded as economic decline and stagnation took hold.

The end of stable, buoyant economic growth was a disaster for African-American aspirations. Indeed, the gap between the 4 or 5 percent annual growth of the previous decades and the 1 or 2 percent annual growth in a "trickle-down" type economy was the difference between an upward moving black social structure and one in stagnation and decline. Blacks, located as they were in precarious unskilled and semi-skilled jobs in the secondary sector, were especially vulnerable. Even black primary sector workers were more likely to be found in declining goods-producing industries like steel, automobiles, and rubber. So, the stable black working class was savaged by plant closings, automation, and export of jobs. Manning Marable argues that the 550,000 black workers forced from the workplace during the early and mid-1970s recessions were victims of a "structurally racist" system (1983, 43).

Black youth were caught in a structural/demographic vise: they entered center city labor markets at a time when these markets were being rapidly transformed from goods production and distributive functions into sophisticated information processing and business services. Industrial restructuring precluded the hiring of an entire cohort of 1970s black youth in the core manufacturing industries. In 1976, for example, 46 percent of black workers, twenty to twenty-four years of age, were employed as blue-collar craft operatives; by generally prosperous 1984, this figure had fallen to 20 percent (Berlin and Sum 1987). The shrinking of smokestack America meant a greatly diminished opportunity structure for African-American young people.

Meanwhile, an impassable chasm in education and skills now stretched between inner city black youth and the mid- to high-echelon positions being produced in real estate, finance, insurance, and such. John Kasarda writes of "the disequilibrium in distressed cities between low skill labor ability and low skill needs" (Peterson 1986, 62). A large proportion of these youth became marginalized and fodder for a lumpen formation, later to be labeled the "underclass." This is a group whose origin lies in structural displacement and cumulative racism: they are essentially unemployed workers beset by automation and the export of historic central city blue-collar jobs elsewhere, inadequate transportation and job information networks, poor educational facilities, and lack of marketable interpersonal skills (Wilson 1987).

African-American middle-class growth tapered off around the mid-1970s. By that time, it had become more difficult for college-educated blacks to translate their training into middle-class incomes (Harrison and Sum 1988, 660–95). Within the vaunted primary sectors of large firms, racial and promotional discrimination still persisted, while public sector employment—earlier, a magnet for black college graduates—stagnated because of financial crises.

Thus, a pattern of steady convergence for the black and white middle classes was reversed; the lower-middle-class black family found two incomes more essential to self-maintenance than its white counterpart did and found maintenance of same-class level increasingly arduous. Bart Landry notes the irony in the way "blacks developed the skills demanded to be middle class" just when "economic conditions that had been transferring the United States into a middle class society and had promised unlimited growth changed abruptly" (1987, 4–8).

By 1980, race convergence was no longer tenable as a paradigm. The decline of the stable African-American working class, the growth of a permanent sub-proletariat, escalating teenage joblessness, and the increasing tendency of black workers to leave the labor market in their prime working years spelled *finis*. Black/white income ratios had begun widening in the seventies, and by 1980, the annual salaries of year-round, full-time black male workers were 70.7 percent—and of black female workers, 51.3 percent—of their white male counterparts (Rothenberg 1988, 72).

Racism remained a major cause of earnings differentials. Even the better trained cohort of young black males entering the labor force from 1975 to 1979 had, by 1980, only 80 percent of the earnings of their white counterparts (Welch 1990, 521). The "cost of being black" could be computed: black men earned about 90 percent of what white men with the same education, work experience, and hours of work earned in 1980s, and black women earned 70 percent of what white men made (Farley 1981, 104). Discrimination at the level of promotions and raises was one major source of this inequality, since "white men are much more highly rewarded for experience than are black men or women" (ibid., 10, 66).

The Reaganist State as Racial State

It had become apparent by 1980 that in a nation of more limited abundance, where social class, professional networks, and educational and political resources had become indispensable to "making it" and "staying there," African-Americans were at a distinct disadvantage. This made state commitments to antidiscrimination policies and interventions to balance an unfavorable market absolutely critical to greater equality. But that same year brought Ronald Reagan—and bold new strategies—to the White House.

Symbolic racism furnished a unifying theme to a disparate Reagan coalition. Reagan had played to states' rights during the campaign, and his crushing defeat of Georgian Jimmy Carter throughout the South confirmed the wisdom of the Southern Strategy. In short, the 1980 election read like a textbook primer of the Kevin Phillips realignment theory.

What the Phillips scenario had not anticipated, however, was the authority of the New Right in such a coalition. Here, we see the politics of resentment, discontent, and insecurity exemplified by Wallace a decade before, only now "disciplined, well-organized and well-financed" (Crawford 1979, 1–5). A major New

Right concern was the restriction of nonwhite roles and power. In its demonology, stereotypic black welfare mothers and street denizens figured as prominent symbols of a fallen America. If the maximum New Right agenda—restoration of untrammeled white supremacy—was unfeasible, then its power could be exerted to block the legitimacy of group rights and to redefine the meaning of social and racial equality. Its prominence in the Republican Party and in a phalanx of think tanks, lobbyists, congressmen, and churches, guaranteed enormous influence (and, in effect, a veto) over Reagan social policy.

The Reaganist state is a classic example of how states organize and shape racial meanings—and of how, despite its intense fragmentation, racial policy in the federal state is hugely impacted by leaders at the apex. The thrust of the mid-1960s (Lyndon Johnson) state had been to acknowledge the historic impact of racism in labor markets and to invoke federal responsibility for creating some degree of equal opportunity. The Reagan administration's "project," in contrast, was to radically undermine the legitimacy of "race" (and therefore, "racism," racial history, discrimination) as valid issues of social discourse and policy. The government would thus deal with its citizens as *individuals*. This stance was wholly compatible with the Reaganite determination to winnow the "deserving" from the "undeserving." The president, himself a master at manipulating the cultural symbols of rugged individualism and self-reliance, pointedly insisted on the need to maintain a "color-blind" government.

This was an administration determined to serve the interests of its upper- and upper-middle-class core constituencies by exalting the entrepreneur and the market. The credo was to reward the financially successful and those situated to be even more so. Federal policy was "explicitly directed toward fostering the inherent dynamism of the private sector" (Council of Economic Advisors to the President 1989).

Thus, the definition of who and what constituted legitimate clients for state services excluded disadvantaged economic, ethnic, or gender groups. Programs oriented to the poor and near poor, such as Food Stamps, Aid to Dependent Children, vocational education, community block grants, Pell grants to disadvantaged students, and federal public housing, were cut severely (Palmer and Sawhill 1984, 180–90). Because of their economic position, this disproportionately impacted the beleagured African-American working class and poor, already hurt by a changing labor market. The first generation of black mayors found themselves confronting huge demands for social services, while federal cutbacks ravaged their budgets (Schorr 1988).

The allocation of social cuts underscored the administration's racial antipathies and its continuing class objective of making the lower classes bear the brunt of restructuring the U.S. political economy.

The larger Reagan policy objective was a partial rollback of the welfare state and assorted public entitlements aimed at providing poor and working-class

Americans some independence from the proverbial "lash of necessity." The reduction of social transfer payments served to restrain labor's wage demands and also moved workers into the labor market on business's terms. The long-term agenda here was a revamping of what state services and "social wages" citizens believe they can reasonably expect. The 1981 tax reduction helped by weakening the state's financial capacity to provide an effective social welfare system. The Reaganite philosophy and political base and the African-American location in the social structure made African-Americans the prime victims of state "color-blindness."

Symbolic racism provides an essential link. What the Reaganist state was expressing, and legitimizing, was the kind of racism which is most functional to privileged racial and economic groups in the post–civil rights era—subtle, nonovert, and directed at enforcing hiring and promotion processes that maintain white bastions and privileges. Here the long tradition of racially segmented labor markets and racial job privilege merge with administration policy to uphold the existing labor market status quo.

In a time of precariousness and deep anxiety for many white workers, the state, by sanctioning existing structures of institutional racism, encouraged the "trench war" being carried out against minorities in the crafts and courts. A spin-off was the general, widespread arousal of "dormant" antiminority attitudes and a marked escalation in racial incidents of all types as the eighties wore on.

African-Americans and the New Economic Order

The realignment of state priorities during the Reagan period overlapped with the advent of a restructured national and global economy. Primary sector business, in response to radically altered market, financial, and technological conditions, intensified earlier restructurings. A major concern was to shore up faltering profit ratios by lowering fixed costs and reorienting the workplace. Earlier labor structures were to be replaced. The sheer strength and resources of Reagan-era business and its access to the levers of state power gave it virtual *carte blanche* to remake the economy to suit its objectives (Kolko 1988, 145–55).

Union bashing and changes in work organization were joined with disinvestment in productive capacity and reduction of the labor component in production. Attracted by market logic and state incentives, bellwether heavy industrial corporations abandoned productive capacity for diversification into financial services and real estate. Federal deregulation of financial markets led to a spree in corporate mergers and takeovers which resulted in pared off divisions and worker layoffs (Bluestone and Harrison 1988, 1–10). While a large number of stable, high-wage, blue-collar jobs disappeared, new manufacturing employment stagnated (Winnick 1987, table 4–4).

In industry after industry, as trade unions retreated, concessionary contracts were negotiated. The six years of celebrated Reaganite economic growth had remarkably little impact on raising wage structures. A new corporate labor force featured a core of full-time regulars surrounded by a growing periphery of part-timers and temporaries, home and subcontracted workers—lacking medical benefits, pensions, and paid vacations, and bearing the costs of market "dislocations." David Harvey (1989) comments: "The American trend in labor markets is to reduce the number of core workers and to rely increasingly on a labor force that can be quickly taken on and equally quickly be costlessly laid off when times get bad."

A sea change in job generation was in motion. Reagan-era job creation, while substantial, was of much inferior quality to that of the pre-1972 period; 85 percent of all new jobs were located in the lower services sector (Mishel and Simon 1988, tables 37, 38). Not only were there a dearth of jobs paying middle-class incomes, but simply being in the middle of the income hierarchy no longer guaranteed the middle-class lifestyle (Levy 1987, 165).

Economic instability and down-mobility became endemic (Newman 1988). Those industries in decline paid more than the ascendant new ones. In the middle eighties, retail services, clerical work, cleaning, waiting and waitressing, all low-wage and lacking career ladders, emerged as the most numerous entry level jobs. The transformed labor market had become hostile to new workers lacking very specialized skills and education.

Median family incomes, virtually unchanged during the Reagan era, were only maintained by the mobilization of millions of new female workers. Inevitably, in an economic landscape marked by job markets and career trajectories that were increasingly cordoned off by education, skills, and incomes, inequalities of class and race were rife (Mishel and Simon 1988, 11). Earlier periods of growth had pushed lower-income Americans—especially racial minorities—into more highly skilled, better paid jobs in the occupational structure. Yet, during each phase of the Reagan business cycle, inequality by class and race rose. State policies and market logic pushed the United States into the most acute class polarization since the end of World War II (Justen 1988, table 57).

African-Americans were among the primary victims of Reagan-era restructuring. Ethnic stratification—despite the persistence of a genuine black middle class—became more rigid; a large percentage of black workers were now dependent upon substandard jobs in the fast-food and health care areas or were altogether superfluous. In terms of the 1973–85 income pattern, a definite racial differential appeared; whites gained 0.3 percent, while blacks lost 2.4 percent (Winnick 1987, table 4–4).

The deteriorating position of relative black incomes did not augur well for the "declining racism" thesis. Between 1980 and 1986, the earnings of full-time, year-round black workers fell from 77 to 73 percent that of whites (Darity and

Shulman 1979). In comparing high school graduates, whites had incomes three to four thousand dollars higher than blacks (Winnick 1987, 100–32). "There is little evidence that increased levels of education reduce racial discrimination," concludes one study (ibid. 129). In many advanced sectors of the primary labor market, stereotypes and nuanced biases limited minority possibilities (Braddock and McPartland 1987, 5–31).

The dual labor system was alive and well. Black and white workers still had different entry ports into the economy, different pay and promotion possibilities. The fact that significantly higher percentages of African-Americans were in the harsher secondary sector means their skills went less rewarded and upgraded (Gordon, Edwards, and Reich 1982, 257). The recessionary early eighties found minority incomes falling faster than those of whites; the ensuing economic "miracle" saw white family income and employment increase more rapidly. In 1984, black per capita income—57 percent of white—was back to what it had been in 1971 (Jaynes and Williams 1989, 274). Throughout the Reagan years, black unemployment and poverty levels hovered between double and triple the white rate (Landry 1987, 151–160; Winnick 1987, 100–132).

The Reagan period marked a continued deterioration in the situation of young black men; the rash of homicides and drug epidemics in inner-city areas caused observers to compare them to an "endangered species." Unemployment of African-American youth assumed what an increasingly somber William Julius Wilson has called "catastrophic proportions" (1987, 36, 60, 104). Because of male joblessness and weak earnings, young black family incomes underwent a precipitous decline; this severely affected the viability of family formation and was a major factor in the extraordinary poverty rates of black, single-parent-headed households. Whereas in 1973, one-third of all young black families had been poor, the figure was one-half by 1986. Although young white families also experienced falling incomes, the black decline was sharper (The Children's Fund 1988, 1–10).

Conclusion

The civil rights movement generated profound hopes for a racially integrated and egalitarian society in the United States; one whose pluralism might be grounded in cultural affiliation rather than racial separation and socioeconomic cleavage. The 1960s and early 1970s witnessed definite advances for African-Americans in the all-important labor market area: the expansion of a stable black working class and the movement of black women from largely domestic to blue-collar and white-collar positions; the emergence of a more widely diffused black professional middle class. This progress was arrested, however, by majority resistance to workplace equality, the coming to federal state power of a coalition committed to upholding the racial status quo, and the new American political economy which rewarded the affluent and educated and punished the poor and working classes. In the absence of a broad-based, interracial political coalition, these forces were dominant.

As the eighties wore on, white workers continued to earn considerably more income than black workers with the same labor market characteristics. Instead of African-American youth taking the first step in the upward mobility process, they lost further ground to their white peers.

This setback proved devastating for U.S. ethnic relations. The burgeoning urban epidemics of poverty, crime, and drugs further isolated whites and African-Americans, deepened white fears and black disillusionments, and set nonwhite minorities in fierce competition for dwindling resources. Ultimately, it gave credibility to the "balkanized fantasies of ethnic and racial destiny being promulgated by a new set of black and white demogogues" (Sleeper 1990).

The connective, mediating element was the continuing racism—if not in principle, then, in practice—of a significant part of the white population. In the wake of official segregation, racism had demonstrated its resilience and capacity to take on diverse new forms. Chief among these was "symbolic racism," a powerful fusion of traditional prejudice, old and refashioned racial stereotypes, and deeply held American values. In essence, this meant that whites overwhelmingly rejected traditional racist notions (for example, "white jobs") *and* voiced opposition to specific plans aimed at improving the black labor market position. Herein lies the core of symbolic racism: *the chasm between the change in racial norms and the absence of commitment to equalizing conditions*. New racial stereotypes appeared to absolve society and majority citizens of blame and place it squarely upon the victims.

Ultimately, the politics of *ressentiment* and gridlock perpetuated a federal state able to block the radical economic restructuring needed to facilitate racial/class equality, while simultaneously carrying on an offensive against minorities and lower-middle-class whites.

What happened and *didn't happen* during the years from 1964 to 1986 set the United States on a firm course toward a most destructive mix of cultural/economic pluralism: "the two societies, one black, one white—separate and unequal . . . ," the Kerner Report had once warned against (National Advisory Commission on Civil Disorders 1969, 1). In retrospect, the proper epilogue for this period occurred some six years later in the spring of 1992, in the burning streets of south central Los Angeles.

REFERENCES

Allport, Gordon W. 1979. *The Nature of Prejudice*. Unabridged 25th anniversary edition. Reading, Mass.: Addison-Wesley Publishing Co.

Althauser, Robert, and S. Spivack. 1975. *The Unequal Elites*. London: Wiley.

Anderson, Benedict. 1991. *Imagined Communities: Reflections on the Origin and Spread of Nationalism*. London: Verso.

Berlin, Gordon, and Andrew Sum. 1987. Toward a More Perfect Union: Basic Skills and Our Economic Future. Unpublished manuscript.

Blau, Peter, and Otis Duncan. 1967. *The American Occupational Structure*. New York: Wiley.

Bluestone, Barry, and Benedict Harrison. 1988. *The Great U-Turn: Corporate Restructuring and Polarizing of America*. New York: Basic Books.

Blumberg, Paul. 1980. *Inequality in an Age of Decline*. New York: Oxford University Press.

Bonacich, Edna. 1989. Inequality in America: The Failure of the American System for People of Color. *Sociological Spectrum* 9: 77–101.

Bowser, Byron, and Ronald G. Hunt. 1981. *Impacts of Racism on White Americans*. Beverly Hills: Sage Publications.

Bradbury, K. 1986. The Shrinking Middle Class. *New England Economic Review* (September–October): 41–45.

Braddock, H., and J. M. McPartland. 1987. How Minorities Continue to be Excluded from Equal Employment. *Journal of Social Issues* 43: 5–39.

Burnham, Walter Dean. 1970. *Critical Elections and the Mainsprings of American Politics*. New York: Norton.

The Children's Fund. 1988. *Vanishing Dreams*. Washington, D.C.: The Children's Fund.

Council of Economic Advisors to the President. 1989. *Annual Report*. Washington: U.S. Government Printing Office.

Crawford, Alan. 1979. *Thunder on the Right*. New York: Pantheon.

Darity, William, and Steven Shulman. 1979. *The Question of Discrimination*. Middleton, Conn.: Wesleyan University Press.

Farley, Reynolds. 1981. *Blacks and Whites: Narrowing the Gap*. Cambridge: Harvard University Press.

Gordon, D. M., R. Edwards, and R. Reich. 1982. *Segmented Work, Divided Workers: The Historic Transformation of Labor in the United States*. Cambridge: Harvard University Press.

Harrison, Benedict, and Andrew Sum. 1988. The Theory of Dual Segmented Labor Markets. *Journal of Economic Issues* 8: 657–706.

Harvey, David. 1989. *The Condition of Post-Modernity*. Oxford: Basil Blackwell.

Hodgson, Godfrey. 1976. *America in Our Time*. New York: Vintage Books.

Jaynes, G., and R. Williams. 1989. *Blacks and American Society*. New York: National Academy Press.

Justen, Thomas F. 1988. The Distribution of Wealth in the United States. *Economic Outlook* 14 (Spring): table 57, col. 4.

Katz, Phyllis, and Dalmas Taylor, eds. 1988. *Eliminating Racism Profiles in Controversy*. New York: Plenum Press.

Killian, Lewis. 1990. Race Relations and the Nineties: Where Are the Dreams of the Sixties? *Social Forces* 69 (September): 1–12.

Kolko, Joyce. 1988. *Restructuring the World Economy*. New York: Pantheon.

Kovel, Joel. 1970. *White Racism*. New York: Random House.

Landry, Bart. 1987. *The New Black Middle Class*. Berkeley: University of California.
Lasch, Christopher. 1978. *Culture of Narcissism: American Life in an Age of Diminishing Expectations*. New York: Norton.
Levy, Frank. 1987. *Dollars and Dreams: The Changing American Income Distribution*. New York: Russell Sage Foundation.
Lewis, Michael. 1978. *The Culture of Inequality*. New York: Meridian.
Marable, Manning. 1983. *How Capitalism Underdeveloped Black America*. Boston: South End Press.
Marr, Warren, and Maybelle Ward. 1976. *Minorities and the American Dream: A Bicentennial Perspective*. New York: Arno.
Mishel, Lawrence, and Jacqueline Simon. 1988. *The State of Working America*. Washington, D.C.: Economic Policy Institute.
Myrdal, Gunnar. 1944. *An American Dilemma*. New York: Harper and Brothers.
National Advisory Commission on Civil Disorders. 1969. *Report*. New York: New York Times Company.
Newman, Katherine. 1988. *Falling from Grace*. New York: Free Press.
Omni, Michael and Howard Winant. 1986. *Racial Formation in the United States from the 1960s to the 1990s*. New York: Routledge, Kegan and Paul.
Palmer, John L., and Isabel V. Sawhill. eds. 1984. *The Reagan Record. An Assessment of America's Changing Priorities*. Cambridge: Urban Institute.
Peterson, Paul E., ed. 1985. *The New Urban Reality*. Washington, D.C.: Brookings Institution.
Phillips, Kevin. 1969. *The Emerging Republican Party*. Garden City: Anchor Books.
Rothenberg, Paula S. 1988. *Racism and Sexism: An Integrated Study*. New York: St. Martin's Press.
Rubin, Lillian. 1972. *Busing and Backlash*. Berkeley: University of California Press.
Schorr, Andrew. 1988. *Common Decency: America After Reagan*. New Haven: Yale University Press.
Sleeper, Jim. 1990. *The Closest of Strangers: Liberalism and the Politics of Race in New York*. New York: W. W. Norton.
Stein, Howard P., and Robert F. Hill. 1978. *Ethnic Imperative: Examining the New White Ethnic Movement*. State College: Pennsylvania State University Press.
Van den Berghe, Pierre L. 1967. *Race and Racism in Comparative Perspective*. New York: Wiley.
Warren, Donald. 1978. *The Radical Center*. South Bend: Notre Dame Press.
Welch, Finis. 1990. The Employment of Black Men. *Journal of Labor Economics* 8 (January): 530.
Wilson, William Julius. 1987. *The Truly Disadvantaged*. Chicago: University of Chicago.
Wilson, William Julius. 1978. *The Declining Significance of Race*. Chicago: University of Chicago.
Winnick, Andrew. 1987. *Toward Two Societies*. New York: Praeger.
Wolfe, Alan. 1982. *America's Impasse: The Rise and Fall of the Politics of Growth*. Boston: South End Press.
Yinger, J. M. 1983. Ethnicity and Social Change. *The Journal of Ethnic and Racial Studies* 6: 399.

4

Language Policy Conflict in the United States

RONALD J. SCHMIDT

Introduction

AS CRAWFORD YOUNG has noted in his introduction to this volume, the United States has experienced heightened ethnic consciousness and political conflict in recent years. With this political saliency of ethnicity has come increased controversy about public policy issues related to cultural pluralism. In addition to the debate raging over multi-cultural curricula on college and university campuses, one of the most volatile of these disputes has centered on *language policy,* especially with respect to three related and overlapping issues: (1) bilingual education for language minority students; (2) "linguistic access" to voting rights through non-English ballots and election materials, along with access to other political and civil rights for language minority persons; and (3) the campaign to designate English as the "official" language of the United States and its political subdivisions. During the past several decades conflict over these issues has divided partisans into two increasingly hostile camps: *pluralists,* who favor bilingual education and measures increasing "linguistic access," and *assimilationists,* who are strongly opposed to these policies and have led the "official English" movement.

The aims of this essay are both descriptive and analytical. The first half of the essay will describe the development of the contemporary politics of language in the United States, and the second half will employ the theoretical constucts outlined in Young's introduction to this volume to interpret and assess this recent political phenomenon. The argument made herein is that, fundamentally, the contemporary conflict over language policy in the United States is not about "language" at all; it is, rather, an *ethnic conflict* in which language has become implicated in several ways. Further, it is argued that these connections between language policy and ethnic conflict are illuminated by all three of the constructs—instrumentalism, primordialism, constructivism—outlined by Crawford Young.

The essay begins, however, with a brief review of the historical background of language policy conflict in the United States and of the recent demographic changes which have helped bring the subject back to the political agenda.

Historical Antecedents

While many Americans may be surprised at the contemporary conflict over language policy, this is by no means a new subject of controversy in U.S. political life. Although the issues of multi-lingualism and multi-culturalism were not prominent on the political agenda between the 1920s and the 1960s, the United States has never been a monolingual or monocultural country. Indeed, racial and ethnic political conflict—including conflict over language use and status—has been endemic through much of the history of the United States.

A large number of languages have coexisted in the U.S., but the language conflict of which European Americans have been most aware has concerned the status of the *German* language in the United States.[1] Even prior to the American Revolution, Benjamin Franklin indignantly asked in a published essay: "Why should the Palantine [German] boors be suffered to swarm in our settlements and, by herding together, establish their language and manners to the exclusion of ours? Why should Pennsylvania, founded by the English, become a colony of *aliens*, who will shortly be so numerous as to germanize us instead of our anglifying them" (quoted by Wagner 1981, 30–31)?

Up through the early twentieth century, German Americans remained the largest non–English-speaking, nonindigenous group in the United States. In addition to publishing houses and newspapers, the Germans sought to provide a variety of other institutional supports for the maintenance of their language and culture. Among the most important of these were churches, clubs, and schools (Kloss 1966). Churches and clubs were the focal points of most German-American communities, and they provided crucial linguistic domains in which the German language and culture were perpetuated. These "adult" institutions were supplemented with schools—both private and public—through which German-Americans worked to reproduce their language and culture in the young. German language education—both "monolingual" in German only (especially in rural areas) and "bilingual" in German and English (in urban areas)—was quite common in the United States until the 1920s (Kloss 1966; Perlmann 1990).

Most of these efforts at linguistic and cultural maintenance by German-Americans (and by many other groups as well) came to an end in the early twentieth century. Beginning with the "Know Nothing" Party of the mid-nineteenth century, a nativist movement had been building in opposition to "foreign" influences in the United States, one which ultimately reached its peak after World War I. Nativists sought to exclude most new immigrants through greater control over the nation's borders and to "Americanize" those "foreigners" already here through an aggressive campaign against "hyphenated Americanism" (Higham 1963). Though the nativist movement was directed against all "foreign" influences on American life, World War I generated a particularly intense level of anti-German sentiment.

The 1920s brought this era of ethnolinguistic conflict to an end. Though there were efforts at resistance, German language maintenance in the United States largely succumbed to the combined onslaught of the nativist political agitation and the anti-German hysteria of World War I (Baron 1990). It is estimated that the number of German-speakers in the United States peaked at nine million in 1910 (Kloss 1966), but by the 1980 census German had dropped to third place among non–English-speakers with fewer than three million recorded (Waggoner 1988).

Recent Demographic Change and the Language Issue

As this discussion of one aspect of the historical background indicates, the politicization of language in the United States often has been associated with *demographic change,* as well as with non-English-language maintenance efforts. Historically, Anglo-Americans have mobilized most frequently on the language question when they have felt most insecure because of mounting numbers of non–English-speaking "newcomers" living and working in "their" communities. Before proceeding to an examination of the contemporary political conflict over language policy in the United States, therefore, it will be useful to summarize briefly the demographic changes in the recent period which are helping to fuel that conflict.

The complete language use results of the 1990 census were not yet available as of this writing. However, one study based on extrapolations of the 1980 census found that over 15 percent of U.S. residents spoke a language other than English in their homes as of 1986 (Waggoner 1988, 105). Moreover, a 1989 Census Bureau survey found a 40 percent increase in non–English-speakers since the 1980 census (Vobejda 1992). Though there were over thirty language groups with more than 100,000 speakers registered by the 1980 census, Spanish speakers now constitute by far the largest language minority group in the nation, with some 15.5 million or 45 percent of non–English-speakers in 1980, and over 52 percent of school-age children from non–English-speaking homes (Waggoner 1988, 82).

As has been true in the past, international migration has become a key factor in the growth of U.S. linguistic diversity in recent years. The rules for immigration were significantly changed in 1965, and partly in consequence the United States has experienced its greatest wave of immigration since the "gates" were almost closed in 1924. Since immigrants tend to concentrate in specific geographic, especially urban, areas it is instructive to examine language use patterns in those cities with the highest numbers of recent immigrants. Examination of some of the data already released from the 1990 census shows significant expansion during the 1980s. The census for New York City, for example, indicates that 41 percent of the 1990 population spoke a language other than English in the home, up from 35 percent in 1980. In Miami, three-quarters of the population live in homes where English is not the usual language, and 67 percent of these reported they do not speak English well. Most strikingly, the census report indicated that the non–English-speaking population of Los Angeles rose from 35.1 percent in 1980 to 49.9 percent in 1990. Statewide, nearly 32 percent of 1990 California residents reported speaking a language other than English in the home. The 1990 census data already released for other cities with large concentrations of non–English-speakers include Paterson, New Jersey, 50 percent; Santa Fe, New Mexico, 40 percent; Hartford, Connecticut, nearly 40 percent; Providence, Rhode Island, 30 percent; and Boston, 26 percent (Vobejda 1992; Lewis 1992; Clifford 1992).

It is further significant that the largest increases in minority language groups have been registered among Latinos[2] and Asian-Americans. Indeed, this has been one of the most notable patterns in the recent migration to the United States; whereas the nineteenth and early twentieth century "waves" of immigration originated overwhelmingly in Europe, some 85 percent of documented immigrants during the 1965–90 period were Latin American and Asian in origin (Fulwood 1990). Along with birth-rate differentials and undocumented migration, these immigration patterns have led demographers to predict that the United States will cease to have a "white" (European-origin) majority population within the next eighty years (Bouvier and Gardner 1986). In view of the long history of racial conflict in America, these demographic trends are important because they introduce a potential linkage between racial diversity and linguistic diversity in the United States which could easily fuel political conflict over language policy for the forseeable future. Before pursuing that point, however, we will turn to an overview of the three issues around which political conflict over language policy has centered in the last several decades.

U.S. Language Policy Issues in Conflict

Bilingual education was the *first* language policy issue to arise in the contemporary period. In 1968 Congress amended the Elementary and Secondary Education Act of 1965 by approving Title VII, known as the Bilingual Education Act. The law was aimed initially at supporting local efforts to stem the relatively high drop-out and educational failure rates of low-income Latino students in the public schools of the Southwest (Lyons 1990). Title VII remained a small, demonstration grant program until 1974 when it was considerably strengthened and expanded in scope.

The year 1974 also witnessed another major event boosting the political fortunes of bilingual education. In *Lau v. Nichols* the U.S. Supreme Court ruled unanimously that the San Francisco public schools had violated the Civil Rights Act of 1964 by attempting to teach Chinese-speaking students in a language they did not understand (that is, in traditional English-only classrooms). On the strength of this decision by the Court, the U.S. Office of Education's civil rights enforcement unit in 1975 issued a set of "Lau Remedies" which strongly encouraged local school districts to establish bilingual education programs for their "Limited English Proficient" (LEP) students. Subsequently, more than half of the states in the United States adopted laws mandating or permitting bilingual instruction in the public schools, and most states made use of Title VII funds for bilingual programs.

Along with this rapid growth, bilingual education quickly generated political conflict. The controversy has operated at all levels of government and on a variety of issues. Underlying and at the center of each of the specific conflicts, however, has been the issue of the goal of the policy with respect to the native languages of students in bilingual programs.

On one side of this question are those—the "assimilationists"—who argue that the *only* legitimate classroom role of the students' home languages is helping them to "keep up" in other subjects until they know English well enough to move into a "mainstream" monolingual English classroom. This *transitional* approach has a remedial orientation in that the child's home language is considered a "crutch" which should be dispensed with as quickly as possible.

On the other side are supporters of a *maintenance* approach to bilingual education. These "pluralists" also seek to enable students to master English and to move quickly into mainstream classrooms, but their orientation to students' native languages is very different. Rather than seeing the home language as a crutch, the maintenance approach views it as a valuable resource which should be nurtured and developed along with other academic skills. Accordingly, maintenance programs continue to teach students in their native tongues long after they become proficient in English. Their goal is mastery of both languages, not just English.

While educators and political activists fought over these questions, legislatures at all levels of government were making it increasingly clear that they would support only the "transitional" aim of the program. By the early 1980s the ground of the debate had shifted somewhat. Citing several disputed evaluation studies which concluded that the (mostly transitional) bilingual education programs being implemented were not any more effective than traditional "submersion" in English-only classrooms, assimilationist critics launched a campaign to provide more "flexibility" to local school districts in their choice of programs (enabling them to use, for example, an "English immersion" approach).

These issues came to a head during the Reagan Administration, when Secretary of Education William Bennett joined in to lead the campaign in support of greater programmatic flexibility for local school districts. In the political conflict that followed, supporters of the "maintenance" aims of bilingual education found themselves in the ironic position of becoming the strongest advocates for "transitional" programs. A compromise bill to extend the federal program was approved in 1988, in which 75 percent of bilingual education funds were "set aside" for "transitional bilingual education programs" and the remaining 25 percent may be used for experimental programs at the local level (which could include both "English immersion" and "maintenance" bilingual education, though the former was thought to be more likely). Upon taking office, meanwhile, President Bush signaled another change in policy by appointing a former lobbyist for bilingual education support groups to head the Department of Education's bilingual programs.

In the 1970s the *second* language policy issue arose, that of *linguistic access* to political and civil rights. The most controversial question of access has been voting rights for non–English-literate citizens. Early in the decade, several Latino political organizations (led by the Mexican American Legal Defense Fund) mounted a successful lobbying campaign to persuade Congress to amend the Voting Rights Act of 1965 to include protections for linguistic minorities.

In its 1975 Extension of the Act, accordingly, Congress found ". . . that voting discrimination against citizens of language minorities is pervasive and national in scope" (U.S. Commission on Civil Rights 1981, 120). As a remedy, Titles II and III of the Voting Rights Act were amended to require that registration forms, ballots, and election materials in a language other than English must be provided if more than 5 percent of the voters in an election district spoke the same non-English language and if the English illiteracy rate in the district was greater than the national illiteracy rate (Leibowitz 1982, 7–9).

Further, the same logic was used by language minority activists to argue that access to other political and civil rights should not be denied by the language barrier. Among the rights targeted in this campaign were access to public social services (Obledo and Alcala 1980), to full understanding of courtroom proceedings (Piatt 1990), and to protection against employment discrimination under the guise of linguistic uniformity rules (Mydans 1990).

It was the so-called "bilingual ballot" issue, however, that generated the most opposition. Monolingual anglophones in many states were incensed that citizens might be allowed to vote in languages other than English, and that their tax dollars were used to print election materials in non-English languages. A voter initiative in California's 1984 general election, directing the governor to send a letter to President Reagan expressing the state's opposition to ballots in languages other than English, for example, won by nearly a two-to-one margin.

In fact, by the end of the 1970s many citizens had become alarmed at what they perceived to be the "bilingualization" of American society and public policy, and they generated the third policy issue by embarking on a campaign to "reclaim" the nation's language. The "Official English" Movement—known to its detractors and to some supporters as the "English-Only" movement—formally began on a national level on 27 April 1981, when Senator S. I. Hayakawa (R-California) introduced into the Senate a proposed Amendment to the U.S. Constitution which would have designated English as the "official" language of the United States. Hayakawa's proposal received little support in the Senate, but it was subsequently joined by a similar measure in the House of Representatives. Though the Congress has continued to show little interest in the issue, a proposed "official English" amendment has been introduced into each Congress since 1981.

Meanwhile, in 1983 Hayakawa (by then retired from the Senate) joined forces with John Tanton, a physician and political activist, to organize a nationwide lobbying group known as "U.S. English." Tanton previously had been president of Zero Population Growth and had also founded the Federation for American Immigration Reform (FAIR), a group dedicated to limiting immigration to the United States. Through a continuous national direct-mail recruitment campaign, U.S. English claimed a membership of over 400,000 by 1990, and was joined in 1987 by another nationwide lobbying group known as "English First."

In their literature, both organizations attacked bilingual education policies and "bilingual ballots" and called for the designation of English as the sole "official" language. Though unsuccessful in Congress, the campaign has won some important votes at the state and local levels. By lopsided margins, for example, state voter initiatives for "official English" were successful in California (1986), Colorado (1988), and Florida (1988). A hotly contested measure with far-reaching implementation language was narrowly approved by voters in Arizona (1988). Victories were achieved as well in several notable local elections, including Miami (1980) and San Francisco (1984). Each of these jurisdictions has experienced rapid growth of non–English-speaking immigrant populations in recent years. By 1990 seventeen states had designated English as their sole "official" language through either voter initiative or legislative action (Marshall 1989; Mydans 1990).

Meanwhile, however, opposing political activists alarmed at the "divisiveness" and "racism" of the "English only" movement organized a new counter-offensive. In 1987 a national coalition of civil rights and educator groups was formed which established the "English Plus Information Clearinghouse" (EPIC) in Washington, D.C., to lead the fight against the "English only" movement. As denoted by its title, the aim of EPIC is to support the mastery of English by all residents of the U.S. *plus* the retention and/or learning of other languages (Henry 1990, 32). This coalition has claimed successes in turning back "official English" campaigns in several states (including Texas), and it supported a successful suit in the Arizona U.S. District Court overturning that state's "official English" law as a violation of the First Amendment (*Yniguez and Gutierrez v. Mofford, et. al.*, 1990).

Pluralism, Assimilation, and Public Values

As the nation entered the 1990s, then, the controversy over language policy showed no signs of abating, and demographic projections indicate continued "re-fueling" for the issue into the forseeable future (see, for example, Meisler 1992). Though there are other possible approaches for resolving language policy conflicts,[3] recent debate in the United States over this policy terrain has focused primarily on arguments between "assimilationists" and "pluralists," as noted above. Assimilationists believe that U.S. linguistic diversity should be resolved through a policy that promotes rapid and efficient assimilation of non–English-speakers into the English language and Anglo-based culture that has dominated the national history. Pluralists also believe that English has been and will remain the predominant public language of the United States, but that public policy should aim to encourage as well the retention and development of other languages long existent in the territory of the United States.

Underlying this conflict between pluralists and assimilationists is a dispute over the meaning and implications of two fundamental public values, "equality" and "national unity." Equality has been the central issue for proponents of ethno-linguistic pluralism. The principal rationale for bilingual education, for example, has been that it is the most appropriate pedagogical vehicle for helping language minority students attain greater equality within the U.S. political economy (Cummins 1989). Assimilationists, on the other hand, have argued that bilingual education does not help language minority children attain higher levels of academic achievement, and that instead it will doom them to continued marginal and subordinate positions in the society (Porter 1990). Similarly, pluralist proponents of "linguistic access" for language minority persons have argued that the principle of equality requires that political and civil rights must be guaranteed to all persons without respect to language barriers. And assimilationists, once again, argue that genuine equality can never be achieved in a multilingual polity.

The second critical value in the debate over language policy is that of national unity. It is this public value which has been most dear to assimilationist proponents of English as the "official" language of the United States. At its most concise, this part of the assimilationist argument is that the adoption of non-English ballots and bilingual education policies has charted this nation onto a new and dangerous course toward ethnolinguistic conflict and deep political division, for which the declaration of English as the sole "official" language is an important corrective measure (Hayakawa 1985). Pluralist opponents of "English-only" laws, on the other hand, charge that it is the strident demand for a single official language which threatens to tear apart the fabric of our civil society, not the ameliorative policies of bilingual education and linguistic access to political and civil rights (Marshall and Gonzalez 1990).

While "equality" and "national unity" are the value issues around which the debate over language policy has centered, the opposing partisans in the debate clearly have differing understandings of the meanings of these protean terms and their relationships to each other. At the center of their clash on these values, however, are fundamentally divergent assessments of the appropriate role of non-English languages in the United States.

Interpretations

How are we to understand the meaning of this contemporary conflict over language policy in the United States? It seems clear that there *is* a genuine political conflict here, and that it is not likely to disappear soon from the political stage. But what is really at stake in this conflict? Why has it developed once again in a country that, as little as thirty years ago, most intellectuals believed to be unquestionably an English-speaking nation?

The first point to be stressed here is that, while *language* has become an important battleground for policy conflict in the United States, the conflict is not centrally about language per se. That is, language is deeply implicated in this debate, but at its heart the conflict is about the place of *ethnic diversity* in American society. Owing much to the Civil Rights Movement of the 1960s and the racial polarization that followed, the ethnic status quo (including the prevailing "melting pot" mythology) in the United States was challenged from a variety of directions in the 1960s and 1970s, as Young has noted in this volume's introduction. Both of the pluralistic language policy initiatives outlined above—bilingual education and linguistic access policies—found their greatest political support among ethnic activists who saw these measures as important avenues to greater ethnic equality in the United States. Similarly, the opposition to these policy initiatives by assimilationists has been focused on the implications of non–English-language retention for continued ethnic conflict, linking the latter to beliefs about the nature of American nationalism.

Accordingly, at its heart this conflict over language policy should be viewed as a conflict about the relationships between language, ethnic identity, and American nationalism. On that assumption, the remainder of this essay will employ the theoretical categories outlined by Young to explore the meaning of the resurgent politics of language in the United States in relation to these themes. Properly understood, it is suggested, each category of analysis offers valuable insights into the nature and meaning of this important political phenomenon.

Language Politics as Instrumentalist

The first analytical concept to be employed here is that of "instrumentalism." Like "primordialism" and "constructivism," instrumentalism aims to uncover the sources of ethnic political conflict. In doing so, it stresses the mutability of ethnic attachments and, especially, the roles of *interest* and *context* in the processes of ethnic conflict. Often, as well, ethnic attachments are seen through the instrumentalist lense as subject to change through rational choice.

Thus, people tend to identify themselves as members of an ethnic group—or to stress their membership in such a group—because it serves their interests to do so in a particular socioeconomic and political context. Similarly, members of one group may define others as an "ethnic group" with certain (negative) characteristics because it helps them to maintain the subordination of those others. But in any case, the key to understanding both ethnic loyalty and ethnic conflict, in the instrumentalist view, is *competition* between groups over scarce material and symbolic resources (Olzak and Nagel 1986; Scott 1990).

How does language policy fit into this interpretation of ethnic conflict? At its most direct and obvious level, it is apparent that contact and intermingling between different language groups introduces costs that must be paid in order for social, economic, and political intercourse between the groups to be facilitated. At a minimum, time and effort must be expended to learn each other's language, or to devise a new patois that is understandable to members of each group. To the extent that language comes to be seen as an important "marker" for ethnic identity, competitive ethnic relations will devolve into a competition over who will bear the greatest "costs" and which group will garner the most "benefits" in the mutual adjustment to multi-lingualism in the political territory which the groups share. In short, each group will attempt to impose the costs of language adjustment onto the other group(s) and to enlarge its own power through the expansion of its linguistic domain (Wardbaugh 1987). In this context, the language policy of the state becomes an important instrument in the competition. Competitive ethnic groups with differing languages seek to use the power of the state in their efforts to gain comparative advantage (see also Weinstein 1983).

Seen through the instrumentalist lense, contemporary U.S. language policy conflict takes on a distinctive and understandable form. Among the primary proponents of a pluralistic language policy are leaders of two diverse ethnic minority communities—Latinos and American Indians—for whom conquest and domination by "Anglo" America have been central historical experiences. That is, American Indians were decimated and systematically pushed onto reservations over a lengthy process that consumed much of the U.S. government's attention for its first hundred years. Long expected to die off or assimilate into the dominant society, they remain distinctive, though numerically small, communities within U.S. territory.

Similarly, the largest Latino nationality groups initially were incorporated into the United States through military conquest: Mexico ceded nearly half its territory to the United States following its military defeat in 1848, and Puerto Rico was acquired in 1898 following the Spanish-American War. Even Cuban Americans, it has been argued, migrated to the United States in large numbers as a direct consequence of this country's long and intimate involvement in Cuba's domestic affairs (and some have applied a similar argument to the recent large migrations from Vietnam, Cambodia, the Phillipines, and Korea).

From the perspective of many members of the conquered and annexed ethnic minority groups, in any case, long-standing efforts by Anglo-Americans to impose English as the sole language of public discourse in the United States are viewed as obvious attempts by a dominant group to impose its will and convenience on weaker groups that have their own legitimate claims to "belonging" in the United States. It is important to emphasize, nevertheless, that most U.S. language minority group members—in contrast, say, to the *québeçois* of Canada—do *not* support a language confederation policy under which they would have their own largely monolingual non–English-speaking territories. Both geodemographic intermingling and the English language are viewed as such overwhelming political and economic realities in the United States that virtually all language minority group members seek mastery of the dominant language for themselves and their progeny.

Instead, most U.S. language minority group members favor a policy of bilingualism, as noted above. There are three central "instrumental" advantages of a pluralistic policy for language minority groups. First and most obviously, a pluralistic language policy will lessen some of the costs heretofore paid by non–English-speakers, shifting some of the burden to the state. Multilingual ballots and election materials, for example, reduce the costs of political participation for language minority members. Second, for reasons too complex to outline here (but see Cummins 1989), many language minority members and language experts are convinced that a bilingual education policy which adds to and builds upon the student's native language will be more effective in generating higher educational achievement levels even in English than do programs seeking to substitute English for the native language. And third, to the extent that bilingual skills become valued in the political economy as a result of a pluralistic language policy, the policy will directly advantage those members of language minority communities who have already invested the time and effort to become bilingual. In particular, they will be advantaged in the competition for public service jobs (for example, teaching, law, law enforcement, health professions, sales). In each case, then, a pluralistic language policy may be seen as in the interest of language minority ethnic groups within the specific context of the United States.

Assimilationist opponents of a pluralistic policy, on the other hand, have sought to counter these perceptions in several ways. First, they have argued that bilingual education policies do not teach English language skills successfully and therefore are not to the competitive advantage of individual language minority group members in the United States (Porter 1990). Second, assimilationists portray the advocacy of pluralist policies as a self-serving political strategy on the part of self-appointed ethnic leaders. These politicians and professionals are accused by assimilationists of cynically condemning their own disadvantaged people to a second-class (non-English) life for their own selfish political purposes, that is to maintain their own positions as ethnic leaders (Chavez 1991).

But perhaps most important from the instrumentalist perspective, assimilationists have sought to counter the legitimacy of the pluralist argument by redefining the beneficiaries of those policies as "immigrants" and not as members of "minority" groups. While it may be illegitimate to ask conquered and annexed peoples to pay the entire price for the country's multi-lingualism, assimilationists believe it is surely legitimate to ask immigrants to do so (Imhoff, 1990).

From an instrumentalist perspective, in short, the assimilationist strategy has not been to deny that language minority group members are at a comparative disadvantage in the U.S. political economy, but rather to assert that in this country assimilationist policies are more advantageous to non–English-speakers and that the costs of linguistic integration appropriately should be assumed by the immigrant speakers of "foreign" languages.

Aside from the question of the effectiveness of bilingual education programs in teaching language minority students English (which will not be pursued further here), the instrumentalist perspective points to a central unresolved issue dividing assimilationists and pluralists: the nature of the American identity. That is, one's understanding of the distribution of "costs" and "benefits" apportioned through language policy is powerfully shaped by one's answer to the question of whether the United States is to be conceived as a monocultural country or as a multi-cultural country.

Further, the stakes on this issue are raised substantially by the large number of recent immigrants to the United States. For in the context of the debate over language policy, the high percentage of non-"white" immigrants keeps in the forefront the important questions of the role that ethnic identity and loyalty will play in their perceptions of who they are in relation to national identity, and what role language loyalty will play in these determinations. With this question, we reach the terrain of the "politics of identity," and this is an aspect of cultural pluralism perhaps best interpreted through the primordialist lense.

Language Politics as "Primordialist"

While the instrumentalist perspective sees ethnic identification and language loyalty as arising out of the competition between social groups for comparative advantage, the primordialist lense scans the innermost recesses of the human psyche in its search for the sources of ethnic loyalties and conflicts. As Young notes in his introduction, primordialists have been particularly successful in explicating the intensely emotional quality of much ethnic conflict. In seeking out the roots of that affective chord, primordialists assert that there is something very "natural," even "spiritual" (Geertz 1973; 260) about ethnic attachments that the materialist emphasis of instrumentalists does not capture.

Stripped of its somewhat ethereal language, the core of the primordialist insight is that human beings become who they are as individuals only as members of groups, and that among the most important of these groups in the contemporary world are those we label *ethnic* and/or *national*. Contrary to the impression created by some Enlightenment liberals, individuals do not come together *de novo* to create political communities; rather the community also "creates" the individual (a position articulated by communitarians from Socrates to Sandel; but see Kymlicka 1989 for a recent liberal defense of this view). The core identity of virtually all human beings, in short, is mediated through the culture of a collectivity.

From a primordialist viewpoint, language often plays a crucial role in this individual identity-formation. This is so because our experience of the reality around us is mediated through words and sounds attached to people, and these come to have an emotional, as well as a rational, meaning for our own sense of self and our world. Political scientist Harold Isaacs (1975, 94–95) articulated the primordialist view of the importance of language as follows:

> That first learned language is, to begin with, the *mother's* tongue, with all that conveys and contributes to the forming of the self and the development of the individual personality. It opens into every aspect of life. . . .
>
> "The world of communicable facts" is the world as it is seen by the family, the group, the culture in which the child enters. It is the world as named and described in the group's language, the tongue in which the child learns what the world is and how it came to be, the words and tones in which the group describes itself, spins its tales of the past, sings its songs of joy or sorrow, celebrates the beauties of its land, the greatness of its heroes, the power of its myths. . . . It thus extends to all who share or have shared this tongue, as Herbert Kelman has put it, "some of the emotional intensity and irreducible quality" attached to "those primordial bonds that tie the child to his mother and immediate kin."

Though his formulation may be somewhat hyperbolic, this depiction by Isaacs may go a long way toward explaining the uncommonly intense emotions often expressed in the political conflict over language policy. A perceived attack on one's language, by the state or by other groups, may be perceived as an attack on one's very identity as a human being as well as an attack on one's people. Viewed in this way, the "stakes" of language policy conflict are very high indeed.

In relation to language policy conflict, the primordialist lense may provide an alternative understanding of the seemingly quixotic behavior of ethnic minority activists who continue to advocate public support for the retention and enhancement of minority languages in the United States against apparently overwhelming odds. The emotional intensity and "primordial" nature of the issue for some Chicano activists, for example, is revealed starkly in the opening lines of Rodolfo Gonzalez's (1967, 3) epic poem, "I Am Joaquin":

> I am Joaquin,
> Lost in a world of confusion,
> Caught up in a whirl of an
> gringo society,
> Confused by the rules,
> Scorned by attitudes,
> Suppressed by manipulation,
> And destroyed by modern society.
> My fathers
> have lost the economic battle
> and won
> the struggle of cultural survival.
> And now!
> I must choose
>
> Between the paradox of
> Victory of the spirit,
> despite physical hunger
> Or
> to exist in the grasp
> of American social neurosis,
> sterilization of the soul
> and a full stomach.

A similar, if less poetic, analysis of the choices faced by Chicanos has been made more recently by political scientist Mario Barrera (1988). In the absence of significant political and policy support for a culturally pluralistic society, the only alternatives for non-Anglo individuals appear to be those of complete cultural assimilation (and loss of "self") or a relatively isolated and subordinated existence on the margins of the society.

As a consequence of the great imbalance in these choices, and despite the increasing number of non-English speakers, most sociolinguists continue to believe that the long-term future of languages other than English is very insecure in the United States. A number of studies (Veltman, 1983; Fishman, 1985) have found that by the third generation the vast majority of Mexican-Americans have lost virtually any facility in the Spanish language—a figure that has held true for most other "newcomer" groups in the past. It is only immigration, these studies indicate, that continues to "feed" non-English-language communities in the United States.

Given these projections and the hegemonically limited choices behind them, attacks by assimilationist critics on the "Latinization" of the United States are taken very personally and are often perceived by Latinos as attacks on their very identity and personal legitimacy as Americans. As one critic of an antibilingual education publication put it: "My ethnic culture is a part of this American culture" (Cardenas 1977, 77). From this perspective, political efforts on behalf of a pluralistic language policy may be perceived as modest (though intensely felt) attempts to preserve valued aspects of the identity of members of ethnic communities increasingly threatened by both hostile political forces and the impersonalism of a highly routinized and bureaucratized society.

What may be more difficult to explain is the apparently "primordial" insecurity of many Anglo-Americans in the face of the virtually global triumph of English in the late twentieth century. For despite the fact that residents of every region in the world—including most immigrants to the United States—are eagerly attempting to learn English to further their life chances, a substantial number of U.S. citizens appear to believe that it is necessary to make English the official language in order to protect its future. Indeed, many assimilationist political leaders appear to believe that the national security of the United States is seriously threatened unless language minority persons not only learn English to the best of their ability, but forego public efforts to preserve their native languages as well (Hayakawa 1985; Lamm and Imhoff 1985). How are these apparently irrational fears to be explained?

Many analysts of the contemporary "official English" movement believe that it is driven by fears about the viability of its members' "national" identity. That is, assimilationists appear to feel deeply that the "unity" of the United States is a very fragile thing, and that—given the immense diversity of the population—the English language is one of the very few unifying factors for a national identity for Americans (Hayakawa 1985, 6). The expansion of non–English-language enclaves, then, is viewed as a threat to the very existence of the nation as they have understood it. Something of the "primordial" nature of this fear may be seen in the following interview response of one Miami proponent of "official English":

> Before we had our revolution [i.e., the influx of Cubans after 1960], it was laid back, you could start out in the morning and go down to Metheson hammock (a local park),

> take the kids down and stop at Shorty's on the way home. Of course, people, their language, it was very easy to conduct your business, and I miss it, I miss it. *I have lost my city*. . . (quoted in Bretzer and Castro 1990, 12; emphasis added)

This sensation of having "lost my city," or even country, then, which in turn is rooted in a deeply felt link between personal and national identity, seems to be a major factor in the intense emotion that often accompanies participation in the "official English" movement.[4] But to put this aspect of the conflict into a larger perspective, it will be useful to turn to the analytical concept of "constructivism."

Language Politics as "Constructivist"

The theme developed above is that part of the conflict over language policy in the United States—the most emotional part—is about the "politics of identity." In struggling for political support for a policy of bilingualism in the United States, many Latino, American Indian, and Asian-American activists are struggling for acceptance of their core "ethnic" identities as authentically "American." In that struggle, language policy has come to symbolize a larger set of issues about the relationship between ethnic and national identity. Particularly since these groups are also "racial" groups for whom linguistic assimilation will not mark the end of easily identifiable ethnic group membership, a far-reaching movement has been evolving for several decades which aims at transforming the core identity of the "American" nationality from that of a "Eurocentric" melting pot to that of a multi-racial, multi-cultural society.

Reacting against the exclusion of "racial" minority groups from the dominant (and largely subconscious) image of "the American people,"[5] this culturally based political campaign is fundamentally about "constructing" a new prototype for full membership in the American political community, a new understanding of the national identity. It may be that language is an important symbol in this "constructivist" effort because racial markers are largely involuntary, and once formal equality between "races" has been codified in law it becomes difficult to discern the degree to which acceptance of minorities as different, but full members of the polity by members of the dominant Anglo group has taken place. Public acknowledgment of language diversity as fully *American,* on the other hand, symbolizes acceptance of "cultural" diversity and therefore of a broader range of the full identities of non-European Americans.

In any case, this "reconstruction" of American national identity means that European-origin Americans are themselves being constructed anew as "ethnics" (for example, as "Anglos" or "Euro-Americans") rather than as "just Americans." A truly multi-cultural and multi-racial understanding of American national identity, in short, would mean that European-origin Americans would be "reduced" from being the standard, the prototype, against which all *Others* are to judge their own "Americanness" to being one ethnic group among many in a "decentered" multi-cultural polity (JanMohamed and Lloyd 1990).

Understood in this way, the strength of the "constructivist" interpretation is that it helps to explain both the strong emotional trigger that language policy has become for protagonists on both sides of the issue (it is about identity) *and* the centrality of *power* in this conflict (it is about who defines identity). That is, like primordialist interpretations, the constructivist lense recognizes the deeply personal and affective nature of ethnic identities and conflicts. Like instrumentalism, however, the constructivist interpretation sees ethnic attachments and identities as deeply implicated in the power relations of the larger society, and as subject to change. In this sense, it should be clear that all three analytical concepts can contribute usefully to an understanding of what is at stake in the contemporary conflict over language policy in the United States.

NOTES

1. There were, of course, important cultural and linguistic conflicts with indigenous groups also, as well as with European-language-speakers who preceded Anglo-Americans into important parts of the territory that became the United States (e.g., Spanish and French speakers). This part of the story will be interpreted below.

2. There is no term which is universally approved to reference the still-emerging ethnic group denoted herein as "Latino." The term is used here to refer to U.S. residents of Latin American origin; this is a very diverse and multi-racial population of which the national origins of the largest groups are Mexican-American, Puerto Rican, and Cuban-American. It is acknowledged that some prefer the appellation "Hispanic," while others object to any pan-ethnic term, preferring to be identified in terms of their national origin or by no ethnic designation at all.

3. In previous essays, I have outlined four alternatives that have been advocated and/or adopted for resolving language policy conflicts in various countries around the world: "domination/exclusion," "assimilation," "pluralism," and "linguistic confederation"; see Schmidt (1991).

4. This interpretation has obvious linkages to earlier attempts to explain "counter-subversive" movements in U.S. history that cannot be developed here; see Bell (1964), Hofstadter (1967), Rogin (1987); see also Citrin et al. (1990), for some survey research evidence which supports this interpretation.

5. To this day, third- and fourth-generation Asian-Americans and Latinos are routinely asked in all parts of the country: "Where did you learn to speak English so well?"

REFERENCES

Baron, Dennis. 1990. *The English-Only Question*. New Haven: Yale University Press.

Barrera, Mario. 1988. *Beyond Aztlan: Ethnic Autonomy in Comparative Perspective*. New York: Praeger.

Bell, Daniel, ed. 1964. *The Radical Right*. New York: Doubleday.

Bouvier, Leon F., and Robert W. Gardner. 1986. Immigration to the U.S.: The Unfinished Story. *Population Bulletin* 41, 4 (November): 3–50.

Bretzer, Joanne M., and Max J. Castro. 1990. Identity and Power: The Curious Question of Language in Miami. A paper prepared for delivery at the Annual Meeting of the Western Political Science Association, Newport Beach, California, March 22–24.

Cardenas, Jose. 1977. Response I. In *Language, Ethnicity, and the Schools: Policy Alternatives for Bilingual-Bicultural Education,* edited by Noel Epstein, 71–84. Washington D.C.: Institute for Educational Leadership, George Washington University.

Chavez, Linda. 1991. *Out of the Barrio: Toward a New Politics of Hispanic Assimilation*. New York: Basic Books.

Citrin, Jack, Beth Reinhold, Evelyn Walters, and Donald P. Green. 1990. The "Official English" Movement and the Symbolic Politics of Language in the United States. *The Western Political Quarterly* 43, 3 (September): 535–60.

Clifford, Frank. 1992. Rich-Poor Gulf Widens in States. *Los Angeles Times,* May 11: A1.

Cummins, James. 1989. *Empowering Minority Students*. Sacramento: California Association for Bilingual Education.

Fishman, Joshua. 1985. The Ethnic Revival in the United States: Implications for the Mexican-American Community. In *Mexican Americans in Comparative Perspective,* edited by Walker Connor, 309–54. Washington, D.C.: The Urban Institute Press.

Fulwood, Sam, III. 1990. "Conferees OK Increase of 45% in Immigration," *Los Angeles Times,* October 25, A1.

Geertz, Clifford. 1973. *The Interpretation Cultures: Selected Essays*. New York: Basic Books.

Gonzalez, Rodolfo. 1967. *I Am Joaquin: An Epic Poem*. Denver: Crusade for Justice.

Hayakawa, S. I. 1985. *One Nation . . . Indivisible? The English Language Amendment*. Washington, D.C.: The Washington Institute for Values in Public Policy.

Henry, Sarah. 1990. English Only: The Language of Discrimination. *Hispanic: The Magazine for and about Hispanics* (March): 28–32.

Higham, John. 1963. *Strangers in the Land: Patterns of American Nativism 1860–1925*. 2d ed. New York: Atheneum.

Hofstadter, Richard. 1967. *The Paranoid Style in American Politics and Other Essays*. New York: Vintage Books.

Imhoff, Gary. 1990. The Position of U.S. English on Bilingual Education. *The Annals of the American Academy of Political and Social Science* 508 (March): 48–61.

Isaacs, Harold R. 1975. *Idols of the Tribe: Group Identity and Political Change*. New York: Harper & Row.

JanMohamed, Abdul R., and David Lloyd, eds. 1990. *The Nature and Context of Minority Discourse*. New York: Oxford University Press.

Kloss, Heinz. 1966. German-American Language Maintenance Efforts. In *Language Loyalty in the United States,* edited by Joshua Fishman et al., 206–52. The Hague: Mouton & Company.

Kymlicka, Will. 1989. *Liberalism, Community and Culture*. New York: Oxford University Press.

Lamm, Gov. Richard D., and Gary Imhoff. 1985. *The Immigration Time Bomb: The Fragmenting of America*. New York: E. P. Dutton.

Leibowitz, Arnold H. 1982. *Federal Recognition of the Rights of Minority Language Groups*. Rosslyn, Virginia: National Clearinghouse for Bilingual Education.

Lewis, Marilyn. 1992. State's Rich Got Richer, Poor Got Poorer. Long Beach *Press-Telegram,* May 12, A1.

Lyons, James J. 1990. The Past and Future Directions of Federal Bilingual Education Policy. *The Annals of the American Academy of Political and Social Science* 508 (March): 66–80.

Marshall, David F. 1989. Up-date and Implications for English Teachers of English Only Legislation. Paper presented to the National Conference of Teachers of English, November.

Marshall, David F., and Roseann D. Gonzalez. 1990. Una Lingua, Una Patria? Is Monolingualism Beneficial or Harmful for a Nation's Unity? In *Perspectives on English-Only,* edited by Karen L. Adams and Daniel T. Brink, pp. 29–51. Berlin and New York: Mouton DeGruyter.

Meisler, Stanley. 1992. "Rising Wind of Migration" Foreseen. *Los Angeles Times,* April 30, A9.

Mydans, Seth. 1990. Pressure for English-Only Job Rules Stirring a Sharp Debate Across U.S. *New York Times,* August 8, A10.

Obledo, Mario, and Carlos Alcala. 1980. Discrimination Against the Spanish Language in Public Service: A Policy Alternative. In *Politics and Language: Spanish and English in the United States,* edited by D. J. R. Bruckner, 155–62. Chicago: The University of Chicago Center for Policy Study.

Olzak, Susan, and Joane Nagel, eds. 1986. *Competitive Ethnic Relations*. Orlando: Academic Press, Inc.

Perlmann, Joel. 1990. Historical Legacies: 1840–1920. *The Annals of the American Academy of Political and Social Science* 508 (May): 27–37.

Piatt, Bill. 1990. *Only English?, Law and Language Policy in the United States*. Albuquerque: University of New Mexico Press.

Porter, Rosalie Pedalino. 1990. *Forked Tongue: The Politics of Bilingual Education*. New York: Basic Books.

Rogin, Michael. 1987. *Ronald Reagan, The Movie . . . And Other Episodes in Political Demonology*. Berkeley: University of California Press.

Schmidt, Ronald J. 1991. Sources of Language Policy Conflict: A Comparative Perspective. An unpublished paper presented at the Annual Meeting of the Western Political Science Association, Seattle, March 21–23.

Scott, George M. 1990. A resynthesis of the primordial and circumstantial approaches to ethnic group solidarity: Towards an explanatory model. *Ethnic and Racial Studies* 13, 2 (April): 147–71.

U.S. Commission on Civil Rights. 1981. *The Voting Rights Act: Unfulfilled Goals*. Washington, D.C.: U.S. Government Printing Office.

Veltman, Calvin. 1983. *Language Shift in the United States*. Berlin: Mouton Publishers.

Vobejda, Barbara. 1992. Land of the Thousand Tongues: English is Increasingly Foreign in America. *Washington Post National Weekly Edition,* April 27, II–37.

Waggoner, Dorothy. 1988. Language Minorities in the United States in the 1980s: The Evidence from the 1980 Census. In *Language Diversity: Problem or Resource?,* edited by S. L. McKay and S. C. Wong, pp. 69–108. Cambridge: Newbury House Publishers.

Wagner, Stephen T. 1981. The Historical Background of Bilingualism and Biculturalism in the United States. In *The New Bilingualism: An American Dilemma,* edited by Martin Ridge, 29–52. Los Angeles: University of Southern California Press.

Wardhaugh, Ronald. 1987. *Languages in Competition: Dominance, Diversity, and Decline.* Oxford: Basil Blackwell.

Weinstein, Brian. 1983. *The Civic Tongue: Political Consequences of Language Choice.* New York: Longman Inc.

5

Demise of an Empire-State: Identity, Legitimacy, and the Deconstruction of Soviet Politics

MARK R. BEISSINGER

THERE HAS BEEN no more spectacular an unraveling of the modern state than that which occurred in the Soviet Union in 1991. A superpower with global commitments and a seventy-four-year record of survival—a polity that had endured two devastating wars, several famines involving millions of deaths, the mass annihilation of its citizens by its own rulers, and a social revolution that brought it into the industrial world—imploded under the weight of its ethnic problems. The breakup of the USSR indeed presents scholars with many paradoxes that challenge our understandings of ethnic politics.

One such paradox was the long refusal of many observers even to contemplate the possibility, let alone the probability, that the USSR might fall apart. Had Western experts been polled in 1986—five years before its dissolution—the overwhelming opinion would have been that the disintegration of the USSR was highly unlikely, if not impossible. Even in 1991, many prominent experts refused to recognize the imminent demise of the USSR. Only months before the events of August 1991, Jerry Hough wrote that "the assumption that the Soviet Union is now revolutionary—and that it may even be disintegrating as a country—contradicts all that we know about revolution and national integration" and was "based on the least comparative perspective." (Hough 1991b, 102).[1] Experts on ethnicity fared no better. David Laitin, in an article written on the eve of the coup, decried "the unjustifiable assumption" that the USSR was on a course towards dissolution; after the August coup, a postscript was added in which Laitin confessed that recent events had made "the image of a rotting empire, discredited in . . . [the] essay, seem intuitively correct." (Laitin 1991, 139–77). Such statements on the eve of the demise of the USSR suggest that many experts were seriously misreading the comparative evidence. They suggest something more as well: the power of the modern state to mesmerize even those who make their careers studying it into believing in its timelessness and immutability.

Another paradox posed by the dissolution of the USSR was the relative lack of violence it involved. The Soviet Union died with a whimper rather than a bang. Among experts there was traditionally a tendency to believe that the breakup of the USSR, if it were to occur, would be an extremely violent, if not cataclysmic event. Indeed, in December, on the eve of the breakup, Secretary of State James Baker warned that the USSR could well turn into a "Yugoslavia . . . with nuclear weapons" (*International Herald Tribune*, December 9, 1991, 1). In reality, when the USSR Congress of People's Deputies formally voted in December 1991 to dissolve the Soviet Union, hardly any deputies bothered to attend. As was noted on December 12 by *Rossiiskaia gazeta,* the newspaper of the Russian parliament, "The former union is no more. And much more important, no one needs it." Even earlier, the August 1991 coup and the events that followed it were striking in the rather minimal violence they involved. The violence that followed the breakup of the USSR was primarily between rival successor groups in the republics rather than between proponents and opponents of preserving the union. Of course, there is a very real possibility that massive violence could occur over the conflicting territorial claims of successor states. But the actual process of the creation of new states out of an old one was much less painful than most experts had predicted.

Behind these paradoxes lie a number of questionable assumptions about the nature of ethnic identity and the character of Soviet politics that are the subject of this essay. The standard argument put forth by those who thought that the Soviet Union was unlikely to break up was that the dissolution of the USSR would have constituted a secession, not much different than the breakup of Nigeria, India, Yugoslavia, or Canada. As many have observed, cases of successful secession have been rare in the modern era, their outcome depending in large part on the reactions of the international community (Horowitz 1985, 265–77).[2] Indeed, if we discount the case of Yugoslavia, which is still running its course, until the dissolution of the USSR, the only unambiguous case of a successful secession since the end of World War II is Bangladesh—a fact often pointed to by those who believed that the dissolution of the USSR was unlikely (Hough 1990, 2).

These arguments ignored two key points. First, before World War II there had been many cases of successful state separatism. It is often forgotten that immediately preceding their independent statehood, Poland had been part of Prussia and Russia from 1793 until 1917, Norway had been part of Sweden from 1814 to 1905, and Iceland was part of Denmark from the late fourteenth century until 1944. The lack of successful secessions in the postwar period was more revealing of the character of international politics than of the inherent stability of the postwar state. Precisely as a result of the Cold War, there was a clear attempt to reify the state system and to freeze its boundaries. In part this was due to a general desire for stability on the part of the Western world in its struggle to contain communism; in part, it was the result of the desire of newly installed postcolonial leaders to denationalize their states, lest the politics of communalism overwhelm them. From the 1960s on, the reification of the state system was also a matter of conscious policy by both superpowers, who feared that they might be drawn into direct confrontation as a result of regional and separatist conflicts.

A second point ignored by those who minimized the possibility of a Soviet breakup was the analogy often made by the Soviet peoples themselves between the demise of the great European empires in the aftermath of the Second World War and the breakup of the Soviet Union. Indeed, even the editor of this volume, in a recent essay that sought to apply theories of ethnicity to the Soviet case, argued that the imperial analogy in Soviet politics was most likely misplaced:

> States perceived in international jurisprudence and dominant political discourse as colonial have been dismantled, but this imagery—however serviceable as cold war lexicon . . . is unlikely to govern the unfolding dialectic between the central institutions of the Soviet state and its non-Russian periphery. . . . [A]lthough there is an undeniable element of "exceptionalism" to the Soviet case, it belongs on balance in the contemporary universe of polities founded on the doctrinal postulates of the "nation-state," and is therefore susceptible of interpretation according to the same empirical inferences as other members of the contemporary body of states. (Young 1992, 91, 97)

By contrast, in the perception of many Soviet peoples, rather than constituting a series of secessions, the breakup of the Soviet Union fell into the category of a decolonization.[3] Indeed, reports on the dissolution of the USSR by non-Russian, Russian, and outside observers alike were enveloped in a litany of empire-imagery that cannot be dismissed entirely as mere political rhetoric.

Should we understand the collapse of the USSR in August 1991 as the collapse of an empire or as the failure of a state—a decolonization or a secession? Behind this question lurks the larger issue of whether the breakup of the USSR represented a broader crisis of the modern state, or simply the end of "the last empire." The answer that this essay will suggest is that it should be understood as both. The Soviet Union always straddled the divide between state and empire. Symbolizing this symbiosis, the events that set in motion the final collapse of USSR began only two days before a treaty constituting a renewed and thoroughly revamped USSR was to be signed. Within the Soviet context, political images of state and empire were intertwined closely with cultural identities, forming the main battleground on which national conflicts were fought. Moreover, empire imagery has not died with the Soviet Union, but continues to live on in the serious national conflicts that plague post-Soviet politics.

The Subjective Bases of Empires and States

Notions such as state or empire have a subjective dimension that too often has been ignored and too easily dismissed by observers. If the history of Soviet multinational politics demonstrates anything, it is that what constitutes a "state" or an "empire" is to a large extent in the eye of the beholder and is closely connected with conceptions of legitimacy and ethnic identity. As David Laitin has written, "it is historically inaccurate to identify the incorporation of Estonia, the Ukraine, Georgia, Uzbekistan, Kazan, and Kazakhstan as examples of the construction of the 'last empire' and to juxtapose Russian imperial expansion categorically to French state building" (Laitin 1991, 173). Violence was as much a part of the state-building process as it was part of empire-building. Given this subjective character of the terms, it is tempting to dismiss them entirely as simply reflecting the prejudices of those who use them, as Laitin indeed does, arguing that they obscure more than they reveal (ibid., 142–43). However, it is *precisely* the subjective dimension that these expressions capture—the perceptions of those who use them—which is the most interesting aspect about them, particularly in view of what they reveal empirically about the subtleties of political and ethnic identities.

The Soviet Union, of course, was frequently referred to as an "empire," particularly as its demise grew imminent and increasingly visible. Relatively few who used the term bothered to define what they meant by it.[4] The use of imperial imagery in scholarly works to describe Soviet politics traces its origins to the study of totalitarianism rather than to the study of Soviet nationalities politics. Empire for most theorists of totalitarianism meant the GULAG and international conquest, both of which were conditioned by a utopian ideology, not by an imperial Russian legacy. The classic works on totalitarianism underplayed the threat of nationalism to the Soviet regime. As Carl J. Friedrich and Zbigniew K. Brzezinski wrote, although nationalism provided the most serious basis for resisting totalitarianism, "after all is said and done, this sort of activity does not seriously threaten the stability of the totalitarian regime. It serves rather to maintain the self-respect of those participating because they share a common danger" (1961, 183).

At the same time, theorists of totalitarianism pointed to a special category of groups, known as "captive nations," explicitly attributing an imperial quality to Soviet rule. The term was used more frequently to refer to peoples of Eastern Europe than those of the Soviet Union; within Soviet borders, it was at times used to describe the Balts, whose annexation by the USSR was never recognized by Western governments. Of course, why the term—in its internal Soviet usage—should have been confined to the Balts when many other groups lying within Soviet borders had long laid claims to independent statehood, had prolonged histories of independence outside of a Russian-dominated political entity, were larger in territory and population, and were better endowed with natural resources than the Baltic republics was never made clear. Any argument for drawing the line for claims to independent statehood at those groups annexed as a result of the Nazi-Soviet pact (and in particular, the Balts) was based entirely on the accidents of history during the three-year period of 1917 to 1920, which ended by providing the Balts with two decades of political independence and separate statehood for the Poles and Finns, but left the remaining peoples of the Tsarist empire stateless.[5] In any "objective" sense, Poles might be considered no less "captive" a nation than Bashkirs or Chechens. This was well understood by Walter Kolarz, whose works constituted a near solitary voice of protest in the 1950s against what he viewed as the Russian imperial legacy in Soviet nationalities policies. While Kolarz saw a connection between Soviet imperialism and communist ideology, unlike most students of totalitarianism he viewed Marxism-Leninism more as an instrument of empire than as its driving force, which was instead Russian nationalism. As he observed: "Communism has become the instrument enabling Russia to resist successfully that liquidation of colonialism carried out elsewhere in the world" (Kolarz 1964, 23; Kolarz 1952).

Kolarz's argument tended to ignore the aspects of Soviet nationalities issues where the fit between the Russian imperial legacy and communism was imperfect. Russian nationalists, for instance, have long argued (and not without justification) that even the Russians were left stateless by the events of 1917–20 and were incorporated instead into an internationalist state that elevated them to the status of "elder brother," but which was in essence an "equal-opportunity repressor." A banner displayed before the White House in August 1991 by Russian demonstrators massed in the tens of thousands symbolized this widespread sense among Russians that they too have been victims of empire; it read: "Down with the Empire of Red Fascism!" The difference between Kolarz's understanding of empire and the non-national version that appeared in most works on totalitarianism represented a basic tension that always ran the full breadth of Soviet politics: the extent to which Russian identities and interests had become synonymous with those of the Soviet Union. When the Soviet Union finally collapsed in August 1991, it was evident that it was brought down as much by pressure from non-Russians for independence as by what Roman Szporluk has referred to as the "de-Sovietization of Russia" (1990, 13).

The idea propounded by Kolarz that communism served simply as a vehicle for the reimposition of Russian dominance formed the basis for most subsequent discussions of the imperial legacy in Soviet nationalities politics. Beginning in the mid-1970s and early 1980s, as it became clear that a nationalities crisis was looming on the Soviet horizon, Western students of Soviet affairs increasingly referred to the imperial dimension of Soviet multinational politics. Richard Pipes asserted that nationality problems in the USSR were similar "to those experienced by the classic empires of the West" and suggested that Soviet nationalities policies were analogous to those pursued by the French in their colonial territories (1975, 455–56). Colin Gray wrote of "the continuing failure to appreciate that the USSR is a true empire. . . . A student of the dynamics of imperialism . . . need look no further than to the contemporary Soviet Union to find a classic example" (1981, 13). Hélène Carrère d'Encausse referred to the Soviet Union after the Second World War as "a new imperial system" and argued that the same forces of nationalism that had led to the breakup of the Russian Empire in the early twentieth century were at work in contemporary Soviet politics (1980, 33, 274). And Guy Imart asserted that the concept of empire was an apt description of the USSR "not in any journalistic or superficial sense but in the technical meaning of the word" (1987, 16). Yet, throughout these discussions none of these authors bothered to define this most slippery of concepts.

It is the argument of this essay that at the base of all conceptions of empire and state are subjective notions of legitimacy and identity. Take, for instance, Michael Doyle's widely accepted and quite generic definition of empire as "sovereignty controlled either formally or informally by a foreign state" (1986, 30). The key word within this formulation is "foreign," for it implies two very important points: (1) a sense of separate ethnic identity among those whose "sovereignty" is being controlled; and (2) a sense that the continued control of that "sovereignty"—at least according to modern notions of national self-determination—is illegitimate (that is, lacking support within society). This does not mean that perceptions of illegitimacy and "foreign" occupation might not be fostered by specific political practices. However, any attempt to define empire in "objective" terms—as a system of stratification, as a policy based on force, as a system of exploitation—fails in the end to capture what is undoubtedly the most important dimension of any imperial situation: perception. Unquestionably, these types of political practices tend to contribute to perceptions of empire. Still, history records many cases in which violence and exploitation have not necessarily resulted in the emergence of widespread resistance. The Soviet case demonstrates quite clearly that "empire-consciousness," if we may call it that, is not necessarily a direct function of the degree to which a group has experienced objectively exploitative or violent policies against it. Nor does empire-consciousness appear to be necessarily connected with a specific system of social or ethnic stratification; after all, the leader of the USSR at the time when its policies most favored Russian national interests was himself a Georgian, and the elite that surrounded him was similarly characterized by a high degree of representation among non-Russians.[6]

The problems involved in applying concepts such as "internal colonialism" to the USSR illustrate the difficulties involved in any "objective" notion of empire. A number of Western observers have suggested that the concept, as used by Michael Hechter, was an apt description of Soviet policies in non-Russian regions (Burg 1990; Hodnett 1974, 60–117). Hechter (1975, 33) defined "internal colonialism" as a system of economic exploitation by which a core group maintained its dominance over the inhabitants of a periphery.

> Commerce and trade among members of the periphery tend to be monopolized by members of the core. . . . The peripheral economy is forced into complementary development to the core, and thus becomes dependent on external markets. Generally, this economy rests on a single primary export, either agricultural or mineral. The movement of peripheral labor is determined largely by forces exogenous to the periphery. Typically there is great migration and mobility of peripheral workers in response to price fluctuations of exported primary products. Economic dependence is reinforced through juridical, political, and military measures. . . . There is national discrimination on the basis of language, religion or other cultural forms.

Indeed, in the last years of existence of the USSR, accusations of "internal colonialism" and economic exploitation gained wide currency in all of the republics and territories of the USSR. Nearly every republic and people, regardless of its level of development, claimed economic exploitation by the center. A closer examination reveals the impossibility of sorting out the bases for these claims, particularly in view of: (1) the market irrationality of the pricing mechanism under central planning, making any comparison of "values" tendentious;[7] (2) the large migrations of Russians and Ukrainians into many non-Russian areas at the same time that native labor forces were relatively sedentary, in contrast to the Hechter model; (3) the higher standards of living of the Baltic and portions of the West compared with Russia; (4) the conscious "affirmative action" policies pursued by the Soviet regime throughout the country; and (5) the claims by Russian nationalists that Russia also witnessed a net drain of resources away from it during the Soviet period.[8] As Ralph Premdas has noted, "In the internal colonialism explanation [of secession], claims of oppression and exploitation tend to be argued and accentuated by a heavy dose of spurious and fabricated data. What is more important than objective facts, however, is the belief among an ethnic group that it is oppressed" (1990, 19). Indeed, in the Soviet case groups which were the most economically developed were actually those that pressed the hardest for the breakup of the Soviet Union, while least developed groups were practically the last to support their own independence.[9]

State-Building and Empire-Consciousness in Soviet History

The above discussion implies that empires and states are set apart not primarily by exploitation, nor even by the use of force, but essentially by whether politics and policies are accepted as "ours" or are rejected as "theirs." Certain policies and behaviors might increase the likelihood of such perceptions. But the fit between practice and perception is always imperfect, being mediated by a series of variables that affect the strengths and weaknesses of political and cultural identities.

It also implies that the transcendence of empire is simultaneously a state-building process involving a fundamental realignment of polity, identity, and legitimacy.

Of course, even polities that are widely perceived as illegitimate are usually not entirely lacking in support. It is well known that European imperial control over its empires, in Ronald Robinson's words, "was as much a function of its victims' collaboration or non-collaboration—of their indigenous politics, as it was of European expansion" (1976, 129, 133). As John Armstrong (1982) documented so well, all empires search for support for their rule within colonial society, creating elaborate myths intended in part to gain adherents who identify with the occupying power and help to maintain it. Weber tells us that it is the search for legitimacy that forms the basis of the modern state. In this small base of support within peripheral society, however minuscule it may be, even empires contain within them the potential seeds of statehood. As the title of one article that appeared in 1990 in a widely read Soviet journal observed: "The Empire—That's People" (*Vek XX i mir,* no. 8, 15–22).

Underlying any sense of legitimacy (and for that matter, of statehood) is a sense of identity, of peoplehood. This point was well-understood by successive Soviet rulers, who over the years constantly but (in the end) unsuccessfully strove to bolster their rule with legitimacy by creating a specifically "Soviet" identity—a *Sovetskii narod,* or Soviet people. It was not Marxism that created the concept of a "Soviet people"; after all, Marxism preached the transcendence of nations, not their creation. Rather the basis for nation-building in Soviet politics must be found in the Union Treaty of December 1922 and Stalin's program of "socialism in one country," put forth shortly afterward. "Socialism in one country" was an expression of the Bolsheviks' determination to build the country without waiting for the foreign revolutions on which they had originally counted. In this sense, it signified the final victory of the concept of the nation-state over what had previously been an internationalist revolution that had denied the utility of states. This victory had been prepared by the gradual erosion of Lenin's orthodox Marxist position on nationalities affairs in the years following the revolution in the face of the persistent state-seeking behavior of the peoples of the Tsarist empire. State forms crept into Marxism-Leninism precisely as a means for preventing various non-Russian nationalities from constructing their own separate states. Thus, the Bolshevik state from the beginning contained within it a co-opting or preempting function. Before the union treaty, a number of republics set up by the communists enjoyed separate statehood and were bound together by means of international treaty, even if they were tightly controlled by Moscow through the Communist Party, much like what continued to be the case in Mongolia and what was the eventual solution pursued in Eastern Europe after World War II. The great concession of federalism to which Lenin acceded against Stalin's advice was essentially viewed as a means for preventing state separatism.

State-building thus was practiced for imperial ends. But state-building within the Soviet context took on a dynamic of its own. As Gerhard Simon observed, "Although in many respects this sovereignty [afforded by federalism] was no more than a legal fiction, the temptation to actually implement it politically has always existed, and many politicians . . . succumbed to this temptation and attempted to implement sovereignty" (1991, 4). Similarly, Gail Lapidus noted that "the very existence of a federal system gave substance to the claims of republic elites that they represented more than mere administrative sub-units" (1989, 211).

Soviet authorities never viewed their own actions as imperial, but rather as state-building—that is, as creating that sense of shared identity and legitimacy necessary for underpinning a legitimate state. This could be done either by seeking legitimate polities around existing cultural entities or by fostering the emergence of an entirely new identity. In confirmation of Walker Connor's observations on the subject, state-building within the Soviet context had both nation-building and nation-destroying implications (1972, 319–55). Stalin's culture-destroying policies of the 1930s and 1940s were the obverse of the flourishing of national communisms that took place in the 1920s. Both flowed equally from the logic of state-building—the first accepting society as it was and seeking to build legitimacy within it, the second seeking to transform identities in society in conformance with the prevailing state system.

Both could also be understood within the context of imperial policies. One could interpret the concessions granted to nationalities in the 1920s as merely a means for defusing separatist nationalism and keeping them in a Russian-dominated state. National communist elites were tolerated in order to mediate domination from Moscow. The thorny question of "whose state?" plagued the Soviet Union from the time of its founding. The answer given was always ambiguous and varied considerably over time. Even at the height of glorification of things Russian in the late 1940s, the Russians were portrayed merely as "elder brothers," not conquerors. Yet, the widespread perception that the Soviet state was fundamentally a Russian state was ever-present.

Coerced legitimacy is an oxymoron, since coercion destroys the free will that stands at the base of any genuine consent. Yet, it was precisely the phenomenon of coerced legitimacy which was the central paradox of the Soviet empire-state. Roman Szporluk (1990) has convincingly argued that the imperial legacy in Soviet politics should not be understood simply as the geographic congruity between the Russian empire and the Soviet Union; after all, it is possible to imagine that such an entity might not be imperial—that is, that it might enjoy a wide-ranging legitimacy. It was the dream of creating a state from an empire that separated Soviet-type imperialism from that practiced by traditional empires. The Soviet regime did much more than simply occupy territories; rather, it was driven to engage in policies aimed at creating a social base for itself and, when one did not exist, to demonstrate the supposed existence of support through coerced legitimacy.

As Szporluk noted, the imperial legacy in Soviet politics essentially manifested itself in the relationship between regime and society—that is, in the creation of a political society based on forced consent and the absence of what is commonly referred to as a civil society. Civil society, when it did emerge, consisted of several layers of societies—of both a Soviet society and a series of national societies—that were in competition with one another for the loyalties of the population. On the one hand, on the eve of the Soviet breakup, Valerii Tishkov could write of what he called "the fatal weakness of the Soviet state"—that is, "the absence of the requisite sense among the citizenry that they belong to a unitary civil society" (1991, 2). On the other hand, an eighteen-year-old Russian college student, Irina Zhuravleva, could tell an American reporter after the breakup: "We don't even know who we are anymore. They tell me I'm a "Russian" now. What does that mean? Does it mean that my parents, who live in Uzbekistan, are foreigners? . . . I think of myself as Soviet. I know nothing about Russia. In school, our history lessons began with the revolution and 1917. I am all for the changes in this country but I am completely confused. What does it mean—"Russian" (*Washington Post*, December 31, 1991). An essential feature of the Soviet empire-state was precisely this confusion over identities.

Confusion over identities was reinforced by the entire thrust of political development after Stalin's death. Much of the post-Stalin period, including developments in nationalities policies, can be understood as an attempt to create a genuine legitimacy in place of the "enforced" or "false" legitimacy of the Stalinist period. De-Stalinization rested on the premise that some alternative means besides force had to be found for integrating Soviet society, some more voluntary means based on consensus. Some Western observers came to refer to these developments as an attempt to create a totalitarianism without terror (Kassof 1964, 558–75). Yet, without terror, the Soviet system was forced to embark upon a greater degree of legitimacy-seeking within society. Leadership was no longer a one-person game, but rather a collective process in which leaders had to build their support more widely within the political elite. This very rudimentary form of legitimacy-seeking gave non-Russian elites new opportunities to influence policies and led to the emergence of policy debates in most spheres of activity, including nationalities questions. So evident was the trend toward "authority-building" in Soviet politics that a number of Western experts concluded that Soviet leadership successions were no longer political crises, but rather needed revitalizations of the system (Breslauer 1982; Bunce 1981).

As legitimacy-seeking diffused more broadly throughout the party elite and the bureaucracy, some observers began to speak of the emergence of an incipient pluralism in Soviet society. Indeed, in the 1960s and 1970s the dominant imagery used by scholars to describe the Soviet Union was that of state rather than empire. It was widely argued that Soviet institutions had achieved a degree of broad-based legitimacy within the Soviet population, irrespective of the national context within which Leninism appeared, and that persuasive methods of rule had replaced state-sponsored intimidation (Hauslohner 1990, 41–90). This perception was not entirely false. Separatist dissidents were relatively few and located on the extreme fringes of society. Most opposition figures did not even conceive of the possible breakup of the USSR, even were it to democratize.[10] Western Sovietologists portrayed cultural pluralism in the USSR as a form of incipient political pluralism that resembled and indeed overlapped with the interplay of self-interested bureaucracies (Hough 1979, 514–15). There was even a sense among many observers of a kind of ethnic representative character to Soviet bureaucratic politics. As Gregory Gleason observed, "[i]n the republics the administrative organizations of government and party became to a large extent the 'captives' of the national ethos of their namesake populations" (1990, 3; see also Burg 1990).

One could argue that such perceptions were illusory and behind the veneer of the years of stagnation stood an empire readying to explode. Yet, these perceptions were widespread enough, both among experts and within the Soviet population, to place the idea of the possible breakup of the USSR along national lines out of the range of conceivable futures for the country in most prognoses. One of the great paradoxes of the breakup of the Soviet Union was that empire-consciousness was not inversely related to efforts at state-building. On the contrary, the Soviet population became the most conscious of the imperial character of the Soviet state precisely at that moment when efforts at legitimacy-seeking by the Soviet regime reached their zenith.

The Plasticity of Soviet Identities

The conceptions of empire and state propounded in this essay are at root attitudinal and behavioral, and therefore, like all attitudes and behaviors, subject to uneven distribution in society. If the key criterion by which to judge the imperial quality of a polity is how its population regards it, then there is no reason why one should expect a consensus to exist over this issue within any given population—or for that matter, ethnic group. From the point of view of one sector of a population or ethnic group, a polity might appear as an empire, while in another it might appear as a state. The long-standing division between Western Ukrainians and Eastern Ukrainians over relations with Russia illustrates that even within existing ethnicities empire-consciousness is unevenly distributed, essentially sociologically determined by cultural, political, and historical factors.

Moreover, if conceptions of state and empire are closely tied with cultural and political identities, then like identities they are subject to constant evolution

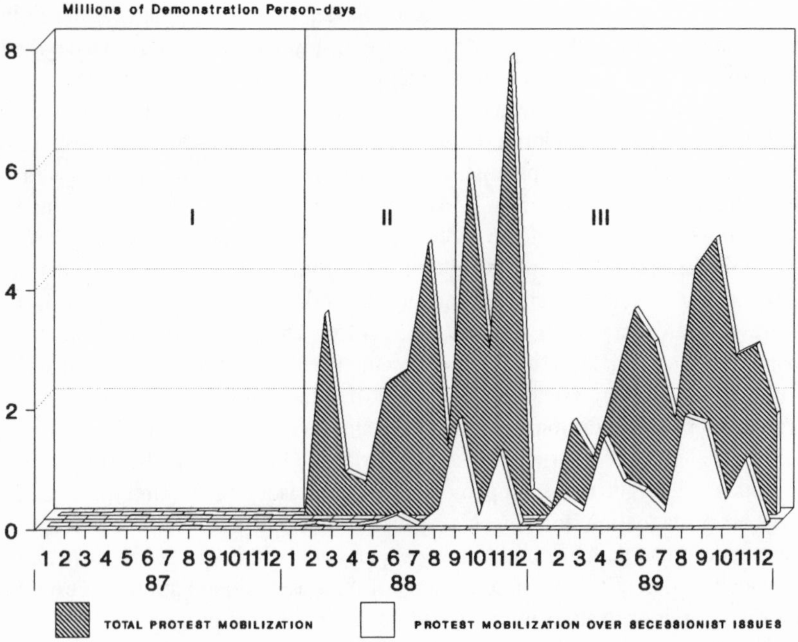

Fig. 5.1a. Total protest mobilization and protest mobilization over secessionist issues. Based on an analysis of 2,158 nonviolent protest demonstrations in the USSR from January 1987 through December 1989, measured in millions of protest person days.

and change. Indeed, if the decolonization process within European empires is any guide, ethnic identities and attitudes toward colonial authorities underwent a very rapid change and politicization on the eve of decolonization. As Robinson described the process: "when the colonial rulers had run out of indigenous collaborators they either chose to leave or were compelled to go. Their national opponents . . . sooner or later succeeded in detaching the indigenous political elements from the colonial regime until they eventually formed a united front of collaboration against it" (1976, 139). Recognition of the imperial quality of European empires by subject populations was always imperfect and varying.

An examination of the temporal development of secessionist protest in the USSR is instructive of how a mass empire-consciousness evolved in the USSR. It did not come about immediately, but rather followed upon the heels of a short but intensive period of protest over "within-system" issues, suggesting in the Soviet case the existence of a relatively brief liminal period in which identities were in a state of flux. Essentially, one can distinguish three stages in the development of secessionist protest; these are described in figures 5.1a and 5.1b, which, on

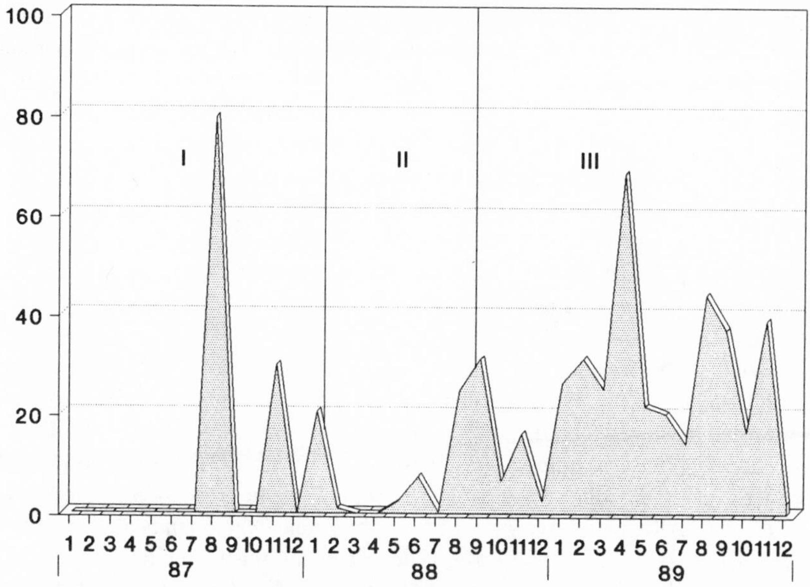

Fig. 5.1b. Percent of total protest mobilization devoted to secessionist issues.

the basis of an analysis of 2,158 nonviolent protest demonstrations, portray the rise of protest mobilization in favor of secession during the 1987–89 period.[11] During stage I, extending through January 1988, secessionist demands often figured prominently in protest activity, but protest did not assume a mass character. During these months, secessionist nationalists, still on the fringes of the political system, attempted to use the issue of empire in order to mobilize populations in support of secession, but without much success. During stage II, covering the very brief period from February 1988 through September 1988, protest mobilization assumed a mass character, but secessionist demands were not those that were mobilizing populations. In this period, protest centered around "within-system" issues that conceivably might have been resolved through the normal policy channels of the state. It is not clear, however, whether the resolution of such "within-system" issues would have prevented the subsequent development of secessionist nationalism. Stage III, beginning around September 1988 and extending through the end of the period examined here, was a time in which protest mobilization was massive and secessionist issues were highly visible among protest demands. In fact, during stage III the rise and fall of overall levels of protest in the country were increasingly driven by the surges and ebbs in secessionist protest.

These temporal patterns suggest extremely rapid change in prevailing notions of state and empire within the consciousness of the Soviet population over the course of 1988 and 1989. By the end of 1989, secessionist nationalism had made its appearance in almost every non-Russian republic, though in some republics it never reached mass proportions. Demonstration effects and widening political opportunity structures would appear to be most logical explanations for the spread of secessionist protest. Indeed, statistical analysis of Soviet protest patterns more generally reveals that opportunity structure, resource-mobilization, and ethnic assimilation played key roles in conditioning differential protest responses by Soviet ethnic groups (Beissinger 1991b). All these explanations in turn suggest that political identities changed relatively quickly and easily in 1988 and 1989. Empire-consciousness and state-consciousness within the Soviet context were plastic and unstable.

Evidence from public opinion polls and voting behavior points to much the same conclusion: the mercurial character of political identities in the *glasnost'* period and the rather short distance that had to be traversed for state-consciousness to be transformed into empire-consciousness.[12] For instance, a survey conducted in August and September 1989 of inhabitants of Ukraine by the USSR Academy of Sciences' All-Union Center for the Study of Public Opinion indicated that only 20.6 percent favored full political self-determination for the republic, up to and including separation from the USSR (*Ogonek,* October 1989, no: 43, 4–5). By contrast, by December 1991, 90.3 percent of these same inhabitants of Ukraine voted in favor of Ukraine's August 24th declaration of independence. Even the heavily Russified Donetsk and Odessa provinces showed 83.9 and 85.3 percent majorities respectively, while 54.1 percent of the voters of Crimea province, populated by a majority Russian population, voted in favor of Ukrainian independence. The transformation in consciousness that this vote signaled has been aptly described by Bohdan Nahaylo (1991, 1–2):

> What appears to have happened is that swiftly and almost imperceptibly, before the revolution that has now taken place through the ballot box, a revolution occurred in the minds of Ukraine's inhabitants. Somehow, during a remarkably short period, the idea of Ukrainian independence, for so long depicted in the Soviet press as the hopeless cause of diehard nationalists in Western Ukraine, took hold throughout the republic.

Public opinion polls similarly document extremely rapid changes in attitudes of Russians toward the need to defend Soviet territorial integrity. In early 1990, 56 percent of the population of Leningrad believed that it was necessary to use the army to put down the revolt against Soviet power then raging in Azerbaijhan. By contrast, a year later 77 percent of Leningraders were against the use of the army to keep the Baltic republics in the USSR (*Ekho Litvy,* February 15, 1991, 4). The key to understanding why the dissolution of the USSR did not involve a violent struggle was that the USSR died without defenders willing to risk their lives to save it. Essentially, this was the result of a relatively swift transformation in consciousness that took place among Russians in 1990 and 1991. This transformation eventually reached the point where even the Director of the Institute of Ethnography of the USSR Academy of Sciences, on the eve of the breakup of the Soviet Union, was referring instinctively to the very government he was advising as an "empire" (Tishkov 1991).

Gorbachev's State-Building Strategy and the Unraveling of the USSR

Gorbachev's tremendous miscalculations concerning the impact of *glasnost'* on ethnic identity were similarly indicative of the enormous confusion over identities that the Soviet empire-state generated, even in the minds of those who ruled it. Gorbachev viewed *glasnost'* as a strategy for recapturing a dwindling and elusive legitimacy. He clearly did not comprehend the degree to which *glasnost'* and democratization would eventually become a vehicle for the expression of secessionist sentiments. The tragedy of Gorbachev was not, as some analysts seem to have suggested, that he failed to grasp that legitimacy assumed a common identity. Rather, it was that he was so hypnotized by the rhetoric of the Soviet regime that he truly believed in the widespread acceptance of a Soviet identity. Gorbachev's understanding of *glasnost'* was probably close to Gail Lapidus's interpretation of it as "an expression of confidence in the legitimacy of the Soviet system and its leadership, and a recognition that the pretense of infallibility is no longer necessary to command popular allegiance and support" (1991, 140). Gorbachev clung to this illusion to the very end and was essentially dragged down by his absolute refusal to part with it. His political career ended not defending the Soviet empire, but rather defending a nonexistent Soviet state.

Ironically, in order to resuscitate the Soviet state, Gorbachev was driven increasingly to recognize its imperial core. Beginning in 1989, when he began to turn his attention to directing nationalities discontent into institutional channels after four years of passive and ineffective leadership on the issue, his state-building strategy was based on the idea of "renewing" the Soviet federation according to the formula "a strong center and strong republics." It soon became apparent that "renewal" would require renegotiating the Union Treaty of 1922. This in itself constituted an explicit recognition of the involuntary origins of the USSR, one which only accelerated demands for the breakup of the country. As power continued to diffuse to the republics, and independence movements gained in strength, Gorbachev dropped the "strong center and strong republics" formula in favor of the idea of an extremely decentralized federalism. By that time, a number of republics had evolved to the position of favoring a confederal arrangement (Lapidus 1991, 201–50). Some republics refused to accept even this position, insisting on nothing less than full independence.

The logic used to support claims to independence was reflective of the hybrid character of the Soviet polity. The Soviet constitution guaranteed republics the right to secede, and that guarantee could have been used to support a departure from the union. Significantly enough, among the six republics that openly sought full independence before August 1991, only Armenia based its argument on its constitutionally guaranteed right to secession. The other five republics that sought full independence based their right to leave not on the Soviet constitution, whose authority they refused to recognize; after all, recognition of the authority of the Soviet constitution would have been an acknowledgment that they were members of a state rather than an empire. Rather, the argument was based on the idea that their incorporation into the USSR amounted to a foreign "occupation." Much as Gorbachev sought to "renew" the Soviet federation, independence-minded republics sought to "renew" their independence. This was, of course, rejected by Gorbachev, and the posturing that took place over the second half of 1990 and early 1991, at times violent in character, essentially revolved around the issue of whose "renewal" would gain ascendancy.

The Novo-Ogarevo agreement of April 1991 temporarily settled the dispute. Since only nine republics agreed to participate in it, it implicitly legitimized the partial dissolution of the USSR, at the same time as it explicitly endorsed a radical decentralization of powers to those republics that remained. For precisely these reasons, the Novo-Ogarevo agreement was despised by conservatives and became, along with the draft of the new union treaty that resulted from the Novo-Ogarevo process, the chief cause of the aborted seizure of power by the State Emergency Committee in August (Beissinger 1991a, 28–29). Throughout the negotiations over the new union treaty, Gorbachev continued to insist upon a federal formula. Indeed, the final draft of the treaty, published on the eve of the coup, described the Soviet government as a "federal" entity, even though the actual content of the treaty was blatantly confederal in character, with republics retaining the right to suspend all-union laws on their territories. Actually, the political institutions that were envisioned in the final version of the treaty were precisely those that were created in the aftermath of the coup, when the central government had completely collapsed. In this sense, Soviet federalism died before the coup took place. Gorbachev was slow to recognize this fact, and it was only on the heels of the declarations of independence by one republic after another at the end of August that he embraced a confederal formula—one with which he was not entirely comfortable.

From what we now know about the decision-making process behind the creation of the Commonwealth of Independent States, it appears to have been an improvised, last-ditch effort to preserve some type of community over the territory of the former USSR in the face of the failure of Ukraine to agree to participate in a renegotiated union treaty based on loose confederal principles. The idea of a commonwealth of independent states was not new; it had been briefly mentioned at least a year earlier by Kirgiz President Askar Akaev as a possible solution to center-periphery relations (*Current Digest of the Soviet Press* 43, 50 [January 15, 1992]: 10), and was the formula supported by the Moldovan government as well. Nevertheless, this solution was by and large ignored until October 1991, when at the Novo-Ogarevo negotiations debate began to focus over the meaning of the word *soiuz,* which in Russian can signify both "union" (implying a state) and "alliance" (implying an international agreement or organization). At that time, the latter connotation was rejected by the participating presidents of the republics. However, Ukraine's continued refusal to agree to any kind of state formation process eventually brought the commonwealth idea back onto the negotiating table. As Russian First Vice-Premier Gennadii Burbulis later noted, "the possibility of signing the latest version of the Union Treaty, including its signing by Ukraine, was discussed" at the Minsk meeting of the presidents of the three Slavic republics in early December 1991. But as a result of Ukrainian intransigence, "only one option was left—the formation of a Commonwealth" (*Current Digest of the Soviet Press* 43, 49 [January 8, 1992]: 3–4). The formation of the commonwealth as an international organization of sovereign states not only signaled the transcendence of the Soviet imperial legacy; it represented the destruction of the Soviet state-building legacy as well.

The Imperial Legacy in Post-Soviet Politics

With the dissolution of the Soviet Union, is the imperial legacy that was widely perceived to stand behind the Soviet polity also extinct? Does the breakup of the USSR mean that we have witnessed the passing of "the last empire"?

The answer, which is clearly no, flows directly from the logic of the arguments presented in this essay, as well as from empirical confirmation. If states and empires are separated largely by a matter of whether politics is accepted as "ours" or "theirs," then the number of situations that might engender empire-consciousness is limited only by the imagination. In early 1992 a group of Polish Seim deputies accused Lithuania of "colonizing" the Vil'nius region, an area of traditional Polish settlement (*Nezavisimaia gazeta,* January 4, 1992, 3–4). The Russian-speaking community in left-bank Moldavia has already declared the creation of its own state in fear of the possibility of what it calls "Romanian occupation" (*Trudovi Tiraspol',* August 29, 1990). Similarly, Russian communities in four provinces of southern Ukraine have called for combining the provinces into a state to be known as *Novorossiia,* or New Russia, in fear of Ukrainian domination (*Nezavisimaia gazeta,* November 16, 1991, 2). A demonstration in the city of Tomsk in 1989 took place under the slogan: "Free Siberia, the largest colony in the world!" In July 1990 the founding conference of the Union for a Siberian Association called for "liquidating the colonial policy of the center toward the region" and for the creation of a Siberian parliament (*Soglasie* 28 [July 9–15, 1990]). A political movement has been founded in favor of the creation of a Urals state with much the same rationale (*Golos naroda* [Sverdlovsk] 6 [1990]). The leadership of Irkutsk province, objecting to the dominance of the center over affairs of the region, has called for vesting all provinces of Russia with state sovereignty (*Nezavisimaia gazeta,* November 11, 1991, 2). The administrative head of Kaliningrad province advocates turning that territory into a fourth Baltic state (*RFE/RL Daily Report* 36 [February 21, 1992]). A meeting held in Alma-Ata in December 1991 called for the creation of a pan-Turkic state that would defend Turkic-speaking peoples against "expansion on the part of Russia" (*Kommersant'* 49 [December 16–23, 1991]). A leader of the Volga Tatar nationalist movement observed: "The big empire has collapsed; the Russian federation will be more difficult, but I think it is inescapable that this empire will also collapse" (*New York Times,* September 8, 1991). In January 1992 the parliament of the Confederation of Mountain Peoples of the Caucasus proclaimed that the Northern Caucasian republics "could not be part of any empire and must strive for full state sovereignty" (*RFE/RL Daily Report* 14 [January 21, 1992]). The Chechens, of course, have already declared their independence from Russia. In other words, the deconstruction of the former USSR remains an ongoing and potentially endless process, even after the USSR formally ceased to exist.

As much as it is true that the central trend of twentieth century history has been the consolidation of the modern state as a political form, empires continue to live with us. Indeed, one might be tempted to argue that change in the modern state system requires the continued existence of empires, for how else, other than on the basis of a lack of fit between polity, identity, and legitimacy, can we justify redrawing state boundaries. So deeply has the state ingrained itself into the modern world that we cannot conceive of any other way of altering its contours than by reimagining states as empires.

But there is another reason why "the last empire" is unlikely to be the last. The mistrust upon which the dissolution of empires is based does not end with imperial dissolution. It lives on into the post-imperial period. When imperialism dies, neo-imperialism still lives. The Moldavian Popular Front's parliamentary group, for instance, has charged that the Moldovan government's pledge to share payment of the USSR's external debt obligations amounted to "reattaching our republic's economy to that of the empire, . . . consigning us and our descendants to an unprecedented financial servitude." The deputies declared that there was no moral or legal justification for "forcing occupied peoples striving for independence to pay the debts of their conquerors" (*RFE/RL Daily Report* 222 [November 22, 1991]). Similar statements have come from Vil'nius and Kiev.

With the new Russian state declaring itself the successor state to the Soviet

Union, would it not also take on the role of successor empire? In an address to the USSR Congress of People's Deputies after the coup, Yel'tsin asserted that "the Russian state, having chosen democracy and freedom, will never be an empire, nor an older or younger brother; it will be an equal among equals." [13] Of course, the reason for locating the headquarters of the commonwealth in Minsk was due to mistrust of the possible imperial intentions of Moscow. As Stanislav Shushkevich, President of Belarus, is said to have noted, "as long as Moscow is the capital, suspicions that the old center is being reconstituted in new garments will be inevitable" (*Current Digest of the Soviet Press* 43, 49 [January 8, 1992]). The creation of a commonwealth was supposed to bury the notion of a center once and for all. As Leonid Kravchuk observed in the aftermath of the Minsk meetings: "We have done everything that we could so that there would never again be a center in our lives and that a center would never again be in charge of our states" (*Nezavisimaia gazeta,* December 10, 1991, 3).

Yet, no sooner had the center been buried than its specter was stalking its familiar territory once again. Only days after proclaiming that the USSR no longer existed, the government of Boris Yel'tsin moved to establish the state emblem of the new Russian state: the two-headed eagle, the symbol of the Tsarist empire, with the proviso, in Gennadii Burbulis' words, that "the eagle not look very evil" (*Nezavisimaia gazeta,* December 19, 1991, 3). The Russian government's takeover of all former Soviet ministries and foreign embassies was seen by many of the former republics as a kind of "imperialism by stealth." And conflicts over ownership of the Black Sea fleet and control of the Crimea have led to complaints in Ukraine over a resurgence of Russian imperialism and a growing nationalist revival within Russia. Russian Vice-President Aleksandr Rutskoi has called for Russia to define itself "as a power, and not as a beggar within the Commonwealth of Independent States." In his words: "Russians' historical conscience does not allow the mechanical association of the borders of Russia and of the Russian federation, thus denying what was a glorious page in Russian history" (*New York Times,* January 31, 1992). As one Russian commentator observed: "Ready pens have appeared suggesting that Russian leaders should embark upon a great power-imperialist course of 'coerced pressure' on the other (smaller) republics . . . and upon a coerced resolution of the national question inside Russia" (*Nezavisimaia gazeta,* January 21, 1992, 5).

This is not to say that a post-Soviet empire is in the making, nor even that the Eurasian state system will not survive in its current, post-Soviet configuration of fifteen plus zero (the union-republics without a center). But the key fact about empires is the need to keep killing them. While empires may die, their memory lives on after them, affecting the perceptions and behavior of those who knew them only too well.

NOTES

Research on protest mobilization in favor of secession was carried out in part under the auspices of a grant from the National Council for Soviet and East European Research, Contract #804-14. The author would like to thank Valerie Bunce for her comments on an earlier version of this chapter.

1. Hough continued to maintain after the coup that "the Soviet Union is not breaking up (except, maybe, in the Baltics—two percent of the Soviet population—and not necessarily there)" (Hough 1991a, 1).

2. Citing Horowitz, Hough argued that secessions in general are rarely successful endeavors. "The most rebellious republics," Hough maintained, "may remain part of the country" (1991b, 106).

3. For one scholarly use of the term "decolonization" to refer to the unraveling of the USSR, see Simon (1991, xiv).

4. As David Laitin observed: "What makes the Soviet Union an 'empire' is not, however, addressed by any author" (1991, 173).

5. There were, of course, the more cynical and pragmatic arguments against the claims to statehood for peoples of the former Soviet Union that formed the basis for much of American policy in the area until the aborted coup of August 1991. These arguments were well paraphrased (but not supported) by Alexander Motyl (1991, 300): "[S]tability must be a key consideration, because the collapse of a superpower can only have portentous consequences for the security of the world. Supporters of unconditional self-determination for the republic thus may justly be criticized by blithely invoking a principle that, if pursued to its logical conclusion, would wreak havoc on the international system of states in general and Eastern Europe in particular." The disintegration of the USSR took place in spite of the strong aversion of policy-makers around the globe to any revision of borders in the "community of states."

6. Several years ago, this author believed that "empire" could be defined objectively and looked toward the system of ethnic stratification in the USSR as its main indicator, or "legacy." Yet, upon closer examination that system of stratification turned out to be extremely complex, varying considerably over time and space (Beissinger and Hajda 1991, 306–9).

7. It is impossible, for instance, to sort out who exploited whom when one considers the extremely low price that was charged for oil inside the USSR. Oil-producing regions, such as Tiumen', Bashkiria, and Azerbaidzhan, have argued that they were subsidizing the rest of the country, at the same time as the rest of the country complained about the low level of prices charged for goods produced in their areas. Both sides were correct.

8. Anatolii Khazanov has noted that "there exist two opinions in the USSR: 1) Central Asia is still an exploited colony, and 2) Central Asia takes more from the Union and is subsidized." See *ACASIA: Newsletter of the Association for Central Asian Studies* 5, 1 (December 1990): 2.

9. My own research on protest mobilization before and during *glasnost'* has shown a strong positive association between the levels of urbanization and education of a nationality and the degree of nonviolent protest in which they engaged (Beissinger 1991b).

10. Amalrik and Solzhenitsyn were exceptions rather than the rule in terms of dissident views on nationalities issues.

11. For more on the methodology behind this analysis, see Beissinger (1990). Secessionist protest was defined as protest in support of one of the following demands: against annexaton of the territory to the USSR or Russia; for redefinition of citizenship along national lines; for creation of national military units; in favor of secession from the USSR; for the right of the republic to separate diplomatic representation abroad; for the withdrawal of the Soviet army from the republic; and for publication or renunciation of the Molotov-Ribbentrop Pact.

12. Game theorists would refer to such a situation as a "tipping game." Indeed, Timur Kuran has used such games to explain why certain major revolutions were unanticipated at the time of their occurrence, but with hindsight appeared inevitable. Kuran argues that this paradox is explained by "preference falsification" by members of society due to repression. "Their silence makes society appear stable, even though it would find itself in the throes of revolution if there were even a slight surge in the size of the opposition" (Kuran 1989, 60). I would argue that in the Soviet case "preference falsification" may explain the rapidity of change in some instances (such as the Balts) where "empire-consciousness" always existed but could not be openly expressed. But as the evidence indicates, within a large portion of the Soviet population a genuine identity change appears to have taken place in a relatively compact period of time. In such cases, what we are dealing with is not "preference falsification," but rather preference change due to inherently ambiguous and overlapping identities. I am indebted to Valerie Bunce for this reference.

13. Moscow Central Television, September 3, 1991. In an end-of-the-year address, Yel'tsin once again denied any imperial intent on the part of Russia. "We do not intend to build the Commonwealth based on Russia; we are equals among equals" (*International Herald Tribune*, December 30, 1991, 1).

REFERENCES

Armstrong, John A. 1982. *Nations before Nationalism*. Chapel Hill: University of North Carolina Press.

Beissinger, Mark R. 1991a. The Deconstruction of the USSR and the Search for a Post-Soviet Community. *Problems of Communism* 40, 6: 27–35.

Beissinger, Mark R. 1991b. Protest Mobilization among Soviet Nationalities. Paper delivered to the plenary session of the annual meeting of the American Sociological Association, Cincinnati, Ohio, August.

Beissinger, Mark R. 1990. Non-Violent Public Protest in the USSR: December 1, 1986–December 31, 1989. Report published by the National Council for Soviet and East European Research, Washington, D.C.

Beissinger, Mark and Lubomyr Majda. 1990. Nationalism and Reform in Soviet Politics. In *The Nationalities Factor in Soviet Politics and Society,* edited by Lubomyr Hajda and Mark Beissinger, 305–22. Boulder: Westview Press.

Breslauer, George W. 1982. *Khrushchev and Brezhnev as Leaders: Building Authority in Soviet Politics*. Boston: Allen and Unwin.

Bunce, Valerie. 1981. *Do New Leaders Make a Difference? Executive Succession and Public Policy under Capitalism and Socialism*. Princeton: Princeton University Press.

Burg, Steven. 1990. Nationality Elites and Political Change in the Soviet Union. In *The Nationalities Factor in Soviet Politics and Society,* edited by Lubomyr Hajda and Mark Beissinger, 24–32. Boulder: Westview Press.

Carrère d'Encausse, Hélène. 1980. *Decline of an Empire*. New York: Newsweek Books.

Connor, Walker. 1972. Nation-Building or Nation-Destroying? *World Politics* 24, 3 (April): 319–35.

Doyle, Michael W. 1986. *Empires*. Ithaca: Cornell University Press.

Friedrich, Carl J., and Zbigniew K. Brzezinski. 1961. *Totalitarian Dictatorship and Autocracy*. New York: Praeger.

Gleason, Gregory. 1990. *Federalism and Nationalism: The Struggle for Republican Rights in the USSR*. Boulder: Westview Press.

Gray, Colin S. 1981. The Most Dangerous Decade: Historic Mission, Legitimacy, and Dynamics of the Soviet Empire in the 1980s. *Orbis* (Spring): 13–28.

Hauslohner, Peter. 1990. Politics before Gorbachev: De-Stalinization and the Roots of Reform. In *Politics, Society, and Nationality: Inside Gorbachev's Russia,* edited by Seweryn Bialer, 41–90. Boulder: Westview Press.

Hechter, Michael. 1975. *Internal Colonialism: The Celtic Fringe in British National Development, 1536–1966*. Berkeley: University of California Press.

Hodnett, Grey. 1974. Technology and Social Change in Soviet Central Asia: The Politics of Cotton Growing. In *Soviet Politics in the 1970s,* edited by Henry W. Morton and Rudolf L. Tokes, 60–117. New York: Free Press.

Horowitz, Donald L. 1985. *Ethnic Groups in Conflict*. Berkeley: University of California Press.

Hough, Jerry F. 1991a. *Politics of Soviet Economic Reform* 1.3 (15 September).

Hough, Jerry F. 1991b. Understanding Gorbachev: The Importance of Politics. *Soviet Economy* 7.2: 89–109.

Hough, Jerry F. 1990. Editor's Introduction. *Journal of Soviet Nationalities* 1, 1 (Spring): 1–13.

Hough, Jerry F. 1979. *How the Soviet Union is Governed*. Cambridge: Harvard University Press.

Imart, Guy G. 1987. A Unique Empire. *Central Asian Survey* 6, 4: 1–22.

Kassof, Allen. 1964. The Administered Society: Totalitarianism Without Terror. *World Politics* 16.4: 558–75.

Kolarz, Walter. 1964. Colonialism—Theory and Practice. In *Communism and Colonialism: Essays by Walter Kolarz,* edited by George Gretton, 14–23. London: Macmillan.

Kolarz, Walter. 1952. *Russia and Her Colonies*. London: George Philip and Son.

Kuran, Timur. 1989. Sparks and Prairie Fires: A Theory of Unanticipated Political Revolution. *Public Choice* 61, 1 (April): 41–74.

Laitin, David D. 1991. The National Uprising in the Soviet Union. *World Politics* 44 (October): 139–77.

Lapidus, Gail. 1991. State and Society: Toward the Emergence of Civil Society in the Soviet Union. In *The Soviet System in Crisis,* edited by Alexander Dallin and Gail W. Lapidus, 130–50. Boulder: Westview Press.

Lapidus, Gail. 1989. Gorbachev and the "National Question." *Soviet Economy* 5, 3:201–50.

Motyl, Alexander. 1991. Empire or Stability? The Case for Soviet Dissolution. *World Policy Journal* 8.3 (Summer): 499–524.

Nahaylo, Bohdan. 1991. The Birth of an Independent Ukraine. *Report on the USSR* 3, 5 (December 13, 1991): 1–5.

Pipes, Richard. 1975. Nationality Problems in the Soviet Union. In *Ethnicity: Theory and Experience,* edited by Nathan Glazer and Daniel P. Moynihan, 453–65. Cambridge: Harvard University Press.

Premdas, Ralph R. 1990. Secessionist Movements in Comparative Perspective. In *Secessionist Movements in Comparative Perspective,* edited by Ralph R. Premdas, W. W. R. Samarasinghr, and Alan B. Anderson, 12–29. New York: St. Martin's Press.

Robinson, Ronald. 1976. Non-European Foundations of European Imperialism: Sketch for a Theory of Collaboration. In *Imperialism: The Robinson and Gallagher Controversy,* edited by William Roger Louis, 128–51. New York: New Viewpoints.

Simon, Gerhard. 1991. *Nationalism and Policy Toward the Nationalities in the Soviet Union: From Totalitarian Dictatorship to Post-Stalinist Society,* translated by Karen Forster and Oswald Forster. Boulder: Westview Press.

Szporluk, Roman. 1990. The Imperial Legacy and the Soviet Nationalities Problem. In *The Nationalities Factor in Soviet Politics and Society,* edited by Lubomyr Hajda and Mark Beissinger, 1–23. Boulder, CO: Westview Press.

Tishkov, Valerii A. 1991. The Soviet Empire Before and After Perestroika. Conference on Ethnic Conflict, United Nations Research Institute for Social Development, Dubrovnik, Yugoslavia, 3–6 June.

Young, M. Crawford. 1992. The National and Colonial Question and Marxism: A View from the South. In *Thinking Theoretically about Soviet Nationalities: History and Comparison in the Study of the USSR,* edited by Alexander J. Motyl, 61–97. New York: Columbia University Press.

6

Azeri Nationalism in the Former Soviet Union and Iran

NADER ENTESSAR

Introduction

IN THIS CHAPTER I propose to examine the genesis and development of Azeri ethnonationalism in the former Soviet Union and Iran. My main thesis is that a distinctive Azeri nationalism did not exist as a political and social force prior to the establishment of the Bolshevik regime in the Soviet Union. I further argue that Soviet irredentist policies toward Iran were the cause for the emergence of secessionist movements in Iranian Azerbaijan. The present-day Azerbaijan Republic (Azerbaijan Soviet Socialist Republic until 1991) was an integral part of Iran, both politically and culturally, until the Russo-Iranian wars of 1804–24 resulted in the ceding of the territory to Russia.

Notwithstanding the process of Turkification that began in Azerbaijan in the eleventh century, Iranian culture continued to remain dominant among the Azeris. Turkification was successful only in the realm of language, where Turkish was superimposed on the local dialect. However, other dimensions of Azeri identity remained Iranian in character—a fact that explains why Azerbaijan has been the hotbed of major Iranian nationalist movements throughout recent history.

As Crawford Young indicates in the opening chapter of this book, theoretical debate over the nature of ethnonationalism has generally evolved around the primordialist and instrumentalist approaches to the study of ethnicity. Ethnic entities, to use Benedict Anderson's words, can also be conceived as imagined political communities to be distinguished "not by their falsity-genuineness, but by the style in which they are imagined" (1983, 15). In many ways, this subjective, emotional attachment to an imagined community has fanned the flames of ethnonationalism in multi-ethnic societies.

In modern times and with the development of strong nation-states, the formation of an ethnic identity has sometimes been influenced by state policies. The expansion of the role of the state as an independent variable and arbiter of competing claims in multi-ethnic societies is a salient feature of contemporary nation-state systems. Until recent times, state control over its peripheral regions was spasmodic and limited. Therefore, as Ludwig Gumplowicz has noted, ethnic group consciousness emerged as a reaction to the imposition of the will of dominant groups through the control of the state apparatus over subordinate and peripheral ethnic groups (1963, 196–99; see also Ringer and Lawless 1989, 16–17). Nowhere is this contention more true than in the case of Azeri nationalism.

The pervasive role of the state in multi-ethnic societies has been manifested in the state's monopolistic control of coercive forces for the purpose of shaping class and/or ethnic identities and relations (Skocpol 1985, 3–37; Caporaso 1989). In the Soviet Union, for example, ethnic rivalries were traditionally promoted and ethnic identities were fostered or altered by the state to advance Moscow's domestic and foreign policy goals. The emergence of Azeri nationalism in the twentieth century should be studied within the framework of the former Soviet Union's foreign policy toward Southern Frontier states, particularly toward Iran.

Nationalism in Azerbaijan

Is Azerbaijan a nation or a state with a distinct history, populated by people who have a long cultural tradition that sets them apart from other nations or states in the region? It is hardly disputable that the Azeri language is a vernacular distinct from both Persian and Turkish and that an ethnic attachment based on language has existed among the Azeri people. However, the concept of a greater Azerbaijan comprising the northwest Iranian province of Azerbaijan and the former Azerbaijan Soviet Socialist Republic is an imagined community created and promoted by the Soviets in the twentieth century. In other words, the concept of a "single Azerbaijan" as a nation or a state that has existed in regions to the north and south of the Aras River from ancient times is a historical fallacy created by Soviet historians in the twentieth century for the political purposes of the Bolshevik state and to justify Russia's irredentist ambitions in Iran and Southwest Asia. This is not to deny that the Azerbaijan Republic has recently developed its own independent political culture and that this may, in the future, have nationalist repercussions among the Iranian Azeris.

Historically, the term "Iran" referred to not only the present country of Iran, but to a larger territory that was Iranian in speech and culture, including Central Asia, the Caucasus, Afghanistan, Baluchestan, Kurdestan, and Iraq (Frye 1968, 13–22). Azerbaijan, or the "Land of Fire" (after the Persian word *azer* or fire) has remained part of the greater Iranian cultural milieu since the time of ancient Medes and the Achaemenid dynasty. Azerbaijan also remained a center of ancient

Iranian Zoroastrian culture and retained its pre-Islamic Iranian character for several centuries after the Arab conquest of Iran and the Islamization of the area. The name of the region north of the Aras River known today as the Soviet Azerbaijan was called "Albania" or "Caucasian Albania" in Greek and Roman texts, and in the Persian and Arabic texts of the Islamic period it was referred to as "Aran." The region located south of the Aras River (Iranian Azerbaijan) was known as "Atropatenes" (a Persian satrap at the time of Alexander the Great) in Greek and Roman texts and as "Azerbaijan" in Islamic and Russian writings (Altstadt 1992, 2–4). These names were used by Russian historians until 1917. The authoritative publication, *Russian Encyclopedia,* still used the name "Aran" to refer to the region north of the Aras River in its last tsarist edition published in St. Petersburg in 1890. The next edition of this encyclopedia, which was published under the title "Soviet Encyclopedia" after the Bolshevik Revolution, used the word "Azerbaijan" in lieu of "Aran." As the noted Russian Orientalist Wilhelm Barthold (Vasillii Vladimirovich) has observed, the change from "Aran" to "Azerbaijan" had no historical justification and was done in the broader context of Leninist/Stalinist nationality policy, which gave titular "nationality" designations to territorial units (Djavadi 1971, 43–82; Matini 1989, 454–59; Reza 1988, 59–63).

The first major demographic change in Azerbaijan occurred in the eleventh century when the Oghuz Turks under the Seljuk dynasty governed Iran. This Turkish influx, along with the wave of Turkish immigrants who came to Iran from Central Asia during the twelfth and thirteenth centuries, transformed Azerbaijan from a Persian-speaking region to a Turkish-speaking land (Frye 1968, 17; Frye 1975, 213–30). In effect, Turkish dynasties ruled Iran from the eleventh century until the advent of the Pahlavi dynasty in the early twentieth century. The common denominator among these Turkish dynasties was that they became Persianized in culture and political loyalties. In short, Iran conquered the ruling Turks culturally. Interestingly, the Turkish rulers of Iran did not adopt Turkish as their own court language, nor did they encourage the use of Turkish vernacular among their subjects (Frye 1979, sec. 13, 308–9). Nonetheless, Turkish dialects became the dominant vernacular of areas such as Azerbaijan that were heavily populated by Turkish tribespeople. Turkification, however, did not create a separate Turkish Azerbaijani national consciousness. The long-standing attachment of Azeri Turks to Iran has remained generally unshakable throughout history (Wimbush 1979, 62; Frye 1953, 21; Cottam 1979, 118–33; Djavadi 1971, 331–658; Taherzadeh Behzad 1984; Higgins 1986, 188–90).

The rise of the Safavid dynasty in Iran at the beginning of the sixteenth century coincided with the rising ambition of the Ottoman Turks in Anatolia. The Safavid Turks, who had their genesis in a Shia dervish order in Azerbaijan, increasingly viewed themselves as the guardians of Shiʿism against the Sunni Ottomans. Furthermore, they proved to be a formidable opponent to the Ottomans whose ultimate goal was to incorporate all Turkish-speaking people in their Sunni empire. In 1499, Ismail, the Safavid leader, declared himself to be the leader of all Shias, and in 1501 took the title of Shah Ismail as the first Safavid monarch. Under the Safavids, Shiᶜism became the official state religion in Iran, and the foundation of the first religiously based Iranian national state was laid. The Azerbaijanis' strong sense of Shia identity coupled with their attachment to Iranian culture accounted for the inability of the Ottoman Turks to separate Azerbaijan permanently from Iran. As S. Enders Wimbush (1979, 63) has noted:

> There would seem to have been little reason for Azeri leaders to seek a real or symbolic separatism from the Iranian state prior to the Russian conquest in the nineteenth century. Since the revival of Iranian statehood by the Samanids in the ninth century, state ideology has been based on three principles. The first is the abstract . . . principle of [governorship] in which the ruler may be of any ethnic origin. . . . Second, a state culture and one literary and administrative language are obligatory. Third, there must be a state religion, which in Iran since the fifteenth century has been Shiism.

The Azerbaijanis have satisfied all three of the aforementioned conditions, hence obviating the need for the development of a strong secessionist or territorially based, distinct national consciousness.

Russian Conquest of Aran

One of the principal goals of Russia's foreign policy since the time of Peter the Great had been to secure an outlet to the warm waters of the Persian Gulf. In this vein, Russia traditionally coveted Iranian territory and waged numerous wars with Iran. In the early nineteenth century, tsarist Russia took advantage of the weak Qajar dynasty (the last Turkish dynasty to rule Iran) and dispatched military units into Iran. It also waged two major campaigns against Iran, resulting in the military defeat of the Qajar forces and the signing of two humiliating treaties with the tsarist rulers. As a result of the treaties of Gulestan (1813) and Turkamanchay (1828), Iran ceded, among other things, the territories of Shirvan (now a part of Russian Azerbaijan), Derbent, Baku, Nakhichevan, Karabakh, and Ganja to Russia and renounced its sovereignty over Georgia.

After the incorporation of Aran and the northern Iranian principalities into the tsarist empire, Russian officials adopted a carrot-and-stick policy vis-à-vis their new Muslim subjects. While suppressing the religious identity of these Turkish-speaking people, the Khans, or feudal lords, of Baku and Nakhichevan were accepted into Russian nobility "with privileges and wealth. Many held high positions in the military and civil service" (Wimbush 1979, 63). For example, the former Khan of Baku was given a prominent position in the tsarist court, while the Khan of Nakhichevan became the commander of Russia's Guard Cavalry Corps.

In the realm of cultural homogenization, attempts were made to familiarize the Turkic subjects with their common origin, pre-Islamic history, and most importantly, language identity. In the early 1830s, for example, the first systematic study of Azeri Turkish was undertaken under the auspices of the tsarist court, resulting in the publication of a comprehensive grammar book in 1839 by Mirza Mohammed Ali Kasimoglo Kazembek, a prominent Turkish linguistic scholar. This was followed by the publication of a Turkish-Arabic-Persian-Russian dictionary under the editorship of Kazembek, Mirza Ja'far Topchibashi, and other Oriental scholars at Kazan University. The primary objective of Russia's "benign" linguistic policy was to facilitate the assimilation and absorption of its Turkic subjects and to pave the way for further expansion of the tsarist domain southward (Altstadt 1986, 275; Frye 1979, sec. 10, 38–51).

Two major intellectual figures of this period who contributed greatly to the historical and literary awakening of Azeri consciousness in Russia were Abbas Kuli Agha Bakikhanli (Bakikhanov in Russian) and Mirza Fath Ali Akhundzade (Akhundov in Russian). As translators in the tsarist bureaucracy, both had become Russified outwardly while promoting the Azeri language. Bakikhanli, who died in 1848 while returning from the *hajj* to Mecca, wrote the first, and still most comprehensive history of the local khanats of Baku and Nakhichevan (Altstadt 1986, 275; Guseinov et al. 1959–62, 102–20). Although Bakikhanli's work was not promoted by the tsars, partly due to the author's religious orientation, and his writings were suppressed after the 1917 Revolution, one of his important essays entitled *Nasihatlar* was republished in 1982 in the Azerbaijan SSR in Azeri and Persian and disseminated widely on both sides of the Aras River (Bakikhanli 1982).

Akhundzade was a nineteenth-century Azeri satirist and playwright who wrote primarily in the vernacular of Azeri masses rather than in the more sophisticated Russian or Persian, notwithstanding his admiration for both of these languages. As the son of a Shia cleric, Akhundzade became one of the most ardent critics of religious clerics, causing the *ulema* to declare him a *mofsid* (corrupt) and *kafir* (heathen). Through his avant-garde writings and plays, Akhundzade became one of the pioneers of modern theatre among the Turks, as well as in Iran. In many ways, as the following description of him indicates, Akhundzade epitomized the contradictions inherent in emerging national consciousness among the Azeri intellectuals and literary figures of the nineteenth century:

> A tsarist official of impeccable loyalty, he described himself as "almost Persian," and his philosophical writings reveal the depth of his preoccupation with all things Persian, both good and bad. Inasmuch as he extolled the pre-Islamic greatness of Persia and castigated the "hungry, naked, and savage" Arabs for having destroyed the kingdom of the Sasanids, he is considered one of the forerunners of modern Iranian nationalism. Nor was he devoid of typically Persian anti-Ottoman sentiments, which were clearly

> reflected in some of his writings. Still he has been recognized as a major figure in the movement for the self-assertion of national identity of Turkic peoples by virtue of his role in the literary revival of the native [Azeri] language . . . (Swietochowski 1985, 24–25).

These contradictions are still apparent in the lives and works of many intellectuals in the Azerbaijan Republic.

The cultural and intellectual awakening of Baku Azeri intellectuals in the mid-nineteenth century had a major impact on the course of events in Iranian Azerbaijan. In particular, it hastened the development of democratic and anti-authoritarian movements that reached their zenith in the Iranian Constitutional Revolution of the early twentieth century. Moreover, the exploitation of the Baku oil fields transformed that Soviet city into an industrial center and magnet for Azeri workers in Iran. In the ten year period from 1880 to 1890 alone, over 30,000 Iranian workers received work permits and obtained employment at the Baku oil fields and factories. If one adds those entering Baku without official permits, the number would be closer to 100,000. By the beginning of the twentieth century, 50 percent of all Muslim workers in Baku were Iranian "guest" workers (Nissman 1987, 14). Cross-border travels further facilitated communication between Iranian Azeris and the Soviets in the realms of culture, literature, arts, philosophy, and above all, politics.

Another dimension of the reemergence of closer ties between Iran and the Muslims of the Caucasus was reflected in the growing number of publications and organizations designed to strengthen solidarity with the Iranian people and to promote modernist, democratic, and socialist ideas (Taqizadeh 1960, 459–65). The liberal democratic thought promoted by these publications provided the catalyst for the first constitutional revolt in Iran in 1905–10 against the despotic Qajar monarch, eventually forcing him to become accountable to a popularly elected *majlis,* or parliament. Some of the more important leaders of the Iranian constitutional revolution were Iranian Azeris, such as Sattar Khan and Baqer Khan, who have become legendary heroes in the annals of twentieth-century Iranian nationalism (Taherzadeh Behzad 1984; Kasravi 1979; Amir Khaizi 1977; Swietochowski 1985, 64–72).

The prominent role played by the Iranian Azeris as the vanguard of constitutional monarchy challenged the pan-Turkic appeals promoted by the Young Turks. For a long time, the Sunni-Shia split in the Islamic world was also reflected in Azerbaijani attitudes toward the Sunni Turks. With the rise of the Young Turks and the emergence of the modernist secular trends in Turkey, a certain segment of the Azeri intelligentsia sought to overcome religious differences and push toward unifying Azerbaijan with a new democratic, secularist state promised by the Young Turks. Pan-Turkic appeals, however, fell on deaf ears in Iran.

In Russia, intellectuals such as Ahmed Agaoglu, Ali Husseinzad, and Mardan Tapchibashy, who had been educated in Istanbul and influenced by the Young Turks, did achieve some initial success in promoting pan-Turanism among the Turks of the Transcaucasus. However, with the establishment in 1918 of the Transcaucasian Federation in Russia, the Russian Azeris joined this federation and declared themselves to be a sovereign state, only to be conquered by the Red Army two years later. In 1922, the area became a part of the newly established Transcaucasian Soviet Federative Socialist Republic, and in 1923, following Stalin's formula for creating republics that were "socialist in content and national in form," the Azerbaijan Soviet Socialist Republic was established (Altstadt 1992, 108–25).

Soviet Marxism and Iranian Azerbaijan

The Azeri intellectuals in Russia became the conduit for the propagation of Marxist thought in Iran. As early as 1904, a group of Baku intellectuals formed the core of a study group called *Hemmat* (Endeavor) which sought to articulate the application of socialist theories prevalent in Russia and Europe to Iran. Two years later, *Hemmat* organized Iranian Azeri workers in Baku into a political party called *Ijtemaiyyun-Amiyyun* (Popular Association). Under the leadership of Nariman Narimanov, an Azeri literary personality who later became the first chairman of the Communist Party of the Azerbaijan SSR, *Ijtemaiyyun-Amiyyun* began to agitate for change in Iranian Azerbaijan. By 1916, the *Ijtemaiyyun-Amiyyun* had transformed itself into a more organized and structured political organization, leading to the formation of the *Adalat* (Justice) Party.

Two important personalities in the *Adalat* Party are worth noting. Both were born in Iran but received most of their education and political training in Russia. The first was Seyyed Ja'far Javadzadeh (Pishevari), and the second was Avetis Mikailian, better known as Sultanzade. Both served on the Central Committee of the *Adalat* Party and were instrumental in transforming the party into the Communist Party of Iran (CPI). Pishevari eventually became better known than Sultanzade because of the former's role as a revolutionary leader in the first aborted socialist movement in Iran—the *Jangali* movement of Mirza Kuchek Kahn in the northern Iranian province of Gilan in the 1920s—and because of his premiership of the so-called Democratic Republic of Azerbaijan in Iran in 1945–46 (Fakhraii 1987; Gerogan 1985; Ghods 1989, 89–92; Abrahamian 1982, 388–415).

Sultanzade's role as a Bolshevik organizer and theoretician has received scant scholarly attention due to the destruction of much of his work during Stalin's rule. Unlike Pishevari and other prominent Azeri revolutionaries who came from a Shia background, Sultanzade, or Mikailian, was born to an Armenian family in the city of Maragheh in Iranian Azerbaijan. His extremely poor peasant parents later converted to Islam, but Sultanzade attended Armenian schools, first in Iran and later in Djamaran, a city near the Armenian capital of Yerevan in Russia (Chaqueri 1984, 57). As a true internationalist, Sultanzade endeavored to bridge the ethnic gap in the CPI. He also challenged Stalin's policy of creating separate linguistic identities in Azerbaijan and elsewhere as counterproductive to the cause of communism in the Soviet Union and Iran. In a series of articles which were published in the CPI's *Setare-e Sorkh* (Red Star) and *Paykar* (Struggle), Sultanzade alienated Soviet Iranologists when he accused them of becoming apologists for Stalin's linguistic divide-and-rule policy and criticized their opportunistic support of the new Pahlavi monarchy in Iran. It was not, therefore, surprising that Sultanzade was purged from the CPI and executed by the Soviet secret police in July 1938, thus becoming the first high-ranking foreign communist to perish in the Stalinist purges of the 1930s (Chaqueri 1984, 66).

While Bolshevism received support among some prominent and rank-and-file Azeris, a genuine anti-Russian national sentiment emerged in Iranian Azerbaijan. Under the leadership of the Muslim clerical reformer, Sheikh Mohammad Khiabani, a key figure in the Iranian Constitutional Revolution of 1905, Iranian Azeris demanded the removal of the pro-Russian governor of Azerbaijan and the establishment of a new and popularly elected parliament. When a response from the central government in Tehran was not forthcoming, Khiabani assumed leadership in Tabriz and established what became known as *Azadistan* (Land of the Free) in Iran in 1920. Although *Azadistan* lasted only three months, this expression of anti-Russian and anti-autocratic nationalism received substantial support from the masses. Khiabani's movement issued documents opposing all foreign presence in Iran, and particularly objecting to both Turkish and Russian efforts to annex Azerbaijan. The Soviet Union, after failing to gain Khiabani's support, began to view him as a serious threat to its own ambitions in Iranian Azerbaijan. Therefore, the Bolsheviks did not object when the Iranian army marched on Tabriz to dissolve *Azadistan* in September 1920, nor did they oppose the subsequent execution of Khiabani by the Shah's army (Nissman 1987, 21–22; Cottam 1979, 122–24).

The Autonomous Republic of Azerbaijan

The most serious attempt to establish a separate Azeri state occurred in 1945 when the Soviet military was in control of northern Iran. Through Soviet support, the *Firqi-e Demokrat-e Azerbaijan* (Azerbaijan Democratic Party), an offshoot of the pro-Soviet *Tudeh* (masses) party of Iran, managed to declare the establishment of an autonomous Azerbaijan republic inside Iran. Soviet Azeri emigrés, such as Pishevari, provided the impetus and the leadership for the new republic (Siavoshi 1991, 261–63; Cottam 1979, 124–29; Abrahamian 1982, 388–415; Ememi-Yeganeh 1984, 5–21; Ghods 1989, 166–73). The *Firqi* disintegrated in 1946 within a year of the establishment of the Azerbaijan Republic. Three major factors contributed to the rapidly declining fortunes of the *Firqi:* (1) the inability of the *Firqi* leadership to penetrate the non-urban Azeri peasant areas where the peasantry had remained deeply religious and suspicious of the collectivist programs of Pishevari and his colleagues; (2) the widening rift between the *Tudeh* and *Firqi* leadership over strategies and tactics to be pursued in Azerbaijan; and (3) Stalin's decision, at least for the time being, to terminate Russia's active support for an independent Azerbaijan in Iran.

Two schools of thought have developed to explain Stalin's behavior and tactical shift in his policy regarding the status of Iranian Azerbaijan. The dominant perspective among both Iranian and Western diplomatic historians is that Stalin was forced to abandon his support for the secession of Azerbaijan and remove the Red Army from northern Iran when President Harry Truman sent him an ultimatum to leave Iran. In fact, this episode is regarded by many scholars as the beginning of the Cold War. The second school of thought attributes different motives for Stalin's behavior in Iranian Azerbaijan and even questions the existence of Truman's ultimatum (Thorpe 1978, 188–95; Cottam 1988, 67–79). According to the revisionist interpretation, Stalin may have used the Azerbaijan crisis as a tactical ploy to obtain two key concessions from the Iranian government: a joint oil exploration scheme in northern Iran and the removal of prime ministers Sadr and Hakimi from Iranian politics. Stalin viewed both as instruments of a post–World War II Western capitalist scheme to encircle the Soviet Union with hostile military and economic forces (Cottam 1988, 67–68).

In fact, it has been argued that the Soviet leadership did not want to promote any genuine secessionist Azeri movement at that time, fearing the spillover effects of Azeri secessionism in Soviet Azerbaijan (Wimbush 1979, 69). It is not my intention in this chapter to examine the merits of these contrasting arguments. What is clear, however, is that the Soviets provided the *Firqi* "little in the way of military equipment. Whereas the Americans refurnished the royalist army with trucks, tanks, and heavy artillery, the Russians provided the Tabriz government with no more than rifles, handguns, and light artillery" (Abrahamian 1982, 411).

Moreover, the treatment of Pishevari and other *Firqi* activists who fled to the Soviet Union after the demise of the Autonomous Democratic Republic of Azerbaijan does not indicate any great admiration on Stalin's part for the *Firqi*. Apprehensive about the spread of independent radical Azeri nationalism in the Caucasus, the Soviet authorities arrested most of the *Firqi* members and sent them to prison camps in Siberia to serve prison terms ranging from fifteen to twenty-five years (Wimbush 1979, 70). Pishevari was allowed to live in the Azerbaijan SSR where he was killed in an automobile accident outside Baku in 1948. Fereydoon Keshavarz, a former member of the Central Committee of the *Tudeh* Party, has accused the *Tudeh* leadership and the Azerbaijan Communist Party of the Soviet Union of masterminding Pishevari's murder and manufacturing the so-called car accident as a cover-up (1979, 65–66).

One final point on the Azerbaijan Democratic Republic is worth noting here. Neither Pishevari nor the Tabriz government demanded the total secession of Azerbaijan from Iran. The eight-point program of the *Firqi,* adopted on 21 November 1945, reiterated that Azerbaijan was an inalienable part of the Iranian nation. But within Iran, it demanded autonomy and the imposition of its own laws and customs. In particular, it demanded that the Azeri language be recognized as the official language of the province (Ememi-Yeganeh 1984, 14–15; *Azerbaijan,* November 26, 1945, 1–2).

The Post–World War II Azerbaijan Question

After the fall of the Azerbaijan Democratic Republic and the onset of the Cold War, the Shah's government adopted a vigorous policy of reducing ethnic sentiments and weakening the Soviet influence in northern Iran. Contacts between Iranian and Soviet Azeris as well as the use of written Azeri were outlawed. At the same time, Azeris were thoroughly reintegrated into mainstream social, economic, and political spheres, and large numbers of Azeris attained prominent positions in government, military, and business circles on the national level.

The developing conflict between the Soviet Union and the Shah's pro–Western posture allowed Moscow to once again use the Azerbaijan issue as a weapon in its cold war with Tehran. The Baku-based Azerbaijan Writers Union and the Azerbaijan Society for Cultural Relations with Foreign Countries were used extensively by Moscow to promote the concept of the national liberation of Azerbaijan from "foreign" occupation. The publication of Mirza Ibrahimov's novel, *Galajak Gun* (*The Coming Day*), which originally was released in 1948 and then underwent a number of revisions in the next three years, signaled the beginning of a sustained Soviet policy of highlighting language specificity and literary writing in their effort to promote "national liberation" movements in Iranian Azerbaijan. Ibrahimov's main political message was that Azeri national consciousness would not die with repressive measures but would become strengthened and would rise like a phoenix from the ashes.

Another political theme emerging in this period has been reflected in the category of poetry called the literature of longing or sorrow (Nissman 1984, 199–207; Javadi 1988, 8–22). Mirza Ibrahimov and Suleyman Rustam exercised a virtual monopoly over the Soviet Azeri literature of longing, with its mixture of patriotism and sorrow for the division of the Azeri people along the Aras River. An interesting but behind-the-scene coordinator of this type of literature has been the Communist Party of Azerbaijan. As David Nissman has pointed out, all Soviet Azeris "who have been prominent in this issue have been party members and some have held, and hold important positions on the All-Union level. Mirza Ibrahimov, for instance, has been a party member since 1930 and Chairman of the Soviet Committee for Solidarity with Asian and African countries since 1977"

(1987, 46). There is little doubt that party politics has determined the role of the literature of longing in keeping the so-called "southern question" on the front burner. Lines from the following poem by Bakhtiyar Vahabzade (quoted in Nissman 1984, 205), a professor of Azeri literature at the Azerbaijan State University, captures the essence of the literature of longing in the Soviet Azerbaijan:

> Your divided motherland
> Expects from this day a slave,
> Brother, your weapons are two,
> By days—the knife, by
> nights—the pen.

The Iranian Azeri response to the literature of longing was to generate its own genre of the literature of sorrow, one which laments principally the suppression of the Azeri vernacular in Pahlavi Iran rather than expresses a longing for unification of "northern" and "southern" Azerbaijan. For example, Reza Baraheni, a highly respected Iranian Azeri literary critic and a leftist opponent of the Shah, expressed in his writings his sorrow and anger about his "repressed nationality as an Azerbaijani Turk whose language was taken away from him by the Pahlavi regime, particularly after 1946, and never given back to him" (1977, 111). The ethnic question appears in Baraheni's essays and poems in the form of allusions. In the following poem, the song of an old man singing in the streets of Tehran displays subtle allusions to Baraheni's ethnic roots. Its form is typical of many other Azeri literary figures in the last decade of the Pahlavi dynasty:

> My father was one of an old king's clowns
> My mother was of the Turkish gypsies
> All my sisters stand
> and dream of that sterile prince
> dream of the arms of powerful mountain men
> And my brothers, yes, my brothers,
> are eunuchs serving the brides of a new king
>
> I was the first son
> My eyes went dry in the city
> an alley woman stole my tambourine
>
> My father was one of an old king's clowns
> My mother was of the Turkish gypsies
> One day my father aged
> no longer made the old king laugh
> They tore out his tongue and threw it to the crows
> They carried this gift to my mother's garden
> her face like a dark rainy sky

her hands like dead birds hanging in the air
her eyes shining wax in deep dark night
her legs stumbling doves
her shoulders made of paper
her breasts lighter than bags full of straw

My mother sang in the streets so long
her voice went blind
My mother was of the Turkish gypsies
at the end of her life no one understood her speech

My father was one of an old king's clowns
My mother was of the Turkish gypsies . . .
(Baraheni 1977, 113–14)

The Islamic Republic and the Azerbaijan Question

With the ouster of the Shah in January 1979, the ban on the writing and reading of the Azeri Turkish was lifted in Iran. The people of Azerbaijan played a decisive role in the revolutionary activities that led to the Shah's downfall, and they have continued to occupy an important position in the Islamic Republic. Mehdi Bazargan, the first post-Shah prime minister of Iran was an Azeri, as was Mir Hussein Mussavi, the last prime minister of the Islamic Republic before the country established a presidential system and eliminated the post of prime minister. Ayatollah Khamenei, the former president and current supreme religious leader, or *faqih*, is a Turkish-speaking Iranian (Izady 1990, 32–33). In fact, the Azeris have been represented in a proportionally higher number in many levels of government, military, and private business sectors than any other single Iranian ethnic group, including the Persians. This was also true during the Shah's reign.

While Azeri representation has remained high in the Islamic Republic, tensions with Tehran have at times been apparent. For example, in the early 1980s, Ayatollah Kazem Shariatmadari, the spiritual leader of the Iranian Azeris and one of the grand ayatollahs, was stripped of his title by the religious clerics in the holy city of Qom. Although Shariatmadari's ouster was a manifestation of the power struggle between the radical and more moderate clergy, it nevertheless had negative repercussions among the Azeris.

Before coming to power in 1979, Ayatollah Khomeini did not seem to have considered ethnic issues as crucial in a Muslim society. In his magnum opus, *Hokumat-e Islami* (*Islamic Government*), Khomeini did not even discuss ethnicity or cultural pluralism in a country that has historically been composed of numerous religious and ethnic minorities. Ayatollah Khomeini's December 1979 statement (quoted in Menashri 1988, 216–17) captures the essence of his views on Muslim minority groups:

> Sometimes the word minorities is used to refer to people such as the Kurds, Lurs, Turks, Persians, Baluchis, and such. These people should not be called minorities, because this term assumes there is a difference between these brothers. In Islam, such a difference has no place at all. There is no difference between Muslims who speak different languages, for instance the Arabs or the Persians. It is very probable that such problems have been created by those who do not wish the Muslim countries to be united. . . . They create the issues of nationalism, of pan-Iranism, pan-Turkism, and such isms, which are contrary to Islamic doctrines. Their plan is to destroy Islam and Islamic philosophy.

On philosophical and religious grounds, the Islamic Republic of Iran had no objections to the blossoming of linguistic and cultural expressions of various Muslim ethnic minorities because religious identity would dominate all other forms of cultural demarcations in an Islamic state. In the first five years of the Islamic Republic, Azeri publications once again blossomed. The most significant of Azeri publications appearing in post-revolutionary Iran was the monthly *Varlig* published by Javad Heyat, a prolific Azeri literary scholar. Other publications of note included three magazines: *Yoldash* (*Comrade*), *Engelab Yolunda* (*On the Road to Revolution*), and *Yeni Yol* (*New Road*). All major Azeri publications, with the exception of *Varlig,* have ceased operation either for financial reasons or because Islamic authorities forced them to close as a result of their espousal of secularist and/or leftist doctrines. However, *Kayhan,* the Iranian newspaper with the largest circulation, continues to publish an Azeri-language insert in its airmail edition.

The revival of Azeri publishing in Iran was welcomed by the Soviets as they tried once again to revive the concept of "one Azerbaijan" through connections some Azeri communists had established with *Yeni Yol* and other publications that fit the Soviet concept of progressivism. They had little success in generating the kind of enthusiasm among the Iranian Azeris they had hoped for, especially after most of these publications were closed down by the Islamic authorities in Iran. Mirza Ibrahimov and other Soviet Azeri figures then sought to portray the action of the Iranian government as a direct attack on the Azeri language, whereas the Iranian crackdown was primarily a manifestation of anti-Soviet and anticommunist impulses of the clerical establishment in Tehran and Tabriz (Nissman 1987, 60–61). Furthermore, the Soviets came to the realization that both Shia Islam and Iranian culture still remained the most formidable obstacles to the dominance of Soviet influence in Iranian Azerbaijan.

Paradoxically, Islamic revivalism in Iran has generated an ideological crisis within the Azerbaijan Republic and other Muslim republics in the former Soviet Union. This crisis is reflected in the growing rift between the state-supported official Islam and the unofficial Islam of the grass roots. Officially, the Azeri Turks in the former Soviet Union, 75 percent of whom are Shia Muslims and 85 percent of whom live in the Azerbaijan Republic (Bennigsen and Wimbush 1986, 133;

Anderson and Silver 1989, table 1, 612), are represented in the religious realm by the head of the Spiritual Administration of the Muslims of the Transcaucasus in Baku. Traditionally, the heads of this organ of official Shiʿism in the former USSR received part of their training under the Iranian *ulema* in the holy city of Qom. Until recent years, they had remained conservative in religious outlook and subservient to the government and party authorities. Islamic revivalism in Iran has brought about some changes in the nature of official Islam in the Caucasus and Central Asia.

In addition to this official Islam, a parallel nonofficial Islam has grown in the Muslim republics of the region. The nonofficial Islam has been reflected in the growing appeal of the Sunni brotherhoods, or *tariqas*, especially Naqshebandi and Qadir orders, and of the Sufi shrines (Bennigsen and Wimbush 1986, 21–23; Nissman 1983, 48–52). In the years preceding the disintegration of the Soviet Union, these shrines became centers for religious activism and symbols of opposition to the Soviet domination of Azerbaijan. In response, *Kommunist*, the daily newspaper of the Communist Party of Azerbaijan, launched a blistering attack against renewed Muslim political activism in general and religious gathering in the shrines in particular.

At the same time, Azeri officials have made certain goodwill gestures toward their Muslim population. For example, the authorities allowed Haj Hassan Sadeq, deputy chief of religious affairs of the Azerbaijan Republic, to travel to Iran in June 1990 as the head of an Azeri delegation commemorating the first anniversary of the death of Ayatollah Khomeini. The Soviet authorities also bowed to Muslim pressure and declared a three-day mourning period in Soviet Azerbaijan for the same occasion (*Tehran Times*, June 6, 1990, 3). Tehran and Moscow also agreed to open their borders at Bilesawar and Jolfa for two days to allow Soviet Azeris unrestricted travel to participate in ceremonies associated with the first anniversary of Ayatollah Khomeini's passing away (*Tehran Times*, June 3, 1990, 2).

Recent Azeri Uprisings and Iran-Soviet Tensions

Gorbachev's policy of *glasnost* had a paradoxical effect on inter-ethnic strife in the former Soviet Union and created an ethnic mosaic of discord (Tishkov 1989, 191–95). Gorbachev tried to deal with this ethnic crisis by removing ethnic elites who had been closely associated with the failed and heavy-handed Brezhnev-Andropov-Chernenko policies of the past. In Azerbaijan, for example, Heider Aliev, an Andropov protégé and a career KGB officer who had become the first secretary of the Azerbaijan Communist Party in 1969 and who had risen to become a member of the Politburo of the CPSU, was eventually replaced as president of the Azerbaijan Republic by Ayez Mutalibov. (Popular pressure against his perceived "soft line" on Armenia later forced Mutalibov out of office.) Mutalibov, who had no known KGB ties but was nevertheless a Communist Party operative, represented the new breed of communist leader in the non-Russian republics whom Gorbachev hoped would defuse, or at least manage, the growing ethnic crisis in the country. Furthermore, in order to give more recognition to the nationality question, Gorbachev included the first secretaries of the communist parties in all the union republics as members of the Politburo of the Communist Party of the Soviet Union when he reconstituted that body in July 1990 (*New York Times*, July 15, 1990, 6).

Ethnic secessionism, which became a powerful force in the Baltic region in the winter of 1987 and spring of 1988, reappeared in the Caucasus in January 1988 with the Armenian-Azerbaijani conflict over the control of the Nagorno-Karabakh autonomous region or *oblast* (NKAO). The Armenians, who constitute the majority of the population of the NKAO, which is located inside the Azerbaijan Republic, had long complained that the region belonged to them and that it had unlawfully been given to the Azeris by Stalin (Walker 1991). In mid-January 1988, the Armenians in NKAO, with strong support from their co-nationals in the Armenian SSR, staged a major revolt in Stepanakert, the NKAO's capital, demanding that the governor of the NKAO be replaced and that their *oblast* be allowed to join Armenia (Alexeyeva 1990, 65; Olcott 1989, 409; Cockburn 1989, 168; Lieven 1988, 23–25; Suny 1990, 245–48). Azerbaijani homes and businesses were attacked, and many Azeris were forced to leave Stepanakert and move to other cities in Azerbaijan. This, along with Azeri charges that Moscow for decades had ignored Armenian attacks in NKAO on the Azeris, including the desecration of graves and obstruction of the observance of their national celebrations and rites, further increased tensions between these two ethnic groups (Samizdat 1988, 142–43).

In order to satisfy some Armenian demands, Moscow replaced V. Kevorkov, the first secretary of NKAO *obkom*, with G. Pogosian. Although both of these individuals were Armenian, Kevorkov had been accused by Armenian nationalists of being closely tied to the Azeri authorities (Olcott 1989, 409). On 26 February 1988, Gorbachev issued an appeal to both sides defending the cultural rights of ethnic minorities and emphasizing the importance of the peaceful resolution of ethnic conflicts. He also promised to set up a committee within the Supreme Soviet to study the implications of the possible transfer of NKAO's control to Armenia. The Azeris, fearing abandonment by Moscow, retaliated by attacking pockets of Armenian minorities in Nakhichevan and Kirovabad (Suny 1990, 247), setting in motion a cycle of attacks and counterattacks that have continued to the present.

The Presidium of the Supreme Soviet, for its part, argued that the redrawing of the country's ethnic borders was not justifiable. It passed a ruling in 1988 which said: "It shall be recognized as unacceptable to resolve complex national territorial issues by exerting pressure on bodies of state authority within an atmosphere of heated emotion and passion and the creation of sundry self-instituted groups advocating the revision of the national-state and national administrative boundaries that the U.S.S.R. Constitution has established" (Redrawing the Border Is Not the Answer, 22). Moscow, however, did announce in January 1989 that NKAO would be placed under its direct supervision—a solution that did not satisfy the Armenians and further alienated the Azerbaijanis. Clashes between the two sides continued to create anarchy and a condition in which for the first time in Soviet history "one republic [was] in a de facto state of war with another" (Suny 1990, 248).

The appearance in the summer of 1989 of a militant Azeri umbrella group—the Popular Front—and its successful coordination of strikes against and boycotts of Armenian targets and virtual encirclement of Armenia compelled Moscow in November to revert the control of NKAO back to the Azerbaijan Republic. This move was also partly in response to the October 1989 passage of the "Law on Sovereignty" by the Azerbaijan Supreme Soviet. This law, while stopping short of declaring independence from Moscow, stated in part:

> Azerbaijan's sovereignty extends throughout its territory including the Nakhichevan Autonomous Republic and the Nagorno-Karabakh Autonomous Oblast which are inalienable parts of the union republic. Its territory . . . cannot be changed without the agreement of the republic expressed by a popular vote (referendum) held by decision of the Supreme Soviet among the entire population. Borders with other union republics can only be changed by mutual agreement . . . (FBIS-SOV, October 10, 1989, 67)

The breakdown of discipline in the Caucasus accelerated in January 1990 when the Azeris in Nakhichevan broke down the Soviet fortifications along the Iranian border and came south to Iran where they were greeted warmly by their co-religionists. The Soviet government then asked the Islamic Republic of Iran to sign agreements for orderly travel between Soviet and Iranian Azerbaijan in exchange for the Soviet construction of bridges over the Aras River. When anti-Soviet and religious publications were smuggled to the Soviet Union, the Soviets temporarily stopped their Aras River bridge construction project.

When the Nakhichevan revolt spread to Baku and resulted in further clashes with the Armenian and Soviet forces, Gorbachev dispatched Soviet troops and tanks to Azerbaijan and put down the revolt by force. Iranian media and officials were unanimous in their condemnation of what they called the Soviet "ethnocide" of Soviet Azeri Muslims (*Jomhuri-e Eslami,* January 24, 1990, 1 and 9; *Ettela'at,* January 23, 1990, 3; *Resalat,* January 18, 1990, 2). The influential Tehran daily *Kayhan* contrasted Gorbachev's approach in dealing with the independence movements in the Baltic region with his iron-fist handling of the crisis in Azerbaijan. The paper, reflecting the views of high-level government figures, concluded that the treatment of the Azeris proved that *glasnost* applied only to the European part of Gorbachev's Soviet Union (*Kayhan,* January 24, 1990, 2). Another Tehran daily, reflecting the views of the clerical centers of power, accused the United States of duplicity and double-standards for supporting Baltic autonomy drives while siding with Gorbachev in his military approach to Azeri sovereignty demands (*Jomhuri-e Eslami,* January 24, 1990, 9).

For the first time since the current Azeri-Armenian crisis started in 1988, the Soviets in July 1990 publicly acknowledged the existence of an Armenian military threat against Azerbaijan. For example, Colonel Valerie Buniyatov, the military commander of Baku, asserted that Armenia had formed a 140,000-man national army "with huge quantities of weapons stolen from Soviet army depots or smuggled into the republic from abroad . . ." (*Chicago Tribune,* July 24, 1990, 4). Soviet military and KGB commanders also acknowledged the increasing number of attacks conducted regularly inside Azerbaijan by the new Armenian army. The Azeris, in turn, launched their own indiscriminate attacks against Armenian targets.

These tragic episodes in the Azerbaijan Republic heightened tension between Moscow and Tehran. Although Soviet authorities accommodated certain demands made by the Azeris, such as allowing more freedom in religious practices and allowing more regular contacts between Iranian and Soviet Azeris, and even declared the Iranian New Year as an official holiday in Russian Azerbaijan, the final resolution of the Azerbaijan crisis and its implications for Russian-Iranian relations are far from certain.

A developing scenario is the growing rivalry between Turkey and Iran in the Caucasus and Central Asia in the aftermath of the demise of the Soviet Union. This new regional "Great Game" may also affect the development of Azeri ethnic nationalism in ways that are too early to forecast. Although outside forces have actively been courting the allegiance of the Azeri Republic since 1991, it is premature to argue that either Turkey or Iran have succeeded in establishing their hegemony over the course of events in that area. As Isa Gambarov, deputy head of Azerbaijan's Popular Front, stated: "We did not fight against Russian domination to place ourselves under the domination of Turkey or Iran" (*Christian Science Monitor,* May 5, 1992, 2).

Another complicating and hitherto unknown factor is the role of Islam in the politics of the Azerbaijan Republic. Although Baku remains secular in its outlook, two competing trends have surfaced in recent Azeri elections. One has been the emergence of Tovbe, a Muslim party which espouses social democratic ideals influenced by Islamic moral values. Another Islamic grouping, which was declared illegal by Soviet authorities, has been heavily influenced by the late Ayatollah Khomeini's vision of an Islamic state. This party is influential outside Baku and in the countryside. The interplay of these two Islamic forces will determine the impact of Islam on Azeri politics in the future. What is certain is that Gorbachev's policy of *glasnost* and the downfall of the Bolshevik system in the independent Azerbaijan Republic increased inter-ethnic and intra-ethnic strife in that country (Tishkov 1989, 191).

Conclusion

It is highly debatable whether what the Russians call "southern" and "northern" Azerbaijan could have been classified as a single nation or state before the creation of the Soviet Republic of Azerbaijan in the early twentieth century. In fact, prior to the Soviet occupation of Baku in 1920, the only articulated group identity of the inhabitants of "northern" Azerbaijan was "that of being Muslim, and their collective consciousness expressed itself primarily in terms of the universalistic ʾumma" (Muslim community; Swietochowski 1985, 191). While the establishment of the Azerbaijan Republic in the former Soviet Union has created an amorphous Azeri identity among the "northern" Azeris, the boundaries of this new identity are not clearly definable. In other words, overlapping, and at times competing, dimensions of this nascent ethnic identity (for example, the purely Shia dimension, the pan-Turkic dimension, the secular and purely Azeri dimensions) have slowed down the formation of a uniquely Azeri identity with well-defined sociopolitical objectives. Although Soviet authorities, historians, and orientalists have sought for over sixty years to cultivate the notion of "one Azerbaijan" in the minds of the Azeris, today the interest of "northern" Azeris in the Iranian Azeris is "more rhetorical than real" (Lemercier-Quelquejay 1984, 54).

Furthermore, no strong sentiments have been manifested by the Iranian Azeris for unification with the "northern" Azeris. Iranian Azeris, whose population of 17 million comprises close to one-third of Iran's total population, are well integrated into Iranian society and Iran's political and economic institutions. Turkish-speaking dynasties that ruled Iran from the eleventh century until the advent of the Pahlavi monarchy in 1925 made the total assimilation of the Azeris in Iran a fact of life. Again, any cataclysmic transformations in Iranian politics may bring about changes in the status of the Azeris, as was the case in the former Soviet Union.

Notwithstanding the Azeri integration in Iran, "the Azerbaijanis tenaciously preserve and adhere to their linguistic distinctiveness. In a gathering of Azerbaijanis, when non-Turkish speaking countrymen are not present, Turkish is almost invariably used as the language of communication" (Kazemi 1988, 213). This is true not only in the case of Azeris, but it also applies to many other Iranian ethnic groups, like Gilanis or Mazandaranis, who use vernacular languages different from Persian. The attachment to one's dialect or language has sometimes been interpreted erroneously by certain observers as a primordial manifestation of political autonomy or secessionism. In reality, language distinctiveness in this context is an expression of what Fredrik Barth has called boundary maintenance between group members and outsiders (1969, 14). However, language distinctiveness may become a major factor in producing the political phenomenon of ethno-nationalism among Iranian Azeris.

In short, Azeri ethnicity and its political manifestations should not be analyzed in a historical vacuum. Rather, they should be studied within the broader context of Iran's long history and culture and of Russo-Iranian relations. A unique feature of Iranian history has been the symbiotic coexistence of ethnic particularism and Iranian nationalism. Azeri ethnic consciousness in Iran, therefore, has been formed within this context. The Azeri identity in the former Soviet Union, on the other hand, has been shaped by what Cynthia Enloe has termed exclusion from "avenues of mobility [and] a sense of common deprivation" (1973, 179), a context which is substantially different from that in which Iranian Azeri ethnicity has grown.

REFERENCES

Abrahamian, Ervand. 1982. *Iran Between Two Revolutions*. Princeton: Princeton University Press.

Alexayeva, Ludmilla. 1990. Unrest in the Soviet Union. *The Washington Quarterly* 13, 1 (Winter): 63–77.

Altstadt, Audrey L. 1992. *The Azerbaijani Turks: Power and Identity under Russian Rule*. Stanford: Hoover Institution Press.

Altstadt, Audrey L. 1986. Azerbaijani Turks' Response to Russian Conquest. *Studies in Comparative Communism* 19, 3–4 (Autumn/Winter): 267–86.

Amir Khaizi, Esmail. 1977. *Qiyam-e Azerbaijan va Sattar Khan* (*The Azerbaijan Revolution and Sattar Khan*). Tehran: Tehran Books.

Anderson, Barbara A., and Brian D. Silver. 1989. Demographic Sources of the Changing Ethnic Composition of the Soviet Union. *Population and Development Review* 15, 4 (December): 609–56.

Anderson, Benedict. 1983. *Imagined Communities: Reflections on the Origin and Spread of Nationalism*. London: Verso Editions.

Bakikhanli, Abbas Kuli Agha. 1982. *Nasihatlar* (*Advice*). Baku: Yaziji.

Baraheni, Reza. 1977. *The Crowned Cannibals: Writings on Repression in Iran*. New York: Random House/Vintage Books.

Barth, Fredrik. 1969. Introduction. In *Ethnic Groups and Boundaries: The Social Organization of Culture Difference*, edited by Fredrik Barth, 9–38. Boston: Little, Brown and Company.

Bennigsen, Alexander, and S. Enders Wimbush. 1986. *Muslims of the Soviet Empire: A Guide*. Bloomington: Indiana University Press.

Caporaso, James A., ed. 1989. *The Elusive State: International and Comparative Perspectives*. Newbury Park, California: Sage Publications.

Chaqueri, Cosroe. 1984. Sultanzade: The Forgotten Revolutionary Theoretician. *Central Asian Survey* 3, 2: 57–73.

Cockburn, Patrick. 1989. Dateline USSR: Ethnic Tremors. *Foreign Policy* 74 (Spring): 168–84.

Cottam, Richard W. 1988. *Iran and the United States. A Cold War Case Study.* Pittsburgh: University of Pittsburgh Press.

Cottam, Richard W. 1979. *Nationalism in Iran.* Updated edition. Pittsburgh: University of Pittsburgh Press.

Djavadi, Chafi. 1971. *Tabriz va Piramoon* (*Tabriz and its Environs*). Tehran: Chehr Publications.

Ememi-Yeganeh, Jody. 1984. Iran va Azerbaijan (1945–46): Divorce, Separation or Reconciliation? *Central Asian Survey* 3, 2: 1–27.

Enloe, Cynthia H. 1973. *Ethnic Conflict and Political Development.* Boston: Little, Brown and Company.

Fakhraii, Ebrahim. 1987. *Sardar-e Jangal* (*The Jungle's Leader*). 3d ed. Tehran: Javidan Publications.

Foreign Broadcast Information Service (FBIS). 1989. *Daily Report, Soviet Union.* (October 10): 67.

Frye, Richard N. 1979. *Islamic Iran and Central Asia (7th–12th Centuries).* London: Variorum Reprints.

Frye, Richard N. 1975. *The Golden Age of Persia: The Arabs in the East.* London: Weidenfeld and Nicolson.

Frye, Richard N. 1968. *Persia.* London: Allen and Unwin.

Frye, Richard N. 1953. *Iran.* New York: Holt.

Gerogan, Hamid. 1985. *Hemase-e Mirza Kuchek Kahn* (*Mirza Kucheck Khan's Heroic Exploits*). Tehran: Ministry of Islamic Guidance.

Ghods, M. Reza. 1989. *Iran in the Twentieth Century: A Political History.* Boulder: Lynne Rienner.

Gumplowicz, Ludwig. 1963. *Outlines of Sociology.* New York: Paine-Whitman.

Guseinov, A. I., et al. 1959–1962. *Istoriia Azerbaidzhana* (*Azerbaijan's History*). Vol. 2. Baku: Elm.

Higgins, Patricia J. 1986. Minority-State Relations in Contemporary Iran. In *The State, Religion, and Ethnic Politics: Afghanistan, Iran, and Pakistan,* edited by Ali Banuazizi and Myron Weiner, 167–97. Syracuse: Syracuse University Press.

Izady, Mehrdad R. 1990. Persian Carrot and Turkish Stick: Contrasting Policies Targeted as Gaining State Loyalty from Azeris and Kurds. *Kurdish Times* 3, 2 (Fall): 31–47.

Javadi, Hasan Ali. 1988. *Azerbaijan va Zaban-e An: Oza' va Moshkelat-e Turki-e Azeri dar Iran* (*Azerbaijan and Its Language: Conditions and Difficulties of the Azeri Turkish in Iran*). Piedmont, California: Jahan Book Company.

Kasravi, Ahmad. 1979. *Tarikh-e Engelab-e Mashruteh-e Iran* (*History of the Iranian Constitutional Revolution*). 2 vols. Tehran: Amir Kabir.

Kazemi, Farhad. 1988. Ethnicity and the Iranian Peasantry. In *Ethnicity, Pluralism, and the State in the Middle East,* edited by Milton J. Esman and Itamar Rabinovich, 201–14. Ithaca: Cornell University Press.

Keshavarz, Fereydoon. 1979. *Man Motaham Mikonam Hezb-e Tudeh-e Iran Ra* (*I Accuse the Tudeh Party of Iran*). Tehran, n.p.

Lemercier-Quelquejay, Chantal. 1984. Islam and Identity in Azerbaijan. *Central Asian Survey* 3, 2: 29–55.

Lieven, Dominic. 1988. Gorbachev and the Nationalities. *Conflict Studies* 216 (November): 1–33.

Matini, Jalal. 1989. Azerbaijan Kojast? (Where Is Azerbaijan?) *Iranshenasi* 1, 3 (Autumn): 443–62.

Menashri, David. 1988. Khomeini's Policy toward Ethnic and Religious Minorities. In *Ethnicity, Pluralism, and the State in the Middle East,* edited by Milton J. Esman and Itamar Rabinovich, 215–29. Ithaca: Cornell University Press.

Nissman, David B. 1987. *The Soviet Union and Iranian Azerbaijan: The Use of Nationalism for Political Penetration.* Boulder: Westview Press.

Nissman, David B. 1984. The Origin and Development of the Literature of "Longing" in Azerbaijan. *Journal of Turkish Studies* 8: 199–207.

Nissman, David B. 1983. Iran and Soviet Islam: The Azerbaijan and Turkmenistan SSRs. *Central Asian Survey.* 2, 4 (December): 45–60.

Olcott, Martha B. 1989. Gorbachev's National Dilemma. *Journal of International Affairs* 42, 2 (Spring): 399–421.

Redrawing the Border Is Not the Answer. 1988. *New Times* (Moscow) 14 (April): 22–23.

Reza, Enayatollah. 1988. *Azerbaijan va Aran* (*Azerbaijan and Aran*). West Germany: Mard-e Emrooz Publications.

Ringer, Benjamin B., and Elinor R. Lawless. 1989. *Race-Ethnicity and Society.* New York: Routledge, Chapman, and Hall.

Samizdat. 1988. Armenia-Azerbaijan Conflict. *Central Asian Survey* 7, 4: 141–44.

Siavoshi, Sussan. 1991. Ethnic Nationalism: The Case of Iran's Azerbaijan. *Current World Leaders* 34, 2 (April): 255–69.

Skocpol, Theda. 1985. Bringing the State Back In: Strategies of Analysis in Current Research. In *Bringing the State Back In,* edited by Peter B. Evans, Dietrich Rueschemeyer, and Theda Skocpol, 3–37. New York: Cambridge University Press.

Suny, Ronald Grigor. 1990. Transcaucasia: Cultural Cohesion and Ethnic Revival in a Multinational Society. In *The Nationalities Factor in Soviet Politics and Society,* edited by Lubomyr Hajda and Mark Beissinger, 228–52. Boulder: Westview Press.

Swietochowski, Tadeusz. 1985. *Russian Azerbaijan, 1905–1920: The Shaping of National Identity in a Muslim Community.* New York: Cambridge University Press.

Taherzadeh Behzad, Karim. 1984. *Qiyam-e Azerbaijan dar Engelab-e Mashrutiyat-e Iran* (*The Azerbaijan Revolt in the Iranian Constitutional Revolution*). Tehran: Eqbal.

Taqizadeh, Seyyed Hassan. 1960. Document: The Background of the Constitutional Movement in Azerbaijan. *Middle East Journal* 4, 4 (Autumn): 456–65.

Thorpe, James A. 1978. Truman's Ultimatum to Stalin on the 1946 Azerbaijan Crisis: The Making of a Myth. *Journal of Politics* 40, 1 (February): 188–95.

Tishkov, Valerii. 1989. Glasnost and the Nationalities within the Soviet Union. *Third World Quarterly* 11, 4 (October): 191–207.

Walker, Christopher J., ed. 1991. *Armenia and Karabagh: The Struggle for Unity*. London: Minority Rights Group.

Wimbush, S. Enders. 1979. Divided Azerbaijan: Nation Building, Assimilation, and Mobilization Between Three States. In *Soviet Asian Ethnic Frontiers*, edited by William O. McCagg, Jr., and Brian Silver, 61–81. New York: Pergamon Press.

7

Nationalism and Ethnic Conflict in Ethiopia

SOLOMON GASHAW

Introduction

MY PURPOSE IN this chapter is threefold: (1) to examine briefly the history and structural components of Ethiopian nationalism; (2) to analyze its mode of interpellating the polyethnic communities of the Ethiopian state; and (3) to assess its weakness and strength to meet the challenges of the contemporary phenomenon of ethnic pluralism.

It is important to keep the following ideas in mind when considering Ethiopia. First, there is a distinct form of Ethiopian nationalism whose influence can be found in the culture of the diverse ethnic groups that constitute the Ethiopian polity. Second, in the modern nation-state there is a new phenomenon of nationalism which champions cultural pluralism as opposed to cultural homogeneity, which is the traditional approach of promoting nationalism. Third, transforming the basis of nationalism from one mode to another will invariably generate a political contest whose outcome depends on a number of variables. Ethiopian nationalism is caught in this transformative process, the outcome of which will certainly have very profound consequences for the destiny of the Ethiopian state and Ethiopian society.

Hegemonic Crises of Ethiopian Nationalism

Abyssinian nationalism, whose traditional organic core was the Tigre/Amhara segment of the population, was a hegemonic doctrine with relation to other ethnic groups. In the last three decades, however, this hegemony faced major political challenges from diverse regional groups. The political agenda of the challengers varied from outright secession to reorganization of the political structure of the state. The conflict has now plunged the nation into a deep political abyss. Consequently, serious doubts have been raised as to the future existence of Ethiopia as a viable nation-state. Its historical destiny now looks to be similar to that of the Hapsburg empire, or of contemporary war-torn Lebanon or Yugoslavia.

Until very recently, political wisdom was that the dismemberment of a nation or state was not an easy task to be readily undertaken. Because it has serious political repercussions, particularly on third world states, where ethnic challenges are the order of the day, the world community of states shunned the idea of splintering a nation-state. In the Ethiopian case, strong countervailing forces against ethnic and regional challenges came from Ethiopian nationalism. The Ethiopian state has existed for over three thousand years. This millennial existence has forged a distinct national identity (nationalism) which cannot easily be dismissed as a myth. Ethiopian nationalism has a time-tested resiliency. It has survived numerous crises and challenges over many centuries, and in times of major crisis the Ethiopian polity has repeatedly shown a strong nationalist response. The successful repulsion time and again of foreign encroachments on Ethiopian territory has created a deep sense of pride in the idea of the Ethiopian nation. For instance in 1579 the Ottoman attempt to expand from a coastal base at Massawa was defeated. In 1868 emperor Yohannes IV repulsed the Egyptians at Gura. And in 1896, at the battle of Adowa, Menelik defeated the Italians. Well into the twentieth century, the European attitude toward Ethiopia was that the "Abyssinians are suffering from 'superiority complex' . . . which may be traced to Gundet, Gura and Adowa" (Crabites 1935, 11).

These historical experiences have helped Ethiopia develop techniques for survival as a nation through the accommodative or assimilative mechanisms of its ethnic groups. The survival of Ethiopia has required that all—the Amhara core culture and groups at the periphery—consider themselves as belonging to one Ethiopian nation. The basic resources of nationalism, however, will erode away if a nation is engaged in a continual political conflict. The ongoing political impasse of recent years has created a crisis of hegemony for Ethiopian nationalism.

Conceptual Framework of Analysis

Nationalism is a universal phenomenon. It is an ideological expression or political belief, based on the real or imagined culture and history of a people. It is an expression of group identity blended from the sum total of individual experiences. As a collective consciousness, it has distinct characteristics of its own. It transcends local, parochial ethnic, and regional attachments. Nationalism overrides isolated regional ethnic sentiments and transforms them into an all-encompassing political expression. Contemporary nationalism is associated with a nation-state, which becomes an embodiment of the collective consciousness, and as such, demands the absolute loyalty of all its citizenry. This unconditional loyalty becomes a motivating force for a relentless drive toward homogeneity.

> This inner impulse toward oneness latent in nationalism brings it into frequent relations of tension with cultural pluralism. The unitarian impulse sires policies aimed at producing greater homogeneity; these measures are a threat to subnational solidarities and mobilize pluralism. The ensuing conflict may reach a level where the unity of the polity is indeed impaired, at which point the dissident groups are either coerced into silence or the homogenizing pressures are slackened. (Young 1976, 72–73)

This observation depicts the current political predicament of the Ethiopian state, a predicament which of course is not unique to Ethiopia. The relation between the state and ethnic groups is very complex. The state is an important element that shapes, forms, and reproduces ethnic identities. When ethnic groups seem to be threatened by the policies of the state, they may resort to communal symbols and identities as a means of shielding themselves or to obtain a bargaining position. In this type of scenario, the state is the most important variable that shapes the consciousness of ethnic groups. The state is never a neutral institution. Its intervention in ethnic politics is, of course, limited by many factors, such as the resources available to it.

Ethnic resurgence has become a common phenomenon in many contemporary societies and is especially prevalent today in third world countries. It was once commonly believed that subnationalities or diverse ethnic groups will in time be assimilated into the dominant nationalism. This view, however, has been found to be untenable since ethnic groups do not wither away, nor are they easily assimilated into the dominant nationalism. The contemporary challenge of nation-building is how to integrate various ethnic groups without eliminating them.

There are some approaches that can be identified in the study of ethnicity. In the introductory chapter to this book, Crawford Young outlines the primordialist, instrumentalist, and assimilationist views of ethnicity. Primordialists emphasize elements of shared culture that have been transmitted over generations (Geertz 1963; Epstein 1978). These shared cultural elements produce predictable responses on the part of the community. Instrumentalists perceive ethnicity as a weapon of elites to be used to achieve desired political or economic goals (Wallerstein 1960). These two approaches, however, are not mutually exclusive. Ethnicity has "both instrumentalist and primordial dimensions" (Young 1982–83, 661). The primordialist emphasis on ethnicity as a quasi-ontological object does not preclude it from being used as a manipulative instrument by elites.

Assimilationists and a fourth perspective, class theorists, predict the diminishment of ethnicity with a rise in the level of modernization. Marxists espouse the eventual primacy of class over primordial loyalty. This assumption, however, has proven to be wrong. As many critiques of Marxist theory have concluded,

Marxism has never been able to comprehend the phenomenon of nationalism, an inability which became Marxism's greatest folly and "great historical failure" (Nairn 1977, 329).

Contrary to what is predicted by modernization theories, urban areas, the symbol of modernity, have become the fertile ground where ethnic associations first take root. This was the case in the mid-1960s in Ethiopia. Regional self-help associations such as the Mecha and Tulema (an Oromo association), Tigre, Sidamo, and Arussi developed in Addis Ababa. This trend alarmed the government. To discourage further development of ethnically based associations, it banned the meetings of some of these associations. They became nonetheless the focal points for new forms of ethnic consciousness.

State and Ethnicity in Ethiopia

Ethiopian nationalism is the legacy of the Axumite state symbolized by the monarchy, a distinct culture blended with Coptic Christian theology, a language with its own written script, and a myth that developed out of its persistent confrontation with foreign encroachment.

The long history of the Ethiopian state is grounded in the mythology that makes Ethiopia one of the oldest states, linked in its legends to King Solomon, David, and eventually to Christ. Its ideological legitimation was articulated in the medieval works *Fetah Negast* and *Fekere Yesus*. In addition to these myths, the strength of the Ethiopian state was rooted in the forms of its operation and in the incorporation of new groups into the system. Historical evidence indicates that in Ethiopia's early history state power was contested and shifted among different ethnic groups. "During this period Ethiopia was not ruled solely by kings and queens of one tribe. Rather numismatic and epigraphic evidence indicates that Axum was the seat of several ethnic dynasties" (Haile 1991, 4). By the tenth century, the center of state power had moved out of the Solomonic line to the Zagwe—an Agew ethnic group with its capital at Lasta. In 1270 a Tigre/Shoan coalition defeated the Zagwe and restored the Solomonic dynasty. In 1600 the Yejju Oromo controlled the kingdom from Gondar. The seat of the kingdom shifted back and forth between Tigre, Last, Gondar, and Shoa, reflecting regional power struggles. In the late 1800s there was a decisive power split between Tigrean and Shoan ruling classes. Shoa became dominant and consolidated its power around Gojjam, Gondar, and eastern and southern Ethiopia. However, despite its preeminence, the Shoan ruling class failed to eliminate challenges to its domination. A Tigre ruling faction remained strong in Tigre and in parts of Eritrea or Bahr Melash. Except for the period of the reign of emperor Yohannes IV, however, the Tigre aristocracy was relegated to the status of a junior partner in the political and cultural domain of the Ethiopian state. The Tigre strongly resented their inferior status. They repeatedly rebelled against Shoan hegemony and contemplated a Tigre kingdom. They even entertained the idea of creating a Tigre kingdom encompassing the northern region. In the early 1940s this plan was strongly endorsed and pushed by Britain.

This shift toward Tigrean autonomy remains very significant in Ethiopian history since it intensified the power struggle between the northerners, led by the Tigre, and the Shoa. Shoan hegemony is commonly presented as Amhara domination. However, it is erroneous to lump all nationalities included in Shoa as Amhara. Shoa is "the most heterogenous of the ancient Ethiopian provinces with several ethnic and religious groups" (Markakis 1974, 19).

Regardless of the chronic conflict for power, the Abyssinian state as symbolized by the monarch remained a powerful integrative force until 1974. The concept of state, however, went beyond the personality of the monarch. It was a highly developed political structure, regulated by distinct legal codes, such as *Serata Mangest*. The Ethiopian notion of *Mangest* conveys the notion of a state separate from the office of king. The state, with its Tigre/Amhara core culture, exercised unchallenged hegemony. It can be argued that the dominant social segment of the Abyssinian society practiced a very loose form of social closure. Although assimilation into Amhara/Tigre culture was required, the system allowed "anyone (and most obviously successful soldiers), to rise to the position of authority by demonstrating a capacity for leadership" (Clapham 1987, 20). Inclusion in the dominant class was possible through marriage or personal valor. Since medieval times succession to the throne was not strictly within the Solomonic line by primogeniture. Emperors Twedros II, Yohannes IV, Menelik II, and Haile Selassie all had dubious connections to the Solomonic line. Mengistu Haile Mariam, who ruled in imperial style without the title, also exemplifies this tradition. The Ethiopian ruling classes cannot be identified with a particular ethnic group. They are a multi-ethnic group whose only common factors are that they are Christians, Amharic speakers, and claim lineage to the Solomonic line. The only interruption was during the brief Zemene Mesafent period, when Oromo became the language of the imperial court.

Antinomies of Provincialism and Nationalism

The beginning of the "age of the Princes" (1769–1855), Fistame Mangest, the end of a monarchical rule, heralded provincialism. The authority of the central state was completely weakened. The various provincial leaders waged an endemic war, which lasted for one hundred years. The contest for political supremacy not only weakened the evolution of centralism, but also contributed to the development of a strong sense of narrow provincialism, which resisted centralizing policies. In spite of its weakened position, the state remained a contested object. Each powerful feudal lord tried to capture the state or force it to recognize his hereditary right to rule over his province.

The Ethiopian Polities

In 1928 in his *Historia di Ethiopia,* the Italian scholar Conti Rossoni characterized Ethiopia as *un museum di popoli*. This notion of a "museum of peoples" gives an accurate sense of Ethiopia's ethnic, religious, and linguistic diversity. The Ethiopian state, despite its possession of an ancient cultural core, has never been a completely homogenous society or political community. It is similar to medieval empires that "claimed a universal domination, and sought to govern any people whom it was able to bring under its control" (Clapham 1987, 23).

The study of the pluralistic society of Ethiopia has been dominated by ethnographers who have studied each community in isolation from the entire society. In most of these studies, the core culture is perceived as the most powerful assimilating center. The Ethiopian Coptic Orthodox church, the state, the imperial dynasty, and the Amhara-Tigre culture are considered to be the great assimilators of the peripheral regions: "the central theme of Ethiopian history . . . has been the maintenance of a culture core which has adapted itself to the exigencies of time and place, assimilating diverse people" (Gabre Sellasie 1975, 1). The state in Ethiopian history, however, has always been more than the imperial bureaucracies. James A. Quirin writes that the "typical technique of provincial rule in Ethiopia, probably going back as far as Axum, has been the classic 'indirect rule,' whenever local elites could be found who would agree—sometimes after and always involving the threat of military force—to cooperate with the central government" (1990, 12). Along the same lines, Donald Levine (1974) identifies what he calls pan-Ethiopian cultural traits that are commonly shared among the various peoples who live within Ethiopia proper, irrespective of their forms of incorporation.

It is possible to argue that ethnic boundaries in Ethiopia are fluid. The prevailing literature, however, portrays the Amhara as a distinct ethnic category which culturally dominates the whole edifice of Ethiopian society, thereby perpetuating their political domination. This is an erroneous view. "Amhara" does not necessarily imply a distinct ethnic category. Amhara was the name of a small region in Wollo province whose inhabitants spoke Amharic. In 1270 king Yekunno Amelak recruited his army from among Amhara peasants. From this time—for reasons that are not clear—the language of the Amhara peasant warriors became the language of the court and also spread into different regions. Those who speak Amharic today do not have any ethnic affiliation to each other. As all French-speaking Africans are not French, likewise all Amharic speakers are not necessarily Amhara. Therefore it is simply wrong to define the Amhara as "the peoples of the northwestern corner of Ethiopia which is coincident with the old Kingdom of Abyssinia" (Baxter 1983, 129). There is no intra-Amhara ethnic consciousness, except among northern settlers in southern Ethiopia. Most Amharic-speaking individuals identify themselves by the place of their birth. For instance, a person is first a Gojjami, a Wolloye, a Gondari, a Menze, then he is an Amhara. It is also common to find distance on the social scale among the Amharic-speaking or "Amhara." There is a strong sense of localism, a tradition of looking down on another "Amhara." For instance an Amhara from Gojjam rarely considers marriage with a Shoan Amhara or vice versa.

There is no distinct sociological profile of an Amhara because there is no such thing as an Amhara with distinct ethnic attributes. As one sociologist has observed, "The isolation of Amhara traits is difficult even in Gondar and Gojjam . . . let alone Shoa, where acculturation between Amhara and Oromo has been occurring since the fifteenth century" (Salole 1981, 23). There is instead a new sociological category of an Amharanized segment of the Ethiopian society, which consists of a metamorphosis of various ethnic and religious groups. The only common link between members of this group is that they speak Amharic, which they either began learning at birth or acquired later on.

In this case, what is Amhara domination? It is a linguistic and cultural domination by a multi-ethnic group who speak Amharic. As Amharic is the language of the state, its knowledge undoubtedly becomes an indispensable asset for upward mobility. Education which opens access to success in life is conducted in Amharic. This situation deprives all non-Amharic speakers from being part of the dominant political, economic, and cultural group of the nation. In effect it reduces them to second-class citizenship. Therefore the Ethiopian social reality encourages Amharanization. "The 'Sociological Amhara' whatever origin" (Salole 1981, 26) considers himself or herself "civilized"—*Silatane*—and like all other urbanized Amhara will look down on peasant Amhara. This is the organic core of Ethiopian nationalism. The consciousness and affiliation of this Amharanized segment transcend their ethnic origins.

Language in Ethiopia is a contested terrain among various ethnic groups. Each ethnic group wants a privileged status for its language, an essential tool for social mobilization and for the creation of a distinct identity. Linguistic division in Ethiopia shows that 37.7 percent of the polity speak Amharic, 35.3 percent speak Oromo, and the remaining 27 percent are divided among seventy languages, including Tigrigna, which is widely spoken in Tigre and Eritrea (Haile 1986, 471). Amharic is a language widely spoken outside the Amhara region. Incorporation of new groups into the Amhara rule was often preceded by a diffusion of Amhara cultural traits. "Amharic became the lingua franca of the elites of all the regions in the Amhara sphere of influence" (Levine 1974, 74).

Most of the regional rulers of the north, including Emperor Yohannes IV, used

Amharic as the official state language. Amharic was *Lisana Nigus,* "the king's language," and even the Muslim invader Ahmed ibn Ibrahim Al-Ghazi (1529–43) from the Harar region did not change it (Haile 1986, 471). In practical terms the existence of a dominant language in a polyethnic society is a distinct political advantage.

Religion, like language, is a powerful element that provides national identity. Since its introduction to the Axumite kingdom in 330 A.D. the Coptic church has been closely associated with the state. Its association with the state has given it a unique and privileged position as compared to Islam, which arrived on the scene centuries later. The Coptic church was the sole provider of education and literature and the custodian of Abyssinian culture and history. Inter-ethnic contact made Christianity "in the local context the supra-ethnic and supra-tribalist religion which legitimized the existence of a state and an imperial dynasty" (Erlich 1980, 405). In Ethiopia, however, religion does not coincide with ethnicity. Historically there has been a constant clash between Christians and Muslims. Ethiopian rulers considered the country a Christian island surrounded by a sea of hostile Muslims. Despite fear of and hostility toward the Muslims, the early Abyssinian state accepted the reality of living with the non-Christians. To "minimize resistance to their rule they abandoned an initial policy of force, which led to the massacre of non-Christians, and resorted to inducements to local chiefs to accept Christianity, rewarding the converts with gifts and recognition of their local position" (Markakis 1974, 19). Conversion of conquered people was "left to time to solve. As long as the military dominance of the Christians lasted, the inhabitants of the conquered areas were slowly and imperfectly absorbed into the new religious framework" (Tamarat 1972, 173). Haile Selassie's statement, "Hager Ye gara now, haymanot yegel now" ("A country belongs to every one while religion is private") reflects Ethiopia's history of religious tolerance. The degree of religious tolerance, however, varied from one region to another.

The Process of Modernization and Its Impact on Nationalism

During his reign from 1930 to 1974, Emperor Haile Selassie pursued a policy of modernization begun by Menelik II. Modernization is a strong force which can either undermine or forge the bases of nationalism. The policy of the state under Haile Selassie was to create a strong centralized nation. Education was perceived as a vehicle to achieve this goal. Haile Selassie carefully and consciously selected the sons of the traditional elites to attend boarding schools in Addis Ababa. He also introduced institutions such as parliament. By appointing provincial elites to the senate, and keeping them in Addis Ababa, he effectively undermined their political power base. In his drive for centralization, he abolished the federal arrangement in Eritrea. The process of modernization also affected even the Ethiopian Coptic church, which began "to be undermined as the most profound expression of nationalism" under the centralization policies of Haile Selassie I (Erlich 1980, 407). Also contributing to the church's loss of influence was its failure to reinvigorate its social responsibilities. It was unable to grasp the changing realities of the time under the process of modernization. These factors made the nascent elites identify the Ethiopian Orthodox church with backwardness. Like all modernizing monarchs, Haile Selassie's vision of progress lagged behind the thinking of the nascent elite who were produced by the very process he initiated. The 1960s marked a watershed in the history of Ethiopian nationalism. Modernization, however small it was, undermined the traditional social structure. Every facet of the traditional forms of political dominance were challenged by diverse groups, ranging from ethnic groups to radical Marxists.

Christianity remained both the strength and weakness of Ethiopian nationalism. Religious pluralism precluded the Ethiopian state from invoking the historical legacy of Christianity to boost nationalist feelings. The historical contribution of Christianity now appeared in contradiction to the diverse religious groups in Ethiopia. Reinterpretation of historical data from a non-Christian point of view gave it a different meaning to non-Christians such as Muslims, who constitute about 40 percent of the population. On the other hand, it is difficult to untangle the experience of Christianity from the course of Ethiopian history.

The Historical Process of Nation Formation

To comprehend the complexities of the Ethiopian polity, it is useful to look briefly into the history of the process of the making of the modern nation-state of Ethiopia and to compare it with other similar processes. The historical making of Ethiopia is dialectically the source of its strength as well as of its problems.

There are two irreconcilable views of the historical emergence of the Ethiopian state. The first is the view of those who reject the entire historical narrative as an accumulation of myth and legend. Those who hold the second view believe in the significance of the historical mythology. Despite their diametrically opposed views, both groups are pathologically nationalist; the first group is referred to as the micronationalists and the second, as the macronationalists (Tibebu 1987).

According to the micronationalists, the southern, southwestern, and the eastern regions of Ethiopia were incorporated during the reign of Menelik II. The north, in particular Eritrea, was left to the Italians. Menelik could have pursued his 1896 victory at Adowa and driven the Italians to the sea. Thus Adowa is an embodiment of victory and defeat, since from it germinated the current Eritrean problem and the view that Ethiopia is a colonial power that annexed and negotiated territories. Micronationalists feel that Menelik gave away Eritrea despite his victorious position because he never considered it as part of his empire, a de facto recognition that Eritrea was not part of Ethiopia.

A distinction should be made between the old and modern forms of state. The historical Ethiopia, or Abyssinia as it used to be called, belongs to the category of ancient states such as Egypt, Persia, or China. The difference between this and the modern form of state may be traced to the levels of centralization and development in bureaucratic administration. Ethiopia was less centralized than the other ancient states, and the class of professional state functionaries was relatively undeveloped. Furthermore, it is worthwhile to look briefly into the process of modern state formation in Europe and Africa and to make a comparative historical evaluation of the different processes at work.

Charles Tilly has aptly said, "war created the state and the state made war" (1975, 34). He further points out: "The high cost of European state-building was its beginning in the midst of a decentralized, largely peasant social structure. Building differentiated, autonomous, centralized organizations with effective control of territories entailed eliminating or subordinating thousands of semi-autonomous authorities" (1975, 7). The history of modern state formation in Europe shows that most of the population resisted the process of incorporation. It took heavy coercion to subdue people under an effective state control (ibid., 8). Modern states in Europe or Africa are the products of violence. They were not formed on the notion of a Rousseauistic Social Contract. Ethiopia clearly fits this pattern.

In the early 1900s, like most historical states, Ethiopia had very diffuse boundaries. For most historical states "peripheral zones were useful to the central core only for occasional extraction of resources through tribute or seizure of men for war or labor or women for procreation" (Young 1976, 67). Historically it was very difficult for Ethiopian monarchies to create a strong centralized state. The strong regional loyalty and sentiment of local leaders led to fierce resistance. Thus if Ethiopia did not exercise effective control in peripheral regions, its failure to do so should not be seen as an exception. Those who argue for the colonial nature of the Ethiopian state focus on the Shoa region. Menelik II was the culprit. Although he consolidated most of Ethiopia's peripheral regions, it was his predecessor, Emperor Yohannes IV, who defined Ethiopia's territorial boundaries to the European powers. The requirement of demarcated boundaries as proof of effective occupation is a recent phenomenon which came with the advent of colonial competition. Yohannes IV wrote to Kaiser Wilhelm I of Prussia: "To the east and the south [southeast] the boundary is the sea. To the west and north, where there are not seas, it is bounded by Nuba, Suakin, Khartoum, Berber, Sennar, Ennaria, Sudan, and Dongola, Haren Dawa, Gash, Massawa, Budun, Shoho and Tiltal. . . . I listed these places so that my country's boundaries be known" (Gabre Sellasie 1975, 258).

For the macronationalists, Ethiopia, as the oldest empire and independent state in Africa, is a source of pride as well as an inspiration not only to all people who live within the current geographical confines of Ethiopia but also to other Africans as well. When in 1936 Ethiopia was invaded by Italy, this act of aggression aroused a sense of anger even among African-Americans in the United States—not only because the invasion offended a simple sense of justice but also because the historically independent Abyssinia was a source of pride for blacks who were politically conscious. For instance, African-Americans demonstrated against Italy and set up committees to collect relief materials as well as to recruit volunteers. For early pan-Africanists like Jomo Kenyata and Kwame Nkrumah, the occupation of Ethiopia was one of the saddest moments in their lives. But to the micronationalist, the 1936 Ethio-Italian war is seen as a struggle between imperial rivals.

An ethnic or regional group may withdraw its membership and legitimacy from the state if the group feels that a change in the socioeconomic structure may put it at a disadvantage. Under given sociopolitical conditions, the group will redefine its positions. Eritrean politics can be cited as an example. Eritrea is a surgical creation of Italy. The African region first came under Italian rule in 1889 through the Treaty of Wuchall which was denounced by Menelik II only four years after he had signed it. In 1935, under Mussolini, Italy invaded Ethiopia and soon thereafter combined Ethiopia with Eritrea and Italian Somaliland to create Italian East Africa. Under Italian rule, national sentiment was nonexistent (Araya 1990, 82). Eritrean consciousness became significant only with the end of Italian rule. When the British Trust Administration replaced the Italians, the possible emergence of controlling constituencies forced the political parties in Eritrea to resort to ethnic and religious mobilization to decide on the political future of the territory. A cleavage was created between two major parties: those who advocated, and those who rejected union with Ethiopia. The unionists invoked the glory of past Ethiopian history. Tedla Bairu, a prominent Eritrean unionist, argued: "We are Ethiopians, but we have been apart from our country for more than sixty years." Mengistu Haile Mariam, until his demise from power in May of 1991, invoked the slogan "mother Ethiopia or death." The same slogan was used among the unionist Eritreans (Araya 1990, 82). The constituents of the anti-unionist movement, the Moslem League, categorically denied any link with Ethiopia, invoking instead the sufferings of Muslims under the Christian rulers of Ethiopia. Although today the Eritrean Peoples Liberation Front (EPLF) claims the nonexistence of ethnic antagonism, such antagonism within Eritrea is not uncommon. Ethnic, linguistic, and religious diversity is alive and well in Eritrea.

The Debate on the National Question

Prior to 1974 the idea of nationalism was discussed only within radical student groups in Ethiopia. The topic was otherwise taboo. Probably Ethiopia as a nation did not face major challenges from any one ethnic group, and even if there was some movement it did not pose a serious threat to the integration of the state. However, the process of political modernization will inevitably force ethnic issues to the forefront. As Samuel S. Huntington has aptly put it, "Ethnic or religious groups which have lived peacefully side by side in traditional society become aroused to violent conflict as a result of the interaction, the tension, the inequalities generated by social and economic modernization" (1968, 39).

Around 1965 discussions of regionalism and nationalism began to surface. Ethiopian students in the period following 1960 were heavily influenced by Marxist ideas. The Ethiopian left readily absorbed Marxism-Leninism and adopted it as a panacea for regionalism and other problems that afflicted the country. The most provocative statement on the question of nationalities was published in November of 1969 in an Addis Ababa University student paper editorial (*Struggle* 17 [1969]: 11). It openly declared that Ethiopia is not a nation but a collection of states ruled by the Amhara/Tigre. It argued for the right of nations to self-determination and for the necessity of armed struggle to achieve these goals. Since its publication, the Ethiopian left has remained obsessed with the question of nationalities. Like their fellow students in Ethiopia, members of the Ethiopian Student Union in North America (ESUNA) were engaged in the debate on the national question. In 1976 ESUNA dedicated a special issue of its journal to the "National Question," in which it supported the right of self-determination.

The Ethiopian left has remained divided on the interpretation of self-determination. To some, self-determination is conditional; it should be supported only if it promotes the rights of revolutionary social classes—in particular, the proletariat. To others, the right to self-determination is unconditional and should be exercised regardless of its impact on other revolutionary social classes. This division in opinion led to an armed conflict between the Ethiopian Peoples Revolutionary Party (EPRP) and the Tigre Liberation Front (TLF), later changed to Tigre People's Liberation Front (TPLF). Both groups conducted guerrilla war against the Dergue from Tigre. The EPRP advocated the primacy of class over ethnicity, while TPLF advocated resolving the national question first. The TPLF, EPLF, and the Dergue, in a rare political agreement, attacked the EPRP and ousted it from the Tigre region. The Oromo Liberation Front (OLF) dismissed the whole episode as a struggle for power among northerners which had nothing to do with the Oromo. With the defeat of the EPRP, the TPLF emerged as a formidable force against the Dergue, one which the Dergue did not recognize as a threat until late. This failure resulted from the fact that, compared to Eritrea, Tigre was considered the heartland of Ethiopia. The Dergue believed that the TPLF's occasional demand for self-determination would not receive wide support. Therefore, the movement would not pose any serious danger to Ethiopia's national integrity. The TPLF, however, gathered together all the anti-Dergue resistance groups under its leadership, calling this new, larger group the Ethiopian Peoples Democratic Revolutionary Force (EPDRF). The EPDRF's policy on the question of nationalities reflects that of its dominant member, the TPLF. It is strongly committed to ethnic representation and the right of Eritrea to be independent.

In 1991, Ethiopian politics of ethnicity changed drastically, beyond the expectations of many observers. The EPLF achieved a military victory and the EPDRF toppled the Dergue. On 1 July 1991, the EPDRF convened a conference of opposition groups to discuss a transitional government. The conference excluded many groups, and the way in which it was conducted created resentment and anger among many. This casts doubt on the possibility of Ethiopia achieving a lasting peace.

Nationalities Perception of the 1974 Revolution

The 1974 social revolution brought ethnic issues to the forefront of political debate. Each nationality began to evaluate the revolution through its own ethnic prism.

Following the revolution of 1974, the Oromo became more visible and active participants in the revolution. An Oromo intellectual, Haile Fida, was appointed as the head of the Provisional Office of Mass Organizational Affairs (POMA). POMA was established in 1976 by the Dergue to lay down the foundation for a workers' party and to conduct political education. Of the fifteen appointed members of POMA, nine were members of the All Ethiopian Socialist Movement (known by its Amharic acronym as MEISON). MEISON was perceived to be an Oromo organization under a Marxist guise. MEISON cadres were appointed to all provincial and district political offices. Both northerners (Amhara and Tigre) and some Western observers considered the Dergue and its political structure to be dominated by Oromo. Northerners seemed to be systematically excluded.

The Dergue saw the north as the bastion of counter-revolution. It was the home of the pro-monarchist opposition groups, Ethiopian Democratic Union (EDU), the EPRP, TPLF, and EPLF. Consequently, regions like Gondar and Gojjam were repeatedly bombed for supporting anti-government groups.

The economic policies of the Dergue, in particular those concerning land reform, produced an unintended effect of exacerbating ethnic tension in Ethiopia. In some regions of the south, the land tenure systems of prerevolutionary Ethiopia were the outcome of the centralization process of the Ethiopian state under Menelik II and Haile Selassie I. The state expropriated part of the land belonging to the local populations and distributed it to soldiers and officials (mostly nonlocals) sent to administer the regions. Therefore, the struggle over the implementation of the 1975 land reform was split along clear-cut ethnic lines. It became a north/south struggle. In this struggle, the northerners, who traditionally have held land, have had the upper hand. In order to enforce the implementation of the postrevolutionary land policies, the Dergue was forced to disarm landowners and create armed peasant militia which could defend themselves. To the northerners this policy was another indication that the Dergue favored the Oromo groups.

In spite of what appeared to be their favored status, the initial support of Oromo for the Dergue began to decline. The Oromo felt that the Dergue did not go far enough in resolving the national question. The Dergue, in its conflicting policies, wavered between praising nationalities groups and then castigating them for raising issues that were narrowly nationalist. The Oromo saw the Dergue as becoming dominated by Amhara/Tigre groups and as unable, therefore, to redress ethnic grievances. The deteriorating relations between the Dergue and the Oromo was worsened by the Ethiopia-Somalia conflict. Somali insurgents were supposedly supported by Oromo in the Harar and Bale regions. This alleged support made the Dergue question the loyalty of the population of those regions. In a reversal of its earlier policy, the Dergue rearmed northern settlers of the region against the opposition of the Oromo.

The revolution was unable to project an image that transcended these contradictory positions. In fact the Dergue, lacking a stable political base, had carefully exploited these underlying tensions. It fostered fear and tension between different ethnic groups to strengthen its political position.

Ethnic Policies of the Dergue

When the Dergue assumed power, resolving Ethiopia's economic problems and protecting its territorial integrity remained the major concerns. Like most military regimes, the Dergue believed the solution to these problems was an eradication of the political and economic corruption of the civilian government. The Dergue saw the most serious challenge to Ethiopia's integrity as the Eritrean problem but thought this challenge was capable of resolution once a clean and progressive government was securely in power. The intelligentsia and the Dergue believed that the various ethnic challengers would lay down their arms and participate in the revolution. The Eritrean fronts were seen as being opposed to Haile Selassie and also appeared to have socialist views. Optimism about Eritrean peace rose even higher when head of state Aman Andom (of Eritrean origin himself) visited the region twice and received wide support from the general public. In his address to mass rallies in Eritrea, Aman said that, "Eritrea had chosen of her own volition to federate with Ethiopia, and by placing the blame for the past misdeeds on the previous administration, . . . he appealed to the Eritreans to join the rest of Ethiopia" (Gabre-Sellassie 1976, 139). The Dergue also pulled back the army from Eritrea to facilitate negotiations. The Eritrean nationalist fronts, however, took advantage of the political chaos of the center and intensified their struggle. In response to Aman's overtures, they responded by calling General Aman Andom "an Eritrean traitor and a stooge of the Ethiopian government" and by claiming that a "political solution cannot be accomplished by means of sending stooges to Eritrea" (Gabre-Sellassie 1976, 139). This rejection, which coincided with an internal political struggle within the Dergue, resulted in the execution of eighty former officials, including General Aman Andom, who was accused of refusing authorization, when minister of defense, to send additional troops to Eritrea, of contacting foreign ambassadors without consulting the Dergue, and of instigating the armed forces to topple the Dergue.

The Dergue pursued a contradictory policy regarding nationalities issues. It advocated various extreme positions, ranging from signaling support for self-determination to an absolute rejection of any compromise on nationalities issues. Behind these inconsistencies, however, there were some persistent policies that the Dergue pursued. The search for a solution to the Eritrean problem was dominated by three considerations: (1) the impact that any concession to Eritrea might have on the other Ethiopian nationalities; (2) the belief in the possibility of weakening the nationalist fronts militarily (this belief was firmly clung to by higher echelon policy-makers primarily because of the domination of Ethiopian political discourse by the armed forces); and (3) the opportunity of using the political differences within the Eritrean fronts to weaken their military strength.

In 1975 a position paper on nationalities issues was prepared by an ad hoc governmental committee. The committee consisted of individuals from six ministries. Its recommendation was endorsed by the Council of Ministers and was then submitted to the head of state, General Teferi Banti. Six alternative solutions were suggested in this recommendation: (1) grant self-administration to all the provinces with their own parliaments and administrators; (2) restore the former status to the province of Eritrea; (3) restore the province of Eritrea, but incorporate the region of Asab to Tigre; (4) create two federal states, one consisting of Eritrea and Tigre and the second compromising all the remaining regions; (5) create a federal structure based on cultural and linguistic similarities, including Oromo, Tigre, Amharic, and Sidama language groupings; (6) create a federal structure based on existing administrative regions. The Dergue quietly shelved this recommendation.

During this phase of the revolution, the Dergue was strongly influenced by the Chinese model of socialism. It was very suspicious of and even hostile toward the Soviets because of the support they gave the Eritreans and Somalia. The Chinese delivered to Ethiopia literally tons of Mao's selected works, which were freely distributed to students and the public at large. They sent thousands of experts to Ethiopia, and the Chinese Ambassador occasionally toured the provinces. When

Mao died, the Dergue suggested erecting a statue of him in Addis Ababa. The course of the revolution as well as the national question was to be resolved according to the Chinese model. As a result, on 20 April 1976 the National Democratic Revolution Program (NDRP) was proclaimed. NDRP, which was based on Chairman Mao's theory of revolution, outlined the stages and the tasks of a revolution. The Ethiopian NDRP contained the first ethnic policy of the state. The document stated that "the right to self-determination of all nationalities will be recognized and fully respected. No nationality will dominate another one since the history, culture, language and religion of each nationality will have equal recognition in accordance with the spirit of socialism. The unity of Ethiopia's nationalities will be based on their common struggle against feudalism, imperialism, bureaucratic capitalism and all reactionary forces." The document correctly stated that ethnic groups in the periphery have been neglected and excluded from the Ethiopian polity. The concrete application of NDRP's policy was to bestow self-government upon each nationality. It envisaged the use of each nationality's own language, autonomous decision-making in internal socioeconomic affairs, and the election of its own administrators. On 16 May 1976, a nine-point peace plan was drawn up based on the new policy to address the Eritrean political problem.

A delegation of Dergue members was sent to various Arab states to explain the new policy and solicit their support. Neither the liberation fronts nor the Arab states, however, paid any attention to the policy. The policy also failed to get support from some leftist political organizations, such as the EPRP, on the ground that it was drawn up without the consultation and involvement of the populations involved.

In June of 1976, Mengestu Haile Mariam made a secret visit to China to solicit arms; he had very limited success. Earlier, another delegation headed by Sisaye Habte, a prominent Dergue member, had been sent to Vietnam to get spare parts for the American-made fighter planes of the Ethiopian Air Force. The delegation returned with no success. In response to these various defeats, a debate was carried on within the Dergue on the practicality of following the Chinese model. The argument was made that within the socialist countries only the Soviet Union had a strong enough influence over "radical" Arab states to stop their support to Eritrea. Therefore, the Soviet Union was the only power that could provide heavy arms in addition to exerting its influence. The Soviet Union, which had been alarmed by the growing influence of the Chinese in Ethiopia, was quick to respond to many requests when approached by the Dergue. Thus the Chinese influence diminished in Ethiopia.

Once the political support of the Soviets was secured, the Dergue began to promote a modified Soviet model for the nationalities problem in Ethiopia. Some Dergue members, including Lieutenant Negussie Negassa, an Oromo, were sent to Yugoslavia to study the nationalities issues. Both the Dergue and the Soviets favored regional autonomy. In a 1979 publication by the Ethiopian Revolution Information Center (p. 70), the Dergue argued that "there was only a quantitative, not qualitative difference between regional autonomy and federation."

The Dergue instructed the Council of Ministers to prepare a document on the nationalities question. The Council in turn created a committee of experts from various ministries to prepare the document.[1] The task of this committee was to revise earlier studies along socialist lines. The committee was instructed to study the experience of eastern European countries, and a study tour to these countries was made. Some Dergue members were sent even to North Korea for consultation.[2]

In March of 1983 an Ethiopian Institute of Nationalities was created. Members of the institute were appointed by the Dergue, and the ideological wing of the party supervised the work of this institute. Most of its work was kept in absolute secrecy. Although there is no official publication of the institute, some members reported that they had concluded a survey of the cultural and ethnic composition in many parts of Ethiopia. The intransigency of both the Dergue and the Eritrean fronts, however, made any possible compromises proposed by the institute difficult to effect. The Dergue worsened the condition by restructuring the old administrative regions as a solution to the nationalities question, creating what it calls self-governing regions. According to this plan: (1) highland Eritrea would be self-governing; (2) highland Tigre, Asseb Dire Dawa, and Ogaden were designated as self-governing areas; and (3) about twenty-four new administrative structures were designated for the rest of the country.

The difference between areas designated as self-governing regions and the others was that the administrations in the self-governing areas would not need approval for promulgating laws and statutes, provided that they were not contrary to the statutes passed by the National Assembly. They could develop plans for economic development and conduct other services such as education, health, and security. The other twenty-four regions would have similar rights, provided they received prior approval by the National Assembly. On 1 February 1987 a new constitution was approved by a national referendum. The new constitution explicitly recognized religious and ethnic pluralism. Article 1.1 stated that "the Ethiopian state has from the beginning, been a multi-national state"; article 2 emphasized centralism by declaring Ethiopia a unitary state which "shall ensure the equality of nationalities, combat chauvinism and narrow nationalism." Pluralism was also reflected in the membership of the 122-seat Central Committee, which included the Patriarch of the Orthodox Church, the chairman of the Supreme Islamic Council, and the heads of the Lutheran and Catholic councils in Ethiopia. In the list of members, thirty-one had Moslem names, fifty-nine had non-Amhara/Tigre names, twenty-one were women, and a number of individuals were from the old nobilities.

The 1974 Revolution and Its Impact on the Question of Nationalism

The old notion of Ethiopian nationalism was unable to transform itself and incorporate new notions of nationalism based on cultural, political, and social equality of its members. Everything that symbolized the old Ethiopian nationalism, such as the Coptic church, the monarch, and ancient histories became irrelevant. The multi-ethnic Ethiopian aristocracy had retained its cohesion through marriages and patronage. The revolution eliminated this segment of society and with it a powerful symbol of the old nationalism, but was unable to create a cohesive ideology of new nationalism.

The hard-line Marxist-Leninist ideology of the Dergue worsened the problem. It alienated religious groups—Christians and Muslims alike. In particular, the Ethiopian Coptic Orthodox Church lost its land as well as its annual government budget. To the dismay of the ecclesiastics, the Dergue also intervened in the election process of the Patriarch.

Many northerners, who were also the reservoir of Ethiopian nationalism, lost their land in the south. In addition to land reform, other nationalization policies of the Dergue greatly antagonized many social groups. This conflict led the northerners to withdraw their recognition of the legitimacy of the regime, an acceptance of which was essential to the strength of the new nationalism. The degree to which individuals identify themselves with the state to a large extent determines its legitimacy, which in turn determines the amount of support a regime can expect. This identification with the state was also undermined in the Christian stronghold of northern Ethiopia when the rumor spread that the Dergue was a Moslem state which was prepared to eliminate the Coptic Orthodox Church and religion. The repressive nature of the regime also greatly alienated various segments of intellectuals, including members of the Ethiopian diaspora. Most intellectuals were caught in the situation where espousing nationalism amounted to supporting a repressive regime. As a result of this political situation, a malaise, or to use Gramsci's phrase a "pessimism of the intellect," grew among Ethiopian intellectuals, a good number of whom are uprooted exiles. Thus beyond the day-to-day issues of survival, Ethiopian intellectuals are no longer engaged in intellectual debates or in problematizing the political situation of Ethiopia. Intellectuals are key to forming, shaping and nursing nationalism. Any new nationalism must be expected to suffer without the intellectuals who are the key to forming, shaping, and nursing its growth. On the other hand, intellectuals and elites of different ethnic groups have been actively engaged in raising ethnic consciousness and ethnic identity. It is difficult to predict where this engagement with ethnicity might lead. Raising ethnic consciousness and identity as a matter of principle cannot be equated with supporting the claims of all members of an ethnic group. In real politics, the elites will tend to fan the sentiments of the masses to maximize their own political positions.

The new Ethiopian intelligentsia is divided and unprepared to face the new problems that inflict the country. As Marina and David Ottoway have noted, "what was most striking in the Ethiopian revolution was not the factionalism of the leftist intellectuals *per se* or the acrimony of their debate, but the fact that they seemed largely disconnected from reality" (1978, 113–14).

The Eritrean problem which poses a challenge to Ethiopian nationalism appears to have a military solution. The EPDRF's open support for Eritrean independence has undermined its legitimacy to a section of the population that espoused Ethiopian nationalism. Besides, other ethnic groups such as the Oromo have openly challenged that the EPDRF is simply a Tigrean front. Thus, the EPDRF is already encountering resistance by various groups. Similarly in Eritrea, the EPLF is facing resistance, in particular from the Afar.

A new Ethiopia is in the process of being formed. The Ethiopian state seems to be afflicted with the current Soviet and Yugoslavian ethnic syndrome. The task ahead of the new builders of Ethiopian nationalism is to synthesize a notion of nationalism that transcends the old and accommodates the new. If this new nationalism should succeed in taking hold, it might even yet sway the Eritreans from seceding. But so far there appears to be no widely agreed upon solution to the ethnic problems of Ethiopia. The various war-weary nationalities have only taken time out from the vocation of war.

NOTES

1. I was a member of this committee representing the Ministry of Land Reform. My participation was cut short after the fourth session of meetings when MEISON used all possible means of coercion to force out non-MEISON political line supporters.

2. North Korea does not have an ethnic or nationalities problem. The Dergue members were sent there because Mengestu Haile Mariam was a strong admirer of the leader of North Korea. He not only made frequent visits, but forced all the political cadres to wear North Korean–style jackets.

REFERENCES

Araya, Mesfin. 1990. The Eritrean Question: An Alternative Explanation. *The Journal of Modern African Studies* 28, 1: 79–100.

Baxter, Paul. 1983. The Problem *of* the Oromo or the Problem *for* the Oromo? In *Nationalism and Self-Determination in the Horn of Africa,* edited by I. M. Lewis, 129–49. London: Ithaca Press.

Clapham, Christopher. 1987. *Transformation and Continuity in Revolutionary Ethiopia*. Cambridge: Cambridge University Press.

Crabites, Pierre. 1935–36. The Abyssinian "Superiority Complex." *Catholic World* 142, 13: 10–17.

Epstein, Arnold L. 1978. *Ethos and Identity*. London: Tavistock Publications.

Erlich, Haggi. 1980. The Horn of Africa and the Middle East: Politization of Islam in the Horn and Depoliticization of Ethiopian Christianity. In *Modern Ethiopia*, edited by Joseph Tubiana, 399–408. Rotterdam: Balkema.

Gabre Sellassie, Zewde. 1976. *Eritrea and Ethiopia: In the Context of the Red Sea*. Woodrow Wilson International Center for Scholars. Unpublished manuscript.

Gabre Sellassie, Zewde. 1975. *Yohannes IV of Ethiopia: A Political Biography*. Oxford: Clarendon Press.

Geertz, C., ed. 1963. *Old Societies and New States: Modernity in Africa and Asia* (New York: Free Press).

Haile, Getachew. 1991. Democracy in Post Dergue Ethiopia. *Imbylta* 1, 3/4: 2–8.

Haile, Getachew. 1986. The Unity and Territorial Integrity of Ethiopia. *The Journal of African Studies* 24, 3: 465–87.

Huntington, Samuel S. 1968. *Political Order in Changing Societies*. New Haven: Yale University Press.

Levine, Donald N. 1974. *Greater Ethiopia: The Evolution of Multiethnic Society*. Chicago: University of Chicago Press.

Markakis, John. 1974. *Ethiopia: Anatomy of a Traditional Polity*. Addis Ababa: Oxford University Press.

Nairn, Tom. 1977. *The Break-up of Britain*. London: New Left Books.

Ottaway, Marina, and David Ottaway. 1978. *Ethiopia: Empire in Revolution*. New York: Africana Publication.

Quirin, James A. 1990. *Ethnicity, Caste, Class and State in Ethiopian History: The Case of the Beta Israel (Falasha)*. Paper presented at NEH Summer Seminar, University of Wisconsin-Madison.

Salole, Gerry. 1981. Who Are the Showans? *Horn of Africa* 3, 1: 20–28.

Tamrat, Tadesse. 1972. *Church and State in Ethiopia: 1270–1527*. Oxford: Clarendon Press.

Teshale, Tibebu. 1987. Process of State Formation in Modern Ethiopia, 1850–1974. *Proceedings: 2nd International Conference on the Horn of Africa*, 13–14. New York: New School of Social Research.

Tilly, Charles, ed. 1975. *The Formation of National States in Western European State-Making*. Princeton: Princeton University Press.

Young, Crawford. 1982–83. The Temple of Ethnicity. *World Politics* 35, 4: 653–62.

Young, Crawford. 1976. *The Politics of Cultural Pluralism*. Madison: University of Wisconsin Press.

8

Ethnicity in Ethiopia: The View from Below (and from the South, East, and West)

■ ■ ■

HERBERT S. LEWIS

IN JUNE 1991, after the fall of Mengistu Haile Mariam's "Dergue," the government that had controlled the empire of Ethiopia since 1974, the Eritrean Peoples Liberation Front (EPLF) made it clear that Eritrea was effectively independent of Ethiopia. On 1 July a totally unprecedented national conference was convened in Addis Ababa in order to reorganize the rest of Ethiopia. Twenty-seven political organizations, nineteen of them explicitly based on ethnic (or "national") groups, emerged from exile or from the countryside to participate in an attempt to reconstruct Ethiopia on a whole new foundation. With no dissent the delegates declared their belief in the human and democratic political rights of individuals, and with only a little argument they affirmed "the right of nations, nationalities, and peoples" to preserve their identities and cultures, administer their own affairs, and exercise the right to independence when they are convinced that these rights are "denied, abridged, or abrogated" ("Ethiopia: A Nation in Transition," *The Ethiopian Mirror* [September/October 1991]; Lewis 1991).

Ethnic opposition groups in Ethiopia had long claimed that they were dominated primarily by one group, the Amhara, and their leaders now declared that this era was finished. The rebellions of various ethnic groups that had begun to take shape in the 1960s had finally resulted in their triumph. The reaction of many members of the educated elite in Addis Ababa, however, was not always so positive. Fears were expressed about the potential breakup (dare one say the "balkanization"?) of Ethiopia. Around the University of Addis Ababa, many well-educated Ethiopians were saying that an attempt to divide the country along ethnic lines would be ridiculous as well as disastrous because so much intermixture and intermarriage had taken place that it was difficult to say who was what, or where one's ethnic homeland might be (Dawit Wolde Giorgis 1989, 117).

Another line of argument denied that the Amhara dominated all the other peoples, claiming instead that the ruling group was actually the "Shoans"—a mixed population from Shoa province composed of Amhara, Tigre, Oromo, and even Eritreans and Gurage. Still others denied that the Amhara comprise a distinctive group at all, or they stressed the social and political distance between the Shoa Amhara and the Amhara of the more northerly provinces, a position taken by Solomon Gashaw in this volume. Or they pointed out, not without some justice, that the Amhara and Tigre peasants had *also* suffered from the monarchical and socialist regimes. (See the discussion of competing views in Triulzi 1983.)

Similarly, the respected student of Ethiopian politics, Christopher Clapham, contends that the Ethiopian central government, "far from being the Amhara preserve, as the mythology of the opposition movements claims, readily provides positions of power for Oromos, Gurages, Aderes, Wollaytas, or Kambattas." (1990, 228). He points to the undeniable fact that some non-Amhara rose to positions of prominence and power both before and after the revolution of 1974. He claims, therefore, that "the system is not ethnically exclusive" (ibid., 222) and considers the cries of the opposition that they have been dominated by the Amhara to be just a stick with which to beat the regime.[1]

In his introductory chapter Crawford Young states that the Ethiopian state mythology has created an "unusually powerful discourse of nationhood." He shrewdly adds, "at least to the intelligentsia." He might also have added, to the *Amhara* intelligentsia in particular, for it is largely, though not solely, their ideology that is recorded in the state mythology.

In this chapter I argue that this "discourse of nationhood" in Ethiopia, and the attempts to downplay ethnic distinctiveness and grievances as well as the extent of Amhara domination, are not based on the realities of life in much of Ethiopia. They represent the partial (in both senses of the word) view of a very influential elite. Although this view may be supported by reason, by personal experiences in elite institutions, and by much of the conventional political wisdom of our time, it is severely limited. It is focused on the north, northwest, and the "modern" sector of Addis Ababa and other major towns and shows no awareness of the conditions of the lives and attitudes of the great majority of the people of Ethiopia who live in the rest of the country.

The conventional wisdom also demonstrates a surprising lack of sensitivity, for the 1990s, to the plight, the feelings, and the reactions of educated elites—all around the world—who come from subordinate ethnic groups. Frequently they have "made it" at the cost of denying their own cultures, languages, and traditions—their own people. Many are not comfortable with this fact, and these days quite a few are rebelling. To others with their own interests, or to those with statist or Marxist commitments, this rebellion may seem like no more than flagrant political opportunism. I suggest that this is not a profitable way to understand what is happening in the 1990s.

By taking a much broader view, one not based on the north and the centers of power, and by trying to get a sense of the experiences and the feelings of the large majority of Ethiopia's peoples, both the country people and the elite, we will be better able to understand the events that are occurring in Ethiopia today.

Origins of the Modern Empire

Although Ethiopia (or Abyssinia) has a history of monarchies stretching back more than two millenia, until the nineteenth century these kingdoms and principalities were restricted primarily to the northwestern part of Ethiopia, especially the regions of Gojjam, Begemder, Tigre, and parts of Shoa, Wollo, and Eritrea. At various times during the past thousand years, northern influence and control of tributaries evidently extended further south and east, but the modern empire was created only during the last 110 years as a result of the rapid southward military expansion of the Amhara rulers of Shoa.

The old Ethiopian empire had fallen apart late in the eighteenth century, and during what is known as "the era of the princes" many rival pretenders fought for supremacy (Abir 1968). These came from three main groups: the Amhara, the Tigre (the Habash or Habesha)—both of which speak related Semitic languages and represent the Ethiopian Christian tradition—and the northernmost Oromo groups, the Azebu, Raya, Yeju, and those of Wollo and northern Shoa. The Oromo (or Galla, as they were generally called then) had joined Ethiopia's political competition in the sixteenth century, but most retained their own language and identity, although some became Christian or Muslim. The Tigre, speakers of the language called Tigrinya, were located in what is today Tigre province and in south-central Eritrea, while the Amhara were divided into a number of groups, notably those in Gondar (Begemder), Shoa, Gojjam, and Wollo.

In 1889 the era of the princes ended as the Amhara king of Shoa, Menelik II, assumed the title of emperor ("king of kings") and established his supremacy over the other northern groups. Even before this, however, he had begun his conquests beyond the confines of the old Abyssinia/Ethiopia. From 1875 to 1898 Menelik expanded his empire to four or five times its original size, almost to the borders it now has (Perham 1948, 294–95; Marcus 1975, 64ff.). It is undeniable and significant that the victorious forces included Tigre and Oromo, as well as members of other populations, both as simple soldiers and as commanders, who saw their chances and took them. But the ultimate control, the glory, and the prevailing influence was to be that of the Shoan Amhara.

The Ethiopian empire was formed during the same period that the British and French African empires were, and with many of the same means: through a series of conquests, some of them quite brutal. If peoples about to be attacked submitted without a fight, they might be permitted to keep their own leaders and some amount of internal autonomy (Lewis 1965; Triulzi 1986). If not, they might be dealt with through massacre, expropriation, and dislocation, as in the case of the Kafa (Perham 1948, 318–22; see Hinnant 1990, 66 ff. on the Guji Oromo region). While keeping Ethiopia free of European domination and creating the "unusually powerful discourse of nationhood," Emperors Yohannis IV, Tewodros II, Menelik II, and Haile Selassie I subjugated many other peoples.

Following the conquest came domination of the new subjects by an alien and exploitative elite, who through the first half-century, at least, took whatever of value they could and gave virtually nothing in return. (For a sense of this rule in various settings, see the chapters in Donham and James 1986.) The vast majority of the newly conquered peoples were not related to their conquerors in language, religion, or other aspects of culture. They had little or no shared history—unless they had been enemies in the past—and frequently had little in common. The new rulers, their natural human ethnocentrism combining with their exalted positions, did not respect their subjects or their cultures. In his book, *Greater Ethiopia* (1974), Donald N. Levine correctly points to certain cultural elements which seem to be shared among many of the peoples of Ethiopia, but these are more readily discerned and appreciated by disinterested anthropologists and historians than by landowners and soldiers who are engaged in struggles for control and worldly gain. Sometimes there were also physical differences between the conquerors and their subjects, and the generally lighter northern highlanders did not lack words to insult and stigmatize the darker peoples of the south and the Sudanese border region.

The vast territories that Menelik's forces conquered had been under the control of autonomous peoples. Some, such as the people of Kafa, Janjero, Male, Hadiya, Kambata, Walamo, and of six different Oromo regions, had their own kings and queens. Others had no states but ran their affairs through a wide variety of sociopolitical arrangements. Among these were political systems based on elections of officials, large assemblies, and various associations such as age-grades (Asmarom Legesse 1973; Baxter and Almagor 1978; Lewis 1974). These systems were especially important to the nonmonarchical groups of the widespread Oromo people. Thus while monarchies had existed among some of the conquered peoples, others had maintained a high degree of egalitarianism. The northern conquerors established their control over peoples who had had a very wide range of structures and practices, and usually ignored or destroyed them.

Whereas most of the northerners professed the distinctive Orthodox Christianity of Ethiopia, many of the conquered peoples, such as the Afar, the Somali, some Gurage, and many Oromo, were Muslim. A great many others held to their own distinctive religions. The new rulers brought in Christian priests, assigned them land for their churches and their maintenance, and accorded them the right to make local people work for them.

Language is the most important single marker of ethnic difference in Ethiopia, and the people of the areas added to the empire speak approximately seventy different languages. These range from those that are spoken by only a few thousand or tens of thousands of people, to those that have hundreds of thousands or a million or more speakers each, to the Oromo with at least fifteen million speakers. There has been no proper census in Ethiopia, and recent population estimates in the range of fifty million are apparently just guesses, projections based on earlier guesses. Any estimates as to numbers or percentages of peoples are likewise of uncertain reliability, but it is widely believed that the Oromo account for perhaps 40 percent of the total population of all of Ethiopia. The other largest groups, perhaps with more than a million each, are the Somali, Wolaita (Walamo), Sidama, Hadiya, and Gurage, along with the Afar, Kambata, and Gedeo (Darasa).[2] Although their numbers then and now are not known with any certainty, and although the extent and nature of ethnic identities and awareness varies greatly, changes over time, and is still being created, one fact stands out: the Amhara and their allies were masters of many peoples who greatly outnumbered them, perhaps by three to one.

These peoples, independent as of 1870, speaking their own languages, following their own customs, political systems, and religions, pursuing their own ecological and economic regimes, were reduced to the status of subject peoples by about 1900. It is necessary to know more about the nature of the regime that controlled them in order to appreciate the complaint that so many have today of "Amhara domination."

Ethiopian Rule in the Conquered Areas of the South, East, and West

There seems to be no debate about the harshness of Ethiopian colonial rule and especially rule at the local level. By all accounts this rule was remarkably basic, crude, and exploitative. The Amhara did not hide behind the cloak of a "civilizing mission" (Shack 1966). From the beginning, local administration was put in the hands of the victorious soldiers, *neft'enya* ("riflemen, armed retainers"), as they are known and execrated. Their only qualifications for the task were their possession of guns and the good fortune to have signed up for the campaigns.

The conquerors established a series of fortified towns (*ketema*) and garrisoned troops in and around them. For their support the new rulers and their troops were apportioned local farmers (*gebbar,* "tribute giver"), who were forced to deliver wealth to their new masters and were expected to provide a wide range of labor services. Not surprisingly their masters tried to extract the maximum profit possible (see Triulzi 1983; Donham 1986; McClellan 1986; and Hinnant 1990 for discussions of *neft'enya* rule; for an outsider's vivid and angry view of Amhara rule in an Oromo area in the late 1960s, see Baxter 1978, 1980, 1983). These landlords, "whether holding official positions or not, exercised administrative, police, and judicial functions within their estates" (Markakis and Nega 1978, 26). There were, of course, many local variations, and in time, in some areas, the *gebbar* system often became a simple sharecropping arrangement, with the descendants of the northern troops as the leading landlords. And some areas, such as Gurage country, were not attractive to northern settlers and thus suffered less (Shack 1966, 25). Regardless of local differences, however, the outlines of this exploitative system are clear.

Usually some indigenous political leaders were also rewarded with grants of land and authority by the emperor. These *balabbat* were meant to serve as further instruments of rule for the emperor and the alien elite. As with the chiefs appointed to similar positions by the European colonial rulers, they were to serve primarily by organizing labor and resources (for the central government and the *neft'enya*), assessing and collecting taxes, and helping to keep order. The manner in which an individual or groups played their roles could vary greatly, of course. Donald Donham (1986) contends that the *balabbat* among the Maale became, in effect, Amharized Ethiopian landlords, while Charles W. McClellan (1986) offers a view of the Gedeo *balabbat* as men in the middle trying, and sometimes succeeding, to be loyal and helpful to their own people.

From the late 1950s on, as the Ethiopian bureaucracy and modern sector developed, more salaried administrators were sent to govern these areas. They were still overwhelmingly either Amhara or other northerners, and anyone who expected to succeed in any government position had to conform to Amhara models and to speak Amharic. Whether they and the *neft'enya* were actually Amhara, or only half Amhara, or came from Gondar instead of Shoa, or were Tigre or Oromo who had adopted the Amharic language, names, religion, lifestyles, and attitudes, they were still alien outsiders. Their precise origins would not matter to a southern *gebbar;* the effect and the impression would be the same: it was the Amhara who ruled them. (Paul Baxter demonstrates this from the perspective of the Arussi [Arsi] Oromo in 1969 [1978, 289–90; 1983, 137–39].) And the emperor and his largely Amhara administration stood behind and enforced the system. (For a reckoning of the origins of high officials in the central government between 1941 and 1966, see Clapham 1969, 75 ff.)

At least until the revolution in 1974 the primary aim of the administration was to keep order, extract as much wealth for the emperor and state as necessary, and for each landowner and government functionary to gather as much profit from the position as he or she could. Except for the development of schools in the larger towns, there were virtually no services provided, and until the 1960s the schools were attended mostly by children of the *neft'enya* (Baxter 1983, 141–42). For the many millions who lived outside of the larger towns even these were lacking. Almost all modern health care outside of Addis Ababa was supplied by missionaries, and their relatively scarce medical centers and little hospitals also had to be located near larger population centers. Little was spent on the improvement of agriculture, although by the late 1950s there were a few educational and research institutions whose personnel struggled with these problems.

The towns were, to a large extent, alien enclaves within the conquered areas. Amharic became the language of the towns even if the people just outside could not speak it at all. The languages used in the schools were Amharic and English. No other languages were acceptable. Thus the children of Amhara speakers had a distinct advantage; all others had to learn it in order to succeed from the first grade on. Educated Oromo describe how they were mocked or punished for speaking Oromo, although theirs was the overwhelming majority language in their area. The same story could be told by speakers of any of the seventy or so other languages, if they managed to get to school. (Similar complaints are lodged by American Indians.) Mission church services, too, had to be in Amharic, whether the congregation could understand it or not.

The court system offers another example of the indignities suffered by those who were not Amhara. In the larger towns the government established courts in which Amharic was the only language used. A person who did not speak Amharic had to hire an interpreter as well as a lawyer, in order to have decisions made by a stranger who had no knowledge of that person's own culture, expectations, traditions, or values. "Even a case between two Oromo before an Oromo-speaking magistrate had to be heard in Amharic" (Baxter 1983, 137). It is no wonder that, whenever possible, these courts were avoided. (See Singer 1975 and Lewis 1990a for more on the avoidance of the courts.)

By the 1960s there were parliamentary elections, but elected officials could do little to aid their people even had they wanted to. There is one interesting and telling account by Paul Baxter (1983, 144), however, which indicates the extent to which local people might be locked out of even these rather futile attempts to obtain some input into the system that ruled them. According to Baxter, the Arussi Oromo of the district in which he was conducting research decided to vote in the 1969 parliamentary elections and elected two Arussi to the available seats. "The Governor however regarded the result as subversion of the proper political order and had one of the candidates disallowed (the other was thought to be protected by Swedish Aid patrons) and ordered a fresh poll. During the second poll Arussi voters were threatened, some imprisoned and the majority prevented from voting so that a Christian northerner was declared elected."

This discussion of schools, courts, and elections may give a false impression of the extent of these trappings of modernity. In fact these institutions barely touched the great mass of the people living anywhere but right in or near the major towns. In the world inhabited by many millions of subjects of the Ethiopian empire, outside of the relatively rare towns and far from all-weather motorable roads, even these tokens of development were lacking.

In 1965–66 I carried out fieldwork in a farming community about seventy miles west of Addis Ababa, just off a good surfaced road, about ten miles from a substantial town. Hardly any but a handful of young students could speak Amharic, and there was no school or modern medical service closer than the nearby town, where there was a high school and a twelve-bed American mission hospital with two doctors and two nurses. The people in the countryside received no services and became aware of the government only if they were involved in an incident that was reported to the police and when they received the annual call to pay taxes. They rarely turned to the local *balabbat* or the courts but had their own extensive system of conflict resolution (Lewis 1990a). For some modicum of leadership they depended upon a dynamic and politically alert spirit medium (Lewis 1970, 1990b; Knutsson 1967). Spirit mediums had become the core of a significant system of belief and ritual, based upon Oromo and borrowed religious ideas. Christianity, either Ethiopian or missionary-based, had virtually no role in the rural area.

While a number of hard-working and shrewd farmers had acquired their own land, most people were sharecroppers, many paying half or three-quarters of their annual crop to landlords who were often outsiders. They rarely met except when the landowners or their stewards came to collect their share of the harvest. Furthermore, in those days there were virtually no radios in use (the broadcasts were all in Amharic in any case), and during the year I was there I was not aware of any discussion of regional or national political matters.

In short, one couldn't really say that these country people participated in a national culture. They had little concept of an Ethiopian state with a glorious history. They recognized that Emperor Haile Selassie I was a powerful ruler. Many thought he had some supernatural power, and with him on the throne they were at least not suffering from famine, epidemic, or war.

This example is not from a remote area but from one not very far from the capital, right off the main road, and only a long walk from a substantial road town. If this is the extent of their national consciousness and involvement with the organs of the state, one can imagine what it was like for the vast majority of peoples of the south, east, and west who were hundreds of miles from Addis Ababa, much further from towns, and nowhere near a motorable road. (The roads of Ethiopia radiate out of Addis Ababa like spokes from a bicycle wheel—which has had most of its spokes removed. There are hardly any connecting links between the major arteries. Thus a large percentage of the people have no direct access to motorable roads.) But even Dilla, a town in the economically important region of Sidamo, "had no secondary school until the 1970s; neither did it have a government hospital nor an airport" (McClellan 1990, 47).

At the other extreme, where contact with *neft'enya* was most intense, in some towns or where major cash crops were grown, this contact might well lead to greater alienation as the northern landowners lorded it over the farmers. Thus the people with little contact may have been the fortunate ones. In summary, for the great mass of the people of the conquered areas, there was little practical, sentimental, or ideological reason to believe in a discourse of Ethiopian nationhood. At best they would have been either ignorant of it or indifferent; at worst, they would have been totally alienated and at least potentially ready for rebellion.[3] And while the "socialist" government of the Dergue may have increased the availability of school and other services for many Ethiopians, it also increased governmental extractions and interference in the lives of all of them markedly.

It should be obvious from this account that there was no way that ordinary, nonelite, rural people who comprise the overwhelming majority of the population of the Ethiopian empire would lose their ethnic identities, their languages, customs, religions, histories. To suggest otherwise is to engage in wishful thinking that runs counter to all we have learned about the dynamics of ethnicity over the past quarter-century. People have learned new things, adopted new patterns (including, more recently, Islam and forms of Christianity introduced by the missionaries), but they have not forgotten who they are, who their ancestors were, and who their kin and fellows are. Some may have "acculturated" in many ways, but there has been far less "assimilation" than is commonly thought (see Shack 1966, 200–3, for his view of the Gurage in the early 1960s; cf. Knutsson 1969, 98).

Although the elite is miniscule in comparison to the many millions who never set foot in a school, those who did receive education were in a somewhat different situation. In the late 1960s and 1970s, many non-Amhara and Tigre students were indeed imbued with a sense of national consciousness. We shall turn to them next.

The Growth of Non-Amhara Leadership and of Modern Politics

Haile Selassie's efforts to transform Ethiopia into a modern state had the consequence of increasing political awareness and activity despite his strenuous efforts to control these undesireable side-effects. After the failed coup attempt of 1960, university and secondary school students became more and more politically conscious and obstreperous. Among these were non-Amhara students who by then were entering schools in increasing numbers.[4] In the main, however, their causes were not at first those of their ethnic groups but were the same issues that concerned other Ethiopian students of all backgrounds.

The impact of schooling on many young people in the 1960s was to give them the sense that they would have a role in the new and modern Ethiopia. To this extent I believe Christopher Clapham and Solomon Gashaw are correct: those who succeeded in rising into the elite during the 1960s and 1970s saw their future and that of their peoples in terms of improving Ethiopia as a whole. (For a sense of the student movement see, for example, the varying accounts of Legesse Lemma 1979; R. Balsvik 1984; Teshome Wagaw 1984.)

Even here, however, individuals varied a great deal as a result of their background and experiences. For example, last June after the Dergue fell I had a long talk with two prominent, educated Oromo, both of whom had spent ten years in prison for "narrow nationalism" after having served successfully in government positions both before and after the revolution. One of them had been raised in a town not far from Addis Ababa, had come to Addis Ababa for schooling at the age of fourteen and, he said, "I didn't see the brutal suppression that others are subjected to." (The aunt with whom he lived had requested that he speak the Oromo language at home, however, and save his Amharic for school.) He went to university, received a law degree, had a successful career, and was awakened to the regime's oppression by others relatively late. His friends who had access to information under the new regime had evidence for the first time of what had occurred under the old, but they felt powerless to remedy similar inequities that were continuing after the revolution. They now came to believe that the northerners, especially the Amhara, were continuing their misrule over the other peoples of Ethiopia.

His friend's experience was different. He came from Wellega, an area much further from the capital, and even though his grandfather had been a *balabbat,* "my family fought Amhara and Italian domination in the 1930s. My father taught me to be anticolonial." He remembers being insulted as a "Galla" by a priest with whom he was studying reading and writing as a child of seven.[5] He tells of being teased in school by teachers and fellow students for his Oromo name. (His father had told him that only bad Oromos changed their names.) Thus from an early age he resisted the Amhara and wanted to associate with Oromo. When he got to the university he sought out other Oromo, and he began to write poetry and articles connected to his concern for justice and social integration in Ethiopia.

During the late 1960s student activists were concerned about students' rights, increasing freedom, and, above all, about land reform. "Land to the Tiller" became their slogan. At this time Oromo and other non-Amhara students could readily identify and participate in these movements. With increasing radicalization they, too, became Marxist, as did that whole generation of Ethiopian students. Young educated Oromo were among the most avid early supporters of the revolutionary regime, which promised to right the old wrongs and create a new society. In addition, after 1969 the student movement embraced the ideal of equality for all nationalities and respect for the languages and cultures of others, as they would all fight the class wars together. Added to the goals of modernization and democratization, this was inspiring and attractive to many non-Amhara.

Before the revolution, in 1967, an episode occurred that was both a portent and a lesson for some educated Oromo, however. An Oromo regional self-help organization, the Mech'a-Tulama association, which was beginning to take on a political dimension, was banned, and its leaders, including General Tadesa Biru, were arrested, tried, and jailed (Clapham 1969, 81; Gilkes 1975, 225). Tadesa Biru had a successful career in the police, was a Shoan Christian, and had seemed "assimilated" until the experience he gained as a result of his high position led him to organize his Oromo brethren. The treatment of Tadesa and the movement had a consciousness-raising impact on many Oromo. According to Bereket Habte Selassie (1980, 81), some members went underground at that time and began to lay the groundwork for the Oromo Liberation Front (OLF) by organizing among Oromo farmers and urban dwellers.

It was not until the late 1970s, when educated young Oromo began to believe that the new regime, despite its promising rhetoric and the initial land reform, did not represent a new deal and equality for the Oromo, that they began to rebel in significant numbers. Some had been very active in the planning and implementation of land reform until, like Tadesa Biru, their proximity to power and information led them to the conclusion that the same old patterns of domination were continuing under the "new *neft'enya*" (as they called them). According to Bereket (1980, 81), among other things the Oromo had hoped for the freedom for farmers to elect their own representatives to the newly formed peasant associations, which the Dergue meant to use as instruments for increasing their control. He reports that when Oromo in the cities of Jimma and Harar held demonstrations in September 1978 demanding that the Oromo language be used for teaching in the early grades, these "were suppressed violently, with some 250 students killed" (ibid., 85). Further Oromo demands for greater use of their language in broadcasting, newspapers, preaching, and government business were rebuffed (Triulzi 1983, 123–25).

Young Oromo began to defect abroad or joined the OLF in the field. The normal route, then, was for a young person, a student, to first become a Marxist and support the revolution, and later, disaffected, turn to the problems and aspirations of his or her own ethnic group. Needless to say, today the Mech'a-Tulama association and its leaders, including Tadesa Biru, who was later killed by the Dergue, play an important role in Oromo nationalist history.

Although I have focused on the Oromo, the same process occurred with people from many other groups as well. A number of national liberation movements were formed, some before and some after the revolution. The most prominent liberation movements were those of the Eritreans, the Somali on the eastern borders, the Oromo, and the Tigre, but many smaller ones were formed by less populous groups, as Tekle M. Woldemikael shows in his chapter on the Eritrean movements (see also Gebru Tereke 1990; Bereket Habte Selassie 1980; also papers in I. M. Lewis 1983). Of course their followers either had to go into exile, hide and fight in the remote countryside, or keep their allegiances secret as they went about their lives. The new regime was no more willing than the old had been to permit any ethnic ("national") organization or activity that they did not directly sponsor and control.

The Development of Oromo Nationalism

The Oromo are by far the largest ethnic (or national) group in Ethiopia, stretching geographically from the far north of Ethiopia to as far south as the Tana River in Kenya, and from the borders of Somalia to those of the Sudan. As noted earlier, they were divided into many individual local groups which might differ from others in many ways: subsistence basis and settlement, the nature and scope of their polities, their religions, their histories (including the extent to which they were involved in Abyssinian politics), and many aspects of their customs and practices. What they shared was a common language and a common genealogy that linked them to the same ancestors. The many far-flung and quite different Oromo groups had no overall integration in the centuries before the Shoan conquest, and different Oromo groups fought each other in the past, but Amhara overlordship had made all Oromo groups (except those in Kenya) subordinate to the same dominant power.

The impact of the colonial yoke on the Oromo varied from place to place. Paul Baxter's articles portray the harsh rule over the Arsi, while, in contrast, the Borana of the far south remained largely nomadic and very remote from the center (Asmarom Legesse 1966). There is every possible variation in between these extremes. But it was rarely completely quiet on the Oromo front.

There were revolts by the Azebu and Raya in the north in 1928–30, in Wellega in 1936, and in Bale province in the 1960s (Gilkes 1975, 206 ff.). Each one of these conflicts was local in scope, but news of the 1964 rebellion against the government and its tax collectors spread from Bale and increased the political awareness of Oromo. Paul Baxter reports that the rebellion "demonstrated that determined Oromo could wage effective guerilla warfare against the Addis Ababa authorities" (1978, 290). He says that the policies of the government created more problems for their rule as they ignored Oromo custom and culture and imposed their own. "As more Oromo became civil servants, Army officers and NCO's and more Oromo school boys became undergraduates, and as more Oromo MPs managed to get elected, each group found that in addition to sharing humiliating experiences, each shared a common language and similar values. The new pan-Oromo consciousness was generated in the army, the University and the Parliament itself" (ibid., 290). These contacts in the "modern sector" made Oromo increasingly aware of "just how numerous, extensive and similar the Oromo peoples were" (ibid.). He continues, "As elsewhere in Africa, as for example among the Ibo, Akan, Somali or Kalenjin, increased education, trade and mobility has fostered wider ethnic sentiments and affiliations" (ibid., 291).

The Dergue sped up this process by organizing and politicizing everything. Whereas Haile Selassie's government did very little but extract wealth and try to keep order according to their lights, the Dergue attempted to penetrate all the corners of society, to organize people and make them do their bidding. The creation of many types of government-controlled organizations, the interference with farmers, traders, students, almost everybody, and the increasing demands on their time and resources increased political awareness everywhere. Most egregiously the Dergue carried out a program of forced resettlement that took northerners speaking totally different languages, with different religions and cultures, and put them on land taken from Oromo. Then they forced Oromo and other southern farmers and herders into compact villages, driving people who were used to living in dispersed homesteads to cluster into settlements that were inappropriate, even disastrous, economically, ecologically, and socially. As before, the Amhara were seen to be dominating the Oromo. (For a discussion of the Dergue's attempts to "capture the peasants," see Stahl 1990; also Poluha 1988 on "central planning and local reality.")

A number of Oromo political movements developed over time, both before and after the fall of Haile Selassie (Gilkes 1975). The largest of these is the OLF, while its major rival is the Oromo People's Democratic Organization (OPDO) which developed under the aegis and as a component of the Ethiopian Peoples Revolutionary Democratic Front (EPRDF). The OLF is the older organization, and many of its leaders have been in exile in Europe and the United States so more is known about its program and ideas.

Judging from the publications which emanated from the Oromo diaspora in Europe and North America, they developed the same sort of rhetoric, symbols, and activities common to similar movements all over the world. Apart from pursuing military action, for example, they initiated campaigns to introduce literacy in the Oromo language in areas they could reach. (They adapted the Oromo language to written form, and today there are two competing systems, the one favored by the OLF using the Latin alphabet while the OPDO introduced one based on the Amharic syllabary.)

In their speeches and publications, they changed place-names back to their Oromo originals, rejecting the Amharic names that had been given them. (Of course they use "Finfini" in place of "Addis Ababa.") New versions of the modern history of Ethiopia are being written to correct what Oromo leaders consider to be the distortions of the Amhara views of the past (see *Oromia Speaks* [1979, vol. 1]; Holcomb and Sisai Ibssa 1990). Accounts of Oromo history and culture are being written that stress Oromo values of egalitarianism and democracy in contrast to Amhara traditions of monarchy and hierarchy (for discussion of the latter, see Hoben 1970). The *gada* system, a "republican" organization of assemblies, election, and rotation of officers, based on age-grades, has been raised to a central ideological place in Oromo nationalism (for example, *Oromia* by "Gadaa Melbaa," a pseudonym taken from *gada;* Lewis 1974). The flag of the OLF features a huge *oda* tree at its center, standing for the meetings of the *gada* assemblies. The role of powerful Oromo chiefs and kings in some areas is played down. (An exception to this is Mohammed Hassen's *The Oromo of Ethiopia* [1990] which deals with the history of the Oromo states of the Gibe regions. But it, too, is written explicitly to correct what the author sees as the record of distortion and persistent undervaluing of the Oromo past and role in Ethiopian history.)

Right after the fall of the Dergue, there was the sense that Oromo from all over the country, many of whom had never had any contact before, were coming together for common organization and action. Not only did they have little opportunity to meet in earlier decades, but they were forbidden to hold any public gatherings by the previous governments in any case. As soon as the Dergue fell, new contacts and organizational activity began. Two significant meetings were held in July of 1991. One was an effort to settle a major dispute between the OLF and the OPDO, the EPRDF-sponsored rival Oromo group, and the other was a feast to celebrate Oromo unity. In these deeply emotional meetings, and in one held soon after by exiles and emigrants in Toronto, one could sense the growing feeling of power, pride, and political potential.

The history of Oromo consciousness follows a common pattern in the development of ethnic nationalism among colonized peoples. When the initial resistance to the empire is overcome by superior force, where there is no realistic hope for rebellion, people settle down to lives of quiet desperation, not liking the outsiders but forced to tolerate them. The roots of ethnopolitics, the identities and the grievances, were there from the beginning but the conditions for organization and the necessary skills were lacking.

In the second stage, as the young gain education and learn about politics, many do, indeed, identify with the largest unit, the state, in this case the Empire of Ethiopia. Young Oromo supported a new revolutionary day for all of Ethiopia, as young Igbo supported a centralized Nigerian state in the early 1960s, before Biafra. But having acted upon these ideals and then discovered that the needs of their own people were not to be met, they become disenchanted. Finding that their own kinfolk and ethnic fellows are still among the insulted and injured, that they lack honor, influence, and economic well-being, and despairing of getting equality through "normal politics" they turn to ethnopolitics.

Political awareness increased late in Haile Selassie's reign. When the Dergue accelerated the process by politicizing everyone, creating associations of peasants, women, students, and urban dwellers, they made it more likely that ethnic political groups would also be formed. And now these ethnic parties are in a position to determine the future of Ethiopia.

The Prospects for Ethiopia

During the 1970s and 1980s Ethiopian politics was notable for the wonderful variety of its factions and ideologies, and especially for all the variations on

Marxist-Leninist themes. But the regime was brought down by the very "narrow nationalists" that the Dergue feared, and it is they who are currently trying to work out a new *modus vivendi,* a completely new deal for Ethiopia.

At the national conference in July 1991, after affirming their support for the Universal Declaration of Human Rights of the United Nations with its emphasis on individual rights, the delegates turned to the rights of the nationalities. Under the direction of Meles Zenawi, the leader of the Tigre Peoples Liberation Front (TPLF), a section of the EPRDF, the assembly agreed to create an ethnically balanced government which no one group dominates and to decentralize the previously totally centralized state. The proclamation issued as a result of the national conference affirmed, in Article 2, the right of a nation, nationality, and people to:

> a) Preserve its identity and have it respected, promote its culture and history and use and develop its language; b) Administer its own affairs within its own defined territory and effectively participate in the central government on the basis of freedom, and fair and proper representation; c) Exercise its right to self-determination of independence, when the concerned nation/nationality and people is convinced that the above rights are denied, abridged or abrogated. ("Ethiopia: A Nation in Transition," *The Ethiopian Mirror* [September/October 1991])

The prospects for these principles to be successfully implemented are still very far from certain. What does seem certain is that there are two deeply divided views in Ethiopia. One is that of the Amhara, not all of them from the elite, who can see only disaster in this formula, and who would undoubtedly reject my portrayal of the Ethiopian ethnic reality. (There are many outside observers of Ethiopia who feel similarly critical and pessimistic. They tend to share a belief in the discourse of Ethiopian nationhood.) They blame the leaders of the TPLF and OLF for pushing the ethnic/national issue to this extent.

The other perspective is that of the representatives of many of the ethnic movements, who would probably present the picture that I have, but more forcefully. There is undoubtedly a middle ground, but what it has to offer is difficult to hear when the contending forces are in full cry. And it is unfortunately true that beyond the grievances of all these groups against the Amhara there are also going to be an endless series of claims that each group has on its neighbors, just as has happened after the breakup of the USSR and Yugoslavia. It will not be a pretty sight, and any specific outcomes are clearly unpredictible. I would make some suggestions about general principles and processes, however.

I suggest that it will do no good to try to argue that a particular group has no reason or right to want to set itself apart for recognition, autonomy, or even independence, on the grounds that it is so similar to another (in this case to the Amhara). Fredrik Barth pointed out in 1969 that it is not cultural content that marks boundaries between ethnic groups and that such boundaries exist despite "objective" similarities or differences. He wrote, "The important thing to recognize is that a drastic reduction of cultural differences between ethnic groups does not correlate in any simple way with a reduction in the organizational relevance of ethnic identities, or a breakdown in boundary-maintaining processes" (1969, 32–33). For an immediate demonstration of this we have the case of the Eritreans, a people whose leaders are arguably as close in every way to the Tigre, and almost as close to the Amhara, as any peoples can be. And yet the Eritreans, both the rural people and the elite, chose to fight a terrible war for thirty years until they gained their independence. The argument from similarity has not done much to keep the peoples of Yugoslavia together, either, nor does it seem to be working with the Slovaks.

Similarly, the Eritrean example should caution those who feel that they can talk others out of their movement because of a "more objective" view of history. Each side will have its own "facts," and the detached observer may prefer one to the other, but once the issue has been joined few of those who feel the grievances will be convinced by the arguments of "the enemy," no matter how scholarly the presentation. It is also unfortunately true that the members of an ethnic elite rarely see the inequalities, the slights, and the insults they inflict upon members of subordinate groups.[6]

As Crawford Young reminds us in the introductory chapter to this book, the world today is awash in ethnopolitics, and it is the "nation-state" that is being increasingly questioned. Over the past twenty years we have witnessed a great new worldwide diffusion of the idea of "self-determination," and the Ethiopian "discourse of nationhood," restricted as it actually was, has little chance of standing against this new discourse *unless* the perceived needs of its many "nations" are met. It is not impossible that they could be met, but it will take much more openness than the opponents of ethnic self-assertion have so far evidenced.

After many years of war and political turmoil, people in Ethiopia want peace, stability, and a chance to rebuild their lives and livelihoods. There are great costs to separation, and people are very aware of this; they do not take the prospect of fighting for independence lightly. They also know that there can be rewards for staying together as a united Ethiopia. But it is unlikely they will willingly accept the sort of system they had before, being ordered around by people who are obviously outsiders, denied what they see as their honor and their rights, and short-changed on services and opportunities. This is a case where justice must be seen to be done and the powerful dynamic of ethnic mobilization addressed. They will require evidence that their felt needs will be dealt with fairly. Nor will it do to merely rail at unscrupulous ethnic leaders. "False consciousness" is a concept that belongs to an earlier era.

The feelings of many educated people from the non-Amhara ethnic groups toward the developments of June 1991 may be represented by the words of one well-educated member of the Sidama Liberation Movement, spoken at the time of the July 1991 conference. According to this young man, "We want to live together, but we want to be respected as human beings, as Sidama, as a people, a culture, a language. We must have a part in this country, not as second class citizens, not as foreigners, but as full partners. Before we didn't want to live with Addis Ababa as our capital, but there is new hope that as priorities shift we can participate as full partners and not be dominated by an elite minority." After speaking of the Sidamo region's wealth in fertile soil, coffee, and gold he said, "Until now we only gave and got nothing in return. No roads, no clinics, no schools. Our resources were taken for the elite, so they could send their children to school in Addis Ababa and abroad. But we no longer will accept this. We want to use these resources, to share with others and get something in return."[7] (Compare McClellan [1990, 47] on the importance of Sidama in Ethiopia's economy and integration.)

In summary, the ethnic politics of Ethiopia are not really very different from those elsewhere in the world in the last decade of the twentieth century. As in so many other places, there are many groups that have in no way lost their sense of identity as distinct peoples—even if in some cases these identities received their modern names and their definition only relatively recently. These identities are no less "real" for that, if people live by them. They are unlikely to be argued out of them. These identities may yield powerful motivations when they are combined with the belief that one's own group has been dominated, exploited, and wronged by another. In today's political climate such domination is no longer seen as inevitable and certainly not as acceptable. The idea of "self-determination" is back in the air once again, and with today's global communication, no place or people in the world will be ignorant of it for long. Whether they approve or not, those concerned about the future of Ethiopia and its peoples must understand these realities.

NOTES

1. In 1969 Clapham offered a different view, however, noting that at that time people from all of the provinces south of Addis Ababa were "largely excluded from the government" (1969, 78).

2. These estimates are partially based on those of M. Lionel Bender (1976).

3. For a few other accounts of relations between northern settlers and local peoples compare, for example: Asmarom Legesse (1966), McClellan (1986, 1990), Baxter (1980, 1978, 1983), Mohammed Hassan (n.d.), Triulzi (1983). Baxter's 1983 account is particularly vivid.

4. Levine (1965, 114) gives percentages for the origins of secondary and college students in Addis Ababa about 1960. He reports 55 percent Amhara, 22 percent Tigre, and 15 percent Oromo. (These figures include students of mixed parentage and are listed

in terms of the father's origin.) As for religion, only 4 percent are listed as Muslim, and 3 percent "other."

5. As is so often the case, the Oromo of one hundred years ago had no single term for themselves, and the Abyssinian name for them, "Galla," came into general use by foreigners as well as other Ethiopians. The name "Oromo," used in a number of areas, was spread increasingly among the people themselves until by the 1970s it came to be the only one accepted all over, and the name "Galla" was rejected as insulting.

6. An Oromo friend told me of an exchange between co-workers in his government office in June 1991. An Amhara man asked a fellow worker, incredulously, "When did you ever feel discriminated against as a Gurage?" This is especially poignant because the Gurage are generally ridiculed because Gurage men used to serve as porters and menial laborers in Addis Ababa, and they have gained a reputation as storekeepers and merchants, occupations that were traditionally looked down upon by Amhara. The night before I heard this story, I witnessed an educated and wealthy Amhara loudly insult his Gurage companion at the bar of the Addis Ababa Hilton for being a grasping Gurage businessman without the honor and pride of the Amhara.

7. For the record, these were the ethnic parties that participated in the National Conference, as listed in *The Ethiopian Mirror* (September/October 1991): Adere Nationality, Afar Liberation Front, BeniShangul People's Liberation Movement, Gambela People's Liberation Movement, Gurage Nationality, Hadiya Nationality, Islamic Oromo Liberation Front, Issa and Gurgura Liberation Movement, Kembatta People, Oromo Abo Liberation Front, Oromo Liberation Front, Ometic Group, Oromo People's Democratic Organization, Oromo People's Liberation Front, Sidama Liberation Movement, Tigray People's Liberation Front, Wolaita Nationality, Western Somalia Liberation Front, Ogaden Liberation Front.

REFERENCES

Abir, Mordechai. 1968. *Ethiopia: The Era of the Princes.* London: Longmans, Green.

Asmarom Legesse. 1973. *Gada: Three Approaches to the Study of African Society.* New York: Free Press.

Asmarom Legesse. 1966. National Integration in Ethiopia: The Borana Galla. Paper delivered at the African Studies Association Conference, Bloomington, Indiana, October 29.

Balsvik, Randi Ronning. 1984. The Ethiopian Student Movement in the 1960's: Challenges and Responses. In *Proceedings of the Seventh International Conference of Ethiopian Studies,* edited by Sven Rubenson, 497–509. Addis Ababa: Institute of Ethiopian Studies.

Barth, Fredrik. 1969. Introduction. In *Ethnic Groups and Boundaries,* edited by F. Barth. Boston: Little, Brown and Company.

Baxter, Paul. 1983. The Problem *of* the Oromo or the Problem *for* the Oromo? In *Nationalism and Self-Determination in the Horn of Africa,* edited by I. M. Lewis, 129–49. London: Ithaca Press.

Baxter, Paul. 1980. "Always on the Outside Looking In": A view of the 1969 Ethiopian Elections from a Rural Constituency. *Ethnos* 45, 1–2: 41–59.

Baxter, Paul. 1978. Ethiopia's Unacknowledged Problem: The Oromo. *African Affairs* 77, 308: 283–96.

Baxter, Paul, and U. Almagor, eds. 1978. *Age, Generation and Time: Some Features of East African Age Organizations*. London: C. Hurst.

Bender, M. Lionel, ed. 1976. *The Non-Semitic Languages of Ethiopia*. East Lansing: Michigan State University African Studies Center, Monograph no. 5.

Bereket Habte Selassie. 1980. *Conflict and Intervention in the Horn of Africa*. New York: Monthly Review Press.

Clapham, Christopher. 1990. Conclusion: Revolution, Nationality, and the Ethiopian State. In *The Political Economy of Ethiopia*, edited by Marina Ottaway, 221–31. New York: Praeger.

Clapham, Christopher. 1969. *Haile-Selassie's Government*. New York: Praeger.

Dawit Wolde Giorgis. 1989. *Red Tears: War, Famine and Revolution in Ethiopia*. Trenton: Red Sea Press.

Donham, Donald. 1986. From Ritual Kings to Ethiopian Landlords in Maale. In *The Southern Marches of Imperial Ethiopia*, edited by Donald Donham and Wendy James, 69–95. Cambridge: Cambridge University Press.

Donham, Donald, and Wendy James, eds. 1986. *The Southern Marches of Imperial Ethiopia*. Cambridge: Cambridge University Press.

Gadaa Melbaa. 1980. *Oromia: A Brief Introduction*. Finfine, Oromia.

Gebru Tereke. 1990. Continuity and Discontinuity in Peasant Mobilization: The Cases of Bale and Tigray. In *The Political Economy of Ethiopia*, ed. Marina Ottaway, 137–55. New York: Praeger.

Gilkes, Patrick. 1975. *The Dying Lion: Feudalism and Modernization in Ethiopia*. New York: St. Martin's Press.

Hinnant, John. 1990. Guji Trance and Social Change: Symbolic Response to Domination. *Northeast African Studies* 12, 1: 65–78.

Hoben, Allan. 1970. Social Stratification in Traditional Amhara Society. In *Social Stratification in Africa*, edited by Arthur Tuden and Leonard Plotnicov, 187–224. New York: Free Press.

Holcomb, Bonnie K., and Sisai Ibssa. 1990. *The Invention of Ethio*. Trenton: Red Sea Press.

Knutsson, Karl Eric. 1969. Dichotomization and Integration: Aspects of Inter-ethnic Relations in Southern Ethiopia. In *Ethnic Groups and Boundaries*, edited by F. Barth. Boston: Little, Brown and Company.

Knutsson, Karl Eric. 1967. *Authority and Change: A Study of the Kallu Institution among the Macha Galla of Ethiopia*. Goteborg: Etnografiska Museet.

Legesse Lemma. 1979. The Ethiopian Student Movement 1960–1974: A Challenge to the Monarchy and Imperialism in Ethiopia. *Northeast African Studies* 1, 2: 31–46.

Levine, Donald N. 1974. *Greater Ethiopia: The Evolution of a Multiethnic Society*. Chicago: University of Chicago Press.

Levine, Donald N. 1965. *Wax & Gold: Tradition and Innovation in Ethiopian Culture*. Chicago: University of Chicago Press.

Lewis, Herbert S. 1991. Ethiopia: Beginning Again. *Africa Report* (September/October): 59–62.

Lewis, Herbert S. 1990a. Values and Procedures in Conflict Resolution among Shoan Oromo. In *Proceedings of the Eighth International Conference of Ethiopian Studies,* edited by Taddese Bayene. Addis Ababa: Institute of Ethiopian Studies.

Lewis, Herbert S. 1990b. Gada, Big Man, K'allu: Political Succession among the Eastern Mech'a Oromo. *Northeast African Studies* 12, 1: 43–64.

Lewis, Herbert S. 1974. Neighbors, Friends and Kinsmen: Principles of Social Organization among the Cushitic-Speaking Peoples of Ethiopia. *Ethnology* 13: 145–57.

Lewis, Herbert S. 1970. Wealth, Influence, and Prestige among the Shoa Galla. In *Social Stratification in Africa,* edited by Arthur Tuden and Leonard Plotnicov, 163–86. New York: Free Press.

Lewis, Herbert S. 1965. *A Galla Monarchy: Jimma Abba Jifar, 1830–1932*. Madison: University of Wisconsin Press.

Lewis, I. M., ed. 1983. *Nationalism & Self-Determination in the Horn of Africa*. London: Ithaca Press.

McClellan, Charles W. 1990. Articulating Economic Modernization and National Integration at the Periphery: Addis Ababa and Sidamo's Provincial Centers. *African Studies Review* 33, 1: 29–54.

McClellan, Charles W. 1986. Coffee in Centre-Periphery Relations: Gedeo in the Early Twentieth Century. In *The Southern Marches of Imperial Ethiopia,* edited by Donald Donham and Wendy James, 175–95. Cambridge: Cambridge University Press.

Marcus, Harold G. 1975. *The Life and Times of Menelik II, Ethiopia 1844–1913*. Oxford: Clarendon Press.

Markakis, John, and Nega Ayele. 1978. *Class and Revolution in Ethiopia*. London: Spokesman Press.

Mohammed Hassen. N.d. Menilek's Conquest of Harar, 1887, and Its Effect on the Political Organization of the Surrounding Oromos up to 1900. In Working Papers on Society and History in Imperial Ethiopia: The Southern Periphery from the 1880s to 1974, edited by D. L. Donham and Wendy James, 227–46. Cambridge African Studies Centre.

Mohammed Hassen. 1990. *The Oromo of Ethiopia: A History 1570–1860*. Cambridge: Cambridge University Press.

Oromia Speaks. 1979. A Publication of the Oromo Liberation Front (OLF). Vol. 1. N.p.: Union of Oromo Students in North America.

Perham, Margery. 1948. *The Government of Ethiopia*. New York: Oxford University Press.

Poluha, Eva. 1988. *Central Planning and Local Reality: A Case Study of Producers Cooperatives in Ethiopia*. Stockholm: Stockholm Studies in Social Anthropology.

Shack, William A. 1966. *The Gurage: People of the Ensete Culture*. London: Oxford University Press.

Singer, Norman J. 1975. The Use of Courts as a Key to Legal Development: An Analysis of Legal Attitudes of the Cambata of Ethiopia. In *Proceedings of the First United States Conference on Ethiopian Studies, 1973,* edited by Harold G. Marcus, 365–83. East Lansing: Michigan State University African Studies Center.

Stahl, Michael. 1990. Capturing the Peasants through Cooperatives—The Case of Ethiopia. *Northeast African Studies* 12, 1: 95–122.

Teshome Wagaw. 1984. The Burden and Glory of Being Schooled: An Ethiopian Dilemma. In *Proceedings of the Seventh International Conference of Ethiopian Studies*, edited by Sven Rubenson, 497–509. Addis Ababa: Institute of Ethiopian Studies.

Triulzi, Alessandro. 1986. Nek'emte and Addis Ababa: dilemmas of provincial rule. In *The Southern Marches of Imperial Ethiopia*, edited by Donald Donham and Wendy James, 51–68. Cambridge: Cambridge University Press.

Triulzi, Alessandro. 1983. Competing Views of National Identity in Ethiopia. In *Nationalism and Self-Determination in the Horn of Africa*, edited by I. M. Lewis, 111–127. London: Ithaca Press.

9

The Cultural Construction of Eritrean Nationalist Movements

■ ■ ■

TEKLE M. WOLDEMIKAEL

ERITREA IS NOW known in the world for its successful nationalist struggle against Ethiopia. However, despite what nationalist slogans might say, Eritrean nationalism is not a given but, like all nationalisms, a social construct. In this chapter I will look at the social composition of the Eritrean nationalist movements and the ways they have dealt with the regional, religious, and ethnic diversity within Eritrean society. There are moments in recent Eritrean history when Eritreans have been able to forge political coalitions based on common national interests. There are other times when divisions along cultural lines have become salient and politicized, causing nationalist movements to founder. I will be examining the history of the relationships between national and subnational sentiments in Eritrea, focusing especially on the cultural solidarities that have been politically activated and mobilized in the last thirty years.

The chapter is divided into five parts. The first part is a critical review of the various perspectives on cultural pluralism in Eritrea. The second section describes the diverse cultural groups in Eritrea, focusing on their language, religion, geographic location, size, and mode of life. The third section analyzes how cultural differences and the politicization of cultural divisions have led to political fissions within Eritrean nationalist movements. It examines the establishment of the two major nationalist movements, the Eritrean Liberation Front (ELF) and the Eritrean Peoples Liberation Front (EPLF), and discusses the cultural basis of the conflict-ridden relationship between the two fronts. The fourth part explores the interaction of the dominant nationalist movement, the EPLF, with the various cultural groups in Eritrea, looking particularly at the division between Christian highlanders and Muslim lowlanders. I argue that the politicization of religious and regional divisions in Eritrea has the potential to form two distinct proto-nationalities within the country: a multi-ethnic grouping of Christian highlanders and a multi-ethnic grouping of Muslim lowlanders. Such proto-nationalist formations are the most potent challenge facing the EPLF today. I also contend that the second major problem facing the EPLF is the question of Afar self-determination. The Afar inhabit territory that crosses the national boundaries of Eritrea, Ethiopia, and Djibouti. In the fifth and concluding section I discuss the tasks the EPLF faces in the near future as it seeks to construct a viable Eritrean state capable of managing its ethnic, regional, and religious diversity.

At present, the major nationalist movement, the EPLF, controls Eritrea after capturing Asmara, the capital city of Eritrea on 24 May 1991 and the port of Assab on 25 May 1991. The EPLF announced on 29 May 1991 that it had formed a provisional government. It promised to transfer power to a popularly elected civilian authority after a popular referendum on the fate of Eritrea is carried out in 1993. The referendum will be internationally supervised and will determine whether Eritrea will remain an integral part of Ethiopia or form a separate independent state.

The nationalist struggle for an independent Eritrea began in September of 1961 when Hamid Idris Awate led an armed band of Beni Amer and Baria fighters from the western lowlands of Eritrea into conflict with government forces. Since the 1960s, however, the politicization of the religious, ethnic, and regional fissions within Eritrea has posed a threat to the emergence of a cohesive national sentiment in Eritrea. The path toward the creation of an independent Eritrea has been blocked by such conflicting solidarities. Moreover, despite the military victory of the EPLF, these subnationalities could threaten the viability and stability of an Eritrean state.

Perspectives on Cultural Pluralism in Eritrea

After decades of neglect, the role of ethnic, regional, and religious divisions in Eritrean politics and the emerging relationship between the nationalist movements and the various cultural groups in Eritrea is gaining attention from scholars (Shumet 1984; Henze 1986; Markakis 1987; 1988; Fessehatzion 1990; Araya 1990; Cliffe 1989; Woldemikael 1991). Scholarly views on nationalism and cultural pluralism in Eritrea can be divided into three perspectives. The first holds that ethnic, regional, and religious cleavages are stronger than nationalist feelings in Eritrean politics (Henze 1986; Araya 1990). Those who hold this view argue that an independent Eritrea would not be viable because it would be embroiled in an endemic civil war.

The second view interprets Eritrean nationalism as a widely shared sentiment that has superceded conflicts based on cultural cleavages (Fessehatzion 1990; Cliffe 1989). This outlook implies that an independent Eritrea will avoid communally based civil war because of the leadership of the EPLF and the shared sense of nationalism among Eritreans forged in the struggle against Ethiopia.

The third perspective is more complex. It considers the cultural and religious divisions in Eritrea to be reflections of competition for scarce resources, especially land and state power (Pool 1983; Gebre Medhin 1989; Markakis 1988). For example, John Markakis examines the case of Eritrea in the context of African colonial and postcolonial history. He notes that the struggle for independence in most parts of Africa consisted of two, often opposing processes: (1) conflict between the colonial subjects and their colonizers, and (2) a "parallel encounter, equally intense but less publicised, . . . fought among ethnic groups and regions, and the parties representing them, for control of the colonial state and the spoils of independence" (Markakis 1988, 51).

According to Markakis, Eritrean nationalism has followed a pattern similar to other independence movements in Africa. The decline of Italian colonial power in Eritrea in the 1940s led to the emergence of internal fissions that divided the society into two camps based on religion (Markakis 1988, 51). This perspective is useful in outlining the general pattern of recent Eritrean political history. But it fails to explain why an Eritrean cultural group may show a greater degree of commitment to one rather than another nationalist movement, even when that movement does not serve the group's economic and political interests. The connection between ethnic groups and movement affiliation is much more complex than this perspective suggests.

These contrasting views on Eritrean politics have limitations. The existence of cultural cleavages will not automatically lead to civil war, nor does the presence of anticolonial nationalist sentiment prevent it. Since "subnational solidarity is of enduring importance as a political determinant" (Young 1976, 11), the future of an independent Eritrea will depend on the past history of communal conflicts and the current policies of the EPLF toward cultural groups in Eritrea. The important questions, thus, are what has been the history of the relationship between national and subnational sentiments in Eritrea, what circumstances have promoted national cohesion, and what circumstances have fostered fissions?

To address the questions raised above, we need a framework that can integrate the symbolic as well as the material meanings of the statements and actions of nationalist movements and cultural groups. The "constructivist" orientation (discussed by Young in Chapter 1 of this volume) offers such a framework. The constructivist claims that cultural groups and nations are imagined communities that are socially manufactured within a particular historical time and social space. A nation is defined as "an imagined political community—and imagined as both inherently limited and sovereign" (Anderson 1983, 15). The terms "subnational" and "cultural identities" are used interchangeably to imply socially constructed identities that could mobilize and politicize individuals in society along ethnic, regional, religious, caste, or other lines that crosscut national ties (Young 1976, 72). A nationalist movement is defined as an organized group, often small, that aspires to create a nation for a given population (Smith 1976, 3). This chapter explores the role of subnational (cultural) identities on the construction of Eritrean nationalist movements.

Every level of group identity, including ethnic, religious, and national identity, is in a constant process of construction. Each can be deconstructed in its own right. I wish to focus on the cultural construction of Eritrean nationalism in the context of competing cultural identities. I analyze the production of Eritrean nationalism by examining the process of interaction, competition, and conflict between the various cultural groups as well as between the cultural groups and the nationalist movements in their efforts to become the sole independence movements in Eritrea and thus gain political control over the emerging Eritrean state. Therefore, the cultural groups that I discuss consist of those that are salient at this time in Eritrean history and society and are recognized as the major ethnic groups by the Eritrean nationalist movements.

Cultural Diversity in Eritrea

The cultural, linguistic, and religious groups in Eritrea are complex and overlapping. They defy neat classification. Unfortunately, since the 1940s, there have been few studies of the cultural composition of Eritreans. Moreover, the ethnic divisions described in the 1940s are not static. My own research draws on personal interviews with many Eritreans and on unpublished and published documents printed in Tigrigna and English by the ELF and the EPLF as well as articles from newspapers, magazines, and journals.

Many Eritreans divide their country into two major geographical areas based on its general physical features: highlands and lowlands. This perception is based on the assumed rough coincidence of mode of life, social organization, and religion among the inhabitants of these two regions. Those known as highlanders (Kebessa) are Christian, sedentary peasants who are socially organized on territorial rather than kinship lines. Lowlanders (Metahit) are pastoral, nomadic Muslims, whose social organization is based on kinship rather than on territorial lines. Thus, the largest and most politically potent division in Eritrean society is the cleavage between Christian highlanders and Muslim lowlanders.

However, the analysis of cultural units in Eritrea in terms of a dichotomy between the highland, Tigrigna-speaking, mostly Christian peasants and the Islamic pastoralist lowlanders is simplistic (Cliffe 1989, 133). There is wide variation within these two main regions. Moreover, Eritreans vary according to multiple languages, religions, castes, ethnic ties, regions, and ways of life. A careful look at Eritrean society shows a great deal of fluidity in its ethnic composition and boundaries. This is explained by widespread ethnic mixing, religious conversions, migration, conquest, and wars in the region as well as by a redefinition of ethnic affiliation and state boundaries. Thus, it is important first to recognize that the physical and cultural maps of Eritrea do not match. Rather the ethnic, religious, and regional divisions in Eritrea are overlapping, intersecting, complex arrangements.

Eritrea has a great deal of physical diversity. Although it is a small country, with an area of 45,754 square miles and over 3.5 million people, of whom 85 percent live in rural areas (*Facts on Eritrea* 1988, 5), Eritrea is composed not of two, but four geographic zones. They are the eastern plains, the western plains, the central plateau, and the northern hills (Nadel 1944, 5). The central plateau is only one-fourth of the total area of Eritrea but is home to almost 50 percent of the total population who are mostly settled farmers. Many of the major cities of Eritrea, including Asmara, the capital city (with an estimated 350,000 population in 1990) are located in this region. The central plateau is divided into three provinces, Akele Guzai, Hamasein, and Serae. The northern hills are divided into two provinces: Sahel in the north and Senhit in the south. Nakfa and Keren are the major towns of Sahel and Senhit, respectively. The western plains consist of Barka province, the biggest and agriculturally the richest region in Eritrea. The province is subdivided into three regions, each named after its major town, including Agordat, in the northeast, Barentu, in the southwest, and Tessenai. The eastern plains, extending along the Red Sea, are divided in two by a narrow extension of the central plateau around the coastal city of Massawa, Eritrea's major port. The northern part of the eastern plains consists of Samhar and Sahel provinces. Semhar includes the Massawa area, but most of Semhar is thinly settled. The southern half falls under Denakil province and stretches south and southwest to Ethiopia and Djibouti (the Territory of Afars and Issas). The capital and the largest city of Denakil is the port of Assab.

Since language is the most accurate basis for identification of the population, I will describe Eritrean ethnicity in terms of language groups. There are nine known language groups that crosscut the four regions of Eritrea. The Tigrigna are Tigrigna-speakers, a language derived from an ancient Afro-Asiatic language called Geez. Most of the Tigrigna inhabit the central highlands. They are largely uneducated peasant farmers, who practice Coptic Christianity, though small numbers are educated Protestants and Catholics. The Coptic religion of Eritrea and Ethiopia has historically been connected with but also distinguished from the Greek and Eastern Orthodox churches in Europe and the Middle East. Living among the Christians is a sizeable Muslim minority known as the Jabarti who specialize in commerce and crafts and speak Tigrigna. The Tigrigna are united by a common religion, language, and a sense of common fate. They constitute a subnationality with a strong sense of solidarity. They are also culturally linked with the Tigrigna and Amharic-speaking Christians in Ethiopia, with whom they share the same overarching self-identification as Habasha (Abyssinians), a name given to them by their Arab neighbors.

The Saho are a small ethnic group who live mostly in the foothills of the central plateau and the northeastern part of Eritrea and have spread into Semhar, Sahel, and the northern hills. The Saho speak Saho, a language akin to another Cushitic language, Afar, which is widely spoken in the eastern plains in Eritrea. Although some Saho are farmers, most are seminomadic herders. The nomads migrate with their herds from the Red Sea coast to the highlands of the central plateau.

The Tigre are made up of a number of independent communities that inhabit mostly Senhit, Sahel, and Semhar.[1] They speak Tigre, a language which like Tigrigna stems from Geez. The Tigre consist of the Maria, who are seminomadic herders and Muslims, the Mensa, who practice agriculture and are mostly Christians, and a small farming group known as Beit Juk who are Muslims. Side by side with the Tigre live independent communities of an ethnic group known as Belien. The Belien, who speak Belien, a Cushitic language of the Agew subfamily also known as Bilien (Thompson 1976, 598), live mostly in Senhit. Most Belien are bilingual (Belien-Tigre) and many are multi-lingual with a perfect command of three languages: Belien, Tigre, and Tigrigna. The Belien are settled cultivators. Historically, the Belien were Orthodox Christians. Now, almost 60 percent are Muslim converts from Christianity. The rest are Christian, most of them Catholics and Protestants, converted recently by missionaries. The Tigre and the Belien share a similar social stratification system based on caste. Caste divisions have diminished in importance over the last fifty years. Historically, the master caste was known as Shumagille, and the serf caste was referred to as Tigre. The masters gave political protection to the serfs, and the serfs paid tribute for the use of grazing or cultivation of the land. Now most ex-serfs have little obligation to the master caste, and the distinctions are maintained primarily in other spheres of social relations such as marriage and social status.

The Rashaida, a small population of recent immigrants from Yemen, who came to northeastern Eritrea (Sahel and Semhar) and the eastern Sudan in the last century, are Arabic-speaking, nomadic pastoralists.

The Kunama and Nara are two small ethnic groups who live in the western plains, around the town of Barentu. Unlike most Eritreans, whose languages are either of the Afro-Semitic or Cushitic language family, the Kunama and the Nara speak Nilotic languages similar to those spoken in southern Sudan and western Ethiopia. They are believed to be the original residents of the region who were marginalized by an influx of the Cushitic and Semitic speakers in ancient times. Both groups are sedentary cultivators. They rarely intermarry. The Nara are mostly Muslims, while the Kunama are a mix of Christians, Muslims, and traditional religions, with Christians becoming more dominant. Both have been victims of expansions by the larger and better organized, Tigrigna and Beni-Amer peoples. The Nara are larger and politically dominate the Kunama. For example, many Kunama chiefs are Nara. While the Nara are found entirely in Eritrea, the

Kunama have spread into Tigray and Begemeder provinces of Ethiopia (Nadel 1944, 24–25).

A large ethnic group known as Beni-Amer occupy the north, west, and southwest of Barka province and parts of Senhit province in the northern hills. They are part of a larger group known as the Beja people, of which the most important are the Hadendewa, Amarar, Besharin, and the Beni-Amer (Paul 1954, 137–39). The Beja are Muslim pastoralists who graze their animals in the entire section of the Red Sea coast and eastern Sudan and the northeastern and western parts of Eritrea. The Beja are not politically united, and feuding among various sectors is common. Only the Beni-Amer are found in significant number in Eritrea, however. Next to the Tigrigna, the Beni-Amer are the largest single ethnic group in Eritrea.

Unlike many other ethnic groups, the Beni-Amer do not share the same language. Some Beni-Amer speak Tigre, locally known as Khasa, while others have maintained their traditional Cushitic language called To-bedawi. Many are bilingual, speaking Tigre and To-bedawi. Tigre seems to be gaining dominance over To-bedawi. The Beni-Amer comprise several subgroups but are politically united in a loose federation under the leadership of a paramount chief called the Diglal. Like the Belien and Tigre, the Beni-Amer have a caste system. The ruling caste group is known as the Nabtab, and the serf caste is called Khasa, Tigre, or *ndessna* (which means "those who belong," in To-bedawi). The power of the Diglal is limited by the existence of a deputy known as Shakh al-Mashaikh usually selected from a leading family (Trimingham 1952, 155–58). From 1942 to 1949, the period during which the British ruled Eritrea, the serfs among the Beni-Amer, the Tigre, and the Belien revolted, demanding emancipation. By 1949, they won complete legal freedom from their traditional obligations (Trevaskis 1960, 72–73). The Beni-Amer are in competition and conflict with the Hadendewa and the Kunama and Nara over grazing land along the Eritrean-Sudanese border and in Barka province.

Danakil consists of Afar who speak Afar, a Cushitic language closely related to Saho (Bliese 1976, 133). The Afar inhabit a large area along the Djibouti-Diredawa railway in the south to the Buri Peninsula in the north, and from the shores of the Red Sea to the eastern slopes of the Ethiopian plateau (Lewis 1955, 155). The Afar are spread into three countries: Ethiopia, Eritrea, and Djibouti. Nomadic pastoralists, they are subdivided into clans and lineage groups, and further divided into two caste groups: the ruling caste of Assaimara ("red men") and the serf caste of Adoimara ("white men"). However, the power of the ruling caste has diminished with the increasing autonomy of the serfs. The Afar share a common language (Afar), a common religion (Islam), and a common heritage of mistrust of and fear of aggression from the highland Ethiopians, all of which have helped sustain their consciousness of their unique identity (Nadel 1944, 51). Because of the dryness of their grazing land, the Afar around Assab tend to migrate deep into Ethiopia. All Afar are united under a kinship-based political leadership which is controlled by the Sultan of Awsa in Wollo province in Ethiopia (ibid., 51).

It should be noted that because Eritrea, as a unit, was a creation of European colonization, most of the nine ethnic and language groups mentioned spill over to the neighboring countries—Ethiopia, Sudan, Djibouti—depending on their geographic location. Moreover, the boundaries between many ethnic groups are fluid, and some groups identify with one ethnic group or another depending on the existence of economic and political opportunities in a given setting.

The Cultural Basis of the Eritrean Liberation Movements

In this section I will focus on cultural solidarities that have emerged as sociopolitically important in recent Eritrean history. I will show how ethnic conflicts have shaped Eritrean perceptions of the nationalist movements, and analyze how the movements have dealt with ethnic conflict and cultural diversity within Eritrean society.

The Emergence of the ELF

The Eritrean Liberation Front (ELF) was founded by a few individuals. Sheik Idris Mohammed Adem, a Beni-Amer from the Nabtab nobility in the Barka region, was the central leader. Idris Mohammed Adem served as the chairman of the Eritrean Assembly from 1955 to 1956 when he was forced to resign by the representative of the Ethiopian government. In 1959 he fled to Egypt. Others were Idris Gelawdewos, a Belien from Senhit, and a lawyer educated in Cairo; Ibrahim Sultan, one of the early Eritrean nationalists who had been living in Cairo since the 1950s; and Osman Salah Sabbe, Saho from Massawa (Semhar province), who was a former teacher and an influential Eritrean nationalist in the Middle East. In Cairo, Idris Mohammed Adem and Idris Gelawdewos designed the agenda and aims of an Eritrean liberation front. Idris Mohammed Adem and Ibrahim Sultan met with King Faisal of Saudi Arabia to ask for financial help to start an armed liberation movement. Then they contacted Sabbe in Jeddah and asked him to join them. These three, Idris Mohammed Adem, Idris Gelawdewos, and Osman Sabbe, formed the core leadership of the Supreme Council of the emerging front, the ELF. All three were Muslim Eritreans, particularly hostile to Christian Ethiopian domination. Idris Mohammed Adem was designated the president of the Supreme Council and his closest ally, Idris Gelawdewos, became the secretary and military advisor, while Osman Saleh Sabbe became the secretary general of the front. However, Sabbe was not close to either of the other two leaders, and most of the decisions of the executive body were made without consulting him (Markakis 1987, 104–10). After his initial participation, Ibrahim Sultan did not have a formal position in the ELF hierarchy.

In 1962, the first recorded armed conflicts between the ELF and the Ethiopian government occurred when a small group of Eritrean forces in western Eritrea, working in small bands, attacked police and other government posts in the Barka and Gash regions. The ELF grew in number, especially among the Muslim lowlanders, and conducted many guerrilla attacks on sites of Ethiopian state power, targeting Ethiopian property and means of communication. The first recorded battle between the ELF forces and the Ethiopian army was the Battle of Togoruba, which took place in a village of that name in Barka province on 15 March 1964 (ELF Foreign Information Centre 1977, 1).

During the 1960s, the ELF defined itself as a pro-Arab, Islamic movement opposing Christian-dominated Ethiopian rule in Eritrea. Its leaders held that the majority (70 to 80 percent) of Eritreans were Arabic-speaking Muslims. ELF presented the fight for Eritrean independence from Christian Ethiopia as a holy war. The leaders used religion to mobilize lowland Eritreans, especially the Beni-Amer in the Barka region and the urban Muslims, and to gain support from neighboring Muslim countries such as the Sudan, Egypt, Saudi Arabia, Syria, and Iraq. ELF restricted the participation of Christian highlanders in leadership positions and closely observed their movements. The few highlanders who joined the ELF were isolated from their Muslim compatriots and prohibited from speaking their native language, Tigrigna, with one another (Yehadego 1971, 1–16). The predominantly Muslim leadership and fighting forces of the ELF distrusted the Christian highlanders for two reasons. First, Eritrean Christians have religious and cultural similarities with the Abyssinians (Habashas) in Ethiopia. Second, Eritrean Christians were accused of uniting Eritrea with Ethiopia in the first place. As the ELF stepped up its guerrilla activities, the Ethiopian state increased its repression of all political activities in the cities. Ethiopian authorities suspected and accused many Christians as well as Muslims of supporting the front. This repression helped ELF to recruit both Christians and Muslims. By 1964 it reached almost one thousand fighters.

As the Ethiopian army put more military pressure on the front, ELF needed to reorganize its fighting forces. In 1965, claiming that they were following the model of the Algerian Front de Libération National that had succeeded in winning independence in 1962, the ELF leadership established four zones along ethnic, religious, and regional affiliations. The first zone consisted of the Barka region, which is the home of the Beni-Amer, Nara, and Kunama. It came under the control of a Beni-Amer named Mohammed Dinai, an appointee of Idris Mohammed Adem. The second zone was in the northern hills of Senhit and Sahel. The population were mainly Tigre and Belien, who mixed farming and pastoralism. Omar Azaz, a Muslim Belien, a follower of Idris Gelawdewos, was chosen to lead this group. The third zone was the highland Christian region of Akele Guzai, Serai, and Hamasien, which consisted of the Christian Tigrigna together with Jabarti and Saho Muslims. This area is densely populated and accounted for almost 50 percent of the Eritrean population. Because Christian participation in the nationalist movement lagged behind Muslim and because the Muslims distrusted Christians, zone three became a zone of mostly Saho under a Saho commander, Abdelkarim Ahmed. The fourth zone was under the command of Mohammed Ali Omero, a Tigre from Sahel, who became the head of Semhar and Danakil provinces. The ethnic groups in this region are the Tigre and Saho in the north and the Afar in the south.

All of the leaders were Muslims, which did little to encourage Christian membership. Moreover, the divisions along ethnic and cultural lines led to competition among the four groups for political control and resources within the movement. Each zone operated as an independent body, and ELF lacked coordinated political and military action. Zone one, with mostly Beni-Amer fighters from the Barka region, was the largest and the most dominant. Zone two, consisting of Belien and Tigre from Senhit, was second in power and resources. This division generated inter-ethnic competition and rivalry. Many Christians, some Saho and Tigre from Semhar and Sahel, and some Afar were alienated from the ELF. Tensions within the lowlander region, in particular between easterners (Samhar, Sahel, and Danakil) and westerners (Barka and Senhit) emerged. The divisions among the lowlanders increased the existing cleavages in ELF.

However, the influx of urban and educated highlanders into the ELF grew, and they began to complain about the lack of Christians in leadership positions. A fifth zone was established in 1966 under the command of Woldai Kahsai, a Christian highlander who was a former unit leader in zone three. This zone consisted of Christian highlanders, Tigre, Christians of the Mensa clan, some Belien, and a significant number of Muslims. Idris Gelawdewos, the military commander of ELF, exerted his own control over the fifth zone by appointing a Muslim Belien named Osman Hishal as the assistant commander. While Woldai Kahsai was on a long trip, Osman Hishal ordered the executions of some ELF fighters, all Christians, presumably on military grounds. The killings convinced Woldai Kahsai that his life was in danger. He defected to the Ethiopian Consul in Sudan, taking with him many Christian fighters. Many more Christians gave themselves up to the Ethiopian Embassy in Sudan and to Ethiopian officials in Eritrea. These defections in turn confirmed the Muslim distrust of the Christians. In revenge, many Christians, by some estimates over two hundred, were killed by the same ELF leaders between 1966 and 1968.

The Emergence of the Eritrean People's Liberation Front

Because of the religious and ethnic strife within the ELF in 1970, some members from the three disaffected zones, including zones three, four and five, broke away from the two dominant zones of the ELF and declared the establishment of a new movement. The members of the three zones met at Sudobha Ala in Danakil and established a united front, the Peoples Liberation Forces (PLF) in June 1971. The PLF included members of the major ethnic and religious groups who vowed to work within an organization under one command. The dominant ethnic groups in the new movement were Muslims from Sahel (Tigre), Semhar (Saho), and Denakil (Afar) regions as well as the Christians from the highlands.

Meanwhile a group of Christian highlanders from the fifth zone, led by Issayas Afeworki and Abraham Tewolde, who were lower commanders in the fifth zone, split from the ELF leadership in March 1969, eluding the Ethiopian army and the ELF. This group issued a manifesto titled "Our Struggle and Its Goals" which outlined what was later to become the basis of the emerging new front, the Eritrean Peoples Liberation Front (EPLF). They declared:

> [The ELF] leaders . . . stirred up some long dead grudges among some of the ethnic groups and started preaching that the Christians were their enemies, that the highlanders were their enemies, and that the Christians wanted unity with Ethiopia. . . . they ordered their forces to plunder the Christian highlands of the country. . . . Further looting and the burning of settlements of innocent civilians were conducted, and those who, in the face of such cruel incidents, demanded the observance of their rights were brutally put to death. . . . In view of this, the highlanders who, more than any other group, suffered from this oppression, resolved not only to renounce "Jebha" [ELF], but even to resist and combat its forces. . . . The agents of "Jebha" . . . issued order[s] to the effect that the remaining Christian fighters in the field should be liquidated. Accordingly, more than one hundred innocent highland revolutionaries were hunted down and killed in the vales of the country. Following the submission of highlanders to the consulate in Kessela [Sudan] and the subsequent killing of valiant revolutionaries, very few Christian fighters remained in the field. Now we are the fighters who chose to sit on the edge of a sharp blade. We are the fighters who made this choice rather than die in the hands of the religious fanatics of "Jebha" [ELF] or flee to Ethiopia. . . . We are freedom fighters and not prophets of Christianity. . . . Should there be any struggle in Eritrea whose aim is to liberate only those who are Muslims, we will oppose it. We are unequivocally opposed to all forms of oppression. We will not close our eyes and remain silent when we see Christians being oppressed for fear that we might be labeled as the defenders of Christians. We are freedom fighters who will not forget our revolutionary responsibility for fear of what might be said about us. (Peoples Liberation Forces 1971, 9–14)

The three forces, including leaders from the breakaway three zones (consisting of Christian highlanders, Afar, Tigre, and Saho), met in Beirut in 1972 and signed an agreement to unite. They nonetheless continued to act as independent and, to a certain extent, even rival forces, maintaining their original ethnic and religious composition. Between 1972 and 1974, the oldest and most powerful liberation movement, ELF, actually waged a military campaign aimed at eliminating the other movements from the Eritrea. Assaults by the ELF, however, forced the PLF to create a strong coalition. They operated as a united front in opposition to the ELF and to the Ethiopian forces. In November 1974, the three forces united to form the Eritrean Peoples Liberation Front.

The EPLF received immediate support from the predominantly Christian highlanders, urbanized and educated Eritreans, urban workers, and Eritrean students in Asmara, Addis Ababa, Europe, and North America. It soon became the major force that represented the interests of the highland Christians and secular Muslim Eritreans.

In 1974, a popular revolution overthrew the forty-four-year long reign of Emperor Haile Selassie, and a new era dawned in Ethiopia. However, the new Ethiopian rulers, the Dergue, escalated the conflict with Eritrea. This external threat brought an end to the civil war within Eritrea. The EPLF and the ELF began to coordinate their attacks against the Ethiopian forces in Eritrea. From 1974 to 1977 both fronts were flooded with new recruits, mostly from the Christian highlands. The composition of the two movements as well as their leadership became increasingly similar and were no longer distinguishable along religious or ethnic lines. In January 1977, the First Organizational Congress of EPLF was held at Sahel. Out of this conference emerged a clear leadership, structure, and purpose for the EPLF. The Congress consolidated the alliance between the Muslim Eritreans from the East, mostly Saho, Tigre, and northern Afar, and the highland Christians. However, the tension between the EPLF and the ELF did not evaporate.

The ELF remained a powerful movement until 1978. From 1978 to 1980, the ELF suffered the brunt of attacks by the Ethiopian army, now supported by the Soviet Union. This battering ultimately weakened the front. In 1980, as the balance of power shifted the advantage to the EPLF, a new civil war began between the two fronts. EPLF forces achieved military victory over the ELF, pushing the ELF fighters out of Eritrea into the Sudan. To this day some ELF factions remain in isolated areas in Eritrea, but, since 1982, the EPLF had established itself as the primary nationalist movement in Eritrea fighting against the Ethiopian army.

It was perhaps inevitable that the war for independence for Eritrea would begin in the Eritrean lowlands, where the people are predominantly semi-nomads and Muslims whose historical and cultural links with Ethiopia were much weaker than those of the highland Christian peasants. In the 1940s, when the fate of Eritrea was being decided by the United Nations, Muslim lowlanders were more clearly opposed to the unity of Eritrea with Ethiopia than were the Christian highlanders. Lowland Muslims correctly perceived that the Christian-dominated Ethiopian state would favor the Christian highlanders and feared that unity with Ethiopia would further tip the scales of economic and political power to the advantage of the Christian highlanders. Equality for Muslims would be more easily achieved in an independent Eritrea. Soon after the federation of Eritrea with Ethiopia in

1952, the Muslim lowlanders were marginalized, while the Christians gained more than their share of educational training and economic opportunities in the Ethiopian-controlled state. The alienation of most Christian highlanders from the Ethiopian state came after 1974, when the Ethiopian government indiscriminately imprisoned, tortured, and killed people in the Eritrean Christian highlands.

Now, the EPLF controls Eritrea and strives to create an organization based on national rather than communal allegiances. The front aims to make Eritrea an independent state, bordering Ethiopia, Sudan, Djibouti, and the Red Sea. Whether or not the EPLF has the resources to meet such a challenge is not clear. The front's highest policy-making body is the Political Bureau. Five of its nine members are Muslims. In addition, thirty-six out of seventy-one members of the Central Committee are Muslims. Until the EPLF's 1987 Congress elected Issayas Afewerki as the secretary general of the movement, the front's top leader was Ramadan Mohammed Nour, a Muslim of Saho background from Semhar (Massawa area). The EPLF uses three languages in its official transactions, including Tigre, Tigrigna, and Arabic. Although Tigrigna and Tigre are more widely spoken, many educated Muslim Eritreans see Arabic as their national language.

Yet, despite these facts the EPLF is perceived as being a Christian-dominated movement. This view comes from two sources. First, lowland Eritreans have historically feared domination by the highlanders who are more educated and urbanized. This fear has a social basis. Although the EPLF leadership has a slight Muslim majority, the rank and file of the movement is largely composed of Christian highlanders. They are the main corps of the EPLF. Except for the Eritrean Naval Forces, which consists of mostly Afar, the Eritrean Peoples Liberation Army speaks Tigrigna. Inside the EPLF-controlled area, Tigrigna predominates over the other Eritrean languages. Moreover, the EPLF has attracted the majority of the Eritrean intelligentsia, who are mostly Christian highlanders. These technocrats are the dominant force in running the various units of the movement. Many of these highlanders have worked as civilian and military technocrats in Ethiopia and have had extensive training and experience in running an effective bureaucracy. Moreover, there are a significant number of highland Christian Eritreans with university or secondary school educations. The dominance of Christian highlanders in the EPLF, however, should not obscure the fact that there was a parallel rise in power of the Christian highlanders even within ELF and the other splinter Eritrean movements, for the same reasons.

The most vocal opponent of the EPLF is the Eritrean Islamic Jihad Movement (EIJM). This movement is based in Sudan and financed by Saudi Arabia. Although the Islamic Jihad has no strong followers in Eritrea, its aim is clearly to challenge the hegemony of the EPLF over Eritrean politics. One supporter of the EIJM, who writes under the pseudonym Abu Jihad Seiful Islam, described the movement's challenge in these terms:

> The Christian-dominated EPLF is waging a war against all Muslim and non-Tigrigna-speaking Eritrean organizations while maintaining strategic alliance and special relationship with the non-Eritrean Christian TPLF [Tigray Peoples Liberation Front]. Their ultimate goal is to merge Eritrea and Tigray which, if achieved, will change the present demographic structure of the region in favor of the Christians. In order to face the EPLF's belligerence and to underbalance the EPLF-TPLF alliance which promises to become a threat to the very survival of Muslims in Eritrea, the Muslims were left no option other than that of uniting their ranks to wage jihad against those who are sworn to annihilate them. Thus was formed the Islamic Jihad Movement. The movement maintains military presence in Eritrea unlike other Muslim organizations. I appeal to all Eritrean Muslims to rally behind the Islamic Jihad Movement. (*Arab News*, March 27, 1990)

His claims are echoed by others who express themselves in a Saudi Arabian financed newspaper. The authors of these letters attack the EPLF as a Christian movement and call for Muslim Eritreans to be mobilized to wage a holy war against Christians. It is not clear who reads these letters, but because this is a time of major political fluidity in Eritrean society, such appeals could incite alienated Muslims, especially those from regions formerly controlled by the ELF.

There are also many other critics of the EPLF. They include some former ELF fighters, both Christians and Muslims, and their followers and a huge number of Muslim Eritreans, especially those with strong religious sentiments. Now, most of them are disengaged from Eritrean politics and show little enthusiasm for the successes of the EPLF. The educated Muslim Eritreans argue that, because the idea of a secular state emerged in Christian states in Europe, Christianity can thrive in a secular state. Thus, the separation of religion from the state works to the advantage of Christian Eritreans. Muslims, however, hold that religion and the state are inseparable. Thus, the secularist EPLF is blamed for weakening Islamic practices. For example, the EPLF has eliminated state-sponsored Islamic laws and holidays, segregation of the sexes, the taboo against Muslims eating meals—especially "Christian" meat—with Christians, the ban against marriage between Christians and Muslims, among others.

In summary, cultural divisions in Eritrea and manipulations of these divisions have played a pivotal role in shaping the origination, the social composition, the leadership, and the ideology of the major Eritrean nationalist movements, the Eritrean Liberation Front and the Eritrean Peoples Liberation Front.

EPLF's Policy Toward Cultural Pluralism

There are few official statements on the EPLF's policy toward the cultural diversity which exists in Eritrea or on the representation of cultural groups within the EPLF. In late August 1990, the EPLF leader, Issayas Afeworki, gave an extensive interview regarding his vision of the future of political pluralism in Eritrea. Concerning the viability of a democratic, multi-party, secular state in a third world country like Eritrea, Issayas said:

> In the case of Eritrea, a prerequisite for a healthy pluralist system is to stipulate by law that eligible political parties must safeguard national unity and interest. Religious parties in Eritrea would, sooner or later, spark civil strife and hence jeopardize national unity. So while the freedom of faith must be respected and religious institutions enabled to proselytize without restriction of any kind, there must be a ban on religious political parties. The same rule must apply to regional and ethnic movements . . . (Interview *Adulis*, 7, 8 [October 1990]: 4–5)

Except for such general statements, the EPLF is unprepared to make specific policy recommendations on ethnic and religious tensions within the society. Its reluctance is understandable. The EPLF was established as a secular organization precisely because religious, ethnic, and regional cleavages had become politicized within the ELF. The EPLF may fear that public policies which especially acknowledge divisions within Eritrean society may lead to the fragmentation of the front, as happened in the case of ELF. In practice, however, the EPLF does recognize these divisions and has pursued policies designed to reduce the importance of religion. The EPLF has decreased the political significance of religious/regional affiliations by recognizing ethnic rather than religious communities and by separating political administration from religion as well as by officially recognizing nine ethnic groups with different languages and cultures in Eritrea.

One practice that yields insight into the EPLF perspective on ethnic diversity within Eritrea is the government-sponsored "cultural show." Cultural shows are performed by a number of artistic units from the EPLF fighting forces for a wide Eritrean audience. In their cultural shows, EPLF artists perform plays, songs, and dances representing the various ethnic groups in Eritrea. Thus, ethnicity is relegated to apolitical folkloric public performance. Although the front recognizes Christian and Muslim presence in its fighting forces, it has designated every Wednesday as a day of rest instead of Sundays as observed by Christians and Fridays among Muslims. The movement does not interfere in intermarriage between Muslims and Christians, something traditionally taboo in Eritrean society. There are a significant number of intermarriages in its ranks as well as among its top leaders. To diminish the sense of cultural connection between Christian Tigrignas in Eritrea and Christian Ethiopians, the EPLF uses the European method of reckoning time, space, and numbers rather than the ancient Geez system. There have even been some proposals to employ Latin characters in writing Tigrigna instead of Geez script, which is also utilized by Amharic and Tigrigna speakers in Ethiopia.

Despite these attempts to mitigate Christian highland cultural hegemony within EPLF, the Muslim lowlanders are underrepresented in the front. For example, the numbers of Beni-Amer in the fighting forces are far from proportionate to their population. There is only one Beni-Amer, from the Barka region, in the Central Committee of the EPLF. The initial spark for armed resistance against Ethiopia led by the ELF came from the Beni-Amer–dominated Barka region. This region has been reluctant to switch its loyalty to the EPLF.

Recently the EPLF has begun to accommodate the Beni-Amer in three ways. EPLF leaders and cadres from the Muslim lowlands are deployed to Barka to win the confidence of the people. The EPLF also has recognized the traditional and religious leaders of the Beni-Amer and asked them to serve as intermediaries between the front and the ordinary Beni-Amers. Moreover, EPLF has started a major integrated development project focusing on afforestation and soil and water conservation through the Mogoraib-Forte Scheme in the Barka province. The project will provide irrigation, water, and agricultural extensions for four and a half thousand families (about thirty thousand people). Similar programs are underway in two other lowland areas—Senhit and Sahel Provinces.

The Afar present a very serious challenge for the EPLF. The EPLF recognizes self-determination for Afar nomadic pastoralists in Ethiopia and Djibouti. However, EPLF support for Afar self-determination in Ethiopia raises the question of the status of the Afar in Eritrea. The EPLF contends that colonial powers broke down ethnic and cultural barriers within Eritrea and gave the people national consciousness as well as political and economic unity. From this view, the Eritrean Afar are merely one of the nine ethnic groups in the single Eritrean state (*Africa Confidential,* July 3, 1985).

Sultan Ali Mireh, the traditional leader of the Afar, and his son, Hanfare Ali Mireh, opposed the land reform initiated by the Dergue and formed the Afar Liberation Front (ALF) in 1975—they have been fighting for Afar self-determination since that time. The ALF aims to bring Afarland in Eritrea, Ethiopia, and Djibouti under Afar rule (Shehim 1985, 344–45). As the son of the Sultan and head of the military wing of the ALF, Ahmed Ali Mireh in a recent press interview stated "We are not against Eritrean self-determination . . . We'd also like the Afars to have the right to self-determination" (Press 1991). Ahmed Ali Mireh stated "We are going to govern our affairs, rule our area, and we'll have an autonomous Afar region in the Afar area . . . The Afar people [in Eritrea] will decide whether they [would] like to join the Afars in the rest of Ethiopia or want to remain within Eritrea" (ibid., 4). Moreover, the economic survival and prosperity of the Assab region of Eritrea has depended on its function as an outlet to Ethiopia's landlocked hinterland. The strong economic linkages between the port of Assab and Ethiopian economic centers threatens the economic integration of the Assab region with the rest of Eritrea. If the Afar in Eritrea wish to remain as part of the Afar in Ethiopia, a potential conflict between EPLF and the Afar could start.

The case of the Kunama is less complex. In the past, the ELF, which had a large following among the Beni-Amer and the Nara, tried in vain to subdue Kunama. In 1977, when the ELF captured most of western Eritrea, the Kunama area remained under Ethiopian control. Even joint military operations by the ELF and the EPLF could not dislodge Ethiopian forces from Barentu in 1978 (*Africa Confidential,* June 23, 1978). Barentu is the center of the Kunama people, who became the Ethiopian government's only consistent ally in Eritrea. Barentu became a symbol of resistance against the Eritrean nationalist movements. In July 1978, Gash and Setit districts and the district capital, Barentu, remained fully controlled by Ethiopian garrisons even after eighteen months of encirclement and siege by the two fronts. In July 1985, the EPLF finally took Barentu but lost it to Ethiopia again on August 25, 1985 (*Africa Confidential,* September 4, 1985.) Its strong Ethiopian garrison was largely composed of and led by local troops, who did not trust the Beni-Amer–led ELF.

The cooperation of the EPLF with the ELF forces in attacking Barentu in 1978 made the Kunama fearful of the EPLF. At present the EPLF fully controls the Barentu area. In order to win the confidence of the Kunama, the EPLF has used local leaders to reconcile the long-standing conflict between the Nara and the Kunama. The EPLF has won significant support among the Kunama by training local cadres and teachers, printing educational texts in Kunama, and teaching the young in their native language.

In contrast to the strained relationship between EPLF and the Kunama, the EPLF won the support of the Nara in the 1980s. This was evident in the Second Congress of the EPLF in March 1987. The Congress was held partly to ratify the unity of the EPLF and the Eritrean Liberation Front Central Leadership (ELF-CL), one of the powerful units of the ELF. One of the top leaders of the ELF force that merged with the EPLF was Ibrahim Toteel, from a ruling Nara family. He brought a large number of Nara fighters, among others, with him. He is now a member of the Central Committee of the EPLF.

At this stage the EPLF faces two serious challenges related to the ethnic, regional, and religious diversity of Eritreans. The first involves the presence of some Muslim fundamentalist movements hostile to EPLF. They are seeking financial and political support from neighboring fundamentalist and theocratic countries, such as Sudan and Saudi Arabia, to stir up the now dormant religious tensions within Eritrea. The fundamentalists have labeled the EPLF as a Christian movement and are trying to mobilize Eritrean Muslims to wage a holy war against the EPLF. The most visible and vocal group are the Eritrean Islamic Jihad Movement. Their success in the future will depend on the external support they receive from conservative Muslim states and on how EPLF handles the deep-rooted religious cleavages in Eritrean society. A key population will be the Muslims in western Eritrea, where the ELF had its inception and enjoys its greatest support.

The second challenge deals with the case of the Afar, whose territory extends from Eritrea across to Ethiopia. The claims of the ALF for self-determination of an Afar nation composed of Afar spanning three countries, Ethiopia, Eritrea, and Djibouti, challenges the Eritrean demand for self-determination. Eritrean nationalist movements have conducted guerilla movements for over thirty years for Eritrean self-determination under the belief that the Afar in Eritrea are one of the nine ethnic groups in Eritrea and not part of the Afar territory under the control of Sultan Ali Mireh, who is based in Awsa, a town located deep in Ethiopia.

Isayas Afeworki, the leader of EPLF, has responded to the question of the policy of EPLF toward the ethnic diversity within Eritrea in the following manner:

> Eritrea remains a heterogenous society with diverse linguistic and religious constituencies. The administrative system envisaged must therefore be highly decentralized with the different regions, delineated on geographical and other criteria, enjoying scope to develop specific institutions that correspond to their cultural particularities. The actual form this takes may vary. But the degree of devolution of the constituent parts needs to be quite high. Political pluralism should take this into account. The whole concept requires careful analysis. (Interview *Adulis* 7, 8 [October 1990]:4–5)

The way the EPLF puts these ideas into practice will determine the politics of ethnic, regional, and religious groups in Eritrea in the near future.

Conclusion

The Eritrean nationalist movements represent Eritrean resistance to Ethiopian sovereignity over Eritrea. Now that Ethiopian hegemony has collapsed, the potential for divisions within Eritrea is even greater than before. The perception among many Eritreans that their country is composed of two major cultural units, highlanders (Kebessa) and lowlanders (Metahit), coincides with the rough split of the population into two major religious groups, Christians and Muslims, of approximately equal size. The Christian highlanders are sedentary peasants and the Muslim lowlanders are nomadic pastoralists. The significance of the division of Eritrean society into two regional/religious subnationalities is, however, undercut by many cultural divisions which overlap and weaken the bipolar split into two regional/religious subnational solidarities. For instance, the unity of the Christian highlanders is countered by the existence of Muslim communities in the highlands, such as the Jabarti and the Saho. Muslim lowlanders themselves are subdivided into eight ethnic groups with distinct social organizations, political leadership, languages, and identities. Moreover, the Eritrean lowlands include many pockets of Christian communities, including Christians among the Belien and the Mensa (a clan within the Tigre ethnic group).

Yet, the perception that Eritreans are divided into two broad cultural units,

Muslim lowlanders and the Christian highlanders, has had serious political consequences. The ELF was supported mostly by the Muslim lowlanders, especially the Beni-Amer and Belien in western Eritrea. It was the most powerful nationalist movement from 1962 to 1980. The aspiration of the lowland Muslim Eritreans coincides with that of the ELF, whose imagined Eritrean community or nation (Anderson 1983) has been an independent Muslim Eritrea, oriented toward the Arab-dominated Middle East states. However, this orientation is not shared by the Christian highlanders, who constitute almost 50 percent of the total population. This conflict led to the breakup of the ELF and the emergence of a new competing liberation movement, the Eritrean People's Liberation Front in 1970. From the beginning, the EPLF has had a significant proportion of its leaders and fighters who were from the Christian highlands. The EPLF views Eritrea as belonging to a community of third world nations that are secular and revolutionary. It seeks fast economic development through revolutionary means rather than by gradual change. The highland Christians, who have kinship and family ties with many of the fighters in the movement, support the EPLF at both the emotional and material level. Moreover, the secularist ideology of the EPLF appeals more to highland Christians than to Muslim lowlanders.

Although a significant number of Saho from Akele Guzai and Semhar, Tigre from Sahil, and Afar from Northern Denakil have joined the EPLF over the years, many Muslim lowlanders have weak kinship or family ties with the main fighting forces of the EPLF. They do not perceive the EPLF as representing their emotional needs and material interests. In order to be perceived as a truly national power, the EPLF has made special efforts to appeal to Muslim lowlanders. It modified its revolutionary approach in dealing with the rural population and is accommodating to the existing local religious and traditional leaders in the lowlands.

I contend, however, that the most serious challenge to the EPLF's state-making ambitions is the persisting cultural factionalism predicated on a Christian-Muslim split and that the religious/regional "subnational solidarity is of enduring importance as a political determinant" (Young 1976, 11) in Eritrea. I make such an argument because of the fact that the religious/regional cleavages divide the Eritrean society into two equal and unranked groups (Horowitz 1985, 23–26), which when politicized and mobilized could polarize the society into two large warring religious/regional proto-nationalist groups and destabilize the very foundation of Eritrean claims to self-determination and independent statehood. Therefore, the EPLF faces the very difficult task of reconciling two conflicting imagined communities. One, to which mostly Christians aspire, seeks the separation of religion from the state. The other, clung to by many Eritrean Muslims, sees such a secularist approach as antithetical to the emotional fulfillment and political and economic interests of its Muslim citizens.

The second important problem the EPLF now faces is the demand by some

Afar leaders for Afar self-determination based on their claims about the unity of all the Afar settled in Eritrea, Ethiopia, and Djibouti. Eritrean nationalist movements, including the EPLF, define Eritrea as a nation, composed of nine ethnic groups including Afar, Tigre, Tigrigna, Belien, Saho, Kunama, Nara, Beni Amer (Beja), and Rashaida, forged out of their common experience during Italian colonial rule from 1889 to 1941. Thus, to permit the Afar in Eritrea to exercise their right to Afar self-determination in conjunction with the Afar in Ethiopia disputes the very foundation of Eritrean nationalist aspirations. The Eritrean "nation," thus far won militarily by the EPLF in the contest with Ethiopia, now must be socially constructed internally by Eritreans if Eritrean self-determination is to be fulfilled.

NOTE

1. Confusion arises because of the similar ethnonyms used to refer to "Tigre" or "Tigreans" in Ethiopia, and the Eritrean Tigre (or sometimes written "Tigrai"). In this chapter, "Tigrinya" is utilized to refer to those speaking that language; they are the same ethnic community as those labeled "Tigre" or "Tigrean" in the chapters dealing with cultural pluralism in Ethiopia. The Eritrean Tigre (Tigrai), as labeled in this chapter, are a distinct ethnic community, with a mode of livelihood and way of life different from those here identified as Tigrinya, though of a related language family.

REFERENCES

Anderson, Benedict. 1983. *Imagined Communities.* London: Verso Editions.

Araya, Mesfin. 1990. The Eritrean Question: An Alternative Explanation. *The Journal of Modern African Studies* 28, 1 (March): 79–100.

Bender, Lionel, ed. 1976. *The Non Semitic Languages of Ethiopia.* East Lansing: Michigan State University Press.

Bliese, Loren. 1976. Afar. In *The Non Semitic Languages of Ethiopia,* edited by Lionel Bender, 133–65. East Lansing: Michigan State University Press.

Cliffe, Lionel. 1989. Forging a Nation: The Eritrean Experience. *Third World Quarterly* 11, 4: 131–146.

ELF Foreign Information Centre. 1977. The Eritrean News Letter. *A Bi Weekly News Report,* no. 5. Beirut, Lebanon.

Eritrean People's Liberation Front. 1977. *The National Democratic Program.* Reprinted in James Firebrace, with Stuart Holland. 1985. *Never Kneel Down: Drought, Development and Liberation in Eritrea,* app. 2, 153–66. Trenton: Red Sea Press.

Fessehatzion, Tekie. 1990. *Eritrea: From Federation to Annexation 1952–1962,* Working Paper no. 2. Washington, D.C.: Eritreans for Peace and Democracy.

Gebre Medhin, Jordan. 1989. *Peasants and Nationalism in Eritrea.* Trenton: Red Sea Press.

Henze, Paul. 1986. Eritrea: The Endless War. *Washington Quarterly* 9 (Spring): 23–36.

Horowitz, Donald. 1985. *Ethnic Groups in Conflict*. Berkeley: University of California Press.

Interview: "Victory Only a Matter of Months." 1990. *Adulis* 7, 8 (October):4–5.

Lewis, I. M. 1955. *Peoples of the Horn of Africa: Somali, Afar and Saho*. London: International African Institute.

Markakis, John. 1988. The Nationalist Revolution in Eritrea. *The Journal of Modern African Studies* 26, 1: 51–70.

Markakis, John. 1987. *National and Class Conflict in the Horn of Africa*. Cambridge: Cambridge University Press.

Nadel, F. S. 1944. *Races and Tribes of Eritrea*. Asmara: British Military Administration.

Paul, A. M. A. 1954. *A History of the Beja Tribes of the Sudan*. Cambridge: Cambridge University Press.

People's Liberation Forces. 1971. Nehnan Alamanan, translated as Our Struggle and Its Goals. In *Liberation* 2, 3 (March 1973): 5–23.

Pool, David. 1983. Eritrean Nationalism. In *Nationalism & Self Determination in the Horn of Africa*, edited by I. M. Lewis, 175–193. London: Ithaca Press.

Press, Robert. 1991. In Ethiopia, a King Ends His Exile. *Christian Science Monitor,* August 8, 1991.

Shehim, Kassim. 1985. Ethiopia, Revolution and the Question of Nationalities: The Case of the Afar. *Journal of Modern African Studies* 23, 2: 331–348.

Shumet, Sishagne. 1984. Notes on the Background to the Eritrean Problem (Early 1950's to the 1960's). *Proceedings of the Second Annual Seminar of the Department of History* 1: 180–213. Addis Ababa: Addis Ababa University.

Smith, Anthony, ed. 1976. Introduction: The Formulation of Nationalist Movements. *Nationalist Movements*. London: Macmillan.

Thompson, David E. 1976. Languages of Northern Eritrea. In *The Non Semitic Languages of Ethiopia,* edited by Lionel Bender, 597–603. East Lansing: Michigan State University Press.

Trevaskis, Gerald. 1960. *Eritrea: A Colony in Transition*. London: Oxford University Press.

Trimingham, J. Spencer. 1952. *Islam in Ethiopia*. London: Oxford University Press.

Woldemikael, Tekle M. 1991. Political Mobilization and Nationalist Movements: The Case of the Eritrean People's Liberation Front. *Africa Today* 38, 2: 31–42.

Yehadego, Tekkue. 1971. Unpublished manuscript, 1–16.

Young, Crawford. 1976. *The Politics of Cultural Pluralism*. Madison: University of Wisconsin Press.

10

Ethnicity, Caste, Class, and State in Ethiopian History: The Case of the Beta Israel (Falasha)

■ ■ ■

JAMES QUIRIN

PEOPLES HAVE THE capability of creating their own identities, but must do so within diverse and changing political-economic and sociocultural contexts. The history of the Beta Israel (Falasha) of Ethiopia offers an extraordinary opportunity to observe such changes in both identity and context over a period of several hundred years. After a consideration of two paradigms of Ethiopian studies, this case study focuses on ethnicity, caste, class, and the role of the state as prisms through which to analyze Beta Israel history.

Ethiopian Paradigms

Ethiopian societal-historical studies used to be characterized by two paradigms which stimulated a great deal of useful research, but which also have resulted in an only partial and inadequate understanding of the whole: the "museum of peoples" approach and the "assimilating core" approach (Levine 1974). In the first, the various peoples in what became the Ethiopian Empire by the late nineteenth century were studied separately, as if the "peoples" were static and discrete groups, divided from each other and isolated from any larger scale political-economic-cultural processes. The assumption of primordialism was implicit.

In the second, the "assimilating core" approach, political-military-religious aspects of the central Ethiopian state and Orthodox Church elite society were analysed, while other peoples—if examined at all—were regarded merely as objects of conquest and presumed assimilation: ". . . the central theme of Ethiopian history . . . has been the maintenance of a cultural core which has adapted itself to the exigencies of time and place, assimilating diverse peoples" (Zewde 1975). This framework has tended to assume the direction of change in Ethiopia was only from the center outward and the top down as diverse peoples were assimilated, acculturated, or incorporated into an expanding core.

An excellent beginning has been made in the effort to understand the histories of the diverse peoples of Ethiopia as well as their relationships with the center (Crummey 1990; Donham and James 1986; Triulzi 1981; Braukamper 1980; McClellan 1988). But many of these studies have been limited by the available sources to a focus on the last century or two, during the process of imperial expansion to the south. A historical analysis of the central and northern highland areas is necessary to a better understanding of the "dominant" ethnicity and nature of the "core" state of Ethiopia (Taddesse 1988a, 1988b).

The framework of cultural pluralism (Young 1976)—when combined with an awareness of material and class factors, and the role of the state—is the most useful means by which to understand the historical emergence of Ethiopia and its peoples. In this framework, the perspectives of "primordialism" and "instrumentalism" need to be supplemented by a third, "constructivist," perspective that sees people as the agents of their own history, but who function within various material, institutional, and ideological constraints and contexts (Anderson 1983; Vail 1989; Bọzzoli 1987, 1–8; Ranger 1983).

The Beta Israel-Falasha shaped their history within the context of an evolving Abyssinian-Ethiopian core state that went through four phases: (1) a strong "conquest" state, 1270–1632; (2) a strong, urban-centered state, 1632–1755; (3) a weak de-centralized state, 1755–1855; and (4) a strong centralizing-"modernizing" state, with some false starts, 1855–1974. During the first phase, the "Falasha" created their own ethnic-religious identity in the face of severe pressures from the state by manipulating their common Old Testament heritage to maintain a degree of independence despite military defeat and land confiscation.

In the second phase, the urban Gondarine Falasha struggled to take advantage of new economic and political opportunities as carpenters, masons, and soldiers while maintaining their own religion and language. They prospered while the monarchy flourished, but as the central state declined in power and wealth during the third phase the Beta Israel struggled against the persecution of the dominant society and the encroachment of foreign missionaries. In this context, they forged a caste relationship with Abyssinian society which allowed them to maintain a degree of social separation and religious integrity despite the lack of protection from the monarchy.

During the fourth phase, up through the twentieth century, the rural Beta Israel remained essentially an artisan caste, but more generally fit into a lower landless class within a new Ethiopia created by the centralizing state. Facing renewed missionary pressure and a lack of government protection or support, the Beta Israel began to refashion their Jewish identity and by 1991 nearly all of them had migrated to Israel.

The Construction of Beta Israel Ethnicity

The constructivist perspective on Beta Israel identity is congruent with processes of ethnic change in Ethiopia as a whole, in which the actual fluidity and flexibility of ethnic "categories" over the centuries belies the occasional use of ethnic propaganda by dominant elements (Crummey 1975). Kinship, language, and religion, as well as control of land and power over people, all combined in flexible ways to define ethnicity.

"Amhara," for example, has a flexible meaning, sometimes including all "Abyssinians" (Crummey 1980) even if they are ethnically Tigre or Agaw. But there are also Amharic-speaking Abyssinian Muslims (Trimingham 1952) and significant mixed areas in Wallo or Shoa provinces where designations of "Amhara" by either religious or kinship criteria are loose and have changed historically (Messing 1957, 63–64; McCann 1987, 25–27; personal observations). As is the case with most pre-nationalist ethnic groupings, neither "Amhara" nor "Abyssinian" suggests a closed descent-based "tribe." People have historically rather easily become Amhara (Donham and James 1986, 3–48) and obtained full land-use rights in the ambilineal descent system (Hoben 1973).

Origins and Terminology

The question of "Falasha origins" and the terminology associated with this group can best be explained from a constructivist perspective. In the debate on Beta Israel–Falasha origins, they have been seen as a "lost tribe" of ethnic Jews, as Agaw "converts" to Judaism, or as "rebels" or dissidents against Orthodoxy and the state (Aescoly 1951, 1–4; Leslau 1951, xliii; Hess 1969, 110–11; Kaplan 1986, 1987b).

The "lost tribe" perspective on Beta Israel origins that asserts the present group of that name descends directly from the ancient *ayhud* ("Jewish," "Jewish group") is untenable because it does not take into account the well-documented Ethiopian Orthodox Christian influences on the Beta Israel, including their liturgy, religious books, and monasticism (Leslau 1951; Halévy 1902; Shelemay 1986a, 1986b; Kaplan 1987c; Gaugine, 1965). In other words, the view that the Beta Israel derive directly from an ancient Jewish group overemphasizes and hence distorts the primordial characteristics of this group. Such a view cannot account for the obvious religious, ethnic, and linguistic changes which have resulted from a profound Ethiopian Christian influence.

On the other hand, the Falasha were not simply "rebels" against Orthodoxy because the evidence from the fifteenth century always refers to the rebels or dissidents as joining an existing *ayhud* group. Moreover, the literary, linguistic, and religious data from Aksum do suggest the presence of a Jewish group of some sort, whether a "lost tribe," or a group of Agaw converts to "Judaism" or "Jewish-Christianity" (Ephraim 1972, 1973). The presence of fundamentally

Hebraic loanwords and Jewish concepts in the Ge'ez language, as well as the well-known "Hebraic-Judaic" influences on Ethiopian Orthodox Christianity support this explanation (Polotsky 1964; Ullendorff 1956, 1968, 36–52; Hammerschmidt 1965; Rodinson 1964; Getatchew 1988).

During various periods of intensive Christian proselytization, some of these Jews or Jewish-Christians refused to go along with the new conversion efforts. These groups then became known in the Ge'ez sources as the *ayhud*.[1] As can be documented for the period after the thirteenth century, these groups were also reinforced by dissident or rebelling Christians who joined them, bringing important new religious and literary elements. In other words, the Jewish aspects of Beta Israel society and religion before the nineteenth century were obtained mostly in a process that filtered through Ethiopian Orthodoxy, rather than descending directly from an ancient normative Jewish source (Shelemay 1986a). It is really a classic case of identity formation and re-formation over the centuries. Some kind of primordial *ayhud* groups existed by the fifteenth century. But the people themselves used the material and ideological elements at hand to forge a new identity during the key fifteenth century and later.

The terminology by which the group has been known reflects their evolving position in the Ethiopian historical context. Although the word *ayhud* continued to some degree up to the mid-nineteenth century (Halevy 1869, 287), during the fifteenth and sixteenth centuries, the word *falasha* began to emerge. The traditional etymology of "Falasha" is said to be from the Ge'ez *falasa,* meaning "to separate," "to emigrate," or "exile," or from *falasyan* ("foreigner"). Both terms, hence, were taken to imply a separation from ancient Israel and migration to Ethiopia (Leslau 1957, 1–2; Conti Rossini 1922, 227; but see Hetzron 1976; Getatchew 1987). On the other hand, a constructivist view suggests the "separation" may simply have been from Christian Ethiopia, not from ancient Israel (Krempel 1972).[2]

By the eighteenth century, the use of the term *beta esra'el* (Beta Israel; "House of Israel") was noted by James Bruce (1790, 1:485) who suggested it began in the fourth century, but its actual origin is unknown. During the twentieth century, "Beta Israel" or just "Israel" became the internally preferred term, though they used "Falasha" too. In the last fifteen years, the term "Ethiopian Jews" has been emerging, particularly for the thousands who have migrated to Israel.

The Fifteenth Century

The "Falasha" emerged as an identifiable, named group during the period from the fourteenth to the sixteenth century (EMML 7334; Kaplan 1985; Chihab 1897–1901; Neubauer 1889) and defended their independence up to the early seventeenth century. The process of ethnic group constructivism occurred in the context of tremendous new pressures on groups of *ayhud* in northwest Ethiopia.

The new pressures were the result of the Abyssinian (Amhara-Tigre) imperial political-economic-religious revival which consolidated central control over many additional regions. A new Amhara dynasty seized power in 1270 and was assisted by Tigrean scribes who completed the final redaction of the *Kebra Nagast* ("Glory of the Kings") about 1320, which provided the ideological justification of the conquest and incorporation of non-Abyssinian peoples into the realm (Levine 1974; Budge 1922; Hubbard 1956). The role of the state during this period, hence, was primarily as "instrument" rather than as either "prize" or "theater" (Harbeson 1988, 22). On the other hand, with regard to conflicts with Muslims which climaxed with the sixteenth-century *jihad* of Ahmad al-Ibrahim ("Gragn"), the state was also a prize.[3]

Although the main conflicts were with the Islamic states located in the southern peripheries, proselytization and eventually war also took place against the *ayhud* in the northwest, the region that was the heartland of the "Falasha." Peaceful proselytization among the *ayhud* was carried out by monks in Shawa, Begamder, and Samen provinces (EMML 4741; Quirin forthcoming; Conti Rossini 1938, 1954).

Some Christians, however, whether for ascetic or theological reasons, were also attracted to the *ayhud* religion. During the reign of Dawit (1380–1412), a Christian ascetic named Qozmos joined the *ayhud* in Samen and led them in an armed revolt against his former Christian community in Begamder (Wajnberg 1936, 50; Conti Rossini 1919–20, 572–77). The evidence suggests the century from the 1380s to the 1480s was marked by an ideological struggle within Orthodoxy that involved actual *ayhud* thinkers, as well as those derogatorily labeled *ayhud* by their opponents (Taddesse 1972; Getatchew 1981a, 1981b). In other words, though the *ayhud* were not a military threat, they were a significant ideological force for which control of the dominant religious idea-system of the state was a "prize."

The reign of Yeshaq (1413–30) was a turning point in the history of *ayhud*-Abyssinian relations. King Yeshaq attempted unsuccessfully to create local clients within the *ayhud* leadership. When these relations broke down, the king personally led the forces which defeated the *ayhud,* who were in possession of the rich agricultural land in the region of Wagara, north of Gondar. As a result of the conquest, both written Christian and Beta Israel oral traditions note that new churches were founded (Basset 1881; interview 2c) and the conquered *ayhud* lost inheritable rights to land unless they converted to Christianity. Yeshaq proclaimed: " 'May he who is baptized in the Christian baptism inherit the land of his father; otherwise let him be uprooted from his father's land and be a stranger (*falasi*).' Since then the [Beta] Israel were called Falashas (*falashoch*)" (EMML 7334, 28b). This passage clearly illustrates the Ethiopian Christian view that the "Falasha" originated by separating from the Christian realm and that in doing so they lost direct access to land. Beta Israel traditions also contain this view of the origin of the name "Falasha" and note that Yeshaq said: "I have taken all your land" (interview 2c; Quirin 1992, 55–56).

As a result of these political, economic, and cultural pressures, some *ayhud* did convert to Christianity and become "Amhara," thereby keeping their land but losing their identity, though some certainly kept their identity secretly, like the Marranos in medieval Spain (Messing 1982, 93–99). Others dispersed to outlying and especially lowland regions. Most were forced to become tenant farmers and to adopt alternative means of survival, such as the artisan crafts of blacksmithing and weaving for the men and pottery-making for the women (interview 2a; Quirin 1992).

But the "Falasha" were not simply the defeated objects of Abyssinian conquest. The religious, political, and economic pressures on the *ayhud* acted as a catalyst by which the people began to construct their own identity and society. Although they were heavily influenced by Christian culture, ironically, this acculturation did not lead to their total incorporation. Rather, a group of formerly Christian monks, acting as culture brokers, adapted the Christian religious literature, liturgy, and liturgical calendar, laying the basis for a new "Falasha" identity that lasted to the twentieth century. The literature was mostly derived from Christian sources. The most important texts were the *Orit* (Pentateuch) and the ancient books of Jubilees and Enoch, as well as the *Te'ezaza Sanbat* ("Commandments of the Sabbath") (Halévy 1902; Kaplan 1987c).

Beta Israel traditions mention several men, but emphasize primarily *abba* Sabra and Sagga Amlak in developing much of their religious life. *Abba* Sabra was a Christian from Shoa who came to the northwest, but later left Christianity, adopted "the faith of the Israelites" (Leslau 1975, 624–25), and established an *ayhud* monastery at Mt. Hohwara. From there he developed and spread almost all elements of the Beta Israel religion (Faitlovitch 1910, 88–89; Luzzatto 1852–53, 96–97; d'Abbadie 1851, 237; Quirin 1988; interviews 2c, 7, 8, 12, 13).

In Beta Israel traditions, Sagga Amlak, an alleged son of king Zar'a Ya'eqob (1434–68), converted to the Beta Israel religion and joined *abba* Sabra at the Hohwara monastery. Though Zar'a Ya'eqob attempted to find him, God hid the Beta Israel settlement from view. The son thereby acquired the name Sagga Amlak ("Grace of God") among the Beta Israel because God had saved him from discovery (Quirin 1988; d'Abbadie n.d., 464, 473; d'Abbadie 1845, 49, 72; Flad 1869a; Halévy 1877; Faitlovitch 1910).

Written (Christian) sources document other examples of Christians joining the *ayhud,* such as Qozmos, and an anonymous case similar to the Beta Israel traditions about Sagga Amlak. In the latter, a Christian cleric joined an *ayhud* community until one day "the ruler of the Christians" sent an army which captured him despite his attempts to hide on the "mountain of the Jews." He was brought to the Christian ruler who executed him and scattered his dismembered body to several regions as an example of what happens to apostates (Getatchew 1986).

It is impossible to correlate precisely the oral and written sources (Quirin 1988), but the very existence of these traditions suggests the significance of such phenomena. Whatever the exact nature of the *ayhud* religious practices before the fourteenth and fifteenth centuries, the Falasha-Beta Israel religion as it has come down to us clearly dates mainly to this critical period of *abba* Sabra and Sagga Amlak during the mid-fifteenth century.

In constructing their new ethnicity, the culture brokers were using the primordial identity of some groups as *ayhud* in an instrumentalist way by adapting elements of their opponents' culture (liturgy, literature) and organization (monasticism) to create a new sense of identity and ability to survive as a group despite military defeat, land expropriation, and acculturation. Ironically, both Orthodox Christians and the Beta Israel were drawing on their common ancient Hebraic heritage. The Christian state, with an imperial ideology embedded in the *Kebra Nagast,* viewed itself as the legitimate successor of ancient Israel with the right to impose its rule over the peoples of the area. The Beta Israel appear to have used the ancient Hebraic heritage as a means of resisting oppression and maintaining a coherent community in the same way that ancient Israel has served as an inspiration for other oppressed peoples in world history (Rodinson 1964; Sundkler 1961; Cone 1970).

Combined with the partially autonomous material base which included artisanry, the new ethnic-religious ideology allowed the Beta Israel to resist conquest until the early seventeenth century. But around 1625, the last Beta Israel leader in the rugged Samen highland area was defeated by the forces of King Suseneyos (1607–32). At that point the "Falasha" nearly disappeared from the written records of the central state and Orthodox church. But the monks kept alive the people's liturgy, history, and sense of identity in oral traditions which were still remembered by a few old priests as late as the 1970s (Shelemay 1986b; Quirin 1992).

The Crucible of Occupational Caste Formation

Ironically, however, even as the Beta Israel created a new ethnic-religious identity, their actions, as well as those of the dominant society and state, began to transform them into a caste position within the broader society. By the mid-nineteenth century, both the "attributional" and "interactional" aspects of caste characterized Beta Israel relations with the dominant Abyssinian society (Marriott 1959; Dumont 1970). Their religio-cultural similarities and political-economic incorporation defined them more as a part of a general "Ethiopian" society than as a separate ethnic group. But their endogamous occupational segregation, which was ideologically justified by mutual concepts of moral purity and fear, maintained their unique caste position.

Castes, like ethnic groups, are not unchanging verities, but emerge through dialectical and diachronic relations, although processes of caste formation are not well known. In general, scholars have utilized two approaches: "conflict" analysis, emphasizing the conquest of a separate ethnic group which then becomes a caste (Cerulli 1922; Maquet 1971); or a "gradualist-integrative" perspective, focusing on internal processes of socio-economic differentiation (Lewis 1962; Levine 1974). Both approaches are necessary to explain Beta Israel caste formation.

The first step was their loss of inheritable land-use rights during the period of conquest between the fourteenth and seventeenth centuries. This land loss pushed them to acquire an alternative means of survival as artisans. Though some continued cultivation as tenants, the group as a whole became known primarily for their essential but despised craftwork as blacksmiths, potters, and weavers.

The establishment of Gondar as the imperial capital in the 1630s and the accompanying processes of urbanization during the next century acted as a crucible for caste formation. The city was built in the Beta Israel heartland, and they played a key role in its construction. Beta Israel men added the occupations of mason and carpenter to their repertoire as blacksmiths and weavers, while the women added activities associated with church decorating, such as paint-making, to their skills as potters. The Beta Israel helped build the castles and churches for which Gondar is still famous (Ludolphus 1682, 73, 390–91; Telles 1710, 38; de Almeida 1954, 54–55; Bruce 1790, 2:634, 3:123, 195; Guidi 1910–12, 98; interviews 2a, 2b, 5a, 5b, 5c, 7, 9). Some Beta Israel also were organized into corps of soldiers (Beccari 1903–17, 14:32, 14:43; Guidi 1903, 19, 21–22; interviews 2a, 2b).

For their work as skilled artisans and soldiers, an elite among them was rewarded with small land grants and titles (interviews 2a, 2b, 3, 4a, 4b, 5b, 5c, 6a, 6b, 7, 10, 11, 13, 14). These rewards resulted in the partial incorporation of the Gondar area Beta Israel into the political-economic and military structures of the Abyssinian kingdom as they became less a distinct ethnic group and more a part of the general society, albeit in clearly defined and generally subordinate roles.

The role of the state in this process was crucial. The monarchs and high officials desired to use Beta Israel skills and to reward them within the Abyssinian system of clientship. Sufficient evidence does not survive of conflicts that may have existed between the Beta Israel and the dominant Abyssinian society, though there are a few hints in the oral traditions. In such cases, the state played more the role of "theater" in mediating potential conflicts. Beta Israel traditions look at the state during the Gondar era as their protector and benefactor and remember the period with a bit of nostalgia as a time of "peace and welfare" (Leslau 1947, 80), a view of peace and harmony echoed by the royal chronicler (Guidi 1910–12, 180).

This partial political-economic incorporation was accompanied by a continuing process of acculturation. By the early nineteenth century, Beta Israel similarities with Abyssinian culture were evident. Each existed within a broad Old Testament ambiance. Both religions were based on essentially the same written texts. Each had the same types of religious practitioners and followed similar religiously sanctioned life-cycle ceremonies of birth, circumcision and excision, marriage, and death (Quirin 1992). Linguistic acculturation accompanied these other influences. Between the seventeenth and twentieth centuries, the Beta Israel gradually lost their indigenous Agaw language and adopted the dominant language in the area where they lived, either Amharic or Tigrigna. (Leslau 1947, 93–94; Bruce 1790, 3:190, 535, 4:27; Beke 1844, 8; Gobat 1850, 468; Steudner 1863, 128; Cohen 1912, 70).

Despite these objective cultural similarities, the two groups became increasingly segregated in the early nineteenth century. Although separation dated back centuries (Guidi 1903, 8; Quirin 1979, 244), the religious-moral ideologies of avoidance became more virulent and obvious during this period.

The weakening role of the central state was crucial to this process. A decline in the wealth and power of the Gondar kings and the growth of regional competition and warfare negatively affected the Beta Israel. As construction work and the monarchy's military declined, the Beta Israel became characterized mainly as blacksmiths and potters, even though a few continued to be masons and carpenters. The Beta Israel became scapegoats in an era of sociopolitical instability which led to a hardening of attitudes and the widespread application of the epithet *buda* ("evil eye") toward them (Reminick 1975, 33–40).

A *buda* in Abyssinian society was considered to be a spirit which possessed certain people, enabling them to cause harm. The *buda* could cause harm or death by using his or her "evil eye" to enter another person and drink his blood or eat his entrails. They were particularly dangerous at night when they could change into hyenas and roam about digging up graves and eating the cadavers (Pearce 1831, 1:287, 2: 340–41; Parkyns 1868, 300–13). The phenomenon is known throughout the Ethiopian highlands and in many other parts of the world (Messing 1957; A. Young 1970; Quirin 1979, 1992; Maloney 1976).

In northwest Ethiopia, the term *buda* became equated specifically with the Falasha (Beta Israel). Though the persecution and fear of blacksmiths can be documented as far back as the fifteenth century, the epithet's association with the Beta Israel became especially virulent in the early nineteenth century (Strelcyn 1965, 88–97; Strelcyn 1973, 171–72; Aescoly 1932, 130). The impact of the stereotype on relations between the Beta Israel and the Abyssinians was to reinforce the ideology of separation.

This ideology of separation, however, was not a one-way street. The Beta Israel were not only kept isolated, but they also separated themselves from the dominant society. Though their desire for separation was long-standing, the segregationist impulse was reinforced by the Beta Israel religious hierarchy in the nineteenth century. This emphasis occurred in the context of a religious revival after a period in which their religion faced severe challenges in the early part of the century. Beta Israel traditions record the decline of their religion, particularly as a result of persecutions by some of the regional warlord king-makers after the decline of the monarchy (Leslau 1947, 80). In addition, the Protestant missionaries who began to work among the Beta Israel in the 1850s created serious internal divisions.

During the early 1860s, a religious dispute between the traditional Beta Israel religious officials and the new Protestant converts was argued before the court of Tewodros II (1855–68). Though the actual results of the dispute were somewhat ambiguous, the Beta Israel felt they had won a victory that supported their view that they should not be forced to convert (Flad 1863, 13; Flad 1869b, 244–45; Leslau 1947, 80; Staiger 1863, 80–81; interviews 1, 2a, 8, 11). The Beta Israel priests defended their right to keep their own religion by using the same texts as the Orthodox Christians.

On the other hand, the Beta Israel saw their practice of the Old Testament religion as being purer and hence more "orthodox" than the practices of Ethiopian Orthodoxy. They venerated the Saturday Sabbath, for example, more strongly than the Christians upheld either Saturday or Sunday (d'Abbadie n.d., 460, 467–78; Flad 1860, 86). They felt the Christians violated the food laws by eating raw meat which they considered such a "barbarous custom" that they "compared those gluttonous savages to dogs" (Halévy 1877, 219). They also felt their stricter sexual practices were more moral. Beta Israel women had to retire to separate "huts of blood" during their menses, and they were more rigidly isolated than Christian women during childbirth. The penalties for adultery by women were more severe than for Christians, including the possibility of death (Flad 1869a, 27; d'Abbadie n.d., 464, 467, 470; Parkyns 1868, 331–32).

These practices and views regarding women in each society support the general perspective that gender may often be used as a marker of ethnic differentiation. The Beta Israel considered their more rigid treatment of women as an indication of a higher level of moral purity than existed in Abyssinian society.

Beta Israel monks and priests used what they called their higher morality to reinforce the separation of the people from Christians. Intermarriage was "strongly interdicted" (Stern 1968, 187). They felt it was " 'forbidden by Moses' law to come near an Amhara' " (Bronkhorst 1862, 3). Impurities that occurred by touching, entering the houses of, or even conversing with non–Beta Israel had to be eliminated by washing themselves and their clothes (Gobat 1850, 279; Halévy 1877, 217, 219; Beke 1844, 8; Steudner 1863, 129). Money paid them for their craft goods was received in a dish full of water (Gobat 1850, 468; Halévy 1877, 217).

In summary, the Christians both despised and feared the "Falasha-*buda*," while the Beta Israel felt they were morally superior to the Christians. These two ideologies of separation hence reinforced each other in creating a religious-moral basis for a caste relationship. The Beta Israel had been institutionally incorporated into the political economy of the broader society in particular occupational roles, the practice of which were both essential and feared or scorned by Abyssinian norms. Their culture seen objectively was quite similar to general Abyssinian patterns. On the other hand, their rather rigid endogamous and occupational separation, which was justified by each group on moral-religious grounds, can be best explained as a caste relationship.

Caste and Class

This internal micro-study of the Beta Israel as an occupational caste helps illuminate some overall features of the evolving Abyssinian-Ethiopian class structure. The pre-1900 Abyssinian polity, in general, "rested upon a moderately developed class structure" (Crummey 1981, 228), primarily based on a division between cultivators who held *rest* ("inherited") land-use rights and rulers who controlled *gult* ("tribute") rights (Crummey 1980, 134). In this hierarchy, exploitation certainly existed, as seen in the taxation and labor dues owed (Addis Hiwet 1975; Cohen 1974), but at least three factors mitigated the degree of exploitation and moderated the emergence of a fully developed class system: (1) the high degree of social mobility (both up and down) between the cultivators and rulers; (2) the lack of horizontal ties among the cultivators and the great significance of dyadic vertical relationships between individuals in each group; and (3) the lack of direct access to the land by the rulers who had to impose tribute rights on a *rest*-holding peasantry which did have direct control over the land (Hoben 1970; Crummey 1980; Ellis 1976).

When a consideration of the endogamous artisan and "slave" groups is added to the analysis of northern Ethiopian society, its class nature becomes much clearer than when the focus is only on the differences between the Abyssinian rulers and cultivators, both of whom had access to land or its products. The Beta Israel had been conquered and thereby lost their inherited land-use rights. They along with other groups, therefore, may be seen as part of an emerging landless "class" in the region, which included the Qemant, Wayto, Zalan, Muslims, "Shanqilla," and other "slaves."

These various landless peoples, however, never saw themselves in any way as one group or even as one category. Hence, "class" can be used to refer to them only in a very rudimentary way (Terray 1975; Marx 1964). They continued to relate to each other as separate peoples, while their degree of separation and distinction from the dominant society allows us to describe them all as "castes" or at least as "castes-in-formation." Each group remained essentially endogamous and occupationally differentiated, though some such as the "Shanqilla" and other "slaves" might be gradually assimilated over several generations (Meillassoux

1973; Gamst 1969, Gamst 1979; Trimingham 1952; Donham and James 1986; Pankhurst 1977; McCann 1986).

"Class" analysis may also be useful in analyzing internal stratification within the "castes." For the Beta Israel, such stratification was related to occupation. Though the Beta Israel valued all artisan work, blacksmiths, for example, occupied an ambiguous position (compare McNaughton 1988, 1–21). Beta Israel priests could not also be blacksmiths, though they could be weavers (d'Abbadie n.d., 255; interviews 2a, 11). This distinction may have followed the Old Testament injunction against priests associating with metal, but it also showed an internal differentiation and was congruent with Christian views of smiths as possessing the "evil-eye."

Class stratification within the Beta Israel caste group was stimulated by the emergence of the Gondar urban area during the seventeenth and eighteenth centuries. Beta Israel masons, carpenters, and soldiers were sometimes rewarded with land grants and titles by the Ethiopian state, which resulted in the partial incorporation of a small secular elite, distinguishable from the traditional Beta Israel religious hierarchy headed by priests and monks.

During the nineteenth and twentieth centuries, the role of the state helped define the Beta Israel position in the overall class structure. The Beta Israel lost their special relationship of protection as the Gondar monarchy declined in power. Despite spurts of special and generally favorable treatment by Tewodros II and Menelik II, the general trend was for the state to turn away from them. One factor in the decline of the special Beta Israel relationship was simply regional.[4] With the Ethiopian shift to Shoa under Menelik, the turn toward the south was confirmed. The shift away from the Beta Israel was simply one small part of the overall de-emphasis on the old and tired north, whatever the ethnic group involved (McCann 1987).

In this southern shift, the Beta Israel were mainly ignored by the state and hence were more open to foreign pressures. The centralizing-"modernizing" state of Menelik II (1889–1913) and later of Haile Selassie (1930–74) had rather different priorities than the Gondar kings. As Ethiopia became an actor on the world stage, an emphasis was put on importing foreign technical skills rather than building on the expertise of internal artisans. The beginnings of a "western" school system were made by Menelik and greatly expanded under Haile Selassie, which ultimately undermined both the primacy of the Orthodox Church school system and many traditional Beta Israel institutions. Many new schools were run by missionaries, who were allowed to proselytize in non-Christian areas (Teshome 1979; Pankhurst 1962, 1967).

The splintering of the Beta Israel and the partial breakdown of the caste relationship were evident by the late nineteenth century. Protestant mission efforts had created a new category of "Falasha converts," rejected by both Orthodoxy and traditional Beta Israel monks who excommunicated them (Crummey 1972; Payne 1972; Kessler 1982; Kaplan 1987a; Quirin 1992).

World Jewry eventually mounted an effort to "save" the Falasha which, however, undermined traditional Beta Israel beliefs and practices (Faitlovitch 1910; Grinfeld 1986; Messing 1982; Leslau 1964; Abbink 1987; Kessler 1982). The Beta Israel began to create a new Jewish identity, in accord with world practices, which eventually resulted in the migration of thousands to Israel (Parfitt 1985). This exodus marks the most visible sign of the splintering and disintegration of the Beta Israel people-caste-religion in Ethiopia that has been occurring for the past century. On the other hand, it also begins a new stage in the evolutionary process of identity formation and re-creation which has been going on for centuries as the "Ethiopian Jews" enter the mainstream of world Judaism on a large scale for the first time in their history.

Conclusion

The literature on cultural pluralism suggests that the development of groups and their relations with others may be seen through several complementary prisms, the most salient of which vary according to time and context. Theoretical frameworks should be devised to fit the complexity of historical change rather than vice-versa.

The case of the Beta Israel illustrates that "ethnicity," "caste," and "class" may be useful frameworks within which to explain their history in different periods and changing contexts. As the Ethiopian state was expanding the territory under its direct control and elaborating an accompanying imperial ideology, the "Falasha" constructed a new ethnic-religious identity utilizing both *ayhud* and Orthodox Christian elements. This new identity, and the accompanying material base, allowed the group to defend itself and remain politically independent up to the early seventeenth century.

Once conquered, however, elements of the group entered into closer ties with the state in an urban environment. They essentially placed themselves under state protection and control as clients who were becoming a caste. The state provided work in stone construction, church decoration, and in the army for which Beta Israel elites received political and material rewards. Although this evolving caste relationship allowed the Beta Israel to flourish, it also began to create secular-religious divisions within the group and may have stimulated the increased antagonism of Abyssinian society.

When the central state faltered after the mid-eighteenth century, the Beta Israel position became increasingly precarious. Caste lines hardened as each side developed more rigid ideologies of revulsion and superiority toward the other even while objective differences of ethnicity and religion were rather slight.

When the state began to strengthen itself again in the late nineteenth and twentieth centuries, the Beta Israel were mostly ignored. Foreign influences proliferated as Ethiopia became more fully incorporated into the world economy, engaged in war and diplomacy on a world stage, and allowed more foreign missionaries, technicians, and advisors into the country. During this period, in contrast to the Gondar era, the technical skills of the Beta Israel artisans were used only marginally by the state in urban areas, although they remained crucial to the rural farming economy of the northwest. Though still a "caste" vis-à-vis the dominant society, the Beta Israel were also clearly part of the lower classes of a centralizing state system. Whereas in the Gondar era, their caste's dominance of highly valued skills allowed them to prosper and obtain a somewhat higher position in the overall class structure than some other minorities, during the twentieth century they were either ignored or suppressed into a definite lower-class ranking. In both cases, the state played a key role in determining the class ranking of the Beta Israel caste. The state manipulated the group's identity to its own ends.

Lacking state support, traditional Beta Israel practices were increasingly threatened by proselytizing Protestant missionaries and their own small group of "Falasha converts." As world Jewry became more concerned with their plight, especially after World War II, the Beta Israel began to reconstruct their identity once again to bring it more in line with international Judaism. This study thus also illustrates an extreme type of ethnic constructivism. Instead of the more usual phenomena of ethnically or territorially based separatist movements within a nation-state or multi-ethnic empire that have characterized the post–World War II revival of cultural pluralism, in this case the group simply left *en masse*. In their new home, the more than forty thousand Ethiopian Jews continue the process of reconstruction of their identity in order to fit into their new Israeli society while retaining a modicum of group identity.

NOTES

1. *Ayhud* had various meanings in the fourteenth and fifteenth centuries, including a derogatory epithet, and I am not arguing that all *ayhud* became "Falasha." See Quirin (1992, ch. 1).

2. Krempel, however, overemphasizes the "rebel" perspective. Another term for the Beta Israel, especially in the Gondar region, was *kayla,* an Agaw term that was first used in the seventeenth century (Esteves Pereira 1892–1900, 1:307; Guidi 1903, 8), but which in recent years has come to have even more derogatory connotations than "Falasha."

3. For a survey of the vast literature on state and society see Lonsdale (1981); Brass (1976); Young (1976). In Ethiopia, at times, the state was the "instrument" of the ruling class, as in periods of conquest (or reconquest) of other peoples or states; at other times, the state was more of a "theater" which mediated between disputing groups; while the

sixteenth-century Muslim-Christian conflict suggests that each side fought to control the state, which was the "prize" in the wars. See John Harbeson's shorthand terminology (1988, 22).

4. The "regional" in Ethiopia is more than simply a "residual" category (Young 1976, 64–65) of cultural pluralism and is often more significant than ethnicity, language, or even religion.

REFERENCES

Abbink, Jon. 1987. An Ethiopian Jewish "Missionary" as Culture Broker. In *Ethiopian Jews and Israel,* edited by M. Ashkenazi and A. Weingrod, 21–32. New Brunswick: Transaction Books.

Addis Hiwet. 1975. *Ethiopia: From Autocracy to Revolution. Review of African Political Economy* (London), Occasional Publ. no. 1.

Aescoly, A. Z. 1961. Notices sur les Falacha ou Juifs d'Abyssinie, d'après le "Journal de voyage" d'Antoine d'Abbadie. *Cahiers d'études africaines* 2: 84–147.

Aescoly, A. Z. 1951. *Recueil de textes falachas. Travaux et mémoires de l'Institut d'Ethnologie* (Paris), vol. 55.

Aescoly, A. Z. 1932. Les noms magiques dan les Apocryphes Chrétiens des Ethiopiens. *Journal asiatique* 220: 87–137.

Anderson, Benedict. 1983. *Imagined Communities*. London: Verso Editions.

Basset, René, ed. 1881. Etudes sur l'histoire d'Ethiopie. *Journal asiatique,* 7th ser., 17:315–434, 18:93–183, 285–389.

Beccari, C., ed., 1903–17. *Rerum Aethiopicarum, Scriptores Occidentales inediti a saeculo XVI ad XIX*. 15 vols. Rome: C. de Luigi.

Beke, Charles. 1844. Abyssinia—Being a Continuation of Routes in that Country. *Journal of the Royal Geographical Society* 14: 1–76.

Berry, LaVerle. 1976. The Solomonic Monarchy at Gonder, 1630–1755: An Institutional Analysis of Kingship in the Christian Kingdom of Ethiopia. Ph.D. dissertation, Boston University.

Bozzoli, Belinda, ed. 1987. *Class, Community and Conflict: South African Perspectives*. Johannesburg: Ravan Press.

Brass, Paul, ed. 1985. *Ethnic Groups and the State*. London: Croon Helm.

Brass, Paul. 1976. Ethnicity and Nationality Formation. *Ethnicity* 3: 225–41.

Braukamper, Ulrich. 1980. *Geschichte der Hadiya Sud-Athiopiens von den Anfangen bis zur Revolution 1974*. Wiesbaden: Franz Steiner Verlag.

Bronkhorst, C. 1862. *Jewish Records* 12 (January): 3.

Bruce, James. 1790. *Travels to Discover the Source of the Nile*. 5 vols. Edinburgh.

Budge, E. A. W., ed. 1922. *The Queen of Sheba and Her Only Son Menyelek . . . A Complete Translation of the Kebra Nagast*. London: Oxford University Press.

Cerulli, Enrico. 1922. The Folk-Literature of the Galla of Southern Abyssinia. In *Harvard African Studies, Varia Africana,* edited by E. A. Hooten and Patricia Bates, vol. 3, Appendix, The Watta: A Low Caste of Hunters, 200–14. Cambridge: Harvard University Press.

Chihab Ed-Din Ahmed ben 'Abd el-Qader (Arab Faqih). 1897–1901. *Histoire de la conquête de l'Abyssinie (XVI siècle),* edited by René Basset. Paris: Ernest Leroux.

Cohen, John. 1974. Ethiopia: A Survey on the Existence of a Feudal Peasantry. *Journal of Modern African Studies* 12: 665–72.

Cohen, Marcel. 1912. Rapport sur une mission linguistique en Abyssinie 1910–1911. *Nouvelles archives des missions scientifique et littéraires,* n.s. 20:1–80.

Cone, James. 1970. *A Black Theology of Liberation* Philadelphia: Lippincott.

Conti Rossini, Carlo, ed. 1954. *Gadla Takla Hawaryat (Acta Sancti Takla Hawaryat). Corpus Scriptorum Christianorum Orientalium, Script. Aeth.* 25: 65–135.

Conti Rossini, Carlo. 1938. Note di agiografia etiopica (Abiya-Egzi, Arkaledes e Gabra Iyesus). *Rivista degli studi orientali* 17: 409–52.

Conti Rossini, Carlo. 1922. Nuovi appunti sui Giudei d'Abissinia. *Rendiconti della Reale Accademia Nazionale dei Lincei* 29: 221–40.

Conti Rossini, Carlo. 1919–1920. Appunti de storia e letteratura Falascia. *Rivista degli studi orientali* 8: 563–610.

Crummey, Donald. 1990. Society, State and Nationality in the Recent Historiography of Ethiopia. *Journal of African History* 31: 103–19.

Crummey, Donald. 1987. Some Precursors of Addis Ababa: Towns in Christian Ethiopia in the Eighteenth and Nineteenth Centuries. In *Proceedings of the International Symposium on the Centenary of Addis Ababa, November 24–25, 1986,* edited by Ahmed Zekaria, et al., 9–31. Addis Ababa.

Crummey, Donald. 1981. State and Society: 19th-Century Ethiopia. In *Modes of Production in Africa: The Precolonial Era,* edited by Donald Crummey and C. C. Stewart. 227–49. Beverly Hills: Sage Publications.

Crummey, Donald. 1980. Abyssinian Feudalism. *Past and Present* 89: 115–38.

Crummey, Donald. 1975. Society and Ethnicity in the Politics of Christian Ethiopia During the Zamana Masafent. *International Journal of African Historical Studies* 8: 266–78.

Crummey, Donald. 1972. *Priests and Politicians: Protestant and Catholic Missions in Orthodox Ethiopia, 1830–1868.* London: Oxford University Press.

d'Abbadie, Antoine. n.d. Journal et mélanges. Bibliothèque Nationale, France Nouvelle Acquisition 21300 (also on microfilm at Institute of Ethiopian Studies, Addis Ababa).

d'Abbadie, Antoine. 1851. Réponses des Falasha dits juifs d'Abyssinie. *Archives Israelites* 12: 179–85, 234–40, 259–69.

d'Abbadie, Antoine. 1845. Extrait d'une lettre de M. Antoine d'Abbadie sur les Falacha ou juifs d'Abyssinie. *Bulletin de la société de géographie,* 3d ser. 4: 43–57, 65–74.

de Almeida, Manoel. 1954. The History of High Ethiopia or Abassia. In *Some Records of Ethiopia, 1593–1646,* edited by C. F. Beckingham and G. W. B. Huntingford. London: Hakluyt.

Donham, Donald, and Wendy James. 1986. *The Southern Marches of Imperial Ethiopia.* Cambridge: Cambridge University Press.

Dumont, Louis. 1970. *Homo Hierarchus, An Essay on the Caste System.* Chicago: University of Chicago Press.

Ellis, Gene. 1976. The Feudal Paradigm as a Hindrance to Understanding Ethiopia. *Journal of Modern African Studies* 14: 275–95.

EMML 4741. Gadla Zena Marqos. Ethiopian Monastic Microfilm Library, Addis Ababa and Collegeville, Minnesota.

EMML 7334. Tarika Nagast, Ff. 28a–28b. Ethiopian Monastic Microfilm Library, Addis Ababa and Collegeville, Minnesota.

Ephraim, Isaac. 1973. *A New Text-Critical Introduction to Mashafa Berhan*. Leiden: E. J. Brill.

Ephraim, Isaac. 1972. An Obscure Component in Ethiopian Church History. *Le Muséon* 85: 225–58.

Esteves Pereira, F. M., ed. 1892–1900. *Chronica de Susenyos, Rei de Ethiopia*. 2 vols. Lisbon: Impressa Nacional.

Faitlovitch, Jacques. 1910. *Quer Durch Abessinien*. Berlin: M. Poppelauer.

Flad, J. M. 1869a. *The Falashas (Jews) of Abyssinia*. London: W. MacKintosh.

Flad, J. M. 1869b. Twelve Years in Abyssinia. *Jewish Intelligence* 9: 244–45.

Flad, J. M. 1863. Journal. *Jewish Records* 28–29 (April–May): 13–20.

Flad, J. M. 1860. *Notes from the Journal of J.M. Flad*. London: James Nisbet and Co.

Gamst, Frederick. 1979. Wayto Ways: Change from Hunting to Peasant Life. In *Proceedings of the Fifth International Conference on Ethiopian Studies, Chicago, 1978,* edited by Robert Hess, 233–38. Chicago: University of Illinois.

Gamst, Frederick. 1969. *The Qemant. A Pagar-Hebraic Peasantry of Ethiopia*. New York: Holt, Rinehart, Winston.

Gaugine, Maurice. 1965. The Falasha Version of the Testaments of Abraham, Isaac, and Jacob. Ph.D. dissertation, University of Manchester.

Getatchew Haile. 1988. The Forty-Nine Hour Sabbath of the Ethiopian Church. *Journal of Semitic Studies* 33: 233–54.

Getatchew Haile. 1987. Review of David Kessler's *The Falashas*. *Journal of Religion in Africa* 17: 187–88.

Getatchew Haile. 1986. The End of a Deserter of the Established Church of Ethiopia. *Ethiopian Studies. Proceedings of the Sixth International Conference, Tel-Aviv, 1980,* edited by Gideon Goldenberg, 193–203. Boston: Balkema.

Getatchew Haile. 1981a. Religious Controversies and the Growth of Ethiopic Literature in the Fourteenth and Fifteenth Centuries. *Oriens Christianus* 65: 102–36.

Getatchew Haile. 1981b. A Study of the Issues Raised in Two Homilies of Emperor Zar'a Ya'eqob of Ethiopia. *Zeitschrift der Deutschen Morganlandischen Gesellschaft* 131: 85–113.

Gobat, Samuel. 1850. Orig. ed. 1834. *Journal of Three Years' Residence in Abyssinia*. New York: Dodd.

Grinfeld, Itzhak. 1986. Jews in Addis Ababa: Beginnings of the Jewish Community until the Italian Occupation. In *Ethiopian Studies: Proceedings of the Sixth International Conference, Tel-Aviv, 1980,* edited by Gideon Goldenberg, 251–59. Rotterdam: Balkema.

Guidi, Ignazio, ed. 1910–1912. *Annales Regum Iyasu II et Iyo'as. CSCO. Script. Aeth.*, 2 vols., ser. alt., vol. 6. Paris.

Guidi, Ignazio, ed. 1903. *Annales Iohannis I, Iyasu I, Bakafa. Corpus Scriptorum Christianorum Orientalium: Script. Aeth.* 2 vols., ser. alt., vol. 5. Paris.

Halévy, Joseph. 1902. *Te'ezaza Sanbat (Commandements du Sabbat)*. Paris: E. Bouillon.
Halévy, Joseph. 1877. Travels in Abyssinia. In *Miscellany of Hebrew Literature*, edited by A. L. Lowy, ser. 2, vol. 2, 175–256. London: Trubner & Co.
Halévy, Joseph. 1869. Excursion chez les Falacha en Abyssinie. *Bulletin de la société de géographie* ser. 5, vol. 17, 270–94.
Hammerschmidt, Ernst. 1965. Jewish Elements in the Cult of the Ethiopian Church. *Journal of Ethiopian Studies* 3, 2: 1–12.
Harbeson, John. 1988. *The Ethiopian Transformation, The Quest for the Post-Imperial State*. Boulder: Westview Press.
Hess, Robert. 1969. Towards a History of the Falasha. In *Eastern African History. Boston University Papers on Africa,* edited by D. F. McCall, 107–32. New York: Praeger.
Hetzron, Robert. 1976. The Agaw Languages. *Afroasiatic Linguistics* 3, 2 (June): 1–45.
Hoben, Allan. 1973. *Land Tenure among the Amhara of Ethiopia: The Dynamics of Cognatic Descent*. Chicago: University of Chicago Press.
Hoben, Allan. 1970. Social Stratification in Traditional Amhara Society. In *Social Stratification in Africa,* edited by A. Tuden and L. Plotnicov, 187–224. New York: Free Press.
Hubbard, D. A. 1956. The Literary Sources of the Kebra Nagast. Ph.D. thesis, St. Andrews University.
Kaplan, Steven. 1992. *The Beta Israel (Falasha) in Ethiopia: From Earliest Times to the Twentieth Century*. New York: New York University Press.
Kaplan, Steven. 1990. *Les Falāshās*. Turnhout, Belgium: Brepols.
Kaplan, Steven. 1987a. The Beta Israel (Falasha) Encounter with Protestant Missionaries: 1860–1905. *Jewish Social Studies* 49: 27–42 (reprinted in *Truman Institute Reprints*).
Kaplan, Steven. 1987b. The Origins of the Beta Israel: Five Methodological Cautions. *Pe'amim* 33: 33–49.
Kaplan, Steven. 1987c. Te'ezaza Sanbat: A Beta Israel Work Reconsidered. *Studies in the History of Religions* 1: 107–24 (reprinted in *Truman Institute Reprints*).
Kaplan, Steven. 1986. A Brief History of the Beta Israel. In *The Jews of Ethiopia. A People in Transition,* 11–29. New York: The Jewish Museum.
Kaplan, Steven. 1985. The Falasha and the Stephanite: An Episode from the *Gadla Gabra Masih. Bulletin. School of Oriental and African Studies* 28: 278–84.
Kessler, David. 1982. *The Falashas. The Forgotten Jews of Ethiopia*. New York: Africana.
Krempel, Veronika. 1972. Die soziale und wirtschaftliche stellung der Falascha in der christlich-amharischen Gesellschaft von Nordwest Aethiopien. Ph.D. dissertation, Free University of Berlin.
Leslau, Wolf. 1975. Taamrat Emmanuel's Notes of Falasha Monks and Holy Places. In *Salo Wittmayer Barron Jubilee Volume, American Academy for Jewish Research,* vol. 2, 623–37. Jerusalem: AAJR.
Leslau, Wolf. 1964. A Falasha Book of Jewish Festivals. In *For Max Weinrich on his Seventieth Birthday,* 183–91. London: Mouton.
Leslau, Wolf. 1957. *Coutumes et croyances des Falachas. Travaux et mémoires de l'Institut d'Ethnologie,* vol. 61: 1–98.
Leslau, Wolf. 1951. *Falasha Anthology*. New Haven: Yale University Press.

Leslau, Wolf, ed. 1947. A Falasha Religious Dispute. *Proceedings of the American Academy for Jewish Research* 16: 71–95.

Levine, Donald. 1975. Menilek and Oedipus: Further Observations on the Ethiopian National Epic. In *Proceedings of the First United States Conference on Ethiopian Studies, 1973,* edited by Harold G. Marcus, 11–23. East Lansing: African Studies Center, Michigan State University.

Levine, Donald. 1974. *Greater Ethiopia: The Evolution of a Multiethnic Society.* Chicago: University of Chicago Press.

Lewis, Herbert. 1962. Historical Problems in Ethiopia and the Horn of Africa. *Annals of the New York Academy of Sciences* 96: 504–11.

Lobo, Jerome, 1789. *A Voyage to Abyssinia by Father Jerome Lobo,* edited by M. Le Grand, translated by Samuel Johnson. London: Elliot and Kay.

Lonsdale, John. 1981. State and Social Processes in Africa: A Historiographical Survey. *African Studies Review* 2, 3: 139–225.

Ludolphus, Job. 1682. *A New History of Ethiopia.* London: J. P. Gent.

Luzzatto, P. 1852–53. *Mémoire sur les juifs d'Abyssinie ou Falashas.* Paris: Extrait des Archives Israelites.

McCann, James. 1987. *From Poverty to Famine in Northeast Ethiopia: A Rural History, 1900–1935.* Philadelphia: University of Pennsylvania Press.

McCann, James. 1986. Children of the House: Slavery and Its Suppression in Lasta, Northwestern Ethiopia, 1916–1975. In *The End of Slavery in Africa,* edited by Suzanne Miers and Richard Roberts, 332–61. Madison: University of Wisconsin Press.

McClellan, Charles. 1988. *State Transformation and National Integration: Gedeo and the Ethiopian Empire, 1895–1935.* East Lansing: Michigan State University Press.

McNaughton, Patrick. 1988. *The Mande Blacksmiths.* Bloomington: Indiana University Press.

Maloney, Clarence, ed. 1976. *The Evil Eye.* New York: Columbia University Press.

Maquet, Jacques. 1971. *Power and Society in Africa* New York: McGraw-Hill.

Marriott, McKim. 1959. Interactional and Attributional Theories of Caste Ranking. *Man in India* 39: 92–107.

Marx, Karl. 1964. *Pre-Capitalist Economic Formations,* edited by E. J. Hobsbawm. New York: International Publishers.

Meillassoux, Claude. 1973. Are There Castes in India? *Economy and Society* 9: 89–111.

Messing, Simon. 1982. *The Story of the Falashas.* Hamden.

Messing, Simon. 1957. The Highland-Plateau Amhara of Ethiopia. Ph.D. dissertation, University of Pennsylvania.

Neubauer, A. 1889. Where Are the Ten Tribes? *Jewish Quarterly Review.* 1: 14–28, 95–114, 185–201, 408–23.

Pankhurst, Richard. 1977. The History of the Bareya, Shanqella and Other Ethiopian Slaves from the Borderland of the Sudan. *Sudan Notes and Records* 59: 1–43.

Pankhurst, Richard. 1967. Menilek and the Utilisation of Foreign Skills in Ethiopia. *Journal of African History.* 5: 29–86.

Pankhurst, Richard. 1962. The Foundations of Education, Printing, Newspapers, Book Production, Libraries and Literacy in Ethiopia. *Ethiopia Observer* 6, 3: 241–90.

Parfitt, Tudor. 1985. *Operation Moses. The Untold Story of the Secret Exodus of the Falasha Jews from Ethiopia.* New York: Weidenfeld and Nicolson.

Parkyns, Mansfield. 1868. *Life in Abyssinia.* 2d ed. London: John Murray.

Payne, Eric. 1972. *Ethiopian Jews: The Story of a Mission.* London: Olive Press.

Pearce, Nathaniel. 1831. *The Life and Adventures.* 2 vols. London: Colburn and Bentley.

Polotsky, H. J. 1964. Aramaic, Syriac, and Ge'ez. *Journal of Semitic Studies* 9: 1–10.

Quirin, James. Forthcoming. Jews in Fourteenth-Century Ethiopia: Data from the *Gadla Zena Marqos.*

Quirin, James. 1993. Oral Traditions as Historical Sources in Ethiopia: The Case of the Beta Israel (Falasha). *History in Africa* 20.

Quirin, James. 1992. *The Evolution of the Ethiopian Jews: A History of the Beta Israel (Falasha) to 1920.* Philadelphia: University of Pennsylvania Press.

Quirin, James. 1988. The Beta 'Esrā'ēl (Falāshā) and *'Ayhud* in Fifteenth-Century Ethiopia: Oral and Written Traditions. *Northeast African Studies* 10: 89–104.

Quirin, James. 1979. The Process of Caste Formation in Ethiopia: A Study of the Beta Israel (Felasha), 1270–1868. *International Journal of African Historical Studies* 12: 235–58.

Ranger, Terence. 1983. The Invention of Tradition in Colonial Africa. In *The Invention of Tradition,* edited by Eric Hobsbawm and Terence Ranger, 211–62. Cambridge: Cambridge University Press.

Reminick, Ronald. 1975. The Structure and Functions of Religious Belief among the Amhara of Ethiopia. In *Proceedings of the First United States Conference on Ethiopian Studies, 1973,* edited by Harold Marcus, 25–42. East Lansing: Michigan State University Press.

Rodinson, Maxime. 1964. Sur la question des 'influences juives' en Ethiopie. *Journal of Semitic Studies* 9: 11–19.

Sabrijian, Dimoteos. 1871. *Deux ans de séjour en Abyssinie,* 2 vols. Jerusalem: Typographie Armenienne.

Shelemay, Kay. 1986a. A Comparative Study: Jewish Liturgical Forms in the Falasha Liturgy? *Yuval. Studies of the Jewish Music Research Centre* 5: 372–404.

Shelemay, Kay. 1986b. *Music, Ritual and Falasha History.* East Lansing: Michigan State University Press.

Staiger, 1863. Journal. *The Home and Foreign Missionary Record of the Church of Scotland,* n.s., vol. 2, 80–81.

Stern, Henry. 1968. *Wanderings Among the Falashas in Abyssinia.* 2d ed. London: Frank Cass.

Steudner, H. 1863. Reise von Adoa nach Gondar, December 26, 1861–Januar 1862. *Zeitschrift fur Allgemeine Erdkunde* 15: 43–141.

Strelcyn, S. 1973. Les nouveaux manuscrits éthiopiens de la Bibliothèque Royale de Bruxelles. *Journal of Ethiopian Studies* 11, 2 (July): 169–88.

Strelcyn, S. 1965. Les écrits médicaux Éthiopiens. *Journal of Ethiopian Studies* 3, 1: 82–103.

Sundkler, Bengt. 1961. *Bantu Prophets in South Africa.* 2d ed. London: Oxford University Press.

Taddesse Tamrat. 1988a. Ethnic Interaction and Integration in Ethiopian History: The Case of the Gafat. *Journal of Ethiopian Studies* 21: 121–54.

Taddesse Tamrat. 1988b. Processes of Ethnic Interaction and Integration in Ethiopian History: The Case of the Agaw. *Journal of African History* 29: 5–18.

Taddesse Tamrat. 1972. *Church and State in Ethiopia, 1270–1527*. Oxford: Clarendon Press.

Telles, Balthazar. 1710. Orig. ed., 1660. *Travels of the Jesuits in Ethiopia*. London: J. Knapton.

Terray, Emmanuel. 1975. Classes and Class Consciousness in the Abron Kingdom of Gyaman. In *Marxist Analyses and Social Anthropology*, edited by Maurice Bloch, 85–135. New York: Halstead Press.

Teshome G. Wagaw. 1979. *Education in Ethiopia: Prospect and Retrospect*. Ann Arbor: University of Michigan Press.

Trimingham, J. S. 1952. *Islam in Ethiopia*. New York: Oxford University Press.

Triulzi, Alessandro. 1981. *Salt, Gold and Legitimacy. Prelude to the History of a No-man's Land. Beta Shangul, Wallagga, Ethiopia (ca. 1800–1898)*. Naples: Instituto Universitario Orientale.

Ullendorff, Edward. 1968. *Ethiopia and the Bible* London: Oxford University Press.

Ullendorff, Edward. 1956. The Hebraic-Judaic Elements in Abyssinian (Monophysite) Christianity. *Journal of Semitic Studies* 1: 216–56.

Vail, Leroy. 1989. *The Creation of Tribalism in Southern Africa*. Berkeley: University of California Press.

Wajnberg, I., ed. 1936. Das Leben des hl. Jafqerena 'Egzi.' *Orientalia Cristiana Analecta* 106: 3–124.

Young, Allan. 1970. Medical Beliefs and Practices of Begemder Amhara. Ph.D. dissertation, University of Pennsylvania.

Young, Crawford. 1986. Nationalism, Ethnicity, and Class in Africa: A Retrospective. *Cahiers d'études africaines* 26: 421–95.

Young, Crawford. 1976. *The Politics of Cultural Pluralism*. Madison: University of Wisconsin Press.

Zewde Gabre-Sellasie. 1975. *Yohannes IV of Ethiopia: A Political Biography*. Oxford: Clarendon Press.

Interviews

1: With Ayyallegne Adgwāchaw and Kebratē Sāmu'ēl, 26 October 1975.
2a: With Berhān Beruk, 3 July 1975.
2b: With Berhān Beruk, 14 August 1975.
2c: With Berhān Beruk, 20 August 1975.
3: With Dassē Yeshaq, 8 January 1976.
4a: With Garimā Tāffara, 4 August 1975.
4b: With Garimā Tāffara, 25 August 1975.
5a: With Gētē Asrass, 3 June 1975.
5b: With Gētē Asrass, 11 June 1975.
5c: With Gētē Asrass, 9 November 1975.

6a: With Jammara Wandē, 21 July 1975.
6b: With Jammara Wandē, 26 August 1975.
7: With Menasē Zammaru and Wandē Iyyāsu, 13 October 1975.
8: With Menasē Zammaru, 15 October 1975.
9: With Mulunah Marshā, Tafari Negusē, and Qanu Ayyalaw, 22 November 1975.
10: With Rattā Zawdē, 10 August 1975.
11: With Webē Akāla, 27 December 1975.
12: With Yehēyyes Madḥanē and Yālaw Siyāmer, 27 October 1975.
13: With Yesḥaq Iyyāsu, 15 December 1975.
14: With Zallaqa Damozē, 28 November 1975.

11

Ethnic Identity and the De-Nationalization and Democratization of Leninist States

■ ■ ■

EDWARD FRIEDMAN

ETHNIC AND REGIONAL resurgence in China is a particular manifestation of a process threatening the disintegration of Leninist and post-Leninist states in general. The Bolshevik conquest of communities previously locked in the Russian Czar's "prisonhouse of nationalities" (Shapiro 1984) was followed by "nativization" (locking the community on a territory) and forced Russification through police terror, resulting in "resistance [which] took the form of retreat into the national culture, refusal to learn or speak Russian, and determined efforts to increase ties with the West" (Suny 1990).[1] Outsiders know of similar resistance in China from the prideful assertions by Tibetans in a historic homeland. However, Leninist rulers in China, seeing themselves as members of a 90 plus percent dominant ethnic group dubbed Han, have suppressed Tibetans in the name of Chinese national unity.[2] But many people in China do not embrace this Han identity as primary. It seems the artificial construction of a discredited rulership. Instead, in keeping with the instrumental needs of some more regional group, Chinese peoples have been imagining themselves in more important terms.

The almost 30 million Muslims who live all over China began, in the post-Mao era, rebuilding and returning to their mosques in an expression of communalist identity as explosive as the Tibetans' (Gladney 1991). The subversive essence of this asserted identity was obvious inside mosques where, within tame Chinese characters, ink brush Arabic strokes conveyed Islamic declarations of faith.

This bold embrace of ethnic identity, a challenge to the Han and their values, is also powerfully revealed in the doubling of registered Manchus between China's 1982 census and its 1990 census, while Han population grew by but 8 percent. The Manchus, the rulers of China's last multi-century dynasty, had been vilified by Leninists as reactionaries. Much of the growth in ethnic population was not a result of high birth rates—although that is how the Han tended to see it—

but the result instead of a conscious choice of a re-valued community. In the Mao era, politically stigmatized Manchus tried to hide their identity and sought to pass as Han, persuading observers that, as modern myth had it, the Han had absorbed nomadic invaders from the north beyond the Great Wall, forgetting that the 1911 revolution that overthrew the Manchus was legitimated by their resistance to absorption. By 1990, the northern steppe Manchus stood up, confidently and publicly asserting an ultimate moral claim higher than that of the dominant Han ruling group whose center was Beijing.

So it was with Mongols too. In Inner Mongolia, where Mongols had been overwhelmed in the Mao era by a massive influx of Han migrants, Mongol informants, according to anthropologist Dru Gladney, reported joy on hearing of the Beijing massacre of 4 June 1989. Finally Han were killing Han instead of the minorities. The Turkish peoples in China's far west suffered a similar Han inundation and persecution. Among Tibetans, Muslims, Manchus, Mongols, and others, a discredited Han ethnic Leninist despotism was challenged. A Harvard researcher in southwest China, seeking to interview a minority, found himself directed to a group he had previously studied as Han. The entire group had abandoned the Han identity. Inadvertently, Leninism brought de-nationalization. The survival and identity of China itself was at issue.

Similar communalist movements exploded against Russians at the end of the 1980s among ethnic groups in the Leninist Soviet Union, in Leninist Yugoslavia against Serbs, and in Leninist Ethiopia against the Amharic. The structured dynamics of Leninist systems inadvertently yet inexorably strengthened ethnic challenges to the nationalistic essence of the previous Leninist despotism, identified, in China's case, as the Han. What cries out for explanation is how the Leninist political system fosters this ethnic assertion against a state-centered group, reexperienced by victims as so oppressive as to be virtually genocidal. To be sure, as the various chapters in this volume exemplify, this ethnic reassertion is well-nigh universal. But Leninist politics, as this essay will show, leaves an extraordinarily deep imprint on identity politics that makes more likely strong, anti-regime forms of consciousness ready to be mobilized.

An inevitable consequence of the unintentionally subversive dynamics of Leninism was the recognition that a far higher priority must be placed on resolving the national question. Strong ethnic reassertions imposed that new political agenda. A Hong Kong reporter finds of China that, as with the former Soviet Union, there can be no "doubt that . . . parts of the country, held together now only by brute force and coercion will want to break off. . . . Ethnic-religious nationalism . . . will spring back to life, once the lid is off" (Pan 1990, 46). The political emergence and ascendance of ethnic communal identities requires a general explanation in terms of shared Leninist dynamics, an explanation that fits China and similar Leninist polities.

Leninism and Its Mark on Ethnic Identity

Leninism, both as institutional structures and policy practices, is driven by a perverse logic that creates the obverse of its proclaimed purposes. The Yugoslav writer Mihajlo Mihajlov explains how the actual dynamics of Leninism are more like racist fascism than like progressive egalitarianism, since "recruitment for the republican police [is] based on ethnic criteria, the bans on the sale of property [are] based on the same principle, etc. Regrettably, very often nationalist savagery is not recognized from a distance. The red star on the helmet of a tank crew totally misinforms . . ." (C.A.D.D.Y. 1991, 2).

Leninists of the dominant group do not see themselves as fascist racists. Rather, Leninists define themselves as anti-imperialists saving a people from parasitic plunder by a death-bed capitalism supposedly temporarily resuscitated only by blood money sucked from the poor nations of the third world. In reality, Leninist rulers therefore opt for economic autonomy. The communities defending against injurious Leninist autarky imposed by the ethnic group at the capital usually seek the blessings offered by open and deep involvement with the world's advanced technology, knowledge, and products. To communities opposing the disastrous economic policies of the center, Leninist anti-imperialism seems a force keeping other communities locked into backwardness and poverty.

Leninist rulers imagine themselves commanding the physical resources of the economy and redistributing them to achieve justice and equity. This is offered in contrast to a hypostatized capitalism that is alleged to operate by a logic of polarization and immiseration in which the rich get richer and the poor get poorer. In practice, the Leninist state distributes a physically confiscated surplus by institution and locale. Groups who are not part of the dominant ethnic bloc at the state center find that distribution by institution means privileging the ruling Leninist party, its governmental ministries, and the military hierarchies, all benefiting the dominant group.

In fact, the Leninist system creates fantastic inequality. W. Brus recounts, "I never saw more inequality than in the Stalinist, pre-reform epoch when distribution was centralized and a large part of remuneration was made in kind. The injustices were in both the relative and in the absolute sense" (Brus 1981, 34). Watching the transformation from Leninist inequalities toward a market-oriented, post-Leninist society, Eric Foner (1990, 800) noted,

> Even those in a position to benefit from this [Leninist] system find it unfair and humiliating. To a large extent, whom you know now determines your standard of living. There is something positively egalitarian about the way money in a market society can erase other social distinctions, about a world in which anybody with the cash can walk into a store and purchase whatever goods he or she pleases, without incurring personal obligations.

Only reform which permits market and mobility and advancement on merit can counter alienating Leninist dynamics. When the Leninist Han center hesitates on reform, it reconfirms the experience of other groups of the dominant group as selfish exploiters. But the ruling group believes it is acting in good faith, taking from its central urban areas to redistribute to the regions dominated by minority language, ethnic, and religious groups. While the minorities find themselves getting last and least, the dominant group feels itself sacrificing to lift up benighted groups. That each and every community feels the loser can facilitate a rapid crumbling of that Leninism when it is finally confronted by a serious challenge. The number, beyond elites and organs of coercion, who ultimately experience themselves as beneficiaries with a stake in the traditional Leninist system turns out to be quite minute. Leninism stands on fragile legs of dessicated legitimacy and shrivelled support.

Who actually benefits from redistribution from the ethnic center to the minority regions? In fact, such regions mainly receive state-imposed, below-market prices for their agricultural products and raw materials. They are forced to self-exploit to fund local education and medicine from remnants left behind by the center's metropolitan-biased pricing system that leaves the minority regions the poorest areas with the least medicine, the worst education, the lowest income, and the highest malnutrition. Hence, what the dominant Han group experiences as the privileging of the inept minorities, providing expensive beef at lower pork prices for Muslims and less strict controls on childbearing, the minorities, in contrast, experience as small change to buy off victims who have been peripheralized and immiserated by the systems of pricing and distribution.

Partial reform produces the worst of all worlds for the center. China's communities in the northwest and southwest find themselves paid below-market prices by an exploitative center, thereby intensifying reasons for alienating from the old center.

Still, it is true that funds from the state center do go to the capitals of the minority regions. But the beneficiaries are mainly the powerholders, usually members of the dominant group. Local turncoats, the equivalents of Indian Indian agents, as one Mongol described them to me, are seen as doing the dirty work of the dominant group. The monies sent from the center tend to stay in the regional capital, whose population increasingly becomes the dominant group, in China's case Han officials, traders, and an occupying army. The minority experiences benefits as going only to the dominant group.

Yet so perverse is the Leninist system that Han beneficiaries experience themselves as poor because so much goes to purportedly lazy, unproductive minorities. People living in Leninist systems learn that reward is related to personalistic politics and not to merit or productivity. The dominant group, in fact, has kept the minorities down. But the dominant group, conscious of its own pain and focused on how the undeserving—including minorities—benefit, is oblivious to the actual sufferings of minorities. Hence in the spring of 1989 when the 27th Army marched from Inner Mongolia to Beijing to crush the movement for democracy, the rumor in Beijing was that an army of minorities was coming to crush the Han. Actually, what arrived was a Han army that had been repressing the Mongol minority.

It is systematic peripheralization of minorities that characterizes Leninist dynamics. Local people are locked into regional poverty by Leninist controls that keep them from fleeing state-imposed, place-specific collectives, a system that also uses internal passports, region-specific food coupons, and police registration in hotels to prevent minorities from even temporarily enjoying the greater resources monopolized elsewhere by the dominant group. The system fosters a divisive process, privileging the dominant group, peripheralizing the minorities. Because a nation-state is a shared space, this absolute geographical split fostered by Leninist structures threatens to split the nation itself. The logic of Leninism is de-nationalization.

Thus the Leninist system creates a situation where the dominant group monopolizes all the best in jobs, education, and residence, while the plundered minority is left with the dregs. A member of the local minority, whether Latvian or Tibetan, waits endlessly on lines and on lists, hoping for key items monopolized and politically rationed to favorites, say, for a new apartment, only to discover that the new and best are given to officials of the alien group from the state center. Consequently, the distribution system commanded by the Leninist apparatus appears as an embodiment of racist injustice. For a minority to be pro-socialist would be to play the fool or to be a traitor, the enemy of one's own community.

In addition, Han officials in the minority area tend to be disgruntled, upset because they failed to obtain postings in Han regions with better services, schools, and housing. They take their disappointment and anger out on the local people they rule. The minority community experiences occupation by an army that hates and ridicules the local community it dominates. Consequences include quotidian degrading treatment of the minorities, resentment, and tension. The rulers find themselves sitting on a powder keg that at times explodes, intensifying the opposing identities and angers.

In a Muslim region of China, "three times government troops came to suppress their revolts against cadres who ruled so callously that their subjects lopped off their hands in frustration and revenge" (Lord 1990, 174). In another Muslim village, in response to protests by the faithful against the closing of a mosque, tanks sent to the village killed "all those living within it. The village itself was reduced to rubble" (Gladney 1990, 64).

Given the polarized identities fostered by the Leninist system, once terror ends and reform begins, local leaders who had been long stigmatized by the ruling group as reactionary agents of imperialism return from exile or prison to be greeted as heroes (Madsen 1989). Long suppressed identities congeal and implode. The occupying army then intensifies communal strife by repressing local cultural reassertion.

> In April 1989 . . . 4,000 policemen armed with electric batons descended upon a Catholic [Chinese] village of 1,700 people; more than 200 were injured, 100 very seriously, including octogenarians and children. Local hospitals were forbidden to treat them. The . . . savagery surpassed even that of the bulldozing of Crossroads and other black townships in South Africa. And the villagers' only offense had been to insist on erecting a tent as a makeshift church (Chan 1990, 7).

The grounding of this oppositional relationship lies in the Leninist project. The impact has fallen both on Koreans in China and in the Soviet Union, and on Lamaists both in China and Mongolia. Koreans under Stalin, about 200,000 of whom had fled Japanese occupation, were forcibly deported in 1937 to barren land in Kazakhstan, where "the dead were taken away in carts every morning for the first six months" (*Far Eastern Economic Review,* July 11, 1991, 18). Two thousand or so were deported to slave labor camps and death, intellectuals were exterminated, teaching in the Korean language outlawed, and assimilation was imposed (ibid.). Likewise, among Chinese of Korean descent, "Several tens of thousands were imprisoned, isolated or investigated," while "about 4,000 persons died due to persecution" (Lee 1986, 89). The official story was that "the use of ethnic language meant cultural degeneration and political retreat. . . . [P]rograms to train minority teaching personnel and to produce minority language textbooks were thoroughly destroyed" (ibid., 91).

In China, the slaughter of some 30,000 Mongols has been admitted. Almost every permanent structure in Inner Mongolia in the late 1960s turned a room into a torture chamber to make Mongols confess that they were foreign agents. In like manner, Stalin's declaration of war on religion devastated Buddhist Lamaism in Soviet-dependent Mongolia, where outside of Tibet live the other people who are Lamaists. Seven hundred plus monasteries were destroyed, religious books were burned, and thousands of Lama Buddhist religious leaders were murdered. It is a general and cruelly oppressive phenomenon of Leninism that requires explanation, not a supposed Han Chinese chauvinism.

V. Zotov, a Soviet analyst, finds: "The key sociological feature of the Stalinist model of socialism to which China had belonged is . . . crowd mentality . . . antagonisms under socialism will be found above all in the ethnical and denominational spheres . . ." (Zotov 1990, 2). Leninism in minority areas brings military occupation by a force felt to be foreign, whose daily conduct intensifies alienation and the primacy of ethnic identity and communalist politics. Consider, for example, this account by a Tibetan refugee (Tibetnet 1990):

> When Tibetans arrive at a check-post and speak Tibetan, the [Han] soldiers will react by telling them they [the soldiers] don't understand and they [the Tibetans] must speak Chinese. They [the soldiers] check all luggage and confiscate knives, keeping them instead of giving them to their officers. The soldiers are also patrolling and when they don't like somebody, they will take this person to the police headquarters, interrogate him and beat him. In the daytime, they beat people in the street with their sticks without any reason, and, at night, this regularly happens. One evening, through my window, I saw five Tibetan pilgrims prostrating on the Barkhor [Lhasa's central market]. Then eight Chinese soldiers came to harass them, treated them badly and took a watch and money that one of them had in his money belt. Another time, in the evening, around the Barkhor, a girl on a bicycle passed Chinese soldiers; Tibetans passing Chinese soldiers have to dismount and bow to show respect to them. She did not, and the soldiers were annoyed; so they started to beat her very badly, even on her breasts. A Tibetan who witnessed the scene and only asked the soldiers not to beat her was also beaten very badly for intervening.

Daily experience reinforces a dichotomy of polarized communalist identities. In China's case, the dominant Han and all others are dichotomized into evil oppressor and innocent victims. In Tibet's case, these cruelties have been extreme, including a famine that forced starving Tibetans to seek survival on the droppings of Han army horses. That is, the dumb beasts of the oppressor were better off than the minority people.

> Parents fed dying children their own blood mixed with hot water and tsampa. Other children were forced to leave home to beg . . . and old people went off to die alone in the hills, thousands of Tibetans took to eating the refuse thrown by the Chinese soldiers to the pigs each Han [military] compound kept, while those around PLA outposts daily pieced apart manure from the soldier's horses looking for undigested grain. (Avedon 1984, 237)

The Han have taken over the non-Han areas and grabbed power, land, and all the best state-run opportunities. In addition, the Han blame the non-Han for the minority community's poverty, claiming, "The one fundamental reason for poverty is the lower quality of the people . . ." (Ellingsen 1991). The system fosters condescension that gives good conscience to those high in the system, making the losers seem naturally inferior. Leninism operates as a racist form of settler colonialism.

While each Leninist state has its particular way of treating minorities, there is a shared content to the system that, over time, delegitimates the national center of the dominant group that has pre-defined the minorities as enemies of the nation and socialism. Leninist rulers believe that only they can save the entire nation from foreign exploitation. Minorities, often on the frontiers and frequently involved with foreigners in a prior era of chaos or openness before the Leninist state was established, seem to Leninists not only incapable of defending the nation against imperialism but often, as with the trade-oriented bourgeoisie and urban workers in port regions, also appear to be allies of imperialism and enemies of "the people." The ultimate expression of this general tendency that defines the cosmopolitan as traitorous was the Khmer Rouge Pol Pot war of annihilation against city dwellers.

In building anti-imperialist nationalism, Leninists define a preexisting *volk* as glorious because of a struggle to hold the land. The actual early story of the Han seizing the territory of other communities and slaughtering minority peoples who once occupied that land is eliminated from the imagined national history. So are the glories of the minority people and their civilization. Seen as dwelling in empty space, the non-Han, a veritable fourth world, find their lands the target of nuclear tests and dominant ethnic group settlers.

Proto-racist Leninist nationalism is similar to the German nationalistic response to French Enlightenment nationalism, an anxious chauvinist response that treats the universal project of freedom as an excuse for expansion. This anxious nationalism is a response to an equivalent of a Napoleon marching into Germany and carrying the promise of republican governance premised on a universalistic legal code. In anti-Enlightenment nationalism, the project of law, freedom, and careers open to talents is experienced as an apologia for foreign domination. The threatened people respond with pride in a particular culture, finding their new nationalism in a rejection of the liberal universalistic project. Hence, national military defense and ideological fundamentalism to preserve the purity of some threatened people become the essence of Leninist anti-imperialist nationalism, an explicit rejection of European expansion, an implicit proto-fascist project proclaiming itself socialist and progressive because it is antiliberal, anti-Enlightenment.

Ironically, Leninism thereby negates the haughty Eurocentric Hegelian-Marxist tradition that saw Europe as the maturity of the human race and perceived Africa and Asia to be its transcended childhood, understanding history as progress in reason and freedom. Instead, as this expanding and chauvinistic Europe defined the non-European other as immature, so the anti-European Leninist response defines its valued essence as the rejection of European categories, commerce, and culture. Survival as a people seems so all-encompassing that stories of Western progress are treated as sources of the death of one's own nation. The oppositional identity rejects the vital baby in throwing out the dirty bath water. Imperialism versus anti-imperialism is a conflict of arrogant irrationalities, a pitting of one haughty chauvinism against another, leaving little space for humane purposes.

Leninist Nationalism in China

In China, Mao Zedong's Leninist movement defined itself as the rejection of the Europe of the Opium War, a Europe represented by Bible-carrying soul stealers and foreign gunboats serving narcotics traffickers. If Hegel and Marx chauvinistically defined China's fate to be submission to European commercial civilization because the latter was superior to alleged Asian fatalism and barbaric customs, in contrast, Chinese Leninists would recreate their nation as a defender threatened with obliteration by murderous Europeans who would devitalize the Chinese people. This anti-imperialist project is manifest in the Mao era film of the Opium War, *Lin Zexu,* in which a heroic people would have successfully defended against foreign narcotics traffickers if not for the betrayal and cowardice of a ruling elite who were afraid to mobilize the people to resist and risk death to save the nation. Constitutional representation or mutually beneficial economic interaction has no part in this nationalist epic of survival through the sacrifice of lives to save the race-people. A militaristic mobilization insists on absolute self-sacrifice as the price of sacred national survival. The technically and scientifically advanced is redefined as a morally bankrupt criminal, enriched only by theft.

Rather than understand how industrially advanced groups applied science and technology to expand wealth at a pace the world had never before witnessed, Leninists explained the accumulation of capital as the plunder of poor laborers. "Under the spur of the vilest and most shameless greed, the bourgeoisie . . . used cruel and remorselessly barbarous devices to suck the blood of millions of laboring people . . ." (Crozier 1990).

But by the end of the twentieth century, Chinese leaders now acknowledge that the problem they confront is not a dying, parasitic capitalism but a new stage in a continuous scientific revolution. Leninist policy has been revealed as a disaster. At first, however, it appeared as an ethical imperative. In the Leninist project, a vulnerable, pure nation needs protection from penetration by the evil and strong foreigner. In China, in response to the Opium War, the conservative cultural advice was to keep the rapacious foreigner out:

> . . . to defend the open ocean is not as good as to defend the seaports, and to defend the seaports is not as good as to defend the inland rivers.
>
> . . . The phrase "enticing the enemy to enter the inland rivers" means that soldiers . . . are sown on land and in the water as if making a pit to wait for tigers . . .
>
> . . . The strength of the British barbarian is on the ocean. . . . On the shore, they will lose their strength.
>
> . . . Except for your ships being solid, your gunfire fierce, and your rockets powerful, what other abilities have you? . . .
>
> . . . If we do not exterminate you English barbarians, we will not be human beings. (Wei 1842, 30–31, 36)

In this view, anyone who reached out to welcome in the values of the Europeans was seen to be on the side of the immoral enemy of the people. Progress in Europe was invisible or tainted. Consequently, a deeply conservative traditionalism infused purportedly modern anti-imperialist Leninist nationalism. The Chinese rejected the European calendar and cosmology and killed Chinese astronomers who found modern science superior. The project of anti-imperialist nationalism was to militarily occupy the threatened borders, the regions of the minorities, and to treat all who trafficked with the foreigners as traitors. This made every minority, from the Muslim traders from the Silk Road to Tibetans dealing with British or Indians, seem similar to compradores working for (meaning selling out to) foreign firms. Nationalists were those who defended the sacred soil from those immoral groups.

The Leninist nation, organizing in self-defense against imperialism, did theoretically include minorities. Yet, such communities, who previously found foreign allies to keep the territorially expanding central group, the Han, at bay, were also redefined as subverters of unity, friends of the new nation's enemies. The Leninist-Stalinist project insisted that it brought modern power by resisting the threat from a parasitic foreign commerce and polluting foreign culture. Stalinism was an autarkic fundamentalism claiming to guarantee military strength and national independence.

The national project was presented by the Han as controlling a national space. Since minorities, in fact, controlled much of that space, the space was redefined as empty, or the minorities as so backward that they had to obey the vanguard ethnic group who could more productively and patriotically employ the space. This vision demanded the suppression of indigenous peoples, redefined as invisible, anachronistic, or traitorous obstacles. Those farthest from the foreign impact, hinterland Han peasants, were valorized as patriots who suffered to keep outsiders out. By stigmatizing what the outside has to offer, Leninists tended toward autarky, import substitution, and the mobilization of mass manual labor. The wealth-expanding world of trade, capital, technology, and knowledge transfer were excluded.

When hinterland Han people turned out to be religious and family-oriented communities whose standard of living required temporary urban jobs, peddling, hauling, and other "bourgeois" economic practices, that made them targets of Leninist fundamentalists out to purify the nation of superstitious, private, parochial, money-oriented pollution. Chinese editions of Marx's work mistranslate his description of religion as an "opium of the people," meaning, according to Marx, "the heart of a heartless world," so that religion is defined by Leninists as a "poison," something that the body politic must be rid of at any cost. The rulers who lead a war on the poison of religion, ethnicity, and family, see themselves as saving lives and purifying an authentic nation. In reality, they are the enemies even of their own community and its culture.

The only morally pure group becomes the party-state leadership of the dominant group engaged in a cultural war against the sacred bonds of all. After all, even the dominant group has a particular culture. Thus, Russians, in the 1990s, who are trying to reclaim a heritage that had been shattered by Leninist tyranny, de-nationalize even Lenin, imagined as anti-Russian, and see him as Mongol, not Russian; and Han Chinese who reject the Leninist system that warred against the sacred rituals of lineage can de-nationalize Deng Xiaoping and see him as Hakka, not Han. Hakka are a community with their own language and culture, who fled south and were forced, many centuries ago, out of the valleys and into the hills, an area from which Mao's earliest guerrillas were disproportionately recruited. Although the Beijing government defines Hakka as Han, antiregime Chinese, especially in the south or east or coasts, often find the regime as backward hinterland, northern conservative, or Hakka, and, therefore, not truly Chinese. Even the dominant group must redefine its communalist nationalism, so morally discredited and isolated does Leninism become.

It is striking how little emotional hold persists in Leninist nationalism beyond antiforeign chauvinism. The culture of the Han anti-imperialist state is artificial and readily discarded, once power and fear are no longer obstacles. Leninist national identity was never integrated into daily life. Its "national holidays, for example, have little cultural meaning and elicit no special behavior whatsoever except for that arranged by local cadres. The contrast with the lunar New Year and other traditional festivals could not be greater" (Cohen 1991, 128). Austere, group marriages were imposed on regime-defined holidays. This alienating artificiality is not a peculiarity of Chinese Leninism. Jacek Koron of Poland's Solidarity finds that Leninism "is a system artificially created and artificially designed, and such a system destroys all life around it" (Koron 1990, 24). Leninism creates a hunger and a need for a genuine community. It leads people to search for truer and deeper identities. Inadvertently but inevitably, it de-nationalizes and recommunalizes.

Morgan, Lenin, and Stalin: The Roots of Leninist Minority Policy

National minority policy in Leninist states combines the ideas of anthropologist Lewis Henry Morgan, adopted by Frederick Engels, with the practices and theories imposed by Lenin and Stalin. The newly dominant group defines its rule as one of civilization replacing barbarism. What is sacred to an ethnic community is thus redefined as ready either for the dustbin of history or for a museum.

With ethnic communities seen as outmoded, mere living fossils, the politics of anthropology in Leninist-Stalinist societies finds little progressive value in the cultures of minority peoples. They are mere economic moments whose time has passed. To be rid of them is like removing the dead but unburied, virtually an apologia permitting genocide. Mao Zedong called for the destruction of the old to make way for the new; his supporters took that as a call to destroy the cultures of those who were not steel factory proletarians. In smashing the bonds of other communities, the central power group experiences itself as merely speeding the pace of history in removing an outmoded economic group that would die anyway. In reducing communities to mere economic moments, a destructive project is proclaimed an advance in the mode of production. Han leaders show no concern that in Buddhist Tibet during the Mao era, as Edward Gargan reports, over six thousand "monasteries . . . were blown up. . . . They burned the scriptures. All the statues were taken away. . . . They drove the monks away. . . ." He continues: "I wondered what the world's reaction would have been if the German occupation of France had left the cathedrals at Chartres, Reims and Rouen in charred ruins. That, and worse, is what had happened in Tibet" (Gargan 1990, 193–94).

This Leninist project of ethnocide is overdetermined. Engels took his anthropology from Lewis Henry Morgan's expression of the chauvinistic and racist myths of his time and European place. Sympathetic to the plight of Amerindians, Morgan saw family societies as the earliest division of labor and Amerindians as tied to a hunting mode of production that could not rise and a prior golden age that Engels could dub primitive communism. While stressing historical contingency rather than biological essence, nonetheless, racist culture and superior technology were linked in Morgan's apologia for his people and time. "The Aryan family represents the central stream of human progress, because it produced the highest type of mankind, and because it has proved its intrinsic superiority by gradually assuming control of the earth" (Jenkins 1984, 19). For Tibetan, Ukrainian, Albanian, Tigrean, who each and all lost their piece of the earth to the Han, Russian, Serb, or Amhara, Leninist rulers act the Aryan role, a threat of genocide.

In 1912 in *Marxism and the National and Colonial Question,* Stalin defined the Leninist nation as "an historically constituted, stable community of people, formed on the basis of a common language, territory, economic life and psychological make-up manifested in a common culture." For China's Leninists, this meant that "those who live together learn the language spoken by the most people" (Chen and Chen 1990, 31). In practice, Leninist Chinese rulers take the language of the capital—a language unintelligible to minorities, southerners, or even most northern peasants—and a sanitized version of its culture as advanced and socialist, and impose it on other regions and cultures, treated as old and backward. Combining Morgan's anthropology with Marx's telos, the Leninist state acts on the colonialist categories of orientalism. The rulers define the people of other regions by an anthropology of advanced and backward, with the most industrialized areas tied to the capital treated as the most advanced. In other regions, people have to make themselves over in the image of an artificial "socialist" culture or be treated as primitive and reactionary. What is demanded is de-culturation. However much people conform on the surface, inwardly, and very deeply, resistance is real. Ever more, people value their martyred and moral community. Once state terror and the charismatic rule of the first anti-imperialist generation evaporate, little is left other than desires for autonomy, revenge, and renewal. A Leninist nationalism that once seemed all powerful suddenly appears as a rejected evil, the target of all communities, even the dominant one.

Not shaping their modernization, ruled by outsiders, forced to destroy their basic identities, in diverse regions, communities resist, finding allies in those who act, speak, dress, or worship truly like them. The enemy is the anti-imperialist center, the old Leninist nationalism. The Leninist war against the market locked people into their places, thus intensifying communal contradictions and the oppositional identities. In market societies, mobility and individuation weaken community identities. In a Leninist order, over time, in contrast, the regional and religious communities grow more conscious of the hypocrisy of the regime's legitimation. To live in truth and justice means to oppose the Leninist center.

When reforms begin, local people experience their group as a previously martyred community. They believe that only they can care for their own, an experience intensified by its invisibility to the people in previously privileged regions. Seeing themselves and their culture also as victims of the Stalinist system, which also repressed parts of its cherished culture, the people of privileged regions do not readily hear the cry of distant victims, whom they have learned, under Leninism, to experience as pampered and undeserving beneficiaries of subsidized largesse. Thus the divisive forces of Leninism that had strengthened ethnic identities and communities allow, or even force, these communities to assert independent claims.

To see just how divisive Leninist nationalism is one should look at what was hidden by invoking the concept of the Han peasant to cover most rural dwellers in China. While Mao praised suffering, sacrificing, ascetic, hinterland Han peasants as the patriots who liberated China, in fact, even before 1949 the Leninists were trying to destroy rural customs and religion, treating diverse community bonds as reactionary obstacles to material progress. Villagers were dismissed as a remnant of a dying mode of production, to be allied with, used, and transformed. Chinese Leninists in the 1920s and 1930s portrayed villagers as victims, exploited and oppressed both by Confucian landlords and Japanese invaders. Mao conceived of the fate of China's peasantry in objectified alternatives defined by Stalinist Russian ideological distortions, kulak oppressors or state-imposed collectives. He simultaneously imagined the obstacle to China's prosperity to be contemptible peasant practices, from family particularism to nonproductive dowries and festive drinking. Rural resisters could be cruelly treated and branded as kulaks who purportedly would return China to polarization and famine. The writer Liu Binyan has noted that the impositions of Mao's unaccountable group of imperious lords actually brought more rape and rapine to the peasantry than did even the pre-Stalinist lords of the land. If peasants of the dominant community are properly understood, as regional historic communities, with rich, diverse cultures, then it is not surprising that their fate is the same as ethnic communities. All particularistic, primary passions that limit commitment to the antiforeign cause are experienced by Leninist rulers as traitorous convictions to be extirpated.

When reforms begin, members of these previously excluded communities surge into privileged redoubts. But Han identity that was legitimated by a war against the foreign, including national minorities, loses meaning as minorities and communities are valorized and the foreign is no longer stigmatized. Each revalorized region tries to maximize its gains against the discredited center. The center finds budget funds slipping through its fingers. A conflict grows over budgets and taxes. In the war between center and regions, barriers are erected in a struggle in which the center seems increasingly foreign to local sufferers. The previously super-centralized Leninist state threatens to fall apart on regional fissures, especially where the fault line coincides with a communalist and group identity. Where there is a joining of cultural, economic, and lingual grievances on "sharply regional lines," political scientist Dankwort Rustow noted in 1970 about political regimes in general, there "secession . . . is likely to result" (Rustow 1970, 354). Because the central regime in Leninist anti-imperialist China has been located in the north and legitimated in terms of a historical narrative that privileges hinterland northern creative dynamism and peripheralizes southern coastal links to world commerce as treason, the regional fault lines tend to pit the south against the north, with the south constructing a new historical discourse that links it to China's future.[3] Whether the outcome is instead a new, cruel central control, or civil war, or federalism, or new self-determinations, a political struggle is unleashed by post-Leninist politics in which regional communities ever more self-confidently contest the legitimacy of a previously dominant center.

That center finds itself threatened and surrounded by atavistic, surging rural dwellers. The fate of the peasantry is struggled over in order to define one's project as properly nationalistic, with different political tendencies imagining different peasantries, but with the center ignoring the powerful identities inherent in regional and lingual and cultural assertions. An almost genocidal wish infuses this imperial nationalism at the center, as urbanites tend to agree that China has too many people, meaning that the number of peasants must be reduced, that it would be better if city people had two children and peasants were restricted to one, so peasant numbers would decline. Rural mobility into cities, followed by urbanization, is almost universally opposed by the urban-based rulers who fear dangerous ex-villagers flooding into cities as criminals who destroy and create disorder.

But peasants do not unite. A notion of a broad national peasant class attracts only a few villagers in diverse regional communities, boundaries of identity being defined by opposition to the next "peasant" culture. Han and Hakka may or may not be antagonistically different. Around the Yangtze River, Subei and

Jiangnan peasant communities are antagonistic worlds. South, coastal Minnan and northern, plains Huabei peoples differ more from each other than many foreign countries do. The political assertions of these revalorized communities could reject a Han racial nationality, which, in fact, is a modern invention, not a genetic essence. Into the twentieth century, while some called for the "race originating in the Yellow River Valley to become the largest unique stock of human beings on earth," actually, according to John Fei and Charlotte Furth, in the early years of the twentieth century, still, "the myth of ethnicity proved less durable than the myth of culture" (Wakeman 1991, 25). That is, the Chinese were not a race, and after progressives de-legitimated inherited culture as an obstacle to national regeneration, the anti-imperialist state could not be premised on a common culture, either. The notion of a Han people who arose thousands of years ago in conquering the Yellow River, who, in 1949, brought Leninists to power to keep out rapacious foreigners is a potted history with a short life span. It can be dispensed with in the communal reassertions of the post-Leninist world.

China in a Post-Leninist World

China in the post-Mao era is no longer envisioned as the longest continuous national civilization, with a unique history from a founding Han people in the loess soil of the North China plain, running without stop from over four thousand years ago to the present. Instead, Chinese history is reconceived to imagine very different national projects, as Zhang Yufa described it in *The Interactions of Divided State(s)* (1989). Maria Hsia Chang (1991, 8) reports that China actually was only unified for 40 percent of the time in its over four-thousand-year history. For an equally long time it was a federation. The rest of the time, China was not even united. The future suddenly is as open as the past. Political history and ethno-national identity are both contested. National identity is contested.

The struggle over national identity reaches from high culture to popular gossip. While cultural identities are truly valued, the struggle over culture is preeminently political. The outcome will be decided in political combat and not merely by continuing cultural consciousness. It is a matter of politics whether the newly politicized ethnic identities lead in a fundamentalist or a federalist direction. The contrast is stark between those valuing community and those seeing no possible good in community. Asking "What Comes After Marxist Regimes?", the Marxist Ralph Miliband (1991, 324) responds: "a nationalism that readily slides into an exclusive, aggressive, xenophobic chauvinism . . . drawing on the most backward and reactionary interpretations of religion." In contrast, the anti-Marxist Alasdair MacIntyre (1981, 262–63) answers the same question, finding "the constitution of local forms of community within which civility and the intellectual and moral life can be sustained . . ." The de-nationalization of identity in a post-Leninist system opens a struggle over the nature of all communities in the territory, with possibilities ranging from racist despotism to federalist pluralism.

The major social science generalization of the twentieth century no longer seems true. It used to be obvious that defensive nationalism was the major, defining political identity and force, the legitimator of a strong, unified state. Yet, as that century ends, so does that political premise. The old, centralized, militarily unified security state is threatened from without and subverted from within. That overly centralized national state was too rigid to respond flexibly to the economic challenges of a penetrating world market with instantaneous finance in an era of post-steel micro-technological lead sectors (Friedman 1991). Whether one looked to the formation of the European Community or the rise of Pacific Rim economies, the defensive, closed premises of Leninist anti-imperialism, import substitution, and dependency theory were revealed as suicidal prescriptions. In addition, that unitary, centralized defensive nationalism was also being subverted from within, as diverse communities and regional groups insisted on their moral and political priority. Penetrated and subverted, ineffective and illegitimate, the old Leninist anti-imperialist nationalism seems to rattle as in its death throes.

Leninist states, such as China, threatened by these international and subnational forces, reveal generalizable dynamic forces building new political forms. East Germany disappeared. North Korea is being forced to accept two Koreas, previously damned as an imperialist plot. Mainly, however, these overly politically centralized, economically rigid, and culturally artificial Leninist states seek, in a post-Leninist era, to benefit from the expansion of the world economy and seek to craft more federal structures. But these are complex tasks. Valorized ethnic communities approach them with the fear of learned experience from the prior era of a cruel Leninism that alienated them, outraged them, and energized them. Communalist demands, often irreconcilable, can explode in bloody and hate-filled fights, or perhaps, lead to truly democratic and communitarian federalist republics.

These new and powerful potentials challenge Leninist China. While reforms permit some decentralization and international economic openness, the Leninist dictators fear the calls for democracy or autonomy, and crush the claimants. It is not obvious, however, that the anti-imperialist Leninist center can hold. It increasingly seems ossified, archaic, and profoundly hypocritical. The regime represses and silences, and yet new communities, new identities, and new political projects keep erupting. It is difficult to see, given the international economics of wealth expansion at the end of the twentieth century, how Han China can prevent the ascension of a reimagined Chinese nation. This newly imagined China is being invented in terms of a south—now tied to Asian Pacific economic dynamism that brings in most of China's foreign exchange earnings and foreign investment—that is now constructed as always having won wealth and progress for China through international exchange.

With finance breaking free of national constraints, there is a virtual guarantee, however, that, in addition to imposing growth-efficiency criteria, international finance will also act in a predatory way that undermines families and threatens communities and thereby unleashes a powerful backlash against money's mobility. Since social life is impossible without value-based bonds, communalist attractions may win out over economic openness and democracy (Sampson 1990, 233). Even a democratic breakthrough can be reversed, as rulers manipulate primordial identities and hates to win backing for communalist tyrannies. That the future is open does not mean it will be better.

Conservatives in China's Communist Party, a political group which began with an attempt to destroy Confucianism and the reactionary interests that the inherited authoritarian culture defended and preserved, were, by 1990, describing authoritarian Confucianism as "the historical guiding principle for the Chinese people's political structure . . . different from any Western model" (Zhang Xinhau 1990, 103–6). Confucianism, Leninist traditionalists found, contained "the essence of humanism and democracy" and was a culture "which aided in the establishment of benevolent and moral government." These "positive ingredients usable by socialism" also were the source of success in the "launching of the East Asian economies." Therefore it made no sense "blindly mouthing empty slogans about 'democracy' and 'freedom' . . . to promote an Enlightenment in China. . . . Compared to the West, China's cultural thinking . . . just might be ahead" (ibid.). The Leninist fundamentalists in power in Beijing have tried to revive the previously vilified culture, especially its most authoritarian features, ally with fundamentalists among the minorities against secularist democrats and political reformers whose cultural creations, such as sex education and uncensored depictions of the body, are damned as foreign cultural pollutions. When the old Han center of Leninist power pridefully and super-patriotically claims to be preserving sacred cultural verities, it, in fact, opposes federalist, democratic, pluralist, and multicultural possibilities. The racist proto-fascism of Leninists, in Serbia, Russia, or China, can readily reemerge in a pure racist, fascist nationalism.

But progressive possibilities also persist. Victims of the Leninist regime, communities of ultimate meaning—family, ethnicity, religion—have bound together to survive and give moral meaning to life against a culturally vacuous Leninism that leaves a profound moral crisis and a widespread popular desire to live in truth. These ethnic communities can build democracies or share in a federal republic. They are not inherently and inevitably reactionary. Envisioning ethnic communities as mere backward irrationality was the Leninist-Stalinist policy understanding that created the ethnic backlash in the first place, leaving "a yawning void to be filled" (Starr 1990, A6). The most intriguing of these proto-communities reaches out from southern and coastal China to embrace the Chinese diaspora. If E. J. Hobsbawm is right that "the area of national studies in which thinking and research are most urgently needed today" is how "national identification . . . can change and shift in time" (1990, 11), then this research suggests that changes in military technologies and wealth-expanding imperatives for shaping political communities that can deliver protection and prosperity with participation in the post-modern world are definers of new national communities that can value openness, self-rule, and pluralism. That is, in the new world of easy physical mobility and immediate long-distance communication, where place-specific bonds of meaning are threatened, the link between national identity and living on a particular piece of land may weaken (ibid., 174). The Chinese nation could come to include what previously had been a diaspora. Market capacity rather than military power could become more central to national identity. Hobsbawm suggests that the rise to international centrality of mini-states such as Singapore and Hong Kong reflects a transcendence of the nineteenth-century vision of "national economies" that supposedly were decisive for Bismarck and Stalin, the paradigmatic leaders of modern centralized despotism. To the large extent that Leninist anti-imperialist nationalism adopted Bismarckian presuppositions of steel and grain autarky as the essence of a nation-state, it is not peculiar that a state system premised on nineteenth-century notions of nation should be dying as humanity enters the twenty-first century.

What this essay suggests, in addition, is that to the extent that symbolic communities permit humans to deal with the joys and pain of life itself, and to the extent that ever more rapid, incomprehensible, unsettling changes impinge on post-steel or post-modern life, the ultimate value of trans-national "national" communities may intensify: perhaps that helps explain the rise of religious nationalism from Sinhalese Buddhists through Amerindians, from Shi'ite fundamentalists to Hindi patriots. As with the Chinese diaspora, territorial exclusivity may, in the post-modern world, be less decisive for experiences of communalist ties. In an age of satellite electronic communication, bonds among people are neither fixed nor bounded by walls at frontiers. If this analysis is accurate, then the old state center can hold only by greatly loosening its grip in an open, democratic, and decentralist direction.

Communities of ultimate identity could be central to a new democratic Chinese identity with roots spread to include diverse, ethnic, and diaspora communities. These communities of recharged ethnic identity that were bloodied and vilified in the Leninist era are, in the reform and post-Leninist era, actors trying to shape their own destiny, and a potential new nation in which Leninist de-nationalization could be the premise of democratization. Still, a future of ethnic warfare beckons if chauvinistic, centralizing Han rulers are incapable of meeting the self-governance demands of regional and ethnic communities. The old center has the power to welcome democratic federation or to practice bloody repression, a de-legitimated repression that can even lead to the breakup of the old nation-state.

NOTES

1. Since Leninist states incited outrage and vengeful passions in ethnic communities, E. J. Hobsbawm (1990, 173) errs in claiming, "it was the great achievement of the communist regimes in multinational countries to limit the disastrous effects of nationalism within them."

2. A good one-volume compilation of the suffering imposed upon Tibetans compiled by the German Greens is Kelly et al. (1991).

3. The emergent construction of a South China regional identity is a momentous new development. For detail, see Friedman (forthcoming).

REFERENCES

Avedon, John. 1984. *In Exile From the Land of Snows*. New York: Random House.

Brus, W. 1981. Is Market-Socialism Possible or Necessary? *Critique* 14: 13–39.

C.A.D.D.Y. (Committee to Aid Democratic Dissidents in Yugoslavia). 1991. Translation of Mihaljo Mhajlov in Borba. *CADDY Bulletin* 65:2.

Chan, Anita. 1990. China's Long Winter. *Monthly Review* 41, 8 (January): 1–14.

Chen, Zhangtai, and Jianmin Chen. 1990. Sociolinguistics Research Based on Chinese Reality. *International Journal of the Sociology of Language* 81: 21–41.

Cohen, Myron L. 1991. Being Chinese. *Daedalus* 120, 2 (Spring): 113–34.

Crozier, Ralph. 1990. World History in the People's Republic of China. *Journal of World History* 1, 2 (Fall): 151–69.

Ellingson, Peter. 1991. Where Poverty Begins at Home or Stays With Scant Relief. *Financial Times,* March 12.

Foner, Eric. 1990. The Romance of the Market. *The Nation* 251, 22 (December 24): 796–800.

Friedman, Edward. Forthcoming. The Eclipse of Anti-Imperialist Nationalism in China and the Rise of a New Southern Nationalism.

Friedman, Edward. 1991. Permanent Technological Revolution and the Vicissitudes of China's Path to Democratizing Leninism. In *Democracy and Reform in China and Their Enemies,* edited by Richard Baum, 162–82. New York: Routledge, Kegan and Paul.

Gargan, Edward. 1990. *China's Fate*. New York: Doubleday.

Gladney, Dru. 1991. *Muslim Chinese*. Cambridge: Harvard University Press.

Gladney, Dru. 1990. The Peoples of the People's Republic. *The Fletcher Forum of World Affairs* 14, 1 (Winter): 62–86.

Hobsbawm, E. J. 1990. *Nations and Nationalism Since 1870*. Cambridge: Cambridge University Press.

Hsia Chang, Maria. 1991. U.S. China Policy and China's Growing Regionalism. Paper presented at the conference of the Western Social Science Association, April 25–27, Sparks, Nevada.

Jenkins, Francis. 1984. *The Ambiguous Iroquois Empire*. New York: Norton.

Kelly, Petra, et al. 1991. *The Anguish of Tibet*. Berkeley: Parallel Press.

Koron, Jacek. 1990. The Overcoming of Totalitarianism. *The Journal of Democracy* 1, 1 (Winter): 72–74.

Lee, Chae-jin. 1986. *China's Korean Minority.* Boulder: Westview Press.

Lord, Bette Bao. 1990. *Legacies.* New York: Knopf.

MacIntyre, Alisdair. 1981. *After Virtue.* South Bend, Ind.: University of Notre Dame.

Madsen, Richard. 1989. The Catholic Church in China. In *Unofficial China,* edited by Perry Link, et al., 103–120. Boulder: Westview Press.

Miliband, Ralph, and Leo Panitch. 1991. *Communist Regimes: The Aftermath.* London: St. Martin's Press.

Pan, Lynn. 1990. Make or Break. *Far Eastern Economic Review* 150 (November 29): 46.

Rustow, Dankwurt. 1970. *Comparative Politics* 2, 3 (April): 337–63.

Sampson, Anthony. 1990. *The Midas Touch.* New York: Penguin.

Shapiro, Leonard. 1984. *The Russian Revolution of 1917.* New York: Basic Books.

Starr, Frederick. 1990. The Disintegration of the Soviet State. *The Wall Street Journal,* February 6, p. A16.

Suny, Ronald. 1990. Nationalities and Nationalism. In *Chronicle of a Revolution,* edited by Abraham Brumberg, 108–28. New York: Pantheon.

Tibetnet. 1990. Interview of a Tibetan refugee by a Swiss Tibetan Support Group, June 13.

Wakeman, Frederic, Jr. 1991. *In Search of National Character.* Berkeley: Center for Chinese Studies.

Wei, Yuan. 1842. In *China's Response to the West,* edited by Ssu-yu Teng and John King Fairbank, 30–36. Cambridge: Harvard University Press, 1954.

Zhang, Xinhua. 1990. On Using Traditional Culture as a Wellspring To Build A Socialist New Culture. *Shehui Kexue* 3 (March 15); translated in JPRS-CAR-90-049 (July 11): 103–6.

Zhang, Yufa. 1989. *The Interactions of Divided State(s)* (in Chinese). Taipei: Institute for International Relations.

Zotov, V. 1990. Political Crisis in China. *Far Eastern Affairs* (Moscow) 2: 64–80.

12

Cultural Pluralism, Revivalism, and Modernity in South Asia: The Rashtriya Swayamsevak Sangh

■ ■ ■

DOUGLAS SPITZ

Introduction

AS SUGGESTED IN Crawford Young's introductory chapter to this volume, until recently modernization theory has been heavily weighted toward the secular assimilative territorial nation-state. Either in its liberal or in its Marxian form, this type of polity was assumed to be the hallmark of, and model for, modernity. According to this view cultural pluralities rooted in religion, region, ethnicity, race, or caste usually were viewed as residual elements of parochial traditions. It was assumed that as national integration progressed these retrogressive traditional elements would be transcended and reduced to political irrelevance by the triumphant nation-state ideology articulated through an increasingly powerful and pervasive state apparatus.

Young goes on to point out that the recent political resurgence of subnational ethnic, ethno-religious, and territorial cultural pluralities has demonstrated their surprising resilience in the face of assimilative pressures, and made ". . . a transforming relationship between cultural pluralism and the nation-state . . . a central drama of our times." In the light of these developments the search for a clearer understanding of the dynamics of the rapidly changing relationship between the nation-state and reemerging cultural pluralities requires a basic rethinking of political modernization theory.

Twentieth-century Indian history richly illustrates aspects of Young's thesis. Since the introduction into late-nineteenth-century India of the novel Western idea of nationalism, there have been sharply differing alternative definitions of national identity, of which the Hindu-Muslim confrontations that culminated in the grisly events of the 1947 partition are only the most dramatic illustration. In this chapter I argue that the concept of Indian nationality articulated by Jawaharlal Nehru that has been officially dominant in post-independence India today faces what may well be its most serious challenge from within the Hindu community.

Among twentieth-century Indian political leaders Nehru stands in the forefront of those who believed the secular assimilative nation-state to be the correct model for constructing a modern Indian nation. In contrast to Gandhi, who defined the Indian polity in terms of the aspirations of India's various religious communities, and to Hindu nationalists such as V. D. Savarkar, B. G. Tilak, and M. S. Golwalkar, who constructed Indian history and nationalism in more narrowly exclusivist Hindu terms, Nehru in *The Discovery of India* (1946) impatiently brushed aside traditional religious modes of thought as at worst divisive, at best irrelevant to the pressing economic and social problems confronting the Indian nation that he hoped to construct.

Not inaccurately called a "man of two worlds," Nehru harbored a deeply ambivalent attitude toward Hindu traditions. On the one hand, his search for a specifically Indian historical cultural identity led him to discover its main source in the Hindu past, as that past had been reconstructed in the nineteenth and twentieth centuries by European Orientalists and Hindu reformers (Frykenberg 1989). He argued that by virtue of its broad tolerationist and nontheocratic principles Hindu India had been able to absorb and Indianize successive waves of invaders, thereby providing a framework for the creation of a distinctive national cultural identity shared by Indians of all religious sects and creeds. It is perhaps not an exaggeration to say that Hindu cultural traditions as he conceived them were the source of such sense of Indianness as Nehru possessed.

On the other hand, Nehru profoundly believed in Western rationalism, science, and democratic socialism as the only path to the realization of his vision of a unified, modern, and economically progressive India. His vision required a radical break with India's past, which in his view had been too much concerned with the supernatural, and too much enmeshed in exclusivist and stultifying caste restrictions:

> . . . we have too much of the past about us and have ignored the present. We have to get rid of that narrowing religious outlook, that obsession with the supernatural and metaphysical speculations, that loosening of the mind's discipline in religious ceremonial and mystical emotionalism, which come in the way of our understanding ourselves and the world. We have to come to grips with the present, this life, this world, this nature which surrounds us in its infinite variety. Some Hindus talk of going back to the Vedas; some Muslims dream of an Islamic theocracy. Idle fancies, for there is no going back to the past; there is no turning back even if this was thought desirable. There is only one-way traffic in Time.
>
> India must therefore lessen her religiosity and turn to science. She must get rid of the exclusiveness in thought and social habit which has become like a prison to her, stunting her spirit and preventing growth. The idea of ceremonial purity has erected

> barriers against social intercourse and narrowed the sphere of social action. The . . . religion of the orthodox Hindu is more concerned with what to eat and what not to eat, whom to eat with and from whom to keep away, than with spiritual values. The rules and regulations of the kitchen dominate his social life. The Moslem is fortunately free from these inhibitions, but he has his own narrow codes and ceremonials . . . which he rigorously follows, forgetting the lesson of brotherhood which his religion taught him. His view of life is perhaps even more limited and sterile than the Hindu view . . . (Nehru 1946, 393–94)

Nehru resolved the tensions that resulted from his straddling of two worlds by boldly prescribing the secularization of Indian political and social life along Western lines, and by finding historical parallels to his secularist ideals in the tolerationist and nontheocratic strands of Hindu traditions, as well as in the accommodationist policies of "Indianized" Muslim rulers such as the Moghul Emperor Akbar. In his reading of India's history a shared sense of Indian cultural nationality which encompassed and transcended religious differences was deeply rooted in India's past. And in his mind this provided the foundation which made the secular nation-state ideology the logical modern outcome of India's historical experience.

Nehru's secularist vision of modernity received widespread and often uncritical support in post–World War II academic circles. For prior to 1970 the prevailing view among students of "third world" countries equated modernity with secularization in political, economic, and social life. Post-independence India's efforts to achieve modernization and national integration under a democratic polity attracted particular attention and inspired a body of literature that dealt with issues related to the problem of transforming India into a secular state on the Western liberal democratic model. For example, Donald Smith in his richly detailed study *India as a Secular State* (1963, 45) argued that:

> The forces of westernization and modernization at work in India are all on the side of the secular state. Industrialization, urbanization, the break-up of the joint family system, greatly increased literacy, and opportunities for higher education—all tend to promote the general secularization of both public and private life. The indifference to religion which characterizes the contemporary western outlook has already made a powerful impact on certain sections of Indian society, and the process is a continuing one. Whether good or bad in terms of the individual, this process tends to strengthen the secular state.

Smith ardently believed that Nehru's vision of a democratic secular polity was essential for India's modernization. While he did not rule out the possibility that India might become a Hindu state, he did not think that this was a likelihood. Yet he conceded that a major difficulty to the realization of the Nehruvian vision was that, in the eyes of India's masses, it was still an abstract ideal that lacked emotional appeal (ibid., 500–501). The weight of Smith's thesis was that this lack of popular emotional commitment to secularism would in time be remedied as the masses became involved in the modernization process.

Despite the hopes of Smith and a generation of scholars who shared his Westocentric premise that secularization was an essential aspect of the modernization process, since the early 1970s there has been in South and West Asia an increasing disillusionment with Western-derived secularizing models of modernity, and with the political elites who promoted these models. Several factors explain this trend: the strains of uneven economic development; the failure of the older secular-oriented political elites to fulfill promises of distributive justice; the tarnished image of the superpowers; and, perhaps most important of all, a growing sense of the loss of community and cultural coherence resulting from rapid, disorienting socioeconomic change. One consequence of this disillusionment has been a heightened ideological ferment which takes the form of a search for a culturally coherent and socially viable definition of modernity in terms of what are considered to be indigenous distinctive cultural values.

The subject of this chapter, the Rashtriya Swayamsevak Sangh (RSS) of India, is one manifestation of this search. It falls under the ethnoreligious cultural category of communalism, defined as the cultural, social, and political mobilization of people on the basis of their religious identity. Communal ideologies are, to use the terminology employed by Young, "manufactured" constructs, created by intellectuals who feel a need to redefine their individual and group identity in response to disorienting social change. Communal groups use shared religious symbols, rituals, and practices to create among their members strong affective ties of community and collective identity. A communal ideology may or may not use a language deemed to be associated with its particular religion as one of its group boundary markers. Depending on the situational context, communal identities may overlap with those of ethnicity or class. In certain political contexts communal groups may define themselves as nationalities.

Communal groups are instrumental in that they define and mobilize themselves to achieve an improved societal position. They are primordial in that they articulate group ideology using religious and cultural symbols which evoke powerful feelings of individual and group identity.

Finally, communal identities and the ideologies that articulate them are flexible. A communal group may reinterpret its religious-cultural symbols in such a way as to expand its boundary markers to include groups previously excluded. In threatening circumstances, it may do the reverse.

The RSS, which defines itself as a cultural organization, seeks to recreate India's national identity according to what it defines as an authentically Hindu *rashtra* (nation). In connection with this project, it aims to mold a cadre of "new men" whose character will exemplify Hindu values and whose activism will regenerate, along Hindu lines, the moral tone of society and polity in India. Its political affiliate, the Bharatiya Jana Sangh (BJS) merged with the Janata Party in 1977 and, after the breakup of the Janata Party, reemerged as the Bharatiya Janata Party (BJP).

The RSS has been one of the most controversial organizations in India. To its enemies on the Marxist Left, as well as to those who believe in the Nehruvian-Congress Party vision of India as a secular democratic state, the RSS is both an Indianized version of Fascism and the epitome of murderously divisive Hindu communalism (Mahendra 1977; Sahai n.d.; Gupta n.d.). Others have seen the RSS as an authentically populist Hindu nationalist organization which has the capacity for revitalizing Indian society and polity (Swamy 1979, 11–13; Elenjimittam 1951, 15).

Historically the main geographical strength of the RSS has been in north and central India. Although present in the southern "Dravidian" states since the early 1940s, its rapid and continuing growth in the south dates from the late 1970s (*Organiser,* February 14, 1982, 4).

The RSS social base of support has been predominantly urban—mainly among the economically vulnerable and socially insecure Hindu salaried middle classes and small businessmen. Through its affiliates it had by the 1970s gained a significant following among Hindu students and urban workers. Since the late 1970s its activities in rural development and in defense of Hindu rights have attracted increasing rural support. Through missionary and social work it has made inroads in tribal areas previously outside the Hindu mainstream. Finally, it has developed branches among overseas Hindu communities, most notably in the United States, the United Kingdom, and Africa.

Founded in 1925 in Nagpur, in the present state of Maharashtra, the RSS was a response to the intensification of Hindu-Muslim communal antagonism caused by the rise of the Indian Nationalist movement and the formation of the Muslim League. It drew its inspiration from the Hindu revivalist movements which had originated in the latter half of the nineteenth century. These movements were in large part a response to the accelerated rate of modernizing change in Indian society. The expansion of English-language higher education, as well as education in the vernaculars, created a scramble for status among the literate castes and classes of Indian society which took the form of increasingly intense competition for access to the expanding modern professions and government services (Seal 1971, 17–24, 114–30). Nervously confronting each other in new urban competitive settings, subject to intrusive currents of Western humanistic thought, and challenged by the work of Christian missionaries, many educated Indians experienced new forms of alienation, as well as of personal and group identity (Jones 1976, 1–29, 154–85).

The Hindu, Sikh, and Muslim religious-cultural movements generated in response to these felt strains, although initially defensive in character, became increasingly assertive both toward opposing groups within their own communities and toward outsiders. Among Hindus these movements may be roughly classified according to three types. First, there were orthodox movements that aimed to preserve both the forms and substance of traditional orthodoxy. Second, there were modernist reform movements motivated by a desire to reinterpret the traditional faith, especially in the light of Western criticisms, in order to make it more relevant to modern conditions. Third, there were revivalist movements which sought to revive what were deemed to be the fundamentals of the original pure faith, which was alleged to be superior to anything the West had to offer.

Of these movements the various revivalist groups were the most activist. Aggressively proselytizing, they were inspired by a vision of a resurgent united Hindu community which they often identified with "Mother India." Acutely aware of the divisive inequities of caste, and of the economic marginality of the Indian masses, they actively sought to create a wider Hindu communal solidarity that de-emphasized caste and other social cleavages. Convinced of the superiority of their Hindu traditions to those of the West and Islam, they were psychologically equipped for aggressive social mobilization and political activism. When Hindu revivalists became politicized in the nationalist movement, they often tended to foster among Hindus antagonistic attitudes toward Muslims. There were three reasons for this. First, Islam was associated with foreign conquest. Second, Muslims by self-definition were outside any boundary marker that defined Hinduism. Third, as the largest and most politically assertive non-Hindu group, Muslims seemed to be potentially the most threatening to Hinduism. The rise of the nationalist movement under the aegis of the Indian National Congress, and of the Muslim League which was founded in 1909 to protect Muslim interests, added a new political dimension that heightened the Hindu-Muslim sense of difference. Most Indians, when they thought of a national identity at all, conceived of it through the lens of their religious-cultural collectivity and its history. This meant that when they thought in terms of nationality they often tended to focus on things that separated them—differences in religion, differing historical memories.

Muslims were aware that they had once ruled most of India and that only in rare instances had Muslims been under the political domination of Hindus. To many the idea of living in a democratic state with an overwhelming Hindu majority was profoundly disquieting. For their part, Hindus could evoke historical memories of powerful and culturally vital Hindu kingdoms of the pre-Muslim "classical age," instances of religious oppression by Muslim rulers, and Hindu martial heroes who had valiantly resisted Muslim rule. They could also evoke positive, deeply felt all-Indian traditional Hindu symbols of "Bharat" (India) as a sacred geographical entity which, even in pre-Muslim times of political division, had always had an overarching cultural unity and a common core in all-Indian deities.

The expansion of national electoral politics in the period from 1909 to 1939 and the emergence of mass agitational politics in connection with the Indian independence movement opened up new political arenas of group competition which had the effect, among others, of intensifying Hindu-Muslim communal hostilities. This was especially true after Gandhi assumed leadership of the independence movement and gave it a mass base by using the idiom of religious symbols of all the communities to mobilize the Indian masses for political agitation.

Gandhi can be viewed from one angle as a Hindu religious revivalist who sought to regenerate Hindu society by freeing it from foreign rule, abolishing the social inequities of caste and poverty, and fostering that strand in Hindu tradition that enjoined a positive appreciation of all religions as worthy approaches to the sacred. His concept of a secular Indian national state under whose protective and nurturing umbrella all the religious communities of India could flourish can be viewed as an ideology of national integration which would encompass the pluralities of Indian society within a framework that would foster religious tolerance based on mutual respect.

To Gandhi's bitter disappointment, the politicization of the masses in the 1920s through the appeal to religious symbols exacerbated communal rivalries in ways which caused Muslim-Hindu riots to increase in number and ferocity. This engendered among many Hindu nationalists a feeling that Gandhi was making too many concessions to Muslim sensibilities, and that Muslim militancy posed a serious danger to Hindus. Moreover, they were increasingly frustrated with the failure of Gandhi's nonviolent strategy of political confrontation to gain Indian self-rule from the British.

Creation and Organization of the RSS

Dr. Keshav Baliram Hedgewar, the founder of the RSS, shared these misgivings. Like many Hindu nationalists, he was profoundly disturbed by what he perceived to be an overwhelmingly numerous but divided and enfeebled Hindu community, lacking the self-confidence either effectively to challenge the rule of a handful of Britishers or to defend itself against the attacks of a seemingly more united and aggressive Muslim community. As Hedgewar saw it, the remedy lay in the creation of a new type of Hindu character modeled on the virtues of past Hindu heroes. Men of such character would be proud of their Hindu nation and would feel a kinship with all its members. They would strive selflessly for its unity and for its moral and physical uplift. They would fearlessly defend it against all enemies. Their moral example and unremitting disciplined, selfless activism for the community would be the leaven that would eventually regenerate all aspects of Hindu society and create a mighty, organically united Hindu nation, no longer divided against itself by caste, class, or sect (Andersen and Damle 1987, 30–41, 58–64; Malkani 1980, 1–32).

To create disciplined cadres of this new Hindu moral elite, Hedgewar founded the RSS, whose highly centralized and organizational forms and basic rituals were by the mid-1930s developed into essentially what they are today.

The RSS sees itself as a family, indeed as the precursor of what will one day be the great, organically united, regenerated Hindu family. At the base of the organization is the *shaka* (branch) which comprises fifty to one hundred participants (*swayamsevaks,* volunteers) and meets daily. According to observers, the majority of the typical *shaka*'s members are young men between eighteen and twenty-five years of age. The highly disciplined *shaka* activities include prescribed games, defensive skills, yogic exercises, patriotic songs, and group discussions on a variety of topics—ideal personal character traits, Hindu history and heroes, the need for Hindu unity, current problems of India. All topics are discussed from the standpoint of RSS ideology. *Shaka* activities are considered to be religious acts of devotional service to the holy, all-nurturing motherland. The opening and closing ceremonies express this, as well as the *swayamsevaks*' commitment to selfless service to the Hindu nation (Andersen and Damle 1987, 84–86, 89–98; Sirsikar 1988, 191–95; Sampradayikta Virodhi Committee n.d., 11–13; Dhooria n.d., 9–27; Park 1966, 2–6; Curran 1979, 63–70; Golwalkar 1980, 511–15; Malkani 1980, 198–207; present writer's personal observations). The emphasis in *shaka* activities is on group solidarity and disciplined cooperative effort to achieve group goals. Close personal bonds with fellow *swayamsevaks* are encouraged, and loyalty to the leadership is stressed. In accordance with the overriding concept of Hindu brotherhood, caste is not recognized in RSS activities, and RSS members have informed the present writer that it would be considered extremely bad form for any member to inquire about another's caste.

An occasional qualified defense of the fourfold *varna* and caste system as a social order that in the past had harmoniously held together Hindu society by organizing the division of labor on the basis of individuals' differing abilities is still expressed in RSS publications (Nijhawan 1990; Sharma 1990). However, RSS spokesmen have condemned the inequalities and rigid hereditary character of caste as perversions of the original intent of Hindu thinkers (Golwalkar 1980, 143, 462–70; Golwalkar 1972, 110; Bharat Prakashan 1955, 50; Deoras 1974, 11–30; Deoras 1982, 11–15; Nene 1988, 74–76). The caste system as practiced today has been criticized by the current RSS leader as an institution whose inequities divide the Hindu community, and one which is incompatible with the requirements of modern society. He and other RSS writers admit that, given the realities of contemporary Hindu society, the elimination of caste will require a long-term effort to alter basic attitudes. They argue that this effort should be carried out by a gradualist strategy of persuasion which emphasizes the unity of all Hindus while working for the social uplift of oppressed castes and backward classes. They feel that only by this strategy can the caste system be pushed toward a natural death without unduly inflaming inter-caste hostilities and further hardening caste divisions which are the major obstacle to the consolidation of Hindu society (Deoras 1974, 11–30; Deoras 1982, 11–15; Goradia 1991).

In line with this approach RSS writers bitterly denounced Prime Minister V. P. Singh's abrupt decision in August, 1990, to implement the Mandal Commission's recommendations for government job and educational reservations for "other backward classes" as a tactic designed, by promoting "caste war," to increase his party's vote bank and to undermine the feeling of Hindu unity that was gathering momentum due to the RSS-BJP campaign to recover for Hindus Lord Ram's birthplace in Ayodhya (*Organiser* August 26, 1990, 1, 15; September 2, 1990, 1, 15, 4, 8; September 23, 1990, 1, 15, 4, 6, 10; December 9, 1990, 8–9; May 19, 1991, 4, 8). In contrast to Singh's divisive strategy, asserted one RSS writer, the RSS-affiliated BJP will implement the Mandal guidelines in a "judicious way" that will presumably minimize the divisive impact on Hindu society while promoting long-term Hindu consolidation by bringing the backward classes into the economic mainstream of Hindu society (*Organiser* April 28, 1991, 9–10).

Although the membership attrition rate is high, the RSS socializing methods seem to have a powerful formative effect on most young men who participate in the organization. Many outside observers, including some hostile to the RSS ideology, have been impressed by the disciplined efficiency of its organization and activities, as well as by its high degree of group and organizational cohesiveness.

The RSS organizational structure is hierarchically centralized, with direct lines of transmission from the center in Nagpur down through the regional, state, district, and local levels. There is constant feedback from the lower to higher levels. The key links in the structure and the core cadre of the RSS organization are the *pracharaks*—a word which, in the context of many RSS writings, often seems equivalent to "missionary." These are full-time workers, who have undergone a rigorous selection process and have committed themselves to devoting their total energies to RSS work.

At the top of the organizational pyramid is the *sarsanghchalak* (Supreme Guide). So far there have been three: Hedgewar until his death in 1940; Madhav Sadashiv Golwalkar until his death in 1973; and the current *sarsanghchalak*, Madhukar Dattatraya Deoras. In public matters the *sarsanghchalak* speaks for the whole organization. In major policy decisions his voice in the inner RSS councils is usually decisive. However, he does not have, or claim to have, dictatorial powers and appears to consult carefully with the inner council of senior *pracharak* advisors before making major policy decisions (Sirsikar 1988, 198; Andersen and Damle 1987, 82, 88–89).

The close personal bonds among *pracharaks*, their sense of intense personal identification with the RSS, and the overriding imperative of loyalty to the organization constitute such powerful social and psychological pressures on the individual that seldom does one feel able to openly challenge the decisions of the senior leadership. A few who have openly challenged the leaders suffered ostracism. Others left the organization and kept silent. However, most who disagree with a policy nevertheless loyally work for its implementation even when they may informally work within RSS circles to get the policy changed. As a result, the RSS so far appears to have been relatively free from the open factionalism typical of many other Indian organizations.

RSS Ideology

I accept the view that ideologies arise in situations of strain and cultural dissonance, and that they serve both to redefine a situation and offer a programmatic way to resolve it (Geertz 1973, 193–233). Since the birth of the nationalist movement in the nineteenth century, Indian society has been undergoing the strain of trying to define its national identity. Post-independence efforts to achieve a viable national integration that can encompass the myriad of India's often mutually antagonistic cultural pluralities have sharpened the sense of strain, as have the pressing problems of economic development and new social and regional cleavages caused by the accelerating politicization of the population.

In viewing RSS ideology as one attempt to identify the sources of strain and cultural dissonance, and to provide a programmatic prescription for action to resolve these conflicts, several basic themes are apparent, ways of thinking which with varying emphasis have been constantly reiterated over the years:

1. A myth of a golden age in the distant past, when the community was united; and its culture, spiritual life, material prosperity, and polity flourished.

2. A contrasting image of the degenerate present, in which the sense of community has been lost; and the community's cultural, spiritual, material, and political life has declined into enfeeblement and slavery to internal vices and external forces.

3. An assertion that even in the worst periods of decline there was always a "saving remnant" of cultural heroes who resisted the causes of decline.

4. An explanation, in terms of internal and external causes, of why this decline occurred.

5. A belief in the existence of powerful malignant external and internal conspiratorial forces which are constantly seeking to undermine the community's welfare; and a sense of urgency that these forces must be vigilantly guarded against and combatted.

6. A call to action to bring about individual and community rejuvenation and solidarity.

In RSS ideology, India (Bharat) as a geographical entity is an aspect or manifestation of the divine, as is the great Hindu race-nation (Golwalkar 1947;

Golwalkar 1980, 159–75). Together they form an indissoluble organic unity. The Hindu nation and its culture (*sanskriti*) have always been the essence of the Indian national soul. Ancient Hindu India was the land of true righteousness (*dharmaboomi*) and of true religion and enlightenment (*punyabhoomi* and *mokshaboomi*)—in short the sacred land of God-realization. It was united and powerful, and its society functioned harmoniously. Its religion, culture, and flourishing civilization were the light of the world. Unfortunately, decline set in when Hindus became selfish, complacent, and divided against themselves. They forgot their national soul (*chiti*), their true *dharma,* and their corporate identity. Thus weakened, they were easy prey for the brutally violent Muslim conquest. The Muslim conquerors looted and destroyed Hindu temples and oppressed Hindu religion. Worse, they either forcibly converted or seduced millions of Hindus into Islam. The wily British rulers made things worse by de-nationalizing the Hindu educated classes and culturally enslaving them with their English educational system. They convinced Hindus that there had never been a unified India or Hindu nation. In depriving the Hindu intelligentsia of their sense of historical nationhood, they destroyed their individual and collective sense of self-respect. And they foisted on them a "composite" identity made up of a forced, artificial syncretism of Indian and Western elements. However, throughout this dark period there was always a saving remnant of Hindu sages and warriors who fought the "thousand-year war" for the Hindu nation and its *dharma*. They kept alive the essence of the divine Hindu national body-soul and waged an unremitting struggle against foreign political and cultural enslavement. Their heroic example provides inspirational role models for all true Indians in today's troubled and dangerous times.

RSS literature over the years has emphasized five major sources of weakness or danger confronting post-Independence India. These, according to RSS literature, have varied in salience over time, but have always been present in an active or latent manner. They may be summarized as follows.

First, Hindu (Bharatiya, Indian) society is still de-nationalized. The moneyed classes ape Western consumerist lifestyles. The self-styled intelligentsia search in alien sources for models of modernity, as well as for definitions of national identity and the good society. Some espouse Marxism with its godless materialism and divisive doctrines of class conflict. Others opt for Western democracy whose essentially capitalistic character stands for selfish individualistic materialism, wasteful consumerism, and ecological destruction. Both of these un-Indian philosophies view man as nothing but a hedonistic materialistic creature. Both ignore the spiritual and moral dimensions of human personality.

Second, the Muslims and Christians, Hindus by blood, have gone over to alien and intolerantly exclusivist "semitic" religious cultures. The primary cultural identities and loyalties of most of them lie outside India, either in Muslim countries or the Christian West. They promote "fissiparous" (antinational) tendencies and inter-communal hostility by constantly demanding privileged treatment from the state, and they serve as a vote bank for politicians who give in to them. The Muslims sympathize with Muslim separatists in Kashmir. With lavish help from Arab oil money, they carry out conversion missionary work among the poorer Hindus, thereby further dividing Hindu society. The Christians also carry out foreign-financed missionary work which promotes separatist tendencies among tribal peoples. If Muslims and Christians could only see that Hinduism tolerates and values all religions, they would realize that being part of the Hindu *rashtra* would be the best guarantee for their religious freedom. In time they could then become true Indians. Meanwhile, their fissiparous activities—particularly their conversion activities among Hindus, should be prohibited by law. And efforts should be made to win them over to a love for, and identification with, Hindu culture.

Third, the Communist parties (the Communist Party of India and the Communist Party Marxist, allied to Russia and China, respectively) represent alien philosophies which promote class and communal conflict and support separatist movements.

Fourth, there is the mainstream Congress Party leadership. With its leftist allies Congress has, in the name of national integration, seduced the Indian people with the false Nehruvian concept that India is a "composite nation" and a Western-type "secular state." Congress treats Indian society as a mere patchwork aggregate of pluralities having no internal moral unity. As a result, minority religions get special privileges which entrench their un-Indian cultures. Under the guise of these false concepts of "pseudo-secularism," corrupt Congress politicians have built up vote banks and fostered fissiparous tendencies. They have coddled the Muslims and prevented their integration into the national life. They have weakly yielded to balkanizing regional movements, especially on language-state issues, and in Kashmir. They have underhandedly played on communal and caste rivalries to undermine electoral opponents, even to the point of encouraging militant Sikh revivalism in the Punjab. In Indira Gandhi's desperate bid to stay in power, they tried to sabotage Indian democracy with a fascist dictatorship in the 1975–77 "Emergency." In foreign affairs Congress has taken a weak line toward aggressive Chinese and Pakistani activities. And it has risked India's military and economic independence by making her too reliant on Soviet arms and Western multi-national corporations.

Finally, there are the foreign threats. There is the Chinese and Pakistani aggression as well as persistent efforts to foster separatist movements on India's borders. The Soviets seek to keep India a dependent satellite. The United States arms Pakistan, and its multi-national corporations foster Indian economic dependency.

According to RSS ideology, the only way to meet these internal and external threats, create a true sense of national integration, and make India into a corporately cohesive, prosperous society with a powerful unitary state is to reconstruct national life as a Hindu *rashtra*. Hindu culture should be recognized as the national Indian culture. Sanskrit should be acknowledged the national classical language and mother of all truly Indian languages. Hindi should be promoted as the national link language. A Hindu *rashtra* would make India a truly democratic state and, because of Hinduism's respect for all religions, a truly positive secular state.

The practical aspects of the RSS national reconstruction program may be summarized as follows. In the sphere of nation-building and social reconstruction, the divisive inequities of caste, and especially the institution of untouchability, should be eliminated. Indian youth, especially the educated youth, should be imbued with the ideals of Hindu *rashtra* and mobilized for service to the nation, particularly for social work among the tribal peoples and the poorer classes. The economy should be decentralized and reconstructed along populist lines that would promote harmony between labor and management, and between the various occupational groups. Workers should be organized into a national labor movement. Through a complex system of autonomous functional units and industrial councils, workers should be given major control over industrial decision-making at all levels, as well as a major voice in national planning for industrial development. In this way a national industrial family would be created, with all groups cooperating in the common enterprise of national economic development. Everyone should be guaranteed employment, and the poorer classes should be brought into the economic mainstream. Gross disparities in wealth should be eliminated by an equitable incomes policy and by restrictions on the excessive consumption of the affluent classes.

In the political sphere political corruption should be sternly repressed. Regional and communal fissiparous tendencies should be firmly suppressed, as should the vote bank politics which foster such tendencies.

In the sphere of defense and foreign affairs India should have a powerful military establishment with a nuclear capability. Pakistani and Chinese aggressive activities should be firmly dealt with. National self-reliance in arms production and in economic development should be stressed and dependence on the superpowers eliminated. In short, India should develop its potential as a world power and frankly assert its position as the dominant power in South Asia.

Growth of the RSS and Its Affiliates

In the climate of rising Hindu-Muslim polarization the RSS expanded rapidly after the mid 1930s, especially in the Hindi-speaking areas of North India. By early 1948 its membership was 600,000–700,000 in 7,000 *shakas*. Although the Congress Party government grudgingly conceded that RSS cadres had done valuable service in aiding Punjabi Hindu refugees and in Kashmir, it banned the RSS from

February 1948 to July 1949 on grounds that it was implicated in the assassination of Gandhi. *Sarsanchalak* Golwalkar was arrested, and an estimated 20,000 *swayamsevaks* were jailed. Nehru and those of the Congress Party who shared his concept of a secular state were intensely hostile to the RSS, which in their view was a dangerous para-military organization that fanned communal frenzy. Despite this the RSS had by the early 1960s achieved a significant measure of national respectability as a disciplined and committed patriotic organization (Andersen and Damle 1987, 49–52, 114; Patel 1969).

Meanwhile, activist young *pracharak* cadres, convinced that RSS "nation-building" effectiveness required an outward thrust into new spheres of activity in various sectors of Indian society, in 1947 began the creation of what has become a sizeable group of RSS-affiliated organizations. In connection with this outward thrust there has also been created a vernacular news service and publishing ventures which have resulted over the years in a proliferation of RSS literature in both the major Indian languages and in English (Andersen and Damle 1987, 114–117, 146).

In terms of numbers and capacity for social mobilization, the most impressive RSS organization achievements have been the *Bharatiya Mazdoor Sangh* (BMS), founded in 1955; the *Akhil Bharatiya Vidyarthi Parishad* (ABVP), founded during the 1948–49 ban on the RSS; and the *Vishwa Hindu Parishad* (VHP), founded in 1964. In the sphere of political party activity the RSS has provided the organizational core of the BJS and, after 1980, the BJP.

Both the BMS and ABVP were initially founded to counteract Communist organizational activities among India's expanding university student and labor populations. Both have experienced a rapid expansion of membership since the 1970s. The ABVP has become an important and sometimes dominant influence in university politics (Andersen and Damle 1987, 120, 122, 129, 148; RSS 1985, 47–49). By 1986 BMS membership was over 1,800,000, making it, according to its own estimate, the second largest national labor organization (Bharatiya Mazdoor Sangh 1981b, March 7, 8, 1981; Andersen and Damle 1987, 132–33). It claims to be particularly concerned to reach the neglected and disadvantaged groups and has been moving into new sections of the unorganized sector of the work force—cottage industries, self-employed labor, and rural labor. Its populist philosophy of a decentralized model of industrial organization, based on the corporate concept of harmoniously cooperating occupational "families" and industrial councils, with workers determining working conditions and production decisions, has been summarized under the slogan:

> Nationalise the Labour
> Labourise the Industry
> Industrialise the Nation.
> (Thengadi n.d., 11)

The VHP was initially founded to bring about unity among the various Hindu sects and promote Hindu values (Andersen and Damle 1987, 133). In the 1980s it took a leading role in massive demonstrations to foster a sense of Hindu unity, mass agitations against Muslim and Christian proselytization, and campaigns to recover mosques that were once allegedly Hindu temples.

The BJS was founded after intense debate within the RSS, whose *sarsanchalak* Golwalkar felt that the RSS should confine itself to the cultural mission of character building and stay aloof from the corrupting effects of party political activity (Sirsikar 1988, 198; Baxter 1969, 54–68; Mishra 1980, 26–30; Low 1968, 330–69; Andersen and Damle 1987, 157–58). It offered itself as a Hindu nationalist alternative. By the early 1970s it espoused a populist-tinged economic program based largely on the ideas of the BMS and had developed ambitions to become a serious national alternative to the ruling Congress party. In 1977 it merged with the Janata Party. After the breakup of Janata, BJS reemerged in 1980 as the BJP.

RSS *pracharaks* have manned the key organizational positions in the BJS and BJP, and RSS *swayamsevaks* have provided the main source of BJS and BJP electoral workers. However, RSS support for the BJP has not been unconditional. In the early 1980s the BJP, in an effort to broaden its electoral base, played down its Hindu nationalist orientation, and instead put its commitment to "Gandhian Socialism" and "positive Secularism" in the forefront of its program (Bharatiya Janata Party 1981; Vajpayee 1980). This engendered some doubts within the RSS as to the genuineness of the BJP's Hindu nationalist credentials (*Organiser,* April 10, 1983, 5; Andersen and Damle 1987, 228–29, 232–33). In the 1984 general election a significant number of *swyamsevaks* entered the Congress Party (Manor 1988, 78, 97). Since 1985 the BJP has reverted to the more frankly Hindu populist nationalist stance of its BJS predecessor, and RSS support for the BJP has again become solid.

In the 1970s RSS cadres, in cooperation with the BJP, BMS, and ABVP affiliates, became increasingly involved in political activism. They played a significant role in the mass mobilization of the J. P. Narayan "total revolution" against the increasingly unpopular Congress Party, which forced Indira Gandhi to declare the "Emergency" dictatorship of 1975–77. Under the "Emergency" the RSS was banned for a second time. As in 1948–49, it went underground. This time it was not alone, and it cooperated with other banned opposition groups to offer effective nonviolent resistance to the government. While estimates vary, it is believed that as many as 100,000 RSS *swayamsevaks* were, at one time or another, jailed. Apparently as a result of the popularity gained from its activities, its role in the Janata Party victory in 1977, and the Hindu resurgence of the 1980s, RSS membership expanded rapidly from 8,500 *shakas* in 1975 to a claimed 20,000 *shakas* in 1985. Its affiliates have expanded rapidly in the 1980s, and its self-confidence has never been higher (Malkani 1980, 91, 93; Andersen and Damle 1987, 213, 241; RSS 1985, 61).

Its optimism received a great boost when, in the general election of late 1989, Congress was again swept from power. The BJP emerged the third largest party with eighty-eight seats in the national legislature (*Organiser,* December 10, 1989, 9). In subsequent state assembly elections, the BJP, claiming to have routed Congress in several of its strongholds, raised its number of seats from 162 to 492. It secured a large majority in two Hindi-speaking states (Madhya Pradesh and Arunachal Pradesh). In the Congress stronghold in the state of Maharashtra, the BJP in alliance with the *Shiv Sena*—the militantly Hindu and rabidly Maharashtrian regional party—made significant gains, claiming to have "almost brought Congress-I to its knees" (*Organiser,* March 18, 1990). The RSS organ *Organiser* hailed the BJP's ". . . big leap forward to emerge as the national alternative" as the "no nonsense Hindu nationalist party of the future" as a triumph of resurgent Hindu nationalism, and as confirming the long-held RSS position regarding the "need to break the Nehruvian straitjacket" of Western-type democratic "negative" secularism (*Organiser,* December 10, 1989, 9; March 11, 1990, 2, 9, 15). In the general election of May-June, 1991, the BJP became the second largest party. It won 119 seats in the Indian Parliament and increased its share of the popular vote from approximately 12 percent in 1989 to 22 percent (*Organiser,* July 7, 1991, 1–2, 4–5, 8–10, 12–15; *Indian Express, Madras,* June 20, 1991, 11; June 21, 1991, 10–11; July 5, 1991, 8; *People's Democracy,* June 23, 1991, 1, 3–5, 11; July 14, 1991, 5, 7).

Future of the RSS and Secular Polity

The RSS faces the future with confidence in playing a major role in shaping India according to its vision of a Hindu *rashtra.* From its perspective several factors favor its program. First, there are the immediately visible trends: the rapid growth of RSS membership all over India; the expansion of the membership and spheres of activity of the RSS affiliates—most notably student, labor, social service, and religious affiliates; and the resurgence of popular Hindu consciousness expressed in a growing popular receptivity to the notion of translating this into political terms, especially in the face of Muslim political assertiveness and Sikh separatist militancy. Second, there is the low morale of the leftist groups—especially the Communist parties—in the wake of the manifest deficiencies of foreign Communist and Socialist systems. Finally, there is the general disillusionment with the Congress Party and the erosion of faith in the Nehruvian vision of a secular state among the Western-type educated minority that has always been its real social base.

This last point merits elaboration. The Nehruvian ideal of a religiously neutral state with its premise of an autonomous sphere of secular polity and culture is rooted in the faith that a rationalist scientific approach is the key to solving India's problems, and that a secular unitary state implementing this approach is the engine for bringing Indian society into modernity. In this view religion is relegated to the private sphere, and the individual citizen qua participant in the polity is, so to speak, a secular animal. As Susanne H. Rudolph (1987) has noted, the Nehruvian view holds that the politicization of religious identities is illegitimate. Conversely, the state has no direct involvement in individual and group identities.

However, this ideal of an autonomous secular category of life activities has no roots in any of the major Indian religious-cultural traditions (Madan 1987; Nandy 1985). In all of these, the spheres of one's life activities are perceived as ideally governed by religiously defined norms. For vast numbers of Indians, one's primary individual and group identity is defined by one's religion, and it is through this identity that one relates to the polity.

This has meant that if the idea of a nation-state is to have a mass base, it must be made meaningful in positive religious terms. Gandhi, because he was religious revivalist, saw this. Out of a deep conviction that all religions are true, he attempted to unite Hindus and Muslims into a nation by drawing on the religious symbols of both. For him the idea of a secular state had positive religious content. As Rudolph has observed, he envisioned an Indian society "built on a community of religious communities" (Rudolph 1987).

More generally, one can argue that in the South Asian context effective political mobilization necessitates the frequent appeal to religious identities and feelings. The increasingly overt politicization of communal issues in the 1980s is disturbing evidence of this situation. Even Congress and leftist politicians, especially in recent years, have not been above resorting to communal appeals. Paul Brass, in noting this and recognizing that India's religious cleavages remain a major unresolved issue, suggests that a major reason for the trend toward overtly communal politics is ". . . the entrenchment of an ideology of the secular state which, in its tolerant face justifies pluralist practices but can also be used to condemn minority demands as a danger to national unity and the integrity of the Indian state" (Brass 1990, 169–70, 202–3). But one can equally well argue that the extent to which the avowedly secularist parties have resorted to communal appeals signifies that even they no longer believe in the secular ideal enough to practice it with consistent conviction. Moreover, the credibility of the Nehruvian secular state has been eroded by its inability to deliver on its promises of distributive justice.

To the degree that these arguments are valid, it would seem that the Nehruvian concept of a secular state has doubtful prospects in India for the near future. That is to say, the concepts of Indian nationhood, as well as of legitimate spheres of secular activity will, if they are to take root in the popular consciousness, need to be redefined in such a way that they are positively meaningful in terms of the religious-cultural concepts of India's various communities. The tragedy is that this task has in post-independence India been left too much the preserve of narrowly communal militants and unscrupulous politicians (Kishwar 1990).

What, if any, role may the RSS have in this? At present it appears that it is likely to remain a widely respected and well-organized presence on the Hindu scene. Within the heterogeneous Hindu community it will likely heighten a sense of Hindu nationalism. In the short term at least this is bound to increase the sense of insecurity of non-Hindus, since most of them also think of themselves in communal terms.

Nevertheless, of all the major religious cultures on the Indian scene Sanskritic-derived Hindu culture has the oldest and richest symbols of "Bharat" as a geographical and cultural entity. Given this, it would seem that any redefinition of Indian national identity in religious-cultural terms would have to draw heavily on the Hindu traditions. Whether this would be done in a narrowly communal or broader inclusive manner (as in the case of Gandhi), and what role RSS avowedly tolerationist concepts of Hindu majoritarian nationalism would play, are open questions.

In the past the RSS has demonstrated some flexibility in softening the salience of certain of its ideological positions. Since the 1970s it appears to have pursued a two-track policy. On the one hand, its message of Hindu nationalism has continued to emphasize the nontheocratic, inclusive, and benignly tolerant elements of the Hindu tradition as true Indian secularism, and on occasion it has sought dialogue with Muslim intellectuals with a view to exploring commonalities among certain strands of Hindu and Muslim traditions. In 1977 it opened its membership to non-Hindus (Deoras 1979; Deoras 1982; Malkani 1980, 99–101; Malkani 1978, 65–81; Beg 1987; Golwalkar 1971; Golwalkar 1972; Andersen and Damle 1987, 223).

On the other hand, it has pursued a track denounced as narrowly communal by its critics. It has continued a strident call for the prohibition of Muslim and Christian conversion activities among Hindus and tribal peoples, while maintaining the right of Hindus to reconvert Muslims and Christians to Hinduism. It has also cooperated closely with its affiliate the *Vishwa Hindu Parishad* in campaigns to recover mosques that were allegedly once Hindu temples—most notably in the current campaign to recover the alleged birthplace of Lord Ram in Ayodhya (*Organiser* February 11, 1990, 11–15; October 21, 1990, 1–39; November 11, 1990, 1–16). These activities as defender of Hindu rights, along with certain rural development activities, appear to be gaining support for the RSS in some rural areas. Finally, the RSS regularly calls for stern measures against Muslim separatist activities in Kashmir, regularly denounces allegedly "antinational" Indian Muslim views regarding Indo-Pakistani relations and Kashmiri separatism, and stridently continues to criticize alleged governmental favoritism toward Muslims. Because of these activities it remains highly suspect among most non-Hindus and is frequently accused of directly and indirectly playing a role in the increasing number of Hindu-Muslim communal riots (Puri 1991).

One of the most serious ideological challenges to the RSS has been the issue relating to the Sikhs. Like most Hindus, the RSS insists that the Sikhs are within the Hindu fold—a proposition that most Sikhs fervently deny. With the emergence of Sikh separatism and Sikh terrorism against the Hindu community in the Punjab, the RSS, while calling for stern repression of Sikh separatism, has consistently tried to take a conciliatory stance toward the Sikh community. This has eroded significantly its support among Hindus in the Punjab, many of whom are deserting to more militant, frankly anti-Sikh Hindu organizations.

Conclusion

In conclusion, the RSS was created at a time when Hindu society was in the throes of acute strain and experiencing a widespread feeling of decline. To many alienated and disoriented urban Hindus of the younger, educated, and economically vulnerable salaried and small business classes, it offered a message based on indigenous beliefs that provided morally coherent ordering principles for their lives, a morally compelling program of action, and a supportive organizational structure for channeling their moral energies and restoring a sense of community. Its denunciation of untouchability and the inequities of the caste system offer a vision of a wider, more unified Hindu community (Deoras 1974, 10–18; Deoras 1979, 20–21; Deoras 1982, 15). Given the manifestly disorienting social strains and divisions in contemporary Indian society, the erosion of belief in secularist ideologies, and the perceived deficiencies of foreign Western and Marxist ideologies, the RSS will likely continue to be an attractive option for a significant number of Hindus who are searching for a sense of community and for a morally compelling individual and collective identity that is both modern and rooted in indigenous cultural values. In this respect the RSS has strikingly similar counterparts in revivalist organizations in the Muslim and Sikh communities, and in other parts of the world.

Whether the RSS will on balance play a divisive and polarizing or an integrative role in the hotbed of Indian cultural pluralism may well determine the future course of Indian politics. RSS-BJP strategies for managing India's cultural pluralism would differ in significant ways from those which Paul Brass describes as having been followed by Nehru and, less consistently, by Indira and Rajiv Gandhi. Brass argues that, in contrast to the model of a culturally assimilative nation-state, post-independence India has been a developing multi-national state in which, "The predominant tendencies . . . have been towards pluralism, regionalism, decentralization, and inter-dependence between the Center and the states" (Brass 1990, 321). He asserts that the Center has on balance accepted these tendencies by adopting policies whereby linguistic demands as well as those for more regional autonomy have been accommodated so long as they stopped short of secession, were not explicitly based on religious differences, demonstrated a broad base of popular support, and were acceptable to the rival ethnic or religious groups concerned (Brass 1974, 16–19, 430; Brass, 1990, 149–52). In addition, Congress governments have implemented provisions of the Indian Constitution that provide special safeguards for religious minorities designated as non-Hindu, especially in the area of personal law.

The RSS ideal of a unitary nation-state based on the assimilation of all Indians into a national Bharatiya culture flatly rejects the concept of India as a multinational state. RSS-BJP theorists do not condemn religious or linguistic pluralism as such. On the contrary, they assert that Hindu culture is inherently pluralistic and religiously tolerationist, and therefore opposed both to a uniformitarian leveling of Indian society and to the creation of an intrusive omnicompetent state that would seek to do this. A harmonious "unity-in-diversity," according to RSS thinkers, has always been the Hindu ideal. Consequently they praise Indian cultural diversities so long as they are not expressed or institutionalized in a divisive "antinational" form that separates religious and linguistic minorities from the mainstream Bharatiya culture and threatens the unity of Indian society (Golwalkar 1972, 57–58; Golwalkar, 1975, 108; Bishikar 1988, 112–23).

In implementing their principles of national integration, RSS-BJP thinkers would like to alter previous policies with respect to four areas of India's cultural pluralism: religion, language, regionalism, and political separatism.

With regard to religion they would, while permitting freedom of religion (but not of proselytization by non-Hindus), like to abolish what they call special privileges for Muslims and Christians. These, assert RSS writers, institutionalize the separate status of these minorities and prevent their integration into the mainstream Bharatiya culture. For example, most RSS writers (but not Golwalkar) would abolish the separate code of personal law for Muslims and have a uniform code for all Indians.

With regard to linguistic plurality, the RSS (many of whose members do not know Hindi) favors the promotion at the lowest local administrative levels of what it considers indigenous Indian dialects, but opposes any special status for Urdu on the grounds that it is a foreign language. It also favors more aggressive policies to promote Hindi as the national link language insofar as this can be done without unduly antagonizing non-Hindi speaking Hindus. Meanwhile, the RSS has accommodated itself to Indian realities, as is evidenced by the fact that some of its major all-Indian publications are in English, and it has had a publication in Urdu.

With respect to regionalism the RSS, deeply concerned that India is being "Balkanized" by the encroachments of increasingly powerful state governments and the creation of linguistic states, would like to arrest these trends and restore to the Center unambiguous sovereignty vis-à-vis state governments. As an ideal some RSS writers advocate the elimination of state governments, and the decentralization of their authority and legislative powers to the lowest homogeneous linguistic dialect units (Bishikar 1988, 183–84; Thengadi 1988, 74–75).

Finally, with respect to the issue of political separatism, the RSS and BJP are far more ready than previous ruling parties have been to allow the Center to use decisive armed action against any separatist nationalist movements—most notably the Sikh Khalistan and Muslim Kashmiri movements. In this connection the RSS, in addition to opposing the creation of the Sikh-dominated Punjabi Suba in the 1960s, has long advocated the abolition of the special constitutional status of Kashmir and the full integration of Kashmir into the Indian Union. It has also called for a more forceful policy against Pakistan to compel that country to cease giving covert support to Kashmiri and Sikh separatist forces.

NOTE

In preparing this paper, I am most grateful to Dr. William Urban and Dr. Carolyn Tyirin Kirk for their editorial criticism; to Mrs. Frances Stauffer for her generous assistance; and to my wife Nellie.

REFERENCES

Andersen, Walter, and Shridar D. Damle. 1987. *The Brotherhood in Saffron: The Rashtriya Swayamsevak Sangh and Hindu Revivalism*. Boulder: Westview Press.

Baxter, Craig. 1969. *Jana Sangh: A Biography of an Indian Political Party*. Philadelphia: University of Pennsylvania Press.

Beg, Moazziz Ali. 1987. Proposals for the Creation of an Institute for Researches on Sufi and Bhakti Tradition as Historico-Cultural and Psychological Basis for National Integration. *Manthan* 8, 11 (November): 9–12.

Bharat Prakashan. 1955. *Shri Guruji: The Man and His Mission: On the Occasion of His 51st Birthday*. Delhi: Bharat Prakashan.

Bharatiya Janata Party. 1981. *Constitution and Rules (as adopted by the National Council on 29th December, 1980 at Bombay and amended on 27th April, 1981 at Cochin)*. Delhi: Nice Printing Press.

Bharatiya Mazdoor Sangh. 1981a. *Constitution and Rules (amended up to March, 1981)*. Delhi: Bharatiya Mazdoor Sangh Central Office.

Bharatiya Mazdoor Sangh. 1981b. *Silver Jubilee Year: Sixth All-India Conference*. Calcutta: New Art Press.

Bishikar, C. P. 1988. *Pandit Deendayal Upadhyaya: Ideology and Perception, Part V: Concept of the Rashtra*. Translated by Y. Kelkar. New Delhi: Suruchi Prakashan.

Brass, Paul. 1990. *The Politics of India Since Independence*. Vol. 4.1 of *The New Cambridge History of India*. New York: Cambridge University Press.

Brass, Paul. 1974. *Language, Religion and Politics in North India*. London: Cambridge University Press.

Curran, J. A., Jr. 1979. *Militant Hinduism in Indian Politics: A Study of the R.S.S.* New Delhi: All India Zuami Ekta Sammeln.

Deoras, M. D. 1982. The Call for Hindu Consolidation: Extracts from the Speech of Sri

Balasaheb Deoras Sarsangchalak of RSS, January 3, 1982. *RSS Karnataka Hindu Sangaman: 1, 2, 3 January 1982*. Bangalore: RSS Karnataka Prakashan Vibhag.
Deoras, M. D. 1979. *Hindu Sangatan: The Need of the Nation*. New Delhi: Suruchi Sahitya.
Deoras, M. D. 1974. *Social Equality and Hindu Consolidation*. Bangalore: Jagarana Prakashana publication no. 11, May 8.
Dhooria, Ram Lall. n.d. *I Was a Swayamsevak*. New Delhi: Sampradayikta Virodhi Committee.
Elenjimittam, Anthony. 1951. *Philosophy and Action of the R.S.S. for the Hind Swaraj*. Bombay: The Laxmi Publications.
Frykenberg, Robert E. 1989. The Emergence of Modern "Hinduism" as a Concept and as an Institution: A Reappraisal with Special Reference to South India. In *Hinduism Reconsidered,* edited by Günther D. Sontheimer and Herman Kulke, 29–49. New Delhi: Manohar Publications.
Geertz, Clifford. 1973. *The Interpretation of Cultures*. New York: Basic Books.
Golwalkar, M. S. 1980. *Bunch of Thoughts*. Rev. 1st ed. Bangalore: Jagarana Prakshana.
Golwalkar, M. S. 1972. *Spotlights*. 2d ed., 1975. Bangalore: Sahitya Sindhu.
Golwalkar, M. S. 1971. Talk with Dr. Saifaddin Jellany. In *Bunch of Thoughts*, 639–46. 2d ed. Bangalore: Jagarana Prakashana.
Golwalkar, M. S. 1947. *We, or Our Nationhood Defined*. 4th ed. Nagpur: Bharat Prakashan.
Goradia, Prafull. 1991. Nullifying Casteism Through "Hindutva." *Organiser,* May 26, 9, 14.
Gupta, N. L. n.d. *RSS and Democracy*. New Delhi: Sampradayikta Virodhi Committee.
Kishwar, Madhu. 1990. In Defense of our Dharma. *Manushi,* September/October, 2–15.
Jones, Kenneth. 1976. *Arya Dharm: Hindu Consciousness in 19th Century Punjab*. Berkeley: University of California Press.
Low, Donald. 1968. Syama Prasad Mookherjee and the Communal Alternative. In *Soundings in South Asian History,* edited by Donald Low, 330–74. Berkeley: University of California Press.
Madan, T. N. 1987. Secularism in Its Place. *The Journal of Asian Studies* 46, 4:748–54.
Mahendra, K. L. 1977. *Defeat the RSS Fascist Designs*. 2d ed. New Delhi: New Age Printing Press.
Malkani, K. R. 1980. *The RSS Story*. New Delhi: Impex India.
Malkani, K. R. 1978. *The Midnight Knock*. New Delhi: Vikas Publishing House Pvt. Ltd.
Manor, James. 1988. Parties and the Party System. In *India's Democracy: An Analysis of Changing State-Society Relations,* edited by Atul Kohli, 62–98. Princeton: Princeton University Press.
Mishra, Dina Nath. 1980. *RSS: Myth and Reality*. New Delhi: Vikas Publishing House Pvt. Ltd.
Nandy, Ashis. 1985. An Anti-Secular Manifesto. *Seminar* (Bombay) 314 (October): 14–24.
Nehru, Jawaharlal. 1946. *The Discovery of India*. 1960 ed., edited by Robert I. Crane. Garden City, New York: Doubleday.
Nene, V. V. 1988. *Pandit Deendayal: Ideology and Perception,* Vol. 2, *Integral Humanism*. Translated by M. K. Paranjape and D. R. Kulkarni. New Delhi: Suruchi Prakashan.
Nijhawan, P. K. 1990. Why the Caste System Endures. *Organiser,* October 7, 5, 8.
Park, Richard. 1966. *Angularities and the Secular State: An Interview With India's RSS*.

Unpublished paper in University of Chicago Regenstein Library pamphlet collection.

Patel, Vallabh Bhai. 1969. Letter to M. S. Golwalkar, September 11, 1948. *Justice on Trial: A Collection of Historic Letters Between Sri Guruji and the Government.* 5th ed. Bangalore: Prakashan Vibhag.

Puri, Anjali. Carnage in Kanpur. 1991. *Indian Express Madras,* June 2, 9.

Rashtriya Swayamsevak Sangh (RSS). 1985. *RSS: Spearheading National Renaissance.* Bangalore: Prakashan Vibhag.

Rudolph, Susanne Hoeber. 1987. Preface to T. N. Madan's Secularism in Its Place. *The Journal of Asian Studies* 46, 4 (November): 748–54.

Sahai, Govind. n.d. (probably 1956). *R.S.S.: Ideology, Technique and Propaganda.* Delhi: Naya Hindustan Press.

Sampradayikta Virodhi Committee. n.d. Excerpts from a diary of an RSS member. In *RSS: Is It a Cultural Organization?* New Delhi: Sampradayikta Virodhi Committee.

Seal, Anil. 1971. *The Emergence of Indian Nationalism: Competition and Collaboration in the Later Nineteenth Century.* Cambridge: Cambridge University Press.

Seshadri, H. V., ed. 1988. *RSS: A Vision in Action.* Bangalore: Jagarana Prakashana.

Sharma, Ashoke. 1990. Caste-based Reservations for OBCs Are Unconstitutional. *Organiser,* September 23, 5, 14.

Sirsikar, V. M. 1988. My Years in the RSS. In *The Experience of Hinduism,* edited by Eleanor Zelliott and Maxine Berntsen, 190–203. Albany: State University of New York Press.

Smith, Donald E. 1963. *India as a Secular State.* Princeton: Princeton University Press.

Swamy, Subramaniam. 1979. The RSS Is Here To Stay. *The Illustrated Weekly of India,* October 7, 11–13.

Thengadi, D. B. n.d. *The Onward March: Bharatiya Mazdoor Sangh.* New Delhi: Bharatiya Mazdoor Sangh Central Office.

Thengadi, D. B. 1988. *Pandit Deendayal Upadhyaya: Ideology and Perception, Part I: An Inquest.* Translated by M. K. Paranjape. New Delhi: Suruchi Prakashan.

Vajpayee, A. B. 1980. *India at the Crossroads.* Delhi: BJP Publication.

13

The Creation of the Modern Maya

ALAN LEBARON

THE MODERN MAYA of Guatemala demonstrate increasing signs of ethnic solidarity, moving toward a new age of pan-Maya awareness and political unity. The Maya intend to put an end to the nearly five centuries of harsh domination by the Euro-Guatemalans, as they simultaneously put an end to the widely held belief that the Maya will eventually be assimilated into Guatemalan national culture. Significant numbers of Maya now claim separate "nationality" from the Guatemalan state. In Guatemala as elsewhere, the rise of cultural pluralism and its challenge to the cohesion of the nation-state has caught many observers by surprise.

The pan-Maya movement developed after 1944, out of changes brought by "modernization" and protracted conflict with the Guatemalan state. Until 1944, the heart of Maya culture remained in separate, often isolated communities, which protected the Maya from unwanted outside influences. After 1944 changing realities would promote Maya contacts far beyond the old communities. When the Maya established communication with the modern world, conditions were created which necessitated change and adaptation. Maya society has not been erased, however, for Maya ethnicity has flourished and strengthened. The pan-Maya ethnonational movement does not hope to resurrect Maya preconquest nations, nor postconquest colonial culture, for although the modern Maya keep many ancient traditions and attitudes, they have increasingly adapted to (not assimilated into) the contemporary culture of Euro-Guatemalans and to global culture. As the Maya became "modern" they obtained the skills to better define and defend their culture. With the birth of Maya solidarity and Maya politics, Guatemala has become a nation divided by cultural pluralism.

Ethnic Identity and the Pan-Maya Movement

Cultural pluralism in Latin America has not been historically salient. No Latin American nation has experienced sustained ethnic political mobilization and conflict as have, for example, Nigeria, India, Malaysia, or South Africa. Latin American societies certainly have been ethnically divided, with the populations containing Indians, Africans, Asians, Europeans, and the "mixed" children of them all. However, Latin American groups rarely mobilized strictly along ethnic lines, nor developed a broad sense of group kinship. Several exceptions may certainly exist. Spanish Americans, before and after independence from Spain in the early nineteenth century, speculated that various Indian revolts manifested ethnic nationalism. The Inca rebellion led by Túpac Amaru II in 1780 and the Maya Totonicapán revolt of 1820 make two fine examples. Modern historians usually have rejected the notion that pan-Indian ethnic unity fueled rebellions, although a recent reinterpretation of the 1780 revolt now accepts nationalism as a primary factor (Stern 1987).[1]

Into the 1960s and 1970s, little evidence of ethnic politics or ethnic unity could be found in contemporary Latin America. Profound differences in language, culture, geographic location, religion, and political institutions separated the indigenous people. Jean Piel (1970, 108) wrote that the word "Indian" in Peru was useless to describe a "racial or ethnic reality," for a cohesive Indian identity "does not exist and has never existed at any time in the history of Peru." In an early study of world cultural pluralism, Crawford Young (1976) concluded that Latin American Indians had developed neither ethnic unity nor nationalism. At the time Young completed his research, most Latin American specialists believed that Indian cultures would eventually be assimilated into the dominant Spanish cultures and thus become extinct. In regards to the Maya, Carol Smith (1990b, 223) found that "in the 1970s no general sense of 'ethnic' opposition—of all Indians versus all ladinos [non-Indians]—existed in Guatemala."

Indian ethnic consciousness in conflict with non-Indians became clearly visible by the late 1970s. Bringing in a new decade, in 1980, the VIII Congreso Indigenista Interamericano (Merida, Mexico) made history with Latin American Indians vehemently demanding political rights and insisting that non-Indians stop their efforts to integrate and assimilate the Indian into national cultures (Bonfil et al. 1982). Inspired by the 1988 International Symposium on Ethnicity and Nation in Latin America, the *América Indígena* (Mexico, January–March 1989) devoted an entire issue to the current development of Latin American ethnonationalism. The magazine's editorial noted that "the Indian movements of Latin America have opted in recent years for self-determination." Mexico, long thought to be a successful example of national ethnic integration, now faces increasing cultural pluralism. Kearney and Nagengast (1990, 87), for example, have documented the case of the Mexican Mixtec, who have developed a "new panMixtec ethnic identity," now used in political activism to "undermine some of the results of their centuries-long oppression."

Maya ethnonational groups visibly emerged in the late 1970s and the 1980s, as did numerous other Latin American Indian groups. The Maya movement indubitably received stimulation from international contacts with other Indians (Bonfil 1981), but Maya ethnonationalism also descended from local circumstances, such as the peasant leagues and political parties of the 1944–54 reform period, and the organizations connected to liberation theology and revolution in the 1960s and 1970s. According to Richard Adams (1990, 158), "A broader Indian identity became . . . clearly evident in the increasing number of Indian professionals and Indians involved in organizing and revolutionary activity in the 1970s and 1980s." Antonio Gallo (1985, 15) notes that the Maya "each day more" become increasingly conscious of their "Maya-being," and more politically active as well. Arturo Arias (1990, 231) speaks of a "remarkable change in worldview of so many Guatemalan Indians" which has produced an "Indian movement that cut across previous lines of language and community." The Maya themselves speak of their movement with special pride; thus the Comisión de Celebraciones Mayas states: "The people of this America are witnessing a Maya resurgence . . . we already have doctors, lawyers, newspersons, teachers, engineers, architects, and other professionals" (*El Gráfico,* January 9, 1991).

The pan-Maya movement is a widespread and growing force that desires to unify the Maya, protect Maya land, culture, and languages, and promote the general well-being of Maya people (Bonfil 1981; Bonfil et al. 1982; COCADI 1989). Maya unity has been based on local and national organizations, which are increasing in number rapidly. Most Maya would approve of the goals of the Council of Ethnic Communities "Runujel Junam": "struggle to advance the goals of democracy, justice, and dignity for the Maya peoples while fighting racial discrimination" (*Central America Report,* May 18, 1990). The Maya have also demanded the use of Maya languages in the schools and the cessation of state efforts to integrate the Maya into the national culture. A separate Maya nation or significant autonomy would be welcome to most Maya, but such talk is dangerous in Guatemala. Much of the current Maya strategy calls for peaceful relations with the Guatemalan state, and a grassroots "bottom up" Maya nationalism which curtails strong, visible leaders. Maya ethnonationalists generally, although sometimes reluctantly, accept the necessity to obtain help and participation from non-Indians. (I use the Guatemalan term "ladino" to designate a person who is not an Indian.) In concurrence with this view, the Comité Campesino de Altiplano believes that both Indian and ladino ethnicity should be respected and protected and that all economically poor Guatemalans should work together to combat oppression (*Report on Central America,* January–March 1989). The Academia de Lenguas Mayas, a well-known national organization, appears to have a viable strategy: while Maya interests are promoted nationally, the Academia also works to further pride, unity, and well-being in each individual language area.

Guatemala's four million Maya have long represented great diversity in society, language, and geographic location, making unity among themselves problematic, and even the Maya do not claim to constitute one culture. Still, Maya and ladinos can be considered separate ethnic groups, with a clear divide between the two. Certainly, a "transition" area of overlapping stands between the two ethnic groups, and certain individuals, might belong to both the world of the Maya and the ladino. The ladino group theoretically consists mainly of people with combined Indian and European and possibly some African ancestry, but it also includes a wealthy white-skinned minority, which besides Spanish may include German, Swiss, French, or other. There also exists a visible and successful Chinese population. Many Maya currently categorize all non-Indians as ladinos, whether or not the "ladino" is from Guatemala. Maya themselves are considered ladinos when they "ladinoize" and reject allegiance to their original culture.[2] Ladinos have long been divided into factions based on extreme economic and political differences. Indeed, the Maya-Ladino nation of Guatemala consists of a number of divisions that have the ability to overlap ethnicity. Political, religious, or ideological beliefs, economic and educational status, military versus civilian status, and urban versus rural demographics all identify groups within Guatemala. What we consider crucial in this essay, however, is the clearly marked divide which has separated the Maya from ladinos since the conquest.

Conflict has been everlasting with much blood spilled over the years. In what Richard Adams (1989) calls the "Conquest Tradition," the Maya and ladinos have been separated even in times of peace by mutual fear and hate. Racism, little abated in the present day, has worked to further divide the two ethnic groups, as ladinos continue to proclaim the racial inferiority of Indians. Both groups demonstrate pride in a different heritage. While ladinos feel civilized with their European-oriented culture, Maya can look back with pride to their preconquest ancestors, who developed hieroglyphic writing, books of fig-bark paper or deerskin, an advanced calendar, knowledge of the planets, and a highly complex society and religion (Coe 1987, 13). The economic divide has been obvious, with most Maya living through subsistence agriculture, plantation labor, and various forms of small capitalism, while ladinos retained the dominant and more lucrative positions. Although relatively wealthy Indians do exist, and many ladinos are economically poor, notions of ethnicity have remained more important than notions of class. Carol Smith (1984, 1) illustrates this point well: "When asked who are their oppressors, what is their class position, what is the nature of stratification in their society, Guatemalan Indians will invariably point to the structural polarity between ethnic groups—Indians and ladinos—rather than to any other division that the outside analyst might see or want to impose." Even when pressed about obvious inequalities among Indians, they will "maintain that ethnicity overrides class, that the oppressors are ladinos not capitalists, that the wealthy Indian is still a member of a community while the poor ladino is not" (ibid.; see also Smith 1990b).

Attempts to describe the Maya have been numerous. A tourist image might conjure up a rural, primitive, stoic, humble people in colorful "costume" hard at work in their cornfields, unless caught up in religious merriment during festivals. Sly, vicious, lazy, drunken, and immoral; these are but a few of the depictions of the Maya long favored by ladinos. One anthropologist's list of supposed Maya characteristics from the 1940s included the traits of passiveness, fatalism, orientation to the group rather than the individual, and a belief in the value of work (Gillin 1951, 121). Modern social scientists analyze Maya culture based on such characteristics as religion, economic and social class, symbols as found in art and dress, and the psychological relationships between Maya and ladino. It is said, for example, that Maya culture emphasizes strong spiritual beliefs, including a sacred sense of time and universal harmony (Gossen 1986, 6–8); that the Maya developed a social philosophy to rationalize their subordination to non-Indians (Warren 1978, 173); and that oppression by the ladinos led many Maya "to perceive exploitation as a function of ethnicity as well" (Handy 1989, 204). In the main, social scientists have long emphasized the rural and "peasant" characteristics of Maya ethnicity. According to the Maya nationalist Pop Caal, Maya ethnic traits would include harmonious living, altruism, love of justice, discipline, and veneration for elders (1981, 146). Modern Maya in general believe their ethnicity reposes on ancient values and traditions, which survived even after the acceptance of modern technological and educational tools.

Who Are the Maya?

Making general assumptions about the Maya has always been difficult. Although in the main the Maya share similar societies and cultures, significant variations occur among the hundreds of local communities. Within the communities, historic divisions have long existed, some of which may have roots in the preconquest era. The Maya proto-language had its home in the Guatemalan highlands, and about 2600 B.C. may have begun to differentiate. Today there exist some twenty-one Maya languages in Guatemala, a few of which are closely related but remain mutually unintelligible. Change has occurred within the Maya culture over time, but the extent of change is unclear and not agreed upon by researchers (Smith 1990b, 4). Many would agree that the Spanish conquest created new realities which necessitated Maya adaptations, prompting the Maya into a process of cultural defense as they simultaneously acculturated to Spanish characteristics. George

Lovell (1988, 32) states that Maya society became a "creative blend of elements of Hispanic culture . . . mixed with elements of pre-Columbian culture" which the Maya "defended and upheld."

Certainly the modern Maya retain much of their ancient culture. In the first centuries following the conquest, sometimes aided by Church and Crown, Maya communities became (or already were) centers of cultural solidarity which insulated the inhabitants from outside influences. Community structures included communal land, religious sodalities dedicated to particular saints, and a political-religious governmental body of elders. However, plantation agriculture such as indigo, sugar, and cochineal, which developed in the fertile regions around Santiago de Guatemala, along the coast, and in the east, so completely dominated the lives of the Maya workers that during the colonial period Maya in these areas became heavily "ladinoized." The surviving Maya in Guatemala today live primarily in the highlands, where scattered haciendas had a more diffuse influence on Maya lifestyles. Isolation in small nuclear communities, however, prevented Maya peoples from developing a wider sense of ethnicity. Nineteenth-century independence wars, ideological turmoil, and economic development put heavy pressures on Maya communities, and in some areas the Maya were forced into closer contact with the European-oriented national culture, which promoted Maya acculturation. Contemporaries of the time recognized this trend. The Guatemalan government in 1851 claimed that some Maya communities were falling apart and the people were abandoning their culture (Skinner-Klee 1954, 30). However, many Maya communities survived, and in spite of continued pressures on Maya societies in the twentieth century, Maya culture remained largely intact at the time President Jorge Ubico was overthrown in 1944.[3]

Social scientists since the 1930s have studied acculturation and the power of urban, modern forces to overcome peasant or non-Western societies. In Guatemala, observers of the Maya assumed that acculturation and modernization would eventually close the door on Maya culture. It was thought that to be Indian was to be rural, ignorant, backward; to become urban, educated, and modern was to reject Indianness and become ladino-Western. The transformation process to modernization was variously referred to as acculturation, assimilation, ladinoization, and nationalization; and more recently as "dismayanization." John Gillin (1951, 3), in his study of the Maya community of San Carlos, perceived a cultural fusion of ladino and Indian traits leading toward a "Modern Culture." Gillin considered San Carlos an example of an emerging "Modern Latin American Civilization." Richard Adams (1956) saw a process starting with "traditional Indians" who remain far removed from the ladino culture, becoming "modified Indians" under ladino influence, then "latinized Indians" who live close to the ladino style, and finally emerging into "new ladinos." Adams believed that the traditional Indian would disappear in a few generations. Arden King (1967, 536) proclaimed that "modern industrial urbanism will undoubtedly destroy present Middle American Indian culture" with the result in Guatemala being a "large rural proletariat which has no cultural identity as Indian."

The theory of modernization remained widely accepted by scholars for several decades, and to this day, continues to exert a powerful influence on contemporary thinking. However, by the 1970s a few social scientists began to see that the Maya stubbornly retained a conscious pride in their ethnicity even as they acculturated to the Guatemalan nation. It became apparent that changes in Maya lifestyles and beliefs did not necessarily cause the death of Maya identity. Although the Maya adapted (or acculturated) to national society by adopting certain characteristics such as language, clothes, and lifestyle, the Maya were not integrated or assimilated. They did not become ladino; they did not stop being Maya. Robert Hinshaw (1975, 141), for example, found that the Maya of Panajachel had "ladinoized economically to a remarkable degree" but strongly retained their sense of being Maya. Sheldon Annis (1987, 28) found in the late 1970s that the Maya of San Antonio Aguas Calientes maintained a "strong Indian identity" even though they had "four hundred years of intense interaction with ladino society, no common indigenous roots, a high level of literacy, and long standing bilingualism."[4] Douglas Brintnall emphatically rejected the theories of ladinoization; he understood that Maya could modernize but retain their identity. Maya people had no "desire to mimic the Ladinos" (1979, 648).

Respect for the tenacity of Maya culture has increased greatly in recent years; authors now tend to praise the Maya resistance to cultural change. "We see in the Maya heritage a remarkable cultural unity and integrity that has been maintained over a sizeable territory" (Willey 1983, 12). "The Maya are remarkable for an extraordinary cohesion" and "most of them have resisted with remarkable tenacity the encroachments of Spanish American civilization" (Coe 1987, 11). The Maya over the centuries have demonstrated a "strong, continuing sense of native autonomy" and "strongly retain the myth that the state of the conquest is not final" (Adams 1989, 123). Maya culture has had "remarkable persistence . . . over the Millennia" (Gossen 1986, 2). The Maya have retained their "essential beliefs" all during the last millennium and have not become a "hollow hodgepodge of forms and symbols, taken on loan" from the European civilization (Guzmán Böckler 1983, 1). Rosalina Tuyuc, a member of the Coordinadora Nacional de Viudas de Guatemala, and a Maya, says "the wisdom in the bosom of the Maya people accumulated during centuries makes it possible for us to endure" (*El Gráfico*, January 9, 1991).

The modernization theory and the resistance theory both correctly identify current processes in Guatemala: (1) the Maya retain a distinctive culture; (2) they at the same time become more "modern" and adapted to (not assimilated into) Guatemalan culture. Modernization then gives knowledge and skills for enhanced ethnic awareness and political skills. This is particularly true of many of the Maya leaders, who are often the most educated and nationally aware. Modern Maya might appear ladino in their style of clothing, Spanish-speaking ability, education, and general lifestyle, but they will remain Maya in other ways, including feelings of enmity toward ladinos. Young Maya often surpass their parents in adapting to Western culture, in part because well-meaning parents have encouraged modernization as a means of advancement and protection from ladino oppression. In some houses children are allowed to speak only Spanish. Irma Otzoy interviewed twenty Maya women university students, all of whom then lived in Guatemala City but had come from the nation's interior. All spoke Spanish, and all but one spoke a Maya language. Each one considered herself Maya or Indian, and each completely rejected the term "ladino" (Otzoy and Sam 1990, 99).[5]

The Historical Creation of the Contemporary Maya

The creation of the modern Maya and the pan-Maya movement has received impetus from numerous sources. From 1944 through the 1980s, the Maya were affected by such diverse factors as national reform movements, religious activity, increasing prosperity and economic modernization for some, increased suffering for others, and civil war. As the old world died, conditions for a new world were made.

The first period of fast change occurred between 1944 and 1954. This "revolutionary" decade brought to national power an outstanding group of young leaders, who worked energetically to bring justice and economic development to Guatemala. They believed that Guatemala could become a strong, wealthy nation-state, but only if the Maya were modernized and integrated into the national culture and structure. The Constitution of 1945 broadened the vote to illiterate males, thereby giving the right of suffrage to that gender of the Maya Indians. New legislation allowed Maya communities to elect their own mayors and town councils. Political parties and labor unions were formed, and Maya were encouraged, at times exhorted, to join. Government organizations, such as the Instituto Indigenista Nacional, were created to improve understanding of the Maya situation, and new laws, including land reform measures, were intended to eliminate economic oppression. Energetic education programs endeavored to teach the Maya not only literacy and basic skills, but also the ideals of liberty and equality. Significant numbers of the Maya became politicized, and communities faced unaccustomed change. For example, in San Luis Jilotepeque, "from 1948 to 1955 a large number of 'advances' were made on the local scene, reflecting a very rapid modernization that was first set in motion in the early days" of the revolutionary period (Gillin 1957, 26). In San Antonio Sacatepéquez, the policies of the revolution caused great "cultural change" (Ewald 1957, 21). In Cantel, political reforms during the decade created competitive political structures "much changed" from the traditional past (Nash 1957, 31). In Chinautla, the revolution brought "accelerated modifications in local culture" (Reina 1960, 101).[6]

During the years from 1944 to 1954, the Maya experienced increased communication and contact with the Guatemalan nation which lay outside their communities. The new reforms and freedoms led to increased conflict between ladinos and Maya, and traditional Maya rulers were challenged by Maya who were younger and newly politicized. The enthusiasm for change and political action embraced by the Maya confused and frightened many non-Indians, and the forces of conservatism worked to counter these feared trends. Incidents of conflict, and rumors of impending conflict, became rife (Adams 1957; Handy 1988). Weakened by internal conflict and opposed by the U.S. government, the reform ladinos were overthrown in 1954 and replaced by an economic oligarchy in alliance with the military. Subsequently many of the reforms of the previous ten years were obliterated.

However, Guatemala continued to change at a fast pace after 1954 and did not return to the pre-1944 past. The Guatemalan national government, with the help of foreign aid, enacted large development programs. Expansion and diversification of the economy brought higher levels of technology, roads and transportation, and mass media. Effects on the Maya varied greatly. Some suffered under the new economic structures, in part because superior health care begun during the revolutionary decade improved birth and survival rates, which in turn created population pressures and forced Maya into urban areas and the subsistence wage economy. Although the economy experienced rapid growth during much of the period from the 1950s to the 1970s, inequalities in wealth increased, and real income for agricultural and urban wage laborers decreased (Booth 1991, 45–46). The size of subsistence landholdings also decreased, while the number of landless rural workers increased (Davis 1988, 20). However, social scientists who observed the Maya often saw improvement on the local level, as increased numbers of Maya gained economic independence and acquired new economic skills and technology. Many communities by the early 1970s were not unlike the small town of Aguacatan, Huehuetenago, where the people had cooperatives, used fertilizers, and marketed their own goods (Brintnall 1983, 14). Most Maya became incorporated into a market economy that was significantly intra-Maya, which according to Carol Smith (1988, 215) provided "the material basis for Indian cultural autonomy and Indian political resistance to the state." As Maya became increasingly modernized and independent, they began to expect a greater future. "Thus, through consumption as well as production, the traditional isolation of the Indian farmers was broken, and they began to forge a wider vision of the social structure" (Arias 1990, 235).

Christian religious activity played a crucial role in the development of the modern Maya. The Catholic church during the 1940s began a reform movement called Catholic Action, which attempted to strengthen orthodox Catholicism by destroying unacceptable Maya practices and to stop the spread of Protestantism and Marxism. Foreign missionaries participated prominently and helped guide the movement into liberal social reform. Eventually Catholic Action established schools, clinics, cooperatives, and in general promoted Maya well-being. Maya were active in these events, and the reforms helped produce a new generation of Maya leaders (Warren 1978; Melville 1983). The Catholic church became "the basis of a fairly strong ethnic revitalization and rural modernization movement" (Davis 1988, 16), even though leaders stressed the Maya's oppressed status rather than their ethnicity.

Protestants in 1944 made up about 2 percent of the Guatemalan population. By 1990, about a third of the people had been converted. Protestant missionaries worked hard in the Maya highlands, teaching literary and technical skills, giving material aid, and offering spiritual guidance. When Catholic Action became a target of the military from the 1960s, thousands of Maya converted to the evangelical religion, particularly in 1982 when the Protestant general Efrain Rios Montt became president. Rios Montt himself publicly exhorted his fellow Guatemalans to accept the new faith; he also encouraged an increase of money and missionaries from the United States (Annis 1987, 8).

Catholics and Protestants competed for Maya loyalties and brought new conflicts to communities. Inner divisions within each of the two religions existed as well. Reform Catholics clashed with conservative Catholics, and the Protestant churches were "divided into a seemingly infinite number of denominations, sects, interdenominational churches and organizations, and alliances" (Barry 1989, 99). It may appear that the pan-Maya movement would be hindered by religious divisiveness, but in fact the religious turmoil added to Maya modernization in significant ways.[7] The Maya increased their contacts to the world outside their communities and obtained new skills and knowledge. They learned Spanish, modern agricultural methods, and organization skills through cooperatives and political committees. A core of young Maya who benefitted from the new opportunities eventually become leading advocates of Maya ethnic pride. Another significant result of religious change was the stripping away of much of the power and influence of the traditional community governments, which had been intertwined with traditional religious structures. In particular, the religious sodalities, which in the recent past had helped maintain the culture and isolation of the communities, declined so rapidly that currently their extinction is expected (Rojas Lima 1988, 19).

Guatemalan ladino intellectuals and altruists have contributed in various and complex nonreligious ways to the growth of Maya pride and ethnonationalism. Until the mid-twentieth century, the most typical ladino response to the "Indian problem" was to ignore it or advocate the extinction of the Maya by assimilation or "whitening" with European immigrants. The reform period which began in 1944 marked a change in attitude for significant numbers of idealists and intellectuals. Ladinos continued to believe in their own superiority and in the need of the Maya to "civilize," but the worthiness of Maya culture was increasingly accepted. Some ladinos were influenced by Mexico's apparent success in identifying Mexican culture with the mestizo, giving equal importance to Indian and Spanish heritage. Guatemalans studied and praised Maya language, history, and culture and wrote books which proudly glorified the ladino cultural connection to the Maya past. Efforts to elevate the status of the Maya succeeded in making 20 February a national day of honor for the Maya king Tecún Umán, while the Maya book, the *Popol Vuh,* was declared Guatemala's national book. Guatemalan currency is engraved with a number of Maya themes, including an image of Tecún Umán on the half-quetzal bill. Ladinos in the 1990s are promoting the use of Maya languages in schools, the preservation of Maya culture, and Maya participation in the political process.

Guatemala: Is there Room for the Maya?

However, ladinos do not desire the development of cultural pluralism in Guatemala. Ladinos claim an ability to respect Maya ethnicity, but demand that Guatemala be united as one nation. For most ladino liberals, class rather than ethnicity remains the principal issue.[8] Maya nationalists, however, believe that ladinos are working toward the elimination of the Maya culture (see, for example, Bonfil 1981). For example, the Maya feel that ladinos agree to the use of Maya languages in education only in order to teach Spanish and thus ladinoize the Maya. But ladino liberals have contributed to a growth of Maya pride by elevating certain Maya symbols and by promoting limited reform.

Maya communities in the 1970s entered a new era of unprecedented self-assertion.[9] Cooperatives gained in strength and numbers, unions and political parties were active, children were sent to school and university in relatively large numbers, and new pan-Maya organizations promoted numerous programs in such areas as religion, politics, or sports. Maya candidates began to win local elections, and in many areas the traditional power of the ladino faced a serious challenge. In 1973, Shelton Davis (1988, 17) discovered that Maya sights no longer centered on just local issues: "To my surprise, events in the national capital were followed closely by people in the relatively isolated and traditional highland Indian towns of northern Huehuetenango." Ladinos felt threatened by the Maya resurgence, and events were unfolding that would supply the rationale for violent suppression.

The ladino leaders of the guerrilla movement that began in the 1960s considered the Maya unorganizable and too passive to make forceful allies in revolutionary struggle, but rebel losses promoted a reconsideration. Thus, rebel leaders of the 1970s made an effort to address Maya problems and incorporate Maya issues into revolutionary ideology. The guerrillas developed energetic programs to educate and politicize the Maya and received recruits to their military cause. Whole villages sometimes supported the rebels (willingly or unwillingly) by giving food, information, guides, and other help. The Maya eventually developed their own leadership, and guerrilla groups consisting of all or nearly all Maya were established. Adams (1988, 286) believes that possibly 500,000 Maya participated in the insurgency, but notes that the "full extent of the Indian participation . . . will never be known." Nor will it ever be easy to know the depth of the Maya commitment to the revolutionary cause, or to what degree they were just victims of the situation.

The military from the late 1970s began an attack on Maya community leaders who were believed to favor or aid the rebels, and the violence quickly escalated. One of the first atrocities occurred in 1978, at Panzós, when the military massacred more than one hundred unarmed Maya children, women, and men. The military claimed that Panzós had been working with the rebels, but the desire of ladino miners and cattlemen for Maya land may have been another reason for the attack (Brintnall 1983, 16). After Panzós, the military stepped up its counterinsurgency war, which lasted through much of the 1980s. The Guatemalan state destroyed some four hundred towns, ruined expanses of crop land, killed tens of thousands of people, and caused thousands to flee to Mexico and elsewhere. Some Maya were forced into newly built villages under army control, where houses were clustered together to better dominate the inhabitants. Army strategy included the reorganization of the highland economy in an effort to terminate Maya economic independence and tie the Maya into the national agroexport business (Smith 1990a; Smith 1990b). The army also directed re-education camps, constructed roads to diminish the safety that the guerrillas had found in isolated areas, and built new army bases.

Civil Patrols were established by the military from 1981 to help combat the rebels and control the Maya. The patrols consisted of Maya and ladino males who acted as a reserve military force, aiding the regular army in its war against the guerrillas. At the height of the war, about 1984, possibly 900,000 boys and men served in the Civil Patrols, which declined to some 500,000 by the decade's end. Patrol leaders were chosen for their trustworthiness to the army, and besides combat duty, patrols were to find and arrest subversives within their own communities. In many of the communities, the patrol leaders became the de facto rulers, replacing the elected governments and traditional power structures. Many of the men entered the patrols unwillingly, but some took advantage of the situation to extort money and obtain illegal and immoral privileges. They established reigns of terror in some places, torturing and murdering as they pleased. Americas Watch (1986, 73) discovered that "there is virtually no community whose familial and cultural traditions have not been altered in some forms by the civil patrols." Military tactics meant to destroy Maya unity actually increased unity in some ways, for the response of many was to "unify in struggle, with the development of an all-highland plantation union, with the growth of all-Indian political organizations, and with support for insurgency groups in the region" (Smith 1990b, 226). But the army was not to be defeated. By 1985, the national army had proven its military superiority, had at least temporarily crushed most of the rebels, and had diminished the help which rebels obtained from Maya communities.[10]

Citizens of the United States have also influenced the pan-Maya movement. Respect for ethnic groups and the promotion of peaceful cultural pluralism, at home and abroad, have become standard ideals for U.S. liberals. When the violence of the 1980s made research in Guatemala dangerous, academics tried to support the Maya by political action, public education, and aid to refugees. Churches in the United States have promoted Maya issues, and Native Americans have also shown an interest in Maya politics.[11] Maya have been sponsored on speaking tours and given scholarships to study in U.S. universities. Maya refugees now live in significant numbers in Florida, Texas, and California, and some continue Guatemalan contacts with family and friends. U.S. missionaries and economic development workers in Guatemala, such as the Peace Corps, have also influenced events.

The creation of the modern Maya thus has been rather recent, occurring in the main after 1944. Until that time, during the four and one-half centuries since the conquest, the final line of Maya defense had been the nuclear strength of their protected communities. From 1944 new realities emerged in Guatemala, bringing varied consequences. One outstanding result was the undermining and weakening of traditional community structures, which left the way open to further change. Maya had little or no control over some of the events occurring from 1944 to 1990, but the Maya themselves produced significant change. When opportunities existed to ameliorate the conditions of their lives, the Maya reached willingly to the tenets of progress and technology. Not all of the post-1944 changes would appear to promote pan-Maya unity. Indeed some changes exacerbated old intra-Maya conflicts, or perhaps created new ones. In the long run, however, change usually contributed to the weakening of the Maya traditional world which had once protected itself by isolation, thereby leaving the path to pan-Maya unity open.

Guatemala's move toward cultural pluralism can be better understood by examining several aspects of ethnicity, namely, ethnic identity, ethnic creation, and ethnic change. In order to establish and sustain identity, one or more cultural "markers" such as religion, phenotype, language, social custom, and heritage must be present. Not every marker is needed. What is important is the discovery of markers that unite friends and differentiate the group from its competitors. The Maya have based their sense of ethnicity on several very powerful markers:

a perceived common heritage, a history of hate and conflict with ladinos, and languages and customs which, although they vary among the Maya groups, are still considered Maya and certainly not ladino.

Self-Definition: The Cultural Markers of the Maya

When language becomes a chosen marker of ethnic identity, it becomes a powerful weapon for leaders (Weinstein 1983, 346). Although the Maya speak some twenty-one languages, they all speak a language that is considered Maya. Recently Maya languages have gained significantly in prestige, as the government begins to experiment with multi-lingual education and Maya organizations make the defense of their languages a priority. The Maya are also working to secure improved Maya language versions of Maya writings, including the "bible of the Quiches," the *Popol Vuh*. Benedict Anderson (1986, 47) points out the powerful influence that the printed word exerts on the formation of ethnic identity. In Europe, "print languages laid the bases for national consciousness," thus promoting the "subjective idea of the nation." Perhaps the Maya will eventually consider themselves what Joshua Fishman (1972) calls a "language community." The important point in the Maya case is that the Maya languages so thoroughly mark the speaker as non-ladino. As might be expected, the Maya leadership encourages the practical use of Spanish as a unifier language to overcome the multiplicity of Maya languages.

Religion as a Maya cultural marker has not become a significant rallying point. Maya Christianity retains customs and beliefs that are peculiar to the Maya, but religion may have become less traditional in the wake of Catholic reforms, the rise of the Protestants, and the weakening or the elimination of traditional religious institutions. Moreover, Christianity was a consequence of the conquest, and the ladinos have always at least nominally shared the same religion. Phenotype also would make an imperfect cultural marker, as the physical characteristics between Maya and ladinos are often indistinguishable.

Ethnic creation denotes the formation of new ethnic groups, some recent examples being Eritrians, Ibo, Chicanos, and the various Central Asian Turkic nationalities. Indians of the United States have been at least partly successful in creating a pan-Indian identity. The concept of ethnic creation indicates the development of an enhanced, widened, or deepened ethnicity, as when previously separated groups become united in a new "pan" ethnicity. Benedict Anderson (1986, 19, 40, 49) believes that the peoples of Europe developed an enhanced sense of ethnic awareness from the late Middle Ages, when material and intellectual advances in science, technology, communication, and ideology enabled the Europeans to better conceptualize their membership in larger communities, that is, in "self-conceived nations" or "imagined communities." In Guatemala, similar phenomena have recently enhanced and deepened a pan-Maya consciousness.

Ethnic change is a natural process for all societies. The creation of the modern Maya underway in Guatemala is the result of the Maya evolving new identities in order to adapt to changing circumstances. Indeed, change appears necessary to insure long-term group survival. Charles Keyes (1981, 28) argues that a radial change in an ethnic group's life circumstances will necessitate the group to alter certain of its characteristics. People may try to respond to changing realities "in terms of their established ethnic identities," but find they cannot because to adapt to new situations "new identities must be evolved." In Guatemala, the deepening of Maya ethnonationalism occurring simultaneously with Maya adaptation (or acculturation) to national culture is the result of symbiotic Maya ethnic adaptations to new situations. Frederick Barth (1969, 10) wisely observed that flux in social systems does not lead to ethnic "liquidation through change and acculturation: cultural differences can persist despite inter-ethnic contact and interdependence."

The pan-Maya movement is solid, growing, and probably unstoppable. Certainly not all Maya realize that a movement exists. Not all Maya contribute to it. Maya seeking political and ethnic unity still face formidable obstacles. Ladinos on all ideological fronts oppose a pan-Maya movement that denies Maya integration into the Guatemalan state. The military stands ready to resume a virtually genocidal repression if Maya threaten the status quo. The Maya themselves remain divided through a variety of languages, customs, geographic areas, ideologies, and religions. A weakening of the movement could eventually occur, as various groups fight over tactics and political spoils, as has occurred with ethnonational movements in Africa and elsewhere. Also, given the profound antagonism between the Maya and ladinos, when the Maya succeed to obtain justice and the termination of ladino oppression, ethnic conflict may still long continue (Horowitz, 1985).

Carol Smith (1988, 1990b, chs. 1, 10, 12) believes that the Maya may once again seek survival within the parameters of their individual communities. Smith notes that the Maya throughout history have succeeded in maintaining culture, language, and some autonomy, within the protective strength of their individual communities. An example of the continued ability of the community to insure relative safety would be the Maya of Totonicapán, who refused to join the pan-Maya movements of the 1970s and 1980s and thus escaped the destruction which the military brought to many other Maya communities. Smith realizes that survival has become more difficult, because in numerous ways the independence of Maya communities has been significantly reduced. In a recent article, Smith notes that "the current pattern of economic restructuring in the highlands, whether guided directly by the military, by international funding organizations, or by the market, has been extremely successful in reducing the economic and political autonomy of Indian communities, the main source of resistance to Guatemala's military state" (1990a, 8). However, Smith believes that Maya community relations remain strong overall, and that the probable method of future Maya resistance will be the "further fragmentation of Indian cultural communities, over which the state would have little ability to maintain control and surveillance" (ibid., 282).

Smith's prediction in this respect is certainly wrong, however, because the momentum of the Maya movement is toward the further crystallization of cultural pluralism in Guatemala. The Maya believe they have little choice but to continue the development of Maya unity. Communities no longer have the protection of isolation, nor the independence of an Indian market economy. Maya continue to be oppressed by an unjust social, political, and economic national system directed by ladinos, and that very system now encloses the Maya to a greater degree than at any time in the past. Nor do Maya wish to become isolated again, for they have already developed national and international perspectives. The pan-Maya movement demonstrates great pride, desire, anger, and sincerity, for the Maya believe their cause is just. Maya ethnonationalism has reached a stage of development that will be difficult to stem; one might say a "take-off" point has been reached in Guatemalan cultural pluralism. Whether or not the Guatemalan state will eventually acquire the ability to justly and harmoniously manage this rise of cultural pluralism remains to be seen.

NOTES

1. Social scientists will long debate the role of ethnicity in the Inca and Maya revolts. See for example the works of Leon Campbell, George Kubler, John Rowe, and Victoria Bricker.

2. Some Guatemalans dislike to be called "ladinos" as the term implies mestizo or assimilated Indian, but I lack convenient alternatives. Maya may call themselves either Indian or Maya.

3. Many scholars have contributed to the subjects in this paragraph, including Sol Tax, Eric Wolf, Murdo J. MacLeod, Robert Carmack, David McCreery, and Severo Martínez Peláez. Hill and Monaghan (1987) found that characteristics of closed Maya communities may predate the conquest.

4. Annis believes, however, that Protestantism may eventually promote a weakening of the Maya sense of identity.

5. I first discovered the deep pride of modern Maya in 1986, when I shared a summer's room and board with a Maya university student. For the first weeks of our acquaintance, I assumed him to be "ladino." I have heard ladinos speak derisively of these modern Maya, claiming "they are not Indians at all." Subsequent visits to Guatemala in 1988 and 1990–91 have indicated to me that the Maya movement continues to mature.

6. On community changes, see the works of Jim Handy and Richard Adams, and my 1988 University of Florida dissertation, "Impaired Democracy in Guatemala, 1944–1951."

7. Roland H. Ebel found that, in one community, growing religious pluralism reduced historic political tensions and factionalism. See Carmack (1988, ch. 7).

8. For further insight into the ladino point of view and ladino attitudes, see Barillas et al. (1989).

9. For community changes in the 1970s and 1980s, see the various chapters in Smith (1990b) and Carmack (1988).

10. For army violence in the 1980s see *Cultural Survival Quarterly* (1983) and Carmack (1988).

11. The potential exists for alliances between Maya and Indian groups outside Guatemala: see, e.g., Bonfil Batalla (1981) and Earle (1988). Barry (1989) says U.S. Indians have promoted Maya nationalism, but I found little substantiating material.

REFERENCES

Adams, Richard. 1990. Ethnic Images and Strategies in 1944. In *Guatemalan Indians and the State: 1540 to 1988,* edited by Carol A. Smith, 141–62. Austin: University of Texas Press.

Adams, Richard. 1989. The Conquest Tradition of Mesoamerica. *The Americas* 46, 2:119–36.

Adams, Richard. 1988. Conclusions: What Can We Know about the Harvest of Violence? In *Harvest of Violence: The Maya Indians and the Guatemalan Crisis,* edited by Robert M. Carmack, 274–91. Norman: University of Oklahoma Press.

Adams, Richard, ed. 1957. *Political Changes in Guatemalan Indian Communities.* New Orleans: Tulane University.

Adams, Richard N. 1956. La ladinoizaión en Guatemala. In *Integración Social en Guatemala,* edited by Seminario de Integración Social Guatemalteca, 213–44. Guatemala: Tipografía Nacional.

Americas Watch Committee. 1986. *Civil Patrols in Guatemala.* Washington, D.C.: Americas Watch Committee.

Anderson, Benedict. 1986. *Imagined Communities: Reflections on the Origin and Spread of Nationalism.* 3d ed. London: Verso Editions.

Annis, Sheldon. 1987. *God and Production in a Guatemalan Town.* Austin: University of Texas Press.

Arias, Arturo. 1990. Changing Indian Identity: Guatemala's Violent Transition to Modernity. In *Guatemalan Indians and the State: 1540 to 1988,* edited by Carol A. Smith, 203–57. Austin: University of Texas Press.

Armstrong, John A. 1982. *Nations Before Nationalism.* Chapel Hill: University of North Carolina Press.

Barillas, Edgar, et al. 1989. Formación nacional y realidad étnica en Guatemala. *América Indígena* 44, 1: 101–29.

Barry, Tom. 1989. *Guatemala: A Country Guide.* Albuquerque: Inter-Hemispheric Education Resource Center.

Barth, Frederick, ed. 1969. *Ethnic Groups and Boundaries: The Social Organization of Cultural Differences.* Boston: Little, Brown and Company.

Bonfil Batalla, Guillermo, et al. 1982. *America Latina: etnodesarrollo y etnocido.* San José, Costa Rica: Ediciones FLACSO.

Bonfil Batalla, Guillermo, ed. 1981. *Utopía y revolución: el pensamiento político contemporánico de los indios de América Latina*. México: Editorial Nueva Imagen.

Booth, John A. 1991. Socioeconomic and Political Roots of National Revolts in Central America. *Latin American Research Review* 26, 1: 33–73.

Brintnall, Douglas, ed. 1983. The Guatemalan Indian Civil Rights Movement. *Cultural Survival Quarterly* 7, 1: 14–16.

Brintnall, Douglas. 1979. Race Relations in the Southeastern Highlands of Mesoamerica. *American Ethnologist* 6, 4: 638–52.

Carmack, Robert, ed. 1988. *Harvest of Violence: The Maya Indians and the Guatemalan Crisis*. Norman: University of Oklahoma Press.

Carmack, Robert M. 1986. Ethnohistory of the Guatemalan Colonial Indian. In *Supplement to the Handbook of Middle American Indians,* vol. 4, edited by Ronald Spores, 55–70. Austin: University of Texas Press.

COCADI (Coordinadora Cakchiquel de Desarollo Integral). 1989. *Cultural maya y políticas de desarrollo*. Chimaltenango: Ediciones COCADI.

Coe, Michael D. 1987. *The Maya*. 4th ed. London: Thames and Hudson.

Cultural Survival Quarterly. 1983. *Death and Disorder in Guatemala*. Cambridge, Mass.: Cultural Survival, Inc.

Davis, Shelton. 1988. Introduction: Sowing the Seeds of Violence. In *Harvest of Violence: The Maya Indians and the Guatemalan Crisis,* edited by Robert M. Carmack, 3–36. Norman: University of Oklahoma Press.

Earle, Duncan M. 1988. Mayas Aiding Mayas: Guatemalan Refugees in Chiapas, Mexico. In *Harvest of Violence: The Maya Indians and the Guatemalan Crisis,* edited by Robert M. Carmack, 256–71. Norman: University of Oklahoma Press.

Editorial. 1989. Étnias y estados nacionales en América Latina. *América Indígena* 49 (1): 5–9.

Ewald, Robert. 1957. San Antonio Sacatepéquez: 1932–53. In *Political Changes in Guatemalan Indian Communities,* edited by Richard Adams, 18–22. New Orleans: Tulane University.

Fishman, Joshua. 1972. *The Sociology of Language*. Rowley, Mass.: Newbury House Publishers.

Gallo Armosino, Antonio. 1985. El yo y la etnia. *Cultura de Guatemala* 6, 3: 11–42.

Gillin, John. 1957. San Luis Jilotepeque: 1942–55. In *Political Changes in Guatemalan Indian Communities,* edited by Richard Adams, 23–27. New Orleans: Tulane University.

Gillin, John. 1951. *The Culture of Security in San Carlos: A Study of a Guatemalan Community of Indians and Ladinos*. New Orleans: Middle American Research Institute.

Gossen, Gary H., ed. 1986. *Symbol and Meaning Beyond the Closed Community: Essays in Mesoamerican Ideas*. Albany: Institute for Mesoamerican Studies, SUNY.

Guzmán Böckler, Carlos. 1983. *Las voces negadas toman la palabra: el pensamiento político indio en la dialéctica social de Mesoamérica*. México: CIESAS.

Handy, Jim. 1989. "A Sea of Indians": Ethnic Conflict and the Guatemalan Revolution, 1944–1952. *The Americas* 46, 2: 189–204.

Handy, Jim. 1988. National Policy, Agrarian Reform, and the Corporate Community during the Guatemalan Revolution, 1944–1954. *Comparative Studies in Society and History* 30 (October): 698–724.

Hill, Robert M., II, and John Monaghan. 1987. *Continuities in Highland Maya Social Organization: Ethnohistory in Sacapulas, Guatemala.* Philadelphia: University of Pennsylvania Press.

Hinshaw, Robert E. 1975. *Panajachel: A Guatemalan Town in Thirty-year Perspective.* Pittsburgh: University of Pittsburgh Press.

Horowitz, Donald L. 1985. *Ethnic Groups in Conflict.* Berkeley: University of California Press.

Kearney, Michael, and Carole Nagengast. 1990. Mixtec Ethnicity: Social Identity, Political Consciousness, and Political Activism. *Latin American Research Review* 25, 2: 61–91.

Keyes, Charles, ed. 1981. *Ethnic Change.* Seattle: University of Washington Press.

King, Arden R. 1967. Urbanization and Industrialization. In *Handbook of Middle American Indians,* vol. 6, edited by Manning Nash, 512–36. Austin: University of Texas Press.

Lovell, W. George. 1988. Surviving Conquest: The Maya of Guatemala in Historical Perspective. *Latin American Research Review* 23, 2: 25–57.

Melville, Thomas R. 1983. The Catholic Church in Guatemala, 1944–1982. *Cultural Survival Quarterly* 7, 1: 23–27.

Nash, Manning. 1957. Cantel: 1944–54. In *Political Changes in Guatemalan Indian Communities,* edited by Richard Adams, 28–31. New Orleans: Tulane University.

Otzoy, Irma, and Enrique Sam. 1990. Identidad étnica y modernización entre los mayas de Guatemala. *Mesoamérica* 19 (June): 97–100.

Piel, Jean. 1970. The Place of the Peasantry in the National Life of Peru in the Nineteenth Century. *Past and Present* 46 (February): 108–33.

Pop Caal, Antonio. 1981. Réplica del indio a una disertación ladina. In *Utopía y revolución: el pensamiento político contemporáneo de los indios en América Latina,* edited by Guillermo Bonfil Batalla, 145–52. México: Editorial Nueva Imagen.

Reina, Ruben E. 1960. Chinautla, a Guatemalan Indian Community. In *Community Culture and National Change.* Middle American Research Institute, Publication no. 24, 55–130. New Orleans: Tulane University.

Rojas Lima, Flavio. 1988. La Cofradia Indígena, reducto cultural de los Mayas de Guatemala. *USAC: Revista de la Universidad de San Carlos* 2 (August): 3–19.

Skinner-Klee, Jorge. 1954. *Legislación Indigenista de Guatemala.* México: n.p.

Smith, Carol A. 1990a. The Militarization of Civil Society in Guatemala: Economic Reorganization as a Continuation of War. *Latin American Perspectives* 17, 4: 8–39.

Smith, Carol A., ed. 1990b. *Guatemalan Indians and the State, 1540 to 1988.* Austin: University of Texas Press.

Smith, Carol A. 1988. Destruction of the Material Bases for Indian Culture. In *Harvest of Violence: The Maya Indians and the Guatemalan Crisis,* edited by Robert M. Carmack, 206–31. Norman: University of Oklahoma Press.

Smith, Carol A. 1984. Indian Class and Class Consciousness in Prerevolutionary Guatemala. Paper presented under the auspices of the Latin American Program of the Wilson Center, Washington, D.C., January 9.

Stern, Steve J., ed. 1987. *Resistance, Rebellion, and Consciousness in the Andean Peasant World, 18th to 20th Centuries*. Madison: University of Wisconsin Press.

Warren, Kay B. 1978. *The Symbolism of Subordination: Indian Identity in a Guatemalan Town*. Austin: University of Texas Press.

Weinstein, Brian. 1983. *The Civic Tongue: Political Consequences of Language Choices*. New York: Longman.

Willey, Gordon R. 1983. The Maya Heritage. *Cultural Survival Quarterly* 7, 1: 12–13.

Young, Crawford. 1976. *The Politics of Cultural Pluralism*. Madison: University of Wisconsin Press.

Index

Index

Abba Sabra (leader in religious development of Beta Israel), 205
Abu Jehad Seiful Islam (pseudonym of EIJM writer), 191–92
Abyssinia: nationalism, 138; monarchy, 142; historical Ethiopia, 147; Falasha in, 201; Gondar, imperial capital of, 207; exploitation of land-use rights in, 210; landless classes in, 210; land-use rights in class system of, 210; evolution of caste, 210–12
Abyssinians: separation of, from Falasha (19th century), 208
Academia de Lenguas Mayas: language goals of, in Guatemala, 267–68
Acculturation: in Ethiopia, 166; in Falasha, Abyssinia, 207–8; linguistic, in Falasha, Abyssinia, 208; in Guatemala, 270
Activism: RSS, 245; in India, 247
—political: BJP, 256; RSS and affiliates, 256; Mexican Mixtec, 267
Adalat Party: in Iranian Azerbaijan, 122
Addis Ababa: urban self-help associations in, 141
Adem, Sheik Idris Mohammed (founder of ELF), 186
Adowa, battle of (1896): Menelik's victory at, 146; mentioned, 139
Afar: resistance to EPLF from, 156; as language in Eritrea, 184; as nomads, 185; caste groups among, 185; language boundaries and caste of, 185; political leadership of, 185; as challenge to EPLF, 194; and self-determination, 194, 196, 198
Afar Liberation Front (ALF), 194
Afeworki, Issayas: as ELF defector, 189; as secretary general of EPLF, 191; on cultural pluralism, 192–93; on ethnic diversity, 196
Africa: self-determination and nationalism of, 10–11; nation-building in, 13; and UN charter on self-determination, 19; and view of economic class, 25; ethnicity in, 29; recent secessionist movements in, 29
African-Americans: as economic class, 56; upward mobility of, in 1960s, 56; access of, to labor markets, 56, 57–58, by 1970, 59, in 1980s, 69; skill levels of, 59; and Jimmy Carter, 61; and American mythology, 62–63; unemployment of, 63; and Reagan administration, 65–67, 69; and new global economics, 67–69; and economic stratification during 1980s, 68–69; and obstacles to economic advancement, 69–70; reaction of, to Italian invasion of Ethiopia, 148; mentioned, 28. *See also* Black women; Blacks
"Afrocentric," 5
Agordat (region of Barka Province, Eritrea), 183
Ahmed, Abdelkarim (ELF third zone leader), 188
Akbar (Moghul Emperor): as Muslim in Hindu India, 244
Akele Guzai (Eritrean province), 183

Akhundzade, Mirza Fath Ali (Akhundov): as promotor of Azeri language, 120–21
Aksum: and data on Ethiopian Jewish group, 202–3
ALF. *See* Afar Liberation Front
Al-Ghazi, Ahmed ibn Ibrahim: as Muslim invader of Ethiopia, 145
Al-Ibrahim, Ahmad ("Gragn"): and 16th century *jihad,* 204
Aliev, Heider, 129
All-Ethiopian Socialist Movement (MEISON), 150
America. *See* United States
American Civil Rights Movement. *See* Civil rights; Civil Rights Act of 1964
"American creed." *See* Myrdal, Gunnar
Americas Watch: and Guatemalan civil patrols, 276–77
Amhara: ethnic and religious groups of, 142; identification of, by birthplace, 143–44; and language, 144–45, 163, 164, 165; and ethnic opposition groups, 158; domination by, 158, 160, 162–63, 164, 167; ethnic groups comprising, 158–59; and colonial rule, 162–63; administration of, 163; mentioned, 138, 143–44, 202, 204, 205
Amhara-Tigre: as culture core, 138, 142, 143; and imperial revival, 203–4
Amlak, Sagga, 205
Andom, Aman (General): peace overtures of, to Eritrea, 151–52; execution of, 152; rejection of, by Eritrean nationalist fronts, 152
Anglo-Americans: and language, 75, 82, 83, 87, 89; mentioned, 88
Anti-colonialism: and nation building, 9; and self-determination, 19; mentioned, 10–11
Anti-imperialism: Leninist definition of, 224; Leninist nationalism as center of, 234; Leninist, 237. *See also* Soviet Union
Anti-imperialist nationalism, 229, 231
Arab states (Ethiopia), 153
Arab women, 43
Arabhood, 28
Aran: renamed Azerbaijan, 118; ceded to Russia, 119; Russian policy towards, 119–20; Russian conquest of, 119–22. *See also* Azerbaijan; Azeri
Armenia: and right to secession, 108; and conflict with Azerbaijan, 130; and clashes with Azeri, 130–31
Arussi: self-help associations in, 141; in 1960s elections, 164; mentioned, 163
Asia: and nation-building, 13; and self-determination, 19
Asmara (Eritrean capital), 183
Assab (Ethiopian region), 194
Assimilation: "costs and benefits" of, 84; in Ethiopia, 166; religious aspects of, 200
"Assimilation" in U.S. bilingual education, 77
Austria-Hungary, 10, 19
Awsa, Sultan of: as political leader of Afar, 186
Axum: ethnic dynasties of, 141; and "indirect rule" of Ethiopia, 143
Ayhud ("Jewish group"): and proselytization, 204; and inheritable land rights, 204, 205; conversion of, to Christianity, 205; and legends, 205–6; mentioned, 203
Ayodhya (alleged birthplace of Lord Ram), 250, 259
Azadistan (part of Iran in 1920), 123
Azaz, Omar (ELF second zone leader), 187
Azerbaijan: republic of, 116, 122; and nationalism, 117; Soviet creation of, 117–18; and Turkish rule, 118; and Ottoman Turk separatist movement, 119; and Soviets (Russians), 120, 121, 123, 124–25, 130, 132; and liberal thought, 121; and Baku Azeri intellectuals, 121, 122; and political organizations, 122, 123–24, 125; development and history of, 122–25; under *Tudeh* and *Firqi* leadership, 123–24, 125; Autonomous Republic of, 123–25; Democratic Republic of, 125–26; as Islamic republic, 127–29; and conflicts with Armenians, 130, 131, 132; as Azeri republic, 132, 133; as Soviet republic, 133
Azebu (Ethiopia): and revolt (1928–30), 169
Azeri: self-consciousness of, 27; and Turkification, 116; 19th century language policy of, 120; and Baku intellectuals, 121, 122; Shah's suppression of, 125; language and literature of, 125–27; prominence of, in Iran, 127; publications of, in Iran, 128; and Soviet-Iran tensions, 129–33; and conflict in NKAO, 130; and Armenian clashes, 130–31; and entrance into Iran, 131; "Law on Sovereignty," 131; identity of, 133. *See also* Azerbaijan

Bahr Melash, 141
Bakikhanli, Abbas Kuli Agha (Bakikhanov): as promoter of Azeri language, 120

Baku: and Iranian guest workers, 121; intellectuals, 121, 122; organized *Ijtemiyyun-Amiyyun* political party, 122; and Soviet occupation, 133–34
Balabbat, 163
Bale (Ethiopian province): and Somali insurgents, 151; and revolt (1960s), 169
Baltic republics, 96–97
Bangladesh: territorial integrity of, 20; and war-related rape, 40–41
Baraheni, Reza (Iranian Azeri poet), 126–27
Barentu (Ethiopia): as symbol of resistance in Eritrean nationalist movements, 195
Barka (Eritrean region), 183
Bazargan, Mehdi (Iranian prime minister), 127
Beijing (China): as center of Han ruling group, 223; democratic movement in, 226; massacre at, 233
Beit Juk (Muslim farmers in Tigre), 184
Beja (Muslim pastoralists in Eritrea), 185
Belgium, 12
Belien (ethnic group in Tigre), 184, 187, 188, 196, 197
Beni-Amer (Eritrean ethnic group), 185, 186, 187, 188, 195, 197; EPLF accommodations to, 194
Bennett, William (U.S. Secretary of Education): and bilingual education, 77–78
Besharin (of Beja people), 185
Beta Israel. *See* Falasha
Bharatiya Jana Sangh. *See* BJS
Bharatiya Janata party. *See* BJP
Bilien. *See* Belien
BJP (Bharatiya Janata Party): and RSS, 256; and elections, 257; mentioned, 246
BJS (Bharatiya Jana Sangh): as political affiliate of RSS, 246; becomes BJP, 256
Bilingual education (U.S.): Bilingual Education Act, 76; and "assimilationists," 77; and states' use of Title VII, 77; Limited English Proficient (LEP), 77; and Reagan administration, 77–78; and "bilingual ballot," 78; and Bush administration, 78; mentioned, 76
Bilingualism: and Belien, 184; and Beni-Amer, 185; and Maya, 271
—in Eritrea, 184–85
—in U.S.: approaches to, 77; and expansion of civil rights, 78; and assimilationists' policy, 80, 84; and pluralism and language, 80–81; and public service jobs, 83–84; and "immigrants," 84; mentioned, 73
Blacks (U.S.): employment opportunities of, 63; in public sector employment, 64; youth, 64; as middle class, 64–65; mentioned, 38. *See also* African-Americans
Black women (U.S.): role difficulty of, 36–38; multiple consciousness among, 37; suffragist organization of, 37
Borana (nomadic Oromo group), 169
Brezhnev, Leonid, 13
British African empire: formation of, 160–61
British Trust Administration (Eritrea), 148
Buda ("evil eye"), 208
Burma, 10–11

Caal, Pop, 269
Cambodia, 11
Capital accumulation: Leninist view of, 230
"Captive nations": in Soviet Union, 96; Baltic Republics as, 96–97
Carter, Jimmy: and African-Americans, 61
Caste: in Tigre, 184; and Afar, 185; and Beni-Amer, 185; and Falasha, 201; and Beta-Israel, 206, 207, 209, 210, 211, 212–13; and formation of, 206–7; deemphasized by Hindu groups in India, 247; RSS opinion of, 249–50, 254, 260; as obstacle to Hindu consolidation, 250
Catholic Action (Guatemala), 273–74; as target of military, 274
Catholic church: and Guatemala reform movement, 273–74
Central Committee. *See* EPLF
China: and "minority" question, 6; as Leninist state, 6; ruling dynasties of, 27–28; and "Han Chinese," 28; and "Middle Kingdom," 28; socialist model of, influences Dergue, 152–53; secret visit to, by Mengestu, 153; ethnic and regional resurgance in, 222; Han ethnic group in, 222; post-Mao Muslims in, 222; increase of Manchu population in, 222–23; ruling group of, as exploiters, 225; exploitation of minority regions in, 225, 226; pricing and distribution policies of, 225, 226; persecution of Muslims in, 226; regional poverty in, 226; oppression of Buddhist Lamaism in, 227; suppression of minority groups in, 227; Leninist nationalism in, 229–32; anti-Westernism in, 230; Hakka Hill community in, 232; destruction of monasteries in, 233;

China *(continued)*
and de-culturation, 233–34; as centralized state, 234, 237; regional conflicts in, 235; misperceptions of unity of, 236; as post-Leninist state, 236–39; as reimagined nation, 237; challenges to, from world markets, 237; new national identification of, 238–39. *See also* Han; Manchu
Christ: Ethiopian legend of, 141
Christianity: and Ethiopian nationalism, 146; in Eritrea, 183
Christians: and ELF in Eritrea, 187, 188; Eritrean, 187–88, 189, 190, 191, 196, 197; in Ethiopia, 190–91; and EPLF, 191, 192, 193, 197; Ethiopian oral traditions, 204; attraction of, to *ayhud,* 204, 205; Jewish heritage of, 206
Civil patrols (Guatemala): and report of Americas Watch, 276–77
Civil rights (U.S.): and white Americans, 58–61; and Democratic Party, 59; as movement, 59; and George Wallace, 59–60; challenges to, 59–60; attitudes of whites toward, 60; and Nixon, 60–61; and Gerald Ford, 61; and Jimmy Carter, 61; language access to, 78
Civil Rights Act of 1964: and *Lau v. Nichols,* 77
Class: neo-Marxist role of, in cultural pluralism, 22; analysis of, 25; definitions of, 25; ideology of, 25; recent phenomena of, in Africa, 25; primordial theory of, 25–26; cultural pluralism of, 25–27; landless, in Abyssinia, 210; and Falasha, 211, 212–13; and ladinos and Maya, 268; and ladino issue in Guatemala, 275; ladino view of, 275
Class, economic (U.S.): and African-Americans, 56; and race, 56; predictors of, 58; middle, and African-Americans, 59, 63, 64; middle, 64; lower middle, 64–65; and Reagan policies, 66; differentials of, 68
Cold War: end of, 3; and secessionist movements, 94–95; beginning of, in Iran, 124
Comisión de Celebraciones (Guatemala), 267
Comité Campesino de Altiplano (Guatemala), 267
Commonwealth of Independent States: and Ukraine, 108–9
Communalism: and RSS, in India, 245
Communalist movements: in Soviet Union, 223
Communications: of Maya, with modern world, 265
Communism (USSR), 97
Communist parties: in Azerbaijan Soviet Socialist Republic, 122; and use of literature of longing, in Azerbaijan, 125–26; in China, 238; in India, 253; Marxist, 253
Communist Party of Iran (CPI), 122, 123
Conflict resolution: in Ethiopia, 165
Confucianism: condemnation and acceptance of, by Communist party, 238
Congreso Indigenista Interamericano (Mexico, 1980), 266
Congress Party (India): and secularism, 16; and vision of secular democratic state, 246; opposition of, to RSS, 246, 253, 254–55; unpopularity of, 256; loss of power of, 257; national disillusionment with, 257; safeguarded in India, 261
Consciousness: rise of, in Latin America, 15; of ethnicity, 22; evolution of, 24; class, 25; of USSR, 99–103; of Soviet population, 105–6; of group and ethnicity, 117; Eritrean, 148; of recent history of Oromo, 171; resurgence of Hindu, 257; Latin American Indian ethnic, 266
Constitution (Ethiopia), 154
Constructivism: and ethnic groups, 23; and gender approach, 38–39; and language policy, 88–89; and American language policy, 89; and Eritrea, 181; and Falasha, 202; mentioned, 21, 24
Control, religious: *sati,* as example of, 46
Coptic Christians: in Ethiopia, 141
Coptic Church (Ethiopia): and education, literature, history, 145; and loss of influence, 146
Coptic Orthodox Church (Ethiopia). *See* Coptic Church
Courts (Ethiopia): and use of Amharic language, 164
Cultural domination: in Arabic states, 28; in Asian states, 28; in Caribbean states, 28; in Mexico, 28; in U.S., and African-Americans, 28–29
Cultural identities: and gender, 38; and USSR, 95
Cultural markers: and Maya, 278–80
Cultural pluralism: Young's analysis of, 3–4; and nation-state, 4; politics of, 6–7; and reduced state role, 18; "instrumentalist" mode of, 21, 22; "constructivist" mode of, 21,

23–24; concepts of, 21–25; importance of "internationalist" role of, 22; and class, 25–27; and gender, 25–27, 37; and race, 26; and violence, 26; and feminism, 26, 38, 49–50; and environmental factors, 27; dynamics of, 27–30; and importance of women, 51–52; and language politics, 82–84; in Soviet Union, 103; in Ethiopia, 138; conflict of, with nationalism, 140; Afeworki interview on, 192–93; and EPLF policy, 192–96; factors of, 212
—ethnicity: as element of, 24; primordial mode definition of, 26
—in Guatemala: rise of, 265; opposed by ladinos, 275; ethnic characteristics of, 277
—in India: and RSS strategies, 260; and RSS-BJB, 261
—in U.S.: and Great Depression, 12; and 1924 Immigration Act, 12; history of, 12
Culture: role of, in dress and mannerism, 42, 44–45; women as carriers of, 46–47, 47–48; in U.S., 62–63; in USSR, 101, 222; historic influence on Azeri's, 118; pan-Ethiopian, 143; in Ethiopia, 165; of minorities, and Leninist-Stalinist view, 232–33; in China, 233, 235–36; in India, 242, 243; Mayan, 265, 269–70, preservation of, 271–72; of European-oriented ladinos, 268

David: Ethiopian legend of, 141
Declaration on the Granting of Independence to Colonial Countries and Peoples, 19–20
"Declining discrimination" school, 56
Decolonization: and USSR breakup, 95; as change in ethnic behavior, 104
De-culturation: resistance to, in China, 233–34
Democratic party (U.S.): and race policy (1960s), 59, 60
Democratization, 18–19
Demographics: in U.S., 17, 75, 76; in Azerbaijan, 118; in Eritrea, 182
Denakil (Eritrean province), 183
De-nationalization: in China under Leninism, 223, 232, 236–37; Leninist theory of, 226; in Russia under Leninism, 231–32; of Hindu educated classes, by British, 252
Deoras, Madhukar Dattatraya (RSS Supreme Guide), 250
Dependency, 237
Dergue (Tigre group): and guerilla warfare with other groups, 149; attack on EPRP, 149; and TPLF threat, 149–50; and organization of POMO, 150; economic policies of, 150–51; and creation of armed peasant militia, 151; and Oromo, 151; lack of political base, 151; in power, 151–54; influenced by Chinese socialist model, 152–53; and Soviet model for nationalities, 153–54; members of, visit North Korea, 154; role of, in Ethiopian Institute of Nationalities, 154; antagonism toward, 155; and land reform policies, 155, 168; fall of (1991), 158; and schools and services, 166; organization and politizing of, 169–70; and Ethiopian rulers, 190. *See also* Sisaye Habte
De-sovietization, 97
Dinai, Mohammed (leader of ELF first zone), 187
Discrimination: in U.S., 78. *See also* Racism
Dissidents: Falasha, 202
Djibouti: (Territory of Afars and Issas), 183
Doctrine, hegemonic: and Amhara and Tigre, 138
"Domestic sovereignty" (U.S.), 21
Dynasty: Amhara, 204

Eastern Europe: and emigration, 16
Economics: and deregulation, 17; in post bipolar world, 17; private sector, as replacement for "statism," 17
—in U.S.: and end of post–World War II prosperity, 63; and race, 63–65, 67; new global, and African-Americans, 63, 67–69; income differentials, 65; and industry changes, 67; reorganization of (1980s), 67; and labor (1980s), 68; and disparities in Soviet Union, 99; policies of Dergue, 150–51
Economies: internal colonialism, 98–99
EDU (Ethiopian Democratic Union), 150
Education: and Maya, 272; language, in India, 246
EIJM (Eritrean Islamic Jihad Movement): base and financing of, 191; challenge of, to EPLF, 191–92, 195; writer Abu Jehad Seiful Islam, 191–92; written appeal of, to Muslims, 192
Elementary and Secondary Education Act of 1965: and Bilingual Education Act (Title VII), 76; expansion of (1974), 76–77
ELF (Eritrean Liberation Front): founders of, 186; and armed conflicts with Ethiopia, 187; and distrust of Christians, 187; as Islamic movement, 187; growth of, 187; four zones

ELF (Eritrean Liberation Front) *(continued)* of, 187–88; fifth zone of, established, 188; cleavages within, 188–89; military campaign of, against other Eritrean movements, 189–90; and EPLF, 190; attacks on, by Ethiopian armies, 190; attempt of, to subdue Kunama, 195; mentioned, 179, 182, 191, 192, 193
ELF-CL (Eritrean Liberation Front Central Leadership), 195
Elites: and nation-building, 9; non-Russian, and policy influence, 102; Ethiopian, 158, 161
Empire: Czarist, 10; in Asia and Africa, 10–11; USSR as, 95, 96–99, 110; and states, 96–99; consciousness of USSR as, 97, 98; European, 97, 100; Michael Doyle's definition of, 98; building of Soviet, 99–103; USSR legacy of, 101–2; and Soviet people, 103; continuation of, 110; French African, 160–61; Ethiopian, 160–61, 164
Engels, Frederick, 232
English: as official language in U.S., 73, 79; in Ethiopia, 164. *See also* "Official English" movement
"English-Only" movement. *See* "Official English" movement
English Plus Information Clearinghouse (EPIC), 79–80
EPDRF (Ethiopian Peoples Democratic Revolutionary Force): commitment of, to ethnic representation, 150; and conference of opposition groups, 150; resistance to, by other groups, 156; support of, for Eritrean independence, 156
EPLF (Eritrean Peoples Liberation Front): denies ethnic antagonism, 148; attacks EPRP, 149; resistance to, by Afar, 156; declares independence from Ethiopia, 158; and ELF, 179, 190; challenges to, 180, 194, 195–97; cultural policies of, 181; manifesto of, 189; First Organizational Congress of (1977), 190; formation of, 190; languages used by, 191; members of, 191; Central Committee of, 191, 194, 195; challenge to, from EIJM, 191–92; as Christian-dominated movement, 191–92, 193–94, 195; as secular organization, 192, 193; and cultural pluralism, 192–96; and ethnic groups, 193; and resource development, 194; and ethnic diversity policy, 195; and Kunama, 195; Second Congress of (1987), 195; support for, 195; and Muslims, 195, 197; goals of, 197; and Afar self-determination, 198
EPRP (Ethiopian Peoples Revolutionary Party): and guerilla warfare, 149; defeat of, 149; as pro-monarchism opposition group, 150; rejects NDRP's peace plan, 153
Eritrea: and self-determination, 20; centralization of, 145–46; and Ethiopia, 148; under British Trust Administration, 148; fronts of, 151, 152, 154; under monarchies, 160; and war for independence, 173, 190; ethnic, regional and religious divisions in, 180, 181; cultural pluralism in, 180–86; and constructivism, 181; and nationalism, 181; demographics of, 182; ethnic composition of, 182–83; geographic zones and provinces of, 183; language groups in, 183–84, 185–86; and ethnic groups in, 184–86; as unit of European colonization, 186; and conflict with Dergue, 190; and EPLF, 191, 193; Christian-Muslim divisions in, 196–97; future challenges for, 196–98; national definition of, 198
Eritrean Islamic Jihad Movement. *See* EIJM
Eritrean liberation: cultural basis for movements of, 186–92. *See also* EIJM; ELF; ELF-CL; EPLF
Eritrean nationalist movements, 181–82
Eritrean Peoples Liberation Front. *See* EPLF
ESUNA (Ethiopian Student Union in North America), 149
Ethiopia: and Oromo, 6; rise of ethnic consciousness in, 6; polyethnic communities in, 138; nationalism of, 138, 139, 149–50, 155, 156; and conflict between nationalism and cultural pluralism, 140; and state formation, 140; ethnicity in, 141–42; regional power struggles in, 141–42; multiethnic ruling classes of, 142; and development of nation state, 146–48; as ancient state, 147; territorial boundaries of, 147; and political modernization, 149; interpretations of self-determination of, by left, 149; students in, and nationalism, 149; and influence of Marxism-Leninism, 149, 155, 171–72; and social revolution (1974), 150–51; and economic policies of Dergue, 150–51; land tenure systems in, 150–51; and conflict with Somalia, 151; and

Chinese influence, 153; Central Committee of, 154; constitution of (1987), 154; National Assembly of, 154; intellectuals of, 155–56, 159; and Eritrean problem, 156; and fall of Dergue, 158; and Eritrea, 158; and national conference, 158; political organizations of, 158; ethnic groups of, 158, 172–73; and Amhara, 158–59; subordinate ethnic groups of, 159; elite in, 159, 173; history of, 160; origins of empire of, 160–62; Orthodox Christianity of, 161; regional autonomies of, 161; subjugation of peoples in, 161, 162; and languages of, 162; and Amhara domination, 162, 163, 164; colonial rule in, 162–63; and Amharic language, 163, 164; schools in, 163, 164; health care in, 163–64; elections in, 164; farmers and share-croppers in, 165; lack of roads in, 165; lack of services in, 165; national culture of, and country people, 165, 166; failed coup in (1960), 166; under Haile Selassie, 166; student political consciousness in, 166, 167; and non-Amhara leadership, 166–68; demonstrations for Oromo language in, 168; national liberation movements in, 168; prospects for future of, 171–74; support of, by Soviet Union, 190; status of Christians in, 191; and Falasha, 202; mentioned, 5–6. *See also* Amhara; Eritrea; Falasha

Ethiopian Democratic Union. *See* EDU

Ethiopian Institute of Nationalities, 154

Ethiopian nationalism: influences on, 138; ethnic and regional challenges to, 139; historical crises and challenges to, 139; role of intellectuals in, 155; and division, 156

Ethiopian Peoples Democratic Revolutionary Force. *See* EPDRF

Ethiopian Revolution Information Center, 154

Ethiopian Student Union in North America. *See* ESUNA

Ethnic group: and community, 23; and constructivism, 23–24; and Soviet Union, 27; and language, 82; self-identification of, 82; in U.S., 87, 88; in Azerbaijan, 133; in Eritrea, 185; and Falasha identity, 206; in China, 222; views at reform, 234; backlash to Leninist-Stalinist policy, 238; in Guatemala, 265, 274, 277–78, 279; in Europe, 278

Ethnic associations (Ethiopia): urban, 141

Ethnicity: rise of, 3; constructivist theory of, 24; ideology of, 24; and tribalism, 29; stigmatized in Africa, 29; "defensive," 60; "new," 60; and language, 74, 116; and language policy, 88; components and types of, 140; modernization effects on, 140; and class theorists, 140–41; and Leninist states, 223; and Leninism, 224–32; Leninist Stalinist view of, 232, 233; consolidation of components of, 278–79; in China, 236

—in Eritrea: political and economic factors of, 186; and cultural shows, 193; and Falasha, 205–6, 236

—in Ethiopia, 141–42; and withdrawal from state, 148

—in Guatemala: and Comite Campesino de Altiplano, 267; Maya and ladinos, 269; preservation of Maya, 271, 272

—in India: and identity and class, 245

—in U.S.: and public policies, 73; and language, 81; and language policy, 82–84

—in U.S.S.R.: and exploitation, 99; and population change and decolonization, 104; and post Soviet coup, 109–12; and Gorbachev, 129–30

Ethnocide, 233

Ethnonationalism: in Western Europe, 12; movements of, in Europe, 15; in Soviet Union, 27; and Azeri, 116; in Latin America, 266; and Maya, 267, 274–75, 279–80

Euro-Americans, 57

Europe: Western, and ethnonationalism, 12; ethnonationalist movements of, 15; Eurocentric Hegelian-Marxist tradition of, 229; ethnic development in, 278

European Community, 237

Faisal (King of Saudi Arabia), 186

Falasha: struggle of, against persecution, 201; and identity, 201, 202, 205, 206, Jewish, 201, 212; as artisan caste in Abyssinian state, 201, 207; migration of, to Israel, 201, 212, 213; origins of, 202–3; and ethnicity, 202–6; oral traditions of, 204; religious development of, 205; occupational segregation of, 206; survival of, 206; and caste, formation of, 206–10, 212, 213; and land grants, 207; and loss of inheritable land use rights, 207; awarded Abyssinian clientship, 207; acculturation of, in Abyssinia, 207–8; effect of

Falasha *(continued)*
buda on, 208; and intermarriage, 209; and religion of, 209; Protestant converts among, 209; purity practices of, 209; rules of, for women, 209; effects of modernization on, 211; internal class stratification of, 211; during Gondar era, 212; class and employment of, 212, 213; role of, in Ethiopian state, 212–13; mentioned, 6
Falasha, Gondarine, 201
Family structure, 26
Fascism, 246; and racism, 224
Feminism: as "problem" for other groups, 5; role of, in third world countries, 49; and cultural pluralism, 49–50; and national and cultural currents, 49–50; as broad-based movement, 50; internationality of, 50
Feminist theory, 26, 38. *See also* Feminism
Firqi-e Demokrat-e Azerbaijan (Azerbaijan Democratic Party), 123–24
Foreign aid: to Guatemala, 273
French African Empire, 160–61

Gada system (Oromo), 170
Galla. *See* Oromo
Gandhi, Indira: forced to declare emergency dictatorship, 256; on cultural pluralism, 260
Gandhi, Mahatma: as model for India, 243; as leader of independence movement, 247–48; and concept of India as national state, 248; nonviolent strategy of, 248; as Hindu revivalist, 248, 258; assassination of, 255; and use of religious symbols, 258
Gandhi, Rajiv: on cultural pluralism, 260
Gelawdewos, Idris: as founder of ELF, 186; control of, over ELF fifth zone, 188
Gender, 6; and cultural pluralism, 25–27, 37; and leadership roles, 26; and relationship and hierarchy, 26; roles and family structure, 26; in cultures, 26–27; in U.S., 37; expansion of study of, 37; and cultural identity, 37–38; feminist theories of, 38; and approach to 'constructivist' theory, 38–39; and everyday life, 43–44; and dress, 44; and cultural conflict, 45; and labor division, 46, 49; in Ethiopia, 209. *See also* Feminism; Feminist theory; Sex-gender
Genocide: Leninist threat of, 233
German Americans, 74–75
Gharbzadeh women (Iran), 45
Glasnost: as strategy of Gorbachev, 107; policy repercussions of, 132–33; mentioned, 13
Gojjam: bombing of, 150; under old monarchies, 160; mentioned, 14
Golwalkar, Madhav Sadashiv: and Hindu nationalism, 243; as RSS Supreme Guide, 250, 256; arrest of, 255
Gondar (Ethiopia): bombings of, 150; as imperial capital, Abyssinia, 207; mentioned, 141
Gorbachev, Mikhail: and glasnost, 107, 132–33; state-building strategy of, 107–9; and ethnic crisis in Soviet Union, 129–30; and ethnic problem in Azerbaijan, 130; and NKAO strife, 130–31, 132; mentioned, 13
Guadalupe: and Mexican myth, 28
Guatemala: and ethnic identity, 265, 266–69; and pan-Maya movement, 265, 266–69, 274; cultural pluralism in, 265, 275, 277–78; and Comité Campesino de Altiplano, 267; Maya and ladinos in, 268, 269, 273, 279; plantation agriculture in, 270; education in, 272, multilingual, 278; and Constitution of 1945, 272; land reform in, 272; foreign aid to, 273; Maya cooperatives in, 273; migration to cities in, 273; overthrow of ladino government of, 273; and Catholic Action, 274; guerrilla movement in, 275–76; status of Maya in, 275–78; state counterinsurgency war against Maya in, 276; civil patrols in, 276–77; and Peace Corps, 277; defeat of rebels by army in, 277; mentioned, 6, 265. *See also* Maya
Gulestan treaty (1831): Iran ceded to Russia, 119
Gult ("tribute rights"), 210
Gura, battle of (1868), 139

Haile Fida: as head of POMA, 150
Haile Selassie (Emperor of Ethiopia): on religion, 145; and policy modernization and centralization, 145–46; and land tenure systems, 150; opposition to, from Eritrean fronts, 151; attempts of, to build modern state, 166; and political awareness growth in reign of, 171; overthrow of, 190; mentioned, 142
Hakka Hill Community (China), 232

Hamasein (Eritrean province), 183
Han: ethnic strategy of, 222, 223; and suppression of ethnic populations, 223; Beijing, as center of, 223; migration of, to Mongolia, 223; as dominant group, 225–26; and exploitation of non-Han areas, 228, and peasants, 234; rural, as target of Leninists, 231
Harar: Somali insurgents, 151
Hayakawa, S. I. (U.S. Senator): and "Official English" Movement, 79
Hedgewar, Keshav Baliram: as founder of RSS, 248; and Hindu goals for RSS, 248–49; as Supreme Guide of RSS, 250
Hemmat (Endeavor): 122
Highlanders: as members of EPLF, 191
Hindu: practice of *sati,* 46; and confrontations with Muslims, 242; Nehru attitude toward, 243–44; communalism, 245; and RSS, view of national identity, 245–46; movements, 247–48; beliefs of, 250
Hishal, Osman: and ELF fifth zone executions, 188
Hong Kong, 239
Humphrey, Hubert: as presidential candidate (1968), 60

Ibrahimov, Miza (Azerbaijan novelist), 125
Identity: as race and language, 5; and constructive cultural pluralism, 24; family, 26; gender and cultural, 26–27, 37; in Latin America, 28; developed through sexual symbolism, 42; racial, in U.S., 56–57; primordialist, 85, 238; language factor of, 85–86, 87–88, 278; Anglo-American, and language insecurity, 89; and de-Stalinization, 102; confusion about, in modern Soviet Union, 102; ethnic, and state policies, 116–17; Azeri, 125–27, 132, 134; in historic Ethiopia, 139; Afar, 185–86; in Eritrea, 186; and primordial *ayhud* groups, 203; Falasha, 203, 205, 206, 212; of post-Mao Chinese Muslims, 222; Han, 222, 223; politics, 223; rejection of Han, by Manchus, 223; ethnic, under Leninism, 224–32; Leninist, in reform, 226–27; as nationalistic, 237; democratic Chinese, 239; national, in India, 242, 247; communal, 245; RSS, 245–46; religious, in India, 258; ethnic, Mexican Mixtec, 266–67; ethnic, in Guatemala, 266–69; Mayan, 267, 269–72; pan-Indian, in U.S., 278; components of, 278–79
Ideology: and nation state, 3; and ethnicity, 24; of separation between Beta Israel and Abyssinians, 208–9; of Leninism, 226–27; Nehru's, of Indian nation state, 244; RSS, 249, 251–54, 259
Ijtemaiyyun-Amiyyun (Popular Association): Baku political party, 122
"Imagined community," 23–24
Immigration (U.S.): and national identity, 5; from Europe, 5; and cultural pluralism, 12; Immigration Act (1924), 12; and policy changes since 1965, 75–76; of Asian-Americans, 76; of Latinos, 76; campaigns to restrict, 79; and language policy, 87; from Guatemala, 277; mentioned, 16
India: and nation-building, 11; decolonization and secularism in, 13; Congress Party of, 13, 16, 246; Muslim League in, 13–14; conflict over Ayodhya temple in, 23; Hindu-Muslim confrontations in, 242; 1947 partition in, 242; Hindu cultural traditions in, 242, 243; Hindu nationalists in, 243; as secular state, 244, 245; and RSS, 245; ethnicity and class in, 245; and rural support for RSS in, 246; languages in education in, 246; political parties in, 246; nationalist movement in, 246, 247–48; and Indian National Congress, 247; Hindus and Muslims in, 247; communal rivalries and riots in, 248; and Mandal Commission, 250; national identity of, 251; de-nationalization of, by British, 252; Muslim conquest of, 252; post-independence RSS, 252; conversion of Hindus in, 252–53; communist parties in, 253, 257; Hindu-Muslim polarization in, 254; emergency dictatorship in, 256; political activism by Hindu groups in, 256; as Nehruvian state, 257–58; religious identity of, 258; Hindu-Muslim riots in, 259. *See also* Ghandi, Mahatma; Nehru, Jawaharlal; RSS; Singh, V. P.
Indians: in Latin America, 266; in U.S., pan-Indian identity, 278
Individualism, 62
Instituto Indegenista Nacional (Guatemalan think tank), 272
Instrumentalism: as mode of cultural pluralism, 21, 22; analysis of, 22; and class, 22; and

Instrumentalism *(continued)*
ethnicity, 22, 140; and U.S. language policy, 82–83
Insurgencies, ethnic, 140
Intellectuals: Azeri, 121, 122; Ethiopian, 155
Intermarriage: EPLF policy toward, 193; Falasha and Christians opposed to, 209
"Internal colonialism": in USSR, 98–99
International Labor Organization, 21
International Symposium on Ethnicity and Nation in Latin America, 266
Iran: Islam as political force in, 15–16; women's role in, 42; dress in, 42, 44, 45; influence of, upon Azeris, 116; historical use of term, 117–18; Turkish rulers of, 118; 16th century Safavid dynasty of, 118–19; territorial secession of, to Russia, 119; Baku transborder migration in, 121; constitutional revolt in, 121, 123; and Azeris, 121, 125, 128, 131, 132; and *Hemmat*, 122; *Jangali* Socialist movement in, 122; and Azerbaijan, 123; nationalism of, 123; and Cold War, 124; and Stalin, 124; Stalin's withdrawal from, 124; fall of the Shah in, 127; and tension with Soviets, 129–33; and Nakhichevan revolt in Azerbaijan, 131–32. *See also* Azeri
Islam: and national identity, 14; and Iran, 15–16; and dress, 42, 44, 45; and women, 46, 51; and ethnicity, 128; revivalism of, 128; and ideological crises in former Soviet Union, 128–29; official vs. unofficial, 128–29; and politics in Azeri, 132; role of, in Azerbaijan politics, 132–33; in Ethiopia, hostility toward, 145
Ismail (15th century Safavid Shah), 119
Israel: and immigration from Soviet Union, 16; Falasha migration to, 201, 212, 213; mentioned, 6
Italy: and invasion of Ethiopia (1936), 148
Italian East Africa: creation of, under Mussolini, 148
Italians: in U.S., 47; and Battle of Adowa in Ethiopia (1896), 146

Japan, 9
Janata Party (India), 246; merger with RSS and breakup, 256
Jangali movement (Iran), 122
Judaism: Falasha conversions to, 202
Javadzadeh, Seyyed Ja'far. *See* Pishevari

Kafa (Ethiopian region), 161
Kahsai, Woldai: (ELF fifth zone commander), 188
Kebessa (Eritrean Christian highlander group), 182
Kebra Nagast ("Glory of the Kings"): as justification for conquest of non-Abyssinian peoples, 204
Kenyatta, Jomo: as pan-Africanist, 148
Kerner Commission (U.S.): report of, on 1968 race riots, 61
Keshavarz, Fereydoon: on Pishevari's death, 124
Ketema (fortified towns): in Ethiopia, 162
Khan, Baqer: as leader of Iranian nationalism, 121
Kahn, Mirza Kuchek: and *Jangali* movement in Iran, 122
Kahn, Sattar: leader of Iranian nationalism, 121
Khiabani, Sheikh Mohammad: and Iranian Constitutional Revolution (1905), 123
Khmer Rouge Pol Pot war, 229
Khomeini, Ayatollah: as former president of Iran, 127; on Muslim minorities, 127–28; death of, 128; and Islam state, 132
Kinship: in Eritrea, 197; in Shoa and Wallo, 202
Kin-work: and Italian-American families, 47; and Jews, 47–48; and U.S. Hispanics, 48
Kolarz, Walter: on Russian nationalism, 97
Korea: war-related rape in, 41
Koreans: persecution of, in China and Soviet Union, 227
Kunama (Eritrean ethnic group), 184–85; ELF attempt to subdue, 195

Labor: gender and division of, 39; gender-biased system of, 46–49; women and organization of, 50; and work stoppages, 60; organizations of, in India, 255
Labor markets (U.S.): and race, 56; challenges to white monopolies in, 57–58; historic discrimination in, 57–58; non-integration of, 59; and change in social contract, 63; changes in (1980s), 63, 68; and blacks, 63–64
Labor unions, Maya, 272
Ladinos (Guatemala): as distinct from Maya, 268; divisions within, 268; European-oriented culture of, 268; as ethnic group, 268–69; and conflicts with Maya, 273; contributions of, to Maya pride, 274–75; and cultural plural-

ism, 275; and oppression of Maya, 280; mentioned, 267
Lamaists: in China and Mongolia, 227
Landlords (Ethiopia), 163
Land reform: in Ethiopia, 167, 168; and Dergue, 194; in Guatemala, 272
Land tenure: in Ethiopia, 150–51; in Abyssinia, 210
Language: and politics, instrumentalist theory, 82–84; skills and instrumentalism, 83; and individual identity, 85–86, 87–88
—in U.S.: and ethnic conflict, 73–74; German, 74–75; and demographic changes, 75–76; Chinese, 77; English, 79–80; policy controversy, 80–81, 83, 88; as ethnic competition, 82; and American Indians, 82–83; as "constructivist" symbol, 88–89; and immigration, 89; in China, 233
—in Azerbaijan: Azeri, 116, 117, 120, 122, 133–34; Turkish, 118, 120, 133; and Soviet policy, 120, 125; and identity, 133–34
—in Eritrea: Afar, 184; Saho, 184; Tigre, 184; Beni-Amer, 185
—in Ethiopia: and Oromo, 142, 164, 168, 170; Amharic, 143, 145, 163, 164; retention of, by groups, 160, 161; English, 164
—in Guatemala: and goals of Academia, 267–68; Maya, 269; importance of, to Maya identity, 278
—in India: Hindi, 261
Language policy (U.S.): and voting rights, 78; and bilingualism, 84; and national interests, 85–86; primordialist, 85–88; long-term perspective of, 86–87; mentioned, 73, 76–80
Laos, 11
Latin America: and nation building, 9; Mayan ethnonationalism in, 27; indigenous peoples of, 216; and Indian ethnic consciousness, 266; and liberation theology, 267; peasant leagues in, 267; political parties in, 267; revolutions in, 267
Latinos (U.S.): and language policy, 83; and military conquest, 83
Lau v. Nichols, 77
Law, international, 20–22
Lenin, Vladimir: Czarist empire salvaged by, 10; and self-determination, 19; on nationalities question, 100
Leninism (in China): and view of Manchus, 222; and Mihajlo Mihajlov, 223; and de-nationalization, 223, 226; and definition of anti-imperialism, 224; and fascist racists, 224; and system of inequality, 224; and ethnic identity, 224–32; and non-meritorious society, 225; and polarized identities, 226–28; and minority groups, 227–29, 231, 232–36; and view of foreign exploitation, 228; and Mao Zedong, 229; as anti-Europeanism, 229; as anti-imperialism, 229, 232; on accumulation of capital, 230; and nationalism, 232; and ethnocide, 233; and threat of genocide, 233; mentioned, 6
Liberalism: as associated with secularism, 13; political, 21
Liberation theology: in Latin America, 267
"Limited English Proficient" (U.S.), 77
"Linguistic access" (U.S.), 73
Lin Zexu, 230
Literacy campaign: in Ethiopia, 170
Literature of longing (Azeri), 125–27

Macronationalists: in Ethiopia, 146, 148
Malaysia: and nationalism, 10–11
Manchus (China): and view of Leninists, 222; identity of, 223; resistance of, to absorption, 223
Mandal Commission (India): guidelines of, for new Hindu society, 250
Mao Zedong: and Leninist movement in China, 229; and destruction of minority cultures, 232–33; attempts of, to destroy rural culture, 234
Maria (Tigrean semi-nomads), 184
Marxism: and Azeri intellectuals, 122; in Iranian Azerbaijan, 122–23; and class primacy, 140–41; challenge to, 146; commitments to, by Ethiopian subordinate ethnics, 159; and Ethiopian students, 167; opposition to, in India, 246
Marxism-Leninism: in Ethiopia, 5–6, 149; ideology of, 8; and Dergue, 155; factions and ideologies of, in Ethiopia, 171–72
Market economy: importance of, in modern world, 18; and Maya, 273
Marriage: and sex-gender, 40
Massawa, battle at (1579), 139
Maya: ethnic consciousness of, 6, 279; Comisión de Celebraciones, 267; ethnonational groups, emergence of, 267; and class, 268; as distinct from ladinos, 268; as ethnic group,

Maya *(continued)*
268; preconquest accomplishments of, 268; variations in local communities of, 269; and culture of, 269–72; and acculturation, 270; plantation agriculture of, 270; during modernization, 270–71; bilingualism among, 271; preservation of ethnicity of, 271; labor unions of, 272; pan-Maya movement, 272, 279; politicization of, 272–73; historical creation of, 272–75; increased communication of, with Guatemalan nation, 273; and conflicts with ladinos, 273, 275–76; and Catholicism, 274; Catholic and Protestant competition for, 274; political success of, 275; self-assertion of, 275; insurgency of, 275–76; and Panzós massacre, 276; military attack on, 276, 277; refugees in U.S., 277; support for, by Native Americans, 277; communities as strengths of, 277, 279–80; language of, as important to identity, 278; religion of, as cultural marker, 278; threat of military repression of, 279

Maya Totonicapán revolt of 1820, 266

Mecha (Ethiopian self-help association), 141

Mech'a-Tulama (Oromo self-help association), 167–68

Mediums, spirit: and Ethiopian beliefs, 165

MEISON (socialist movement in Ethiopia), 150

Meles Zenawi (TPLF leader): and rights of nationalities, 172

"Melting pot" in U.S., 12

Menelik II (Emperor of Ethiopia): and battle of Adowa, 139; and Eritrea, 146; consolidated peripheral regions, 147; denounces Treaty of Wuchall (1889), 148; and centralization of state, 150; creates empire, 160; and treatment of Falasha, 211

Mengistu, Haile Mariam: as Ethiopian leader, 5, 20; and Ethiopian imperial style, 142; and Eritrean unionist movement, 148; secret visit of, to China (1976), 153; and fall of Dergue (1991), 158

Mensa (Tigrean farmers), 184

Menze, 144

Mestizo: Mexico, influence of, on ladinos, 275

Metahit (Eritrean Muslim lowlander group), 182

Mexican Mixtec: new ethnic identity of, 266–67; political activism of, 267

Mexico: and cultural domination, in myth, 28; cultural pluralism in, 266–67; Mestizo influence on ladinos, 275

Migration: of Falasha to Israel, 201; Guatemalan urban, 273

Mihajlov, Mihajlo (Yugoslav writer): on Leninism, 224

Mikailian, Avetis. *See* Sultanzade

Minority cultures: destruction of, by Mao Zedong, 232–33

Minority policy: of Leninism, 232–36

Mireh, Hanfare Ali: opposition of, to Dergue land reform, 194

Mireh, Sultan Ali: Afar leader, 194

Modernity: Nehru vision of, for India, 244

Modernization: and diminishment of ethnicity, 140; in Ethiopia, under Haile Selassie, 145–46; and ethnic issues in Ethiopia, 149; effect of, on Falasha, 149, 211, 213; and disillusionment, in India, 245; of Maya in Guatemala, 270–72; and pan-Mayan movement in Guatemala, 274

Moldavian Popular Front, 110

Monarchies: in Ethiopia, 160

Monasticism: and Falasha, 202

Mongols: and Han, 223

Morgan, Lewis Henry: and Leninist minority policy, 232; on Aryan family, 233; on minorities, 233

Multi-culturalism: in U.S., 12; and curricula in U.S. higher education, 73; mentioned, 5

Multi-national empire: post World War I, and Wilson's ideas, 19

Multi-lingual education: in Guatemala, 278

"Museum of peoples": Ethiopia as, 143; as paradigm, of Ethiopian historical studies, 200

Muslim(s): in India, 13–14; in Pakistan, 14; role of women, in Iran, 42; in Ethiopia, 146, as conquered peoples, 161; in Eritrea, 183; among Belien, 184; among Tigre, 184; and ELF, 187; and war for Eritrean independence, 190; on EPLF central committee, 191; hostility to EPLF, 192, 195; and Amharic languages, 202; and conflicts with Amhara, 204; as landless class, in Abyssinia, 210; post-Mao identity of, in China, 222; suppression of, by Han, in China, 223; persecution of, by Chinese, 226; and confrontations with Hindu, 242; assertive, in India, 246–47, 257; and conquest of India, 252; separatists in Kashmir, 253

Muslim Brotherhood: in Egypt and Sudan, 14
Muslim League: as anti-unionist movement, in Ethiopia, 148; response to, by RSS, 246; as protection of Muslim interests, in India, 247; mentioned, 13–14
Mussavi, Mir Hussein (Iranian prime minister), 127
Mussolini, Benito: and invasion of Ethiopia, 148
Mutalibov, Ayez (President of Azerbaijan Republic), 129–30
Myrdal, Gunnar: on racism in U.S., 57
Myth: mestizo, consolidated by, Mexican Revolution, 9; and cultural domination, in Mexico, 28; Guadalupe, in Mexico, 28; Quetzalcoatl, in Mexico, 28; in Ethiopia, 146; chauvinistic and racist, of Lewis Henry Morgan, 233
Mythology: and racism in U.S., 57; African-American, and racism, 62–63; role of, in Ethiopia, 159

Nagorno-Karabakh. *See* NKAO
Nakhichevan revolt: in Soviet Azerbaijan (1990), 131–32
Nara (Eritrean ethnic group), 184–85; support of, for EPLF, 195
Narimanov, Nariman (chairman of Communist Party of Azerbaijan), 122
Nation: idea of and movements toward, 8; and early U.S. sovereignty, 9; Stalin's definition of, 233; mentioned, 3
Nation-building: importance of, 8–9; and elites, 9; and self-reinvention, 9; historical elements of, 9; in Central America, 9; in Ethiopia, 9; in Haiti, 9; in Japan, 9; in Mexico, 9; in Thailand, 9; in U.S., 9; in Western hemisphere, 9; as anti-imperial weapon, 9–10; in China, 9–10; in Austria-Hungary, 10; in Ottoman-Empire, 10; post–World War I, 10; in post-independent Africa, 13; breakdown of, 14–19; and secession movements, 94–95; and suppression of state forms, in Soviet Union, 100
Nation-state: rise of, 3; and cultural pluralism, 4; early post–World War II, 7; emergence of, 7–11; development of, in Europe, 8; and Lenin, 10; and Stalin, 10; and self-determination, 10–11; and ethnicity, 116–17; loyalty of citizens to, 139–40; Ethiopian, development of, 146–47; Nehru model of, 243; Gandhi's concept of, 248
National Democratic Revolution Program. *See* NDRP
National identity: and immigration, 5; and Islam, 13–14; as Arabhood, 28; and American immigration, 88–89; in China, 236
National liberation movements (Ethiopia): of Eritreans, Somali, Oromo, and Tigre, 168
"National question": in Soviet Union, 5
Nationalism: forms of, 7; colonial order as, 11; in Nigeria, 11; and assimilation, 11–14; in Soviet Union (1980s), 12–13; and secularism, 13–14; in Africa, 15; and self-determination, 19; and cultural pluralism, in third world, 22; and role of women, 43; and totalitarianism, in Soviet Union, 96; as resistance to totalitarianism, 96; and Russia, in Soviet Union, 96, 97, 101; secessionist, in Soviet Union, 104–5, 106; in Azerbaijan, 117–19; in Abyssinia, 138; transformation of, 138; ethnic and regional challenges to, 138, 139; historical crises of, 139; characteristics of, 139–40; conflict of, with cultural pluralism, 140; Marxist incomprehension of, 140–41; discussion of, by students, 149; in Ethiopia, 149–50; and role of intellectuals, in Ethiopia, 155; division of, in Ethiopia, 156; predictions for, in Ethiopia, 156; in Eritrea, 156, 181; and Oromo, 169–71; ethnic-religious, in China, 223; and Leninist proto-racist policies, 229; Leninist anti-imperialist definition of, 229; and Chinese Leninists, 229–32; Leninist, in China, 229–32, 234; post-Marxist, 236; and political identity, 237; fascist, 238; religious, 239; introduction of, in India, 242; and Hindu, and RSS, 259; as factor in Latin American revolts, 266
Nationalist movement: in Eritrea, 192
Nationalists: Hindu, in India, 243; Maya, 275. *See also* Nationalism; Nationalist movement
Nationalities: policies of Soviet Union, 97, after Stalin, 102–3; policies of Dergue, 152; in Ethiopia, declaration of at Ethiopian national conference (1991), 158, 172; Maya, as separate from Guatemalan state, 265
Nationality questions: in Soviet Union, 12–13
Nationhood: idea of, used by Lenin, 10; myth of, in Ethiopia, 159; Ethiopian, 165–66; in India, 258

Native Americans: and "termination policy," 12; in U.S., 28; support of, for Maya, 277
Native peoples: and self-determination, 21
Nativist movement: in U.S., 14–15
Nazi-Soviet pact, 97
NDRP (National Democratic Revolution Program) (China), 153
Neft'enya ("riflemen"): and Amhara rule, 162–63
Negussie Negassa, Lt.: visit of, to Yugoslavia, 153
Nehru, Jawaharlal (India's first prime minister): nationalist vision of, 11; and concept of Indian nationality, 242–43; advocated break with India's past, 243–44; on religion, 243–44; prescribed secularization of Indian life, 244–45; hostility of, to RSS, 255; and ideal of state, 257–58; mentioned, 6
Neo-Marxism, 22
"New Economics": in U.S. (1960s), 58; in China, 237
"New Ethnicity": in U.S., 60
New Right coalition: agenda of, 65; and restriction of nonwhites, 66
Nigeria: nationalism in, 11
Nixon, Richard: and civil rights, 60–61
NKAO (Nagorno-Karabakh *oblast*), 130–31
Nkrumah, Kwame: as pan-Africanist, 148
Nomads (Eritrea): Saho, 184; Afar, 185
Nour, Ramadan Mohammed (EPLF leader), 191

Obafemi Awolowo (Nigerian nationalist), 11
"Official English" movement, 79–80; and S. I. Hayakawa, 79; and anti-assimilation, 87–88
OLF (Oromo Liberation Front), 149; organization of, 168; leaders of, exiled in U.S. and Europe, 170; as rival of OPDO, 170, 171
Oligarchy: in Guatemala (1954), 273
Omero, Mohammed Ali (ELF fourth zone commander), 188
OPDO (Oromo People's Democratic Organization): as rival of OLF, 170, 171
Oppression: of Maya, by ladinos, 280
Oral traditions: Christian and Falasha, 204; and conflicts between Beta Israel and Abyssinian society, 207
Oromo: in Ethiopia, 6; Yejju, 141; language, 142, 144; in 1974 revolution, 150; support of, for Dergue, 150, 151; challenge EPDRF, 156; regional autonomies of, 161; disillusion of, with regime (1970s), 168; youths, 168; as ethnic group, 169; nationalism, 169–71; and *gada* system, 170; revisionist history of, 170–71; and ethnopolitics, 171; organization of, after fall of Dergue, 171. *See also* OLF; OPDO
Oromo Liberation Front. *See* OLF
Oromo People's Democratic Organization. *See* OPDO
Orthodox Christians (Ethiopia): influence of, on Falasha, 202–3
Ottoman Turkey: Wilson's ideas on, 19; battle at Massawa (1579), 139

Pacific Rim: economies of, 237
Pakistan: and war-related rape, 40–41; mentioned, 11, 13
Palestine: and Soviet emigration, 16
Pan-Arabism: and self-determination, 11
Pan-Ethiopian culture, 143
Pan-Indian: identity of, in U.S., 278
Pan-Maya movement (Guatemala): as response to modernization in Guatemala, 265; goals and demands of, 267; sources of, 272; and religious divisiveness, 274; influence on, of U.S., 277; growth of, 279; characteristics of, 280
Pan-territorial ethnoculture, 11
Pan-Turanism: influence of, on young Turks, 122
Peace Corps: influence of, in Guatemala, 277
Peasant leagues: in Latin America, 267
Peasantry (China): fate of, 234–35; lack of unity among, 235
Perestroika, 19
Persecution: of Falasha, 201; of Turkish peoples, in China, 223
Phillips, Kevin: and "Southern Strategy," 60–61
Pishevari (Seyyed Ja'far Javadzadeh): as leader of CPI, 122; as leader of new autonomous republic of Azerbaijan, 123; death of, 124
Pol Pot. *See* Khmer Rouge Pol Pot war
Politicization: of Dergue, 169–70; effect of, in India, 248; of Maya, 272–73
POMA (Provisional Office of Mass Organizational Affairs), 150. *See also* Haile Fida
Population: minority, in U.S., 5; reproduction rates of African, 16; reproduction rates of,

in Soviet Union, 16–17; patterns of, in U.S., 17; estimates of, in Ethiopia, 162; Manchu, in China, 222–23; Maya, 273
Pracharak: RSS workers, 250; RSS senior advisors, 250–51
Primogeniture: in Ethiopia, 142
Primordial, identities: manipulation of, by rulers, 238
Primordial integration, 23
Primordial theory: and class, 25–26; ethnically defined, 26
Primordialism: and cultural pluralism, 22–23; and sociobiology, 23; and emotionality, 23; and class theory, 25–26; definition of, 26, 85
"Primordialist" school: analysis and importance of, 22–23; and anthropology, 23; definition of, 85; and role of language, 85–87; and language policies, 85–88; and ethnicity, 140
Princes, Age of (1769–1855), 142. *See also* Fistame Mangest
Promonarchists (Ethiopia), 150
Protest: nonviolent, in USSR, 105–6
Protestants: and conversion of Falasha, 209; activism of, in Guatemala, 273; in Guatemala, under Efrain Rios Montt, 274
Provisional Office of Mass Organizational Affairs. *See* POMA

Qajar: revolt against (1905), 121
Qozmos: Christians joining *ayhud,* 204
Quetzalcoatl: Mexican myth, 28

Race: and national identity, 5; and cultural pluralism and class, 26; in Latin America, 28
—in U.S.: black women, 37; and discrimination, 55, 56, 65; and political economy, 55–58; and social and cultural stability, 56, 57; and labor markets, 56, 63–64; and mythology, 57; and policies (1960s and 1970s), 58–61, 63–65; and Democratic politics, 60; and "New Ethnicity," 60; and working class, 64; black youth, 64; and Reagan administration, 65–67, 69; and economic policy (1980s), 68; and income loss (1980s), 69
Racism: in Guatemala, 268
—in U.S.: during 1960s, 55; and political economy, 55–58; and national culture, 56–57; and belief system, 57; and Euro-Americans, 57; Gunnar Myrdal on, 57; political use of, 60–61, 62–63; stereotyping of, 61; dichotomy of, 61–62; symbolic, 61–63, 67; substitution forms of, 62; and income differentials, 65
Rape: in Pakistan, 40, 41; in Bangladesh, 40–41; war-related, 40–41, in Korea, 41; societal and political importance of, 41; as male violence, 41–42. *See also* Sex-gender
Rashaida (immigrants to Eritrea from Yemen), 184
Rashtriya Swayamsevak Sangh. *See* RSS
Raya: revolt by, in Ethiopia (1928–30), 169
Reagan, Ronald: and privatization, 17; policy of, toward blacks, 65–67; and class interests, 66; and New Right agenda, 66; economic policies of, and race (1980s), 68, 69; and black youth, 69
Religion: and secularism and nationalism, 13–14; and state formation, 15; importance of, in state craft, 16; in Iran, 118, 119, 128; in Soviet Union, concessions to Islam, 129; in Ethiopia, 145; in Eritrea, Christians and Muslims, 190, 191, 192, 195; and Falasha, 203, 207–9; and school missionaries, in Ethiopia, 211–12; Leninist view of, 231; Marxist-Leninist view of, 231; Nehru's view of, 243–44; and cultural movements, in India, 246–47; Hindu-Muslim differences in, 247, 248; and conversion of Hindus, 252–53; and Christian missionaries in India, 253; RSS opinions on, 261; Catholic and Protestant, in Guatemala, 274. *See also* Catholic Action; Hindu; Islam; Protestants; Secularism
Reproduction rates: among nationalities, 16; among Slavs, 16; in Soviet Union, 16–17, "Republican motherhood," 49. *See also* Demography
Republican Party (U.S.): and "Southern Strategy," 60–61, 61–62; mentioned, 66
Resettlement: of Oromo, by Dergue, 170
Resources: competition for, in Eritrea, 181; Leninist command and redistribution of, 224
Revolts: local, in Ethiopia, 169; in Latin America, 266
Revolution: and Mexican and mestizo myth, 9; and overthrow of Haile Selassie (1974), in India, 190; in Latin America, 267
Riots: Hindu-Muslim, 248
Rios Montt, Efrain (General): president of Guatemala (1982), 274

Rossoni, Conti: and Ethiopia as "museum of peoples," 143
RSS (Rashtriya Swayamsevak Sangh): Indian cultural organization, 245; and national identity, in Hindu mold, 245–46, 250–51, 259; as controversial organization, 246; branches of, in U.S., UK, and Africa, 246; geographical strength of, 246; formation and origins of (1925), 246, 248–54; and vision of Hindu brotherhood, 249; criticizes caste system, 249–50; denounces Singh, 250; organizational structure and activities of, 250, 252; role of *pracharaks* of, 250–51; ideology of, 251–54, 259; sees weaknesses of India, 252–53; and foreign threats to India, 253; conflicts of, with communist parties in India, 253; and Congress Party, 253, 254–55; and Hindu-Muslim polarization, 254; and national construction program, 254; growth and affiliates of, 254–57; hostility toward, by Nehru, 255; literature of, 255; and BJP, 256; banned under emergency dictatorship, 256; economic program of, 256; membership expansion of, 256; merges with Janata party, 256; future of, 257–60; religious position of, 259; and Sikhs, 260; goals of, for Hindus, 260; rejects idea of India as multinational state, 260; and cultural pluralism, 261; political separatism of, 261–62
Russia: Wilson's ideas on tsarist, 19; post-Soviet, 110–11; and policy of assimilation of Aran, 119–20; and policy of linguistic integration, 120; and Azerbaijan-Iran ties, 121; and de-nationalization of Leninism, 231–32
Russification: forced upon nationalities, 222
Russo-Iranian relations, 134
Rustam, Suleyman: and literature of longing, 125
Rutskoi, Aleksandr (Russian vice president), 111

Sabbe, Osman Salah (ELF founder), 186
Sahel (Eritrean province), 183
Saho (Eritrean province), 184
Sarsanghchalak (Supreme Guide): of RSS, 250
Sati: Hindu practice, in India, 46
Saudi Arabia: and financing of EIJM, 191
Savarkar, V. D.: Hindu nationalist, 243
Secession: predicted in USSR, 94–95; as political challenge, Tigre/Amhara, 138
Secessionist movements: in Africa, 29; in Soviet Union, 104–5
Secularism: in Western Europe, 13; link of, to modernization, 14, 242; and Congress Party in India, 15, 266; in Iran, 16; in India, 244–45
Secular state: and disillusionment, in India, 257
Segregation: of Falasha, by occupation, 206
Sekou Toure, 13
Self-determination: and Asia, 10–11; and nation-building, 10–11; and pan-Arabism, 11; and Africa, 11, 19, 20, 29; and U.N. charter, 11, 19–20; and anti-colonization, 19; and Soviet Union, 19; and Wilson's ideas, 19; and World War I, 19; as by-product of nationalism, 19; post–World War II, 19–20; of "captive nations," in Soviet Union, 20; and International Labor Organization, 21; and native peoples, 21; and secession movements, 21; and sovereignty claims, 21; and Ethiopia, 149; and world-wide diffusion, 173; and Afar, 195
Self-government: NDRP policy of, 153
Seljuk dynasty: in 11th century Iran, 118
Semhar (Eritrean province), 183
Senhit (Eritrean province), 183; as independent community in Tigre, 184
Serae (Eritrean province), 183
Sex-gender: and cultural puralism and blood ties, 39; systems, 39–43; and group access, 40; and marriage, 40; as question in U.S. slavery, 40; role regulation, 40; and rape, 40–41; male, 42; identification and ethnic markers of, 44–45; and politics of control, 45–46
Shaka, 249
Sharecroppers: in Ethiopia, 165
Shariatmadari, Ayatollah Kazem: spiritual leader of Iranian Azeris, 127
Shawa: kinship and historical change of, 202; and proselytization, 204
Shia: in Iran, 128
Shiᶜism, 118, 119; in Iran, 129
Shoa: and regional power struggles, 141, 142; Ethiopian region, 147; mentioned, 160, 202, 205, 211
Shoan Amhara, 160
Shumagille (master caste in Tigre), 184
Sidama, 174
Sidama Liberation Movement, 174

Sidamo (Ethiopian region), 174; self-help association in, 141
Sikhs: religious-cultural movement of, 246–247; militancy of, 257; as ideological challenge to RSS, 259–60; separatism of, 260
Singapore, 238
Sisaye Habte (Dergue leader): visit of, to Vietnam, 153
Socialization: in sex-gender roles, 43
Social reform: and Catholic Action, in Guatemala, 274
Socialism: association of, with secularism, 13
"Socialism in one country," 100
Sociobiology: and "primordialism," 23
Solomon, King: Ethiopian legend of, 141
Somalia: and conflict with Ethiopia, 151
"Southern Strategy": in U.S. presidential campaign (1968), 60–61; use of, by Reagan (1980), 65–66
Soviet Union: dissolution of (1991), 5, 93–94, 95; as nation state, 7–8; and Marxist-Leninist ideology, 8; and nationalism, 12–13; emigration from, 16; reproductive rates of, 16–17; and self-determination, 19; "captive nations" of, 20; and collapse of state socialism, 27; and manipulation of ethnics, 27; and role of ethnonationalism, 27; summary history of, 93; and ethnic question, 94; secession, predicted, 94–95; as state and empire, 95, 96–99, 101–2; and totalitarianism, 96; "elder brothers" in, 97, 101; nationalities policies of, 97–98; empire consciousness of, 98, 99–103; and "internal colonialism," 98–99; and republics' economic dissatisfaction, 99; and "socialism in one country," 100; emergence of state forms in, to suppress nationalities, 100; identity of, 100, 102, 103–7; and state building, 101, under Gorbachev, 107–9; nationality concessions (1920), 101; empire legacy of, 101–2; and civil society, 102; government of, after Stalin, 102; modern identity crisis of, 102; legitimacy-seeking rule of (1960s and 1970s), 102–3; and cultural pluralism (1960s and 1970s), 103; relations of, with Ukrainians, 103; secessionist movements in, 104–5, 107, 108; nonviolent era of, 106–7; and Union Treaty of 1922, renegotiation, 107; federalization of, 107, 108; and republic and independence claims, 108; and secession claim of Armenia, 108; State Emergency Committee in, 108; as Commonwealth of Independent States, 108, 109; Novo-Ogarevo agreement (1991), 108, 109; continued disintegration of, 109–10; and post-Soviet policies, 109–11; post-coup ethnic conflicts in, 109–12; and Azerbaijan Soviet Socialist Republic, 117; and ethnic policy of, 117; and Azerbaijan, 125–26, 128, Republic of, 133; concessions of, to Islam, 129; and Armenian-Azerbaijan conflict, 130; and Gorbachev and ethnic problem, 130; and agreement with Iran, 131; "Law on Sovereignty" (1989), 131; Nakhichevan revolt in Azerbaijan (1990), 131–32; influence of, on Azeri territory, 132; influence of, on Arab states, 153; political support of, for Ethiopian nationalities, 153; and Dergue requests, 153–54; support of, for Ethiopian army, 190; nativization of, 222. *See also* NKAO; Russia
Spain: and ethnic nationalism, 266
State: formulation of, 8; post–World War II, 8; modernization of, and secularism, 14; and socialism, 17, 18; Reaganist, 66; and demise of Soviet, 93; imperfect relationship of, with empire, 97, 98, 99; subjectivity of, 98; and Lenin, 100; building of Soviet, 101; and empire, 103–4, 105–6; separate Azeri (1945), 123–25; Ethiopian, 141, 147; formation of modern European, 147; status of, at end of 1920s, 237
State secessions: pre–World War II, 94; post–World War II and Cold War, 94–95
State socialism: collapse of, 17; collapse of, in Soviet Union, 27
Stalin, Joseph: ideas of, on nation-state, 10; and cultural destruction, 101; Azerbaijan linguistic policy of, 123; and Azeri secessionist movement, 124; and *Firqi* movement leaders, 124; and withdrawal from Iran, 124; and definition of Leninist nation (1912), 233
Stereotyping: racial, in U.S., 57, 61; as depersonalization of race, in U.S., 62–63; of blacks during Reagan presidential campaign (1980), 66, 68–69; of relations, between Beta Israel and Abyssinians, 208–9
Students: Marxist influence on (1965), 149; Ethiopian, and political consciousness, 149, 166, 167; Ethiopian, and Marxist influence, 167; Hindu, and RSS, 246
Sudan: as base of EIJM, 191

Suffrage movement (U.S.), 37, 50
Sultan, Ibrahim (founder of ELF), 186
Sultanzade (Avetis Mikailian): as member of Central Committee of *Adalat* Party, 122; biographical information, 122–23; and Stalin's linguistic policies, 123
Sunni: in Iran, 118, 119; brotherhoods (*tariqas*) of, as nonofficial Islam, 129
Suseneyos, King: and defeat of Falasha, 206
Swayamsevaks (volunteers): of RSS, 249
Symbolic racism: meaning of, 70
Symbols: sexual, in national identity, 42; use of, by Reagan, 66, 67; use of, by ethnic groups against state, 140; religious, used by Gandhi, 248, 258; Hindu, 259

Tadesa Biru, General (leader of Mechᶜa-Tulama association), 167–68
Tanton, John: and "U.S. English" lobbying group, 79
Tedla Bairu (Ethiopian unionist), 148
Teferi Banti, General (head of Ethiopian state), 152
Tessenai (region of Barka province, Eritrea), 183
Tewodros II: as Ethiopian emperor, 142; and subjugation of peoples, 161; and religious dispute, between Beta Israel and Protestants, 209; and treatment of Falasha, 211
Tewolde, Abraham: defection of, from ELF, 189
Thatcher, Margaret: and privatization, 17
Third World: debt of, 17; and cultural pluralism, 22; ethnic insurgencies in, 140
Tibet (Tibetan): resistance of, to China, 222, 223; refugee account of persecution by Chinese, 227–28; monasteries destroyed, 233
Tienanmien Square, 18
Tigre: and Abyssinian nationalism, 138; in Eritrea, 184; language of, 184, 284; ethnic association of, 141; and regional power struggles, 141–42; and guerilla war against Dergue, 149; social stratification of, 184
Tigre Peoples Liberation Front. *See* TPLF
Tigrigna (Eritrean people), 183; language of, 183, 184, 187
Tilak, B. G. (Hindu nationalist), 243
Togoruba, battle of (Ethiopia), 187
Totalitarianism: and Soviet Union, 96; and "captive nations" in Soviet Union, 96–97
Toteel, Ibrahim (ELF leader): as member of EPLF Central Committee, 195
Tovbe (Muslim party in Azerbaijan): and Azeri elections, 132
Tribalism: and ethnicity, in Africa, 29; mentioned, 13
Tudeh Party, 124
Tulema: Ethiopian self-help association, 141
Túpac Amaru II: and Inca rebellion in 1780, 266
Turkey: influence of, on Azeri, 116, 118
Turkic people: persecuted in China, 223
Turk rulers: in Azerbaijan, 118; and Qajar dynasty, 119

Ubico, Jorge (Guatemalan president): overthrow of (1944), 270
Ukraine: and self-determination, 106; and Commonwealth of Independent States, 108–9
Unionist party (Ethiopia), 148
United Nations: and rights of nationalities, 172; Universal Declaration of Human Rights, 172
United Nations Charter: and self-determination, 11; and Africa, 19; anti-colonial justifications of, 19–20
United Nations Commission on Human Rights, 21
United Nations General Assembly, 19
United States: national identity of, 5; population minorities of, 5; and nation-building, 9; and pre-independence rights, 9; and cultural pluralism, 12; and termination policy, 12; multiculturalism of, 12; 1924 Immigration Act, 12; demographics of, 17, 75, 76; and class ideology, 25; and race and cultural pluralism, 26; and cultural dominance, 28–29; history of black women in, 37; suffragist organization and black women in, 37; treatment of blacks in, 38; Italian-American families in, 47; Hispanic community in southwest, and kin-work, 48; and "republican motherhood," 49; suffrage movement in, 50; and racism and political economy, 55–58; and employment in (1960s), 56; race and economic class in, 56, 57; labor market and blacks in, 56, 57–58, 59, 63–65; and mythology and race, 57; as "classless" society, 57; racism in, 57, 59–60; and federal government activism and civil rights, 58–59; civil rights movement in, 58–59; policies

and race, 58–61; Democratic Party and civil rights in (1960s), 59; civil rights in, under Nixon and Ford, 61, under Carter, 61; and racism dichotomy, 61–62; economics and new global position of, 63–64; racial policy in, under Johnson, 66; and trade unions, 67–68, 69, 70; and ethnic consciousness, 73; and language policy, 73, 74–75, 76–80, 81, toward American Indians, 82–83, and immigration, 87; "Know Nothing" party in, 74; and nativist movement, 74–75; racial conflicts and language in, 76; and bilingualism, 78, 79, 80; "English-Only" movement in, 79; political conflict and language in, 81; new immigration to, 88–89; and overthrow of ladinos, in Guatemala (1954), 273; and Maya refugees, 277; influences of, on pan-Maya movement, 277. *See also* Bilingual education; Bilingualism: in U.S.; Carter, Jimmy; Civil rights; Language: in U.S.; Reagan, Ronald; Wallace, George
Universal Declaration of Human Rights, United Nations, 172
Urbanization: in Abyssinia, 207; in China, 235

Vietnam: and Democratic Party in U.S., 59; visited by Sisaye Habte, 153; mentioned, 11
Violence: and cultural pluralism, 26; male expression of, 40–41; lack of, in demise of Soviet Union, 94; as part of state building, 96; modern states as product of, 147; of ethnics, in Ethiopia, 149; against minorities, 234; military, against Maya in Guatemala, 276
Vote: extended to illiterate males in Guatemala (1945), 272; in Soviet Union (1989, 1990), 106
Voting Rights Act of 1965 (U.S.): 1975 extension of, 78

Wallace, George: as U.S. presidential candidate (1964 and 1968), 59–60
Wallo (Ethiopian province): kinship and historical change in, 202
Wellega (Ethiopia): revolt in (1936), 169
Williams, Patricia: personal story of, 36–37, 51–52
Wilson, Woodrow: and self-determination, 19; ideas on multi-national empires, 19
Wollo (Ethiopia): under monarchies, 160
Women: role of, in Iran, 42; role of, in society, 42; dress of, as form of control, 42, 44; role of, dominated by men, 42–43; Arab, 43; as cultural carriers, 43, 47; role of, in nationalism, 43; role of, in work, 46–49; in Hispanic community, 48; as missionaries of "traditional" American culture, 48–49; and citizenship, 49; and "modernization," 49; and labor organization, 50; and cultural pluralism, 50–51; and Islam, 51; Falasha rules for, 209
Work of kinship: and Italian American families, 47
World War I: post, and empire dissolution, 10; and self-determination, 19
World War II: post, and nation-state, 3; and dissolution of empire, 8; and nation-building, 9; and U.S. cultural pluralism, 12; and self-determination, 19–20
Wuchall, Treaty of (1889): denounced by Menelik II, 148

Yekunno Amelak (King of Ethiopia), 143
Yemen: immigrants from, in Eritrea, 184
Yeshaq (Abyssian king): and war against *ayhud,* 204
Yohannes IV (emperor of Ethiopia and Tigre): and use of Amharic language, 144–45; defined Ethiopia's boundaries, 147; and subjugation of peoples, 161; mentioned, 141, 142

Zagwe (Agnew ethnic group), 141
Zemene, Mesafent: in Ethiopia, 142